The Harrowsmith

COOKBOOK

Volume Three

More Classic and Creative Cuisine

By the Editors & Readers of Harrowsmith Magazine

Compiled from the private recipe collections of the Editors, Readers, Contributors and Staff of *Harrowsmith*, the Award-Winning Magazine of Country Living and Alternatives

CAMDEN HOUSE

© 1987 by Camden House Publishing
(a division of Telemedia Communications Inc.)

Reprinted: 1990; 1994

Canadian Cataloguing in Publication Data

Main entry under title:
The Harrowsmith cookbook
"Editor, Pamela Cross; associate editors, Jennifer Bennett,
James Lawrence."

Includes index.
ISBN 0-920656-80-3 (v. 3; bound)
ISBN 0-920656-78-1 (v. 3; pbk.)

1. Cookery. I. Cross, Pamela. II. Bennett, Jennifer.
III. Lawrence, James. IV. Harrowsmith.

TX715.H39 1981   641.5   C82-004954-9 rev

Library of Congress Catalogue Card Number: 87-72352

Published by Camden House Publishing
(a division of Telemedia Communications Inc.)

Camden House Publishing
7 Queen Victoria Road
Camden East, Ontario K0K 1J0

Camden House Publishing
Box 766
Buffalo, New York 14240-0766

Printed and distributed under exclusive licence
from Telemedia Communications Inc. by
Firefly Books
250 Sparks Avenue
Willowdale, Ontario
Canada M2H 2S4

Firefly Books (U.S.) Inc.
P.O. Box 1338
Ellicott Station
Buffalo, New York 14205

Colour separations by
Herzig Somerville Limited
Toronto, Ontario

Printed and bound in Canada by
D.W. Friesen & Sons Ltd.
Altona, Manitoba

Cover illustration by Roger Hill

The Harrowsmith
COOKBOOK
Volume Three

Editor
PAMELA CROSS

Contributing Editors
JOANNE CATS-BARIL, RUX MARTIN

Test Kitchen Coordinators
MEREDITH GABRIEL, RANDI KENNEDY

Testers
BRUCE MORGAN, PAT NOVOTNY,
ELIZABETH WELTIN, PETER DUNDAS

Art Director
LINDA J. MENYES

Photography
ERNIE SPARKS

Food Design
MARIELLA MORRIN

Illustrations
MARTA SCYTHES

Graphic Artist
SUSAN GILMOUR

Copy Editing/Typesetting
EILEEN WHITNEY, WENDY S. RUOPP, PATRICIA DENARD-HINCH,
CATHERINE DeLURY, MARY PATTON, CHARLOTTE DuCHENE,
LYNN MILLER, SUZANNE SEIBEL, SARA PERKS

Contents

Introduction

"I never get any home cooking. All I get is fancy stuff . . . "

—The Duke of Edinburgh

As far as grumbling dukes go, we think we like this one, a man who, we suspect, might share some of our views on the current state of the culinary world: microwave dinners, ersatz Cheddar, faux lobster, burger-chain breakfasts – food trends rippling across the land, ascending and declining and being replaced as fast as new fads can be spawned and spotted.

Were it within our power, we would be deeply pleased to introduce the disgruntled royal to an extraordinary family of "home cooks" – the thousands of contributors throughout North America who collaborated on the production of this, the third volume of *The Harrowsmith Cookbook*.

"God sends meat and the Devil sends cooks," is an old English proverb that might seem appropriate for a project involving some 6,000 recipes submitted by as diverse a crowd of food lovers as has ever been gathered between the pages of a single cookbook: men and women, vegetarians and hunters, world travellers and farmhouse grandmothers, classically trained culinarians and commonsense home cooks.

What makes this unlikely cooperative authorship work is not a single easily defined theme but, rather, an informal *Harrowsmith* philosophy about how food should be prepared and what makes it good. As mailbag after mailbag full of recipes came tumbling into the offices of our food editors, an immediate winnowing process began,

with automatic rejection for:

1. Recipes with highly processed ingredients (Dream Whip, Jell-O, Spam and the like).
2. Recipes taken directly from newspapers or other cookbooks.

Beyond this, our editors looked for things they would want to try in their own homes, recipes which made use of healthy, obtainable ingredients and which did not generally require long preparation times and complicated procedures. At the same time, they ruthlessly eliminated the Communard Specials – dishes with unimpeachable nutritional qualities but unpalatable tastes and textures. The final selections, if they can be classified as a group, tend to be intimately connected with the garden, the countryside, the woods and the family food traditions of our readers.

"These recipes are my inheritance from a grandfather I knew and a grandmother I never knew," wrote Delmas Freeman. "They are steeped in memories of scoldings for snitching ingredients, after which my mother would always happen to have 'just a little too much for the pot,' of smells wafting through the house and of the final reward of the meal. They are finally reduced to print after 100 years of oral tradition."

Similarly, another contributor sent a recipe for Crusty Blueberry Batter Cake, originally made by her grandmother and painstakingly recreated from memory by her mother. Another parted with a recipe for Dakota Prairie Pumpkin Pie, which had been in the family for six generations. More contemporary treasures include Frittata Fairbanks, an Alaska creation from Mark Boberick, who describes it as "the most delectable omelette I have ever eaten and one of the most beautiful dishes imaginable"; Susanna Barnett's Ten-Year Granola – the result of a decade's worth of evolution and breakfast-table testings; and Mandarin Hot & Sour Soup, perfected by Barb McDonald after she lived in China for two years.

Simplicity prevails in most of these recipes, and many can be prepared quickly, in the presence of impatient children and/or after a long day at work. Others, such as Apple Meringue Pie With Hazelnut Pastry, are intended for those times when cooking can be more leisurely or more elaborate in preparation for a special occasion.

In either case, the directions for these recipes are presented in a clear, straightforward manner. We do not believe there needs to be any mystique to the preparation of even exotic dishes. Each recipe, as well as being tested for accuracy, is proofread by several individuals, some of whom are not gourmet cooks and never hesitate to inform us if something just doesn't make sense.

To be sure, evidence of recent food trends can easily be found in this collection – even some of what a duke might regard as "fancy stuff." We have attempted to ensure, however, that mere novelty is absent here.

We also offer two new chapters in this book. Breakfasts and Snacks finally gives a real home to waffles, pancakes, muffins and cookies. And the Holiday chapter gathers together those very special recipes that we cook only once or twice a year.

It is clear that many of our readers like to travel and experiment with foreign dishes, and as a result, recipes from Mexico, the Far East, Africa and Europe rub shoulders with good old-fashioned North American country cooking.

Perhaps the most encouraging – and surely the most potentially enduring – of the new food waves is the "discovery" of fresh, unadulterated local ingredients, North American game and wild foods. Readers of the earlier *Harrowsmith* cookbooks will find nothing new in this, and in the best home-cooking tradition, many recipes herein make good use of the local abundance – an explosion of blackberries in a wet season, a too prolific row of zucchini, a haunch of venison or a harvest of woodland mushrooms.

Also apparent is the international flavour of this volume, the result of the parallel efforts of the Canadian edition of *Harrowsmith* and its new American counterpart. With test kitchens in a former farmhouse in Camden East, Ontario, and in what was once a creamery in Charlotte, Vermont, all recipes included were rated for taste, appearance, texture and ease of preparation. Interestingly, two editors of this project had formerly owned and managed cafés that blended music with a wholesome-foods orientation: Pamela Cross's Carden Street Café in Guelph, Ontario, and JoAnne Cats-Baril's Sunprint in Madison, Wisconsin. The coincidences continued with the chief recipe testers: Randi Kennedy, who runs the Canadian kitchen, lives and works on a cooperative lamb farm, while Meredith Gabriel, who manages food preparation in Vermont, is also an experienced raiser of sheep and a veteran natural-foods chef.

Additional testing was done in home kitchens by a number of friends and staff members, foremost among them Rux Martin, whose work has appeared in *Food & Wine* and in *Harrowsmith*, and Bruce Morgan, a recent graduate of a culinary management programme and a professional chef-to-be. Readers will notice that some recipes appear without a byline. These are recipes developed in our test kitchens or from the private collections of the editors.

As in earlier volumes, the brilliant food photography was done by Ernie Sparks, with food preparation and presentation by *cordon bleu* cooking instructor Mariella Morrin.

The results of all this testing had to pass the critical scrutiny of our editors, graphic artists, circulation personnel, advertising sales staffers and various journalists, sales people and bankers who happened to be passing through our offices at lunchtime. During the height of the testing, midmornings were marked by mass risings from office desks, as staff members in two countries moved simultaneously toward two kitchens, drawn by the aromas of freshly baked Upside-Down Rhubarb Muffins, White Chocolate Mocha Java Bars and the like. Again, at midafternoon, taste-testing duties were often required. Waistlines expanded. Even the most resolute dieters routinely had their resistance broken by offered samples of just-made pecan ice cream with hot strawberry sauce. In making final evaluations, the ultimate question of tasters was: "Would you want this recipe for yourself?" Those with an overwhelming "yes" response are to be found in these pages.

We think the results are worthy of your attention, and, if previous *Harrowsmith* cookbooks are any indication, the pages that follow are destined to become dog-eared, dusted with flour, stained with oil, scented with herbs and dripped on with chocolate (or carob, as the case may be). A soiled cookbook is a loved cookbook, and we sincerely hope this one has a well-smudged fate in your own home kitchen.

Breakfasts & Snacks

"I'll cook beautifully for you, a perfectly beautiful breakfast, if only you won't have me for supper."

—*Bilbo Baggins*
The Hobbitt

For a generation that grew up scolded about the nutritional deficiencies of Sugar Frosted Flakes, Cocoa Puffs, Froot Loops and their ilk, it may come as a shock to learn that the beginnings of our modern-day cereal industry can be traced to an evangelical vegetarian and nutritional visionary named Dr. John Harvey Kellogg.

A Seventh Day Adventist, Kellogg began developing grain and nut products in 1876 to enhance the diet of his patients at the Battle Creek Sanitarium in Michigan. By boiling wheat, then running it through his wife's noodle machine and baking it, a process that came to him in a dream, Kellogg created one of the first manufactured health foods and called it Granola, then Granose. The new breakfast food proved an instant success, and Toasted Corn Flakes, peanut butter and 70 other breakfast foods followed. Impressed by the good doctor's success, a patient at the same clinic, C.W. Post, came up with Elijah's Manna, another high-fibre cereal product that was speedily renamed Grape-Nuts.

One suspects that both Kellogg and Post would be shocked at the sugary turn breakfast has taken in North America today. Still, the concept of breakfast as the nutritional keystone of the day remains strong. In one major scientific study, students who ate breakfast concentrated better and made fewer mistakes late in the morning; calories consumed early in the day are much less likely to become stored fat than those ingested at night; and people who eat breakfast may actually live longer than those who do not.

The recipes that follow should provide ample inspiration for breaking one's fast without resorting to the old bacon-eggs-hash-browns-buttered-toast routine. Most of the pancake, waffle and muffin recipes can be made in as little as half an hour, and the quick breads and coffee cakes can be served hot from the oven by early-rising cooks. (For a special treat, try Grandma's Scottish Potato Scones, quickly made using a few boiled potatoes from the previous evening.) Many of the recipes can be started the evening before, leaving only the final assembly or baking for the morning.

This is a new chapter for the *Harrowsmith Cookbook* series, and we have chosen to include snacks in this section. Carrot Zucchini Squares and Wonderful Oatmeal Raisin Cookies are wholesome enough to be eaten anytime, while the White Chocolate Mocha Java Bars and others clearly ought to be saved for later in the day.

The days of entire families gathered around the kitchen table for a daily calorie-loading feast may be gone forever, but there is no reason why we cannot all leave the house in the morning well nourished and with a healthful, homemade snack in a brown bag for those midafternoon doldrums.

BANANA MUFFINS

1 cup white sugar
½ cup butter
1 egg, beaten
1 cup mashed bananas
1½ cups flour

1 tsp. baking soda
½ tsp. nutmeg
½ tsp. vanilla
salt

Cream sugar and butter, then add egg and mix well. Add bananas and flour. Dissolve baking soda in 1 Tbsp. hot water, then add to creamed mixture along with nutmeg, vanilla and salt. Spoon into greased muffin cups and bake at 350 degrees F for 20 minutes.

Makes 12 muffins.

—Ann Coyle
Fergus, Ontario

OAT MUFFINS

"I FIRST MADE THESE WHEN I WAS 10, AND I MAKE AND ENJOY THEM TO THIS DAY." THEY ARE light muffins with an even, spongy texture.

1 cup rolled oats
1 cup buttermilk
1 cup flour
1 tsp. baking powder
½ tsp. baking soda

½ tsp. salt
½ cup brown sugar
1 egg, beaten
¼ cup oil **or** melted butter

Soak oats in buttermilk for 1 hour. Combine flour, baking powder, baking soda, salt and sugar and mix well. Stir egg and oil into oat mixture. Make a well in dry ingredients, pour in liquid and stir quickly until just mixed. Pour into greased muffin cups and bake at 400 degrees F for 20 minutes.

Makes 12 muffins.

—Faye Cassia
Deroche, British Columbia

BLUEBERRY BRAN WHEAT GERM MUFFINS

"THESE MUFFINS PASSED MY DAUGHTER'S TEST, AND SHE DOES NOT CARE FOR BRAN OR WHEAT germ." We thought they were great – really moist and flavourful.

3 eggs
1 cup brown sugar
½ cup oil
2 cups buttermilk
1 tsp. vanilla
1 cup wheat germ

1 cup bran
2 cups flour
2 tsp. baking powder
2 tsp. baking soda
½ tsp. salt
1½ cups blueberries

Beat eggs well, add sugar and beat, then add oil, buttermilk and vanilla and mix well. Stir in wheat germ and bran.

In smaller bowl, combine flour, baking powder, baking soda and salt, then stir in blueberries. Pour into liquid ingredients and stir until just mixed. Spoon into greased muffin cups and bake at 400 degrees F for 20 to 25 minutes.

Makes 24 muffins.

—Sandy MacLennan
Millgrove, Ontario

VIRGINIA CORN MUFFINS

"MY GRANDMOTHER FROM TENNESSEE TAUGHT ME THIS RECIPE. WHY SHE CALLED IT 'VIRGINIA' Corn Muffins, I don't know."

1 cup white cornmeal	¾ tsp. salt
½ cup flour	1 egg
¼ cup sugar	½ cup milk
5 tsp. baking powder	2 tsp. oil

Mix together cornmeal, flour, sugar, baking powder and salt. Beat together egg, milk and oil. Quickly stir liquid into dry ingredients. Place in 12 greased muffin cups and bake at 375 degrees F for 25 minutes.

Makes 12 muffins.

—Ruth Ellis Haworth
Toronto, Ontario

ORANGE PECAN MUFFINS

1 cup buttermilk	1⅓ cups flour
¼ cup melted butter	⅓ cup demerara sugar
1 egg	1½ tsp. baking powder
½ tsp. vanilla	½ tsp. baking soda
juice & grated rind of 1 orange	½ tsp. salt
1 cup rolled oats	⅔ cup coarsely chopped pecans

Combine buttermilk, butter, egg, vanilla, orange juice, orange rind and rolled oats and let stand for 15 minutes. Combine remaining ingredients and add to liquid mixture. Mix lightly. Fill greased muffin cups ⅔ full. Bake at 375 degrees F for 15 to 20 minutes.

Makes 12 muffins.

—Beth Caldwell
Marysville, British Columbia

UPSIDE-DOWN RHUBARB MUFFINS

OUR VERMONT TESTER SAYS, "THESE MUFFINS ARE TERRIFIC — NOT TOO SWEET, WITH A GOOD combination of tastes and textures."

1 cup finely chopped rhubarb	1½ cups flour
¼ cup melted butter	2 tsp. baking powder
½ cup packed brown sugar	½ tsp. salt
⅓ cup soft butter	½ tsp. nutmeg
⅓ cup sugar	½ cup milk
1 egg	

Combine rhubarb, melted butter and brown sugar in small bowl and mix well. Place in 12 greased muffin cups.

Beat together butter, sugar and egg until fluffy. Combine flour, baking powder, salt and nutmeg and add to creamed mixture alternately with milk. Stir just to moisten, then spoon on top of rhubarb mixture.

Bake at 350 degrees F for 20 to 25 minutes. Invert on cooling rack and leave pan over muffins for a few minutes so all rhubarb moisture runs out. Serve warm.

Makes 12 muffins.

—Joan Airey
Rivers, Manitoba

AUNT NELL'S HUSH PUPPIES

LIGHT AND FLAVOURFUL, CRISPY OUTSIDE AND MOIST INSIDE, THESE HUSH PUPPIES ARE QUICK and easy to make.

1 cup cornmeal
1 tsp. baking soda
1 cup flour
2 Tbsp. sugar

1 clove garlic, crushed
1 egg
1 large onion, chopped
1 cup buttermilk
fat for frying

Combine all ingredients. Let rise for 30 minutes. Drop by tablespoonsful into deep hot fat and fry until golden brown.

Makes approximately 18 hush puppies.

—Carolee Gosda
Lincoln, Illinois

PUFF BALL DOUGHNUTS

ALSO KNOWN AS BEAVER TAILS AND ELEPHANT EARS IN OTHER PARTS OF CANADA, THESE ARE A real treat. Roll in sugar, roll up with grated cheese as a filling, or brush with garlic butter.

3 eggs
1 cup sugar
2 cups milk
lemon extract

3 cups flour
3 tsp. baking powder
½ tsp. salt
oil for deep-frying

Beat eggs, add sugar and beat well. Add milk and lemon extract. Sift together flour, baking powder and salt and fold into egg mixture. Using two spoons, drop into oil heated to 375 degrees F. Fry until golden brown. Dough should turn by itself. If not, turn with a fork, making certain not to pierce dough.

Serves 4 to 6.

—Myrna Smith
Carroll, Manitoba

THISTLE-DOWN PLACE SCONES

½ cup raisins
2 cups flour
3 Tbsp. sugar
2 tsp. baking powder
½ tsp. salt
½ tsp. baking soda

5 Tbsp. butter
1 cup sour cream
1 egg, separated
1 tsp. sugar
½ tsp. cinnamon

Cover raisins with warm water and let stand for 5 minutes. Drain well and set aside.

Combine flour, sugar, baking powder, salt and baking soda. Cut in butter to make a coarse crumb texture. Stir in raisins.

In another bowl, combine sour cream and egg yolk. Make well in centre of dry ingredients and pour in egg-cream mixture. Stir just until dough clings together.

Turn out onto floured surface and knead gently 10 or 12 times. Pat into ½-inch-thick circle and cut into 4-inch rounds. Place on ungreased baking sheet, brush with egg white and sprinkle with sugar and cinnamon. Cut each round into quarters but do not separate. Bake at 425 degrees F for 15 minutes, or until golden.

Makes 16 scones.

—Irene Louden
Port Coquitlam, British Columbia

GRANDMA'S SCOTTISH POTATO SCONES

"ON ALL OF HER VISITS, GRANDMA WOULD TAKE LEFTOVER POTATOES FROM THE DAY BEFORE and make us potato scones to have hot, slathered with butter, as a bedtime snack." Our tasters thought these scones good enough to warrant purposely cooking extra potatoes.

Mash cold potatoes well on well-floured surface. Knead in as much flour as potatoes will absorb. Add salt to taste. Roll out to ¼-inch thickness and cut into large circles. Quarter circles and cook on slow griddle, turning when lightly flecked with brown.

Eat hot with butter or honey.

—Lesley-Anne Paveling
Mozart, Saskatchewan

GERMAN BREAD GRIDDLE CAKES

OUR CAMDEN EAST TESTER DECLARED THESE TO BE "DELICIOUS! ESPECIALLY LIGHT. JUST excellent." We agreed and thought they made a tasty, light alternative to pancakes.

1½ cups milk	½ cup flour
2 Tbsp. butter	4 tsp. baking powder
1½ cups stale bread crumbs	½ tsp. salt
2 eggs, well beaten	oil for cooking

Scald milk, then add butter and stir until butter has melted. Pour over bread crumbs and let soak for 30 minutes. Beat in remaining ingredients. Cook in hot oil over medium heat until golden brown.

Serves 2 to 3.

—Jean Perkins
Sauquoit, New York

GINGERBREAD WAFFLES

A FLAVOURFUL WINTER BREAKFAST, THESE WAFFLES ARE ALSO CAKEY ENOUGH TO BE SERVED (perhaps dusted with confectioners' sugar) as part of an afternoon tea.

2 cups flour	¼ tsp. cloves
½ tsp. salt	1 cup molasses
1 tsp. baking powder	¾ cup milk (approximately)
2 tsp. ginger	1 egg, beaten
1 tsp. cinnamon	½ cup oil

Combine flour, salt, baking powder, ginger, cinnamon and cloves. Mix together molasses, milk, egg and oil and stir into dry ingredients, adding additional milk if necessary. Bake in hot waffle iron until golden brown. Serve with sweetened whipped cream.

Serves 4.

—Sybil D. Hendricks
Plymouth, California

ORANGE WAFFLES

USE UNPEELED ORANGES FOR THIS RECIPE – BUT WASH THEM WELL AND REMOVE SEEDS FIRST. If your oranges are not very juicy, you may need to add a bit more liquid.

1½ cups flour
½ tsp. salt
1½ tsp. baking powder
2 eggs, separated

1 cup milk
¼ cup oil
2 oranges, quartered

Sift dry ingredients together. Blend egg yolks, milk and oil well in blender or food processor. Add orange quarters one at a time and blend well. Beat egg whites until stiff. Add orange mixture to dry ingredients and stir well. Gently fold in egg whites. Bake in waffle iron until golden brown.

Serves 4.

—George Driscoll
Dutton, Ontario

FINNISH OVEN PANCAKE

"THIS PANCAKE PUFFS UP, THEN COLLAPSES. IT IS GOOD HOT OR COLD. I SERVE IT WITH SYRUP and sliced fresh fruit."

3 eggs
1 cup milk
½ cup flour
2 Tbsp. sugar

¼ tsp. salt
1 tsp. vanilla (optional)
¼ cup butter

Beat eggs until fluffy. Add remaining ingredients, except for butter, beating continuously. Melt butter in ovenproof skillet, then pour in batter. Bake at 400 degrees F for 20 to 25 minutes, or until knife inserted in middle comes out clean.

Serves 2.

—Jeanne Reitz
Yreka, California

FRUIT PANCAKE

"THIS IS OUR FAVOURITE LEISURELY MORNING BREAKFAST. I USE APPLES, PLUMS OR PEACHES – fresh or frozen." Add a brandy sauce, and this pancake becomes a tasty dessert.

¼ cup butter
¼ cup brown sugar
1 tsp. cinnamon
4 apples, plums **or** peaches
4 eggs, separated

⅓ cup sugar
⅓ cup flour
½ tsp. baking powder
⅓ cup milk

Heat oven to 400 degrees F and melt butter in 10″ round baking dish. Remove from oven and sprinkle with brown sugar and cinnamon. Slice fruit and arrange in dish, then return to oven for 8 to 10 minutes.

Meanwhile, beat egg whites until foamy and gradually beat in sugar until stiff. In another bowl, combine flour and baking powder, beat in milk and yolks, then fold in egg-white mixture. Spread evenly over fruit.

Bake for 20 minutes. Loosen edges and invert onto serving plate.

Serves 2 to 3.

—Adele Dueck
Lucky Lake, Saskatchewan

BUCKWHEAT PANCAKES

ONE CUP OF BLUEBERRIES CAN BE ADDED TO THIS RECIPE. THE PANCAKES ARE TENDER, MOIST and delicate.

½ cup buckwheat flour	3 eggs
½ cup flour	2 Tbsp. oil
2 tsp. baking powder	1 cup milk
1 Tbsp. sugar	oil for cooking

Combine flours, baking powder and sugar. Beat together eggs, oil and milk, then beat into dry ingredients. Heat oil in skillet, and cook pancakes over medium heat, turning when bubbles form on uncooked side.

Serves 2 to 3.

—Lorna Palmer
Gloucester, Ontario

APPLE PANCAKES

"THESE PANCAKES FREEZE WELL. THE RECIPE IS OF POLISH ORIGIN AND HAS BEEN HANDED DOWN through my family for three generations."

2 Tbsp. yeast	4 eggs, beaten
2 cups warm water	6 cups flour
½ cup honey	½ tsp. salt
2 cups milk	6 apples, peeled & thinly sliced
¼ cup butter	oil for cooking

Proof yeast in water and honey for 10 minutes. Add remaining ingredients and mix well. Knead briefly, then let rise for at least 1 hour. Fry in hot oil over medium heat until golden brown.

Makes 2 dozen large pancakes.

—Karen Havelock
Gimli, Manitoba

BANANA BRAN BREAD

VARY THIS RECIPE BY SUBSTITUTING DARK RUM FOR THE ORANGE JUICE OR WALNUTS FOR THE raisins. This is a delicious bread with a wonderful texture.

¾ cup butter	3 cups flour
1½ cups brown sugar	4 tsp. baking powder
3 eggs	1 tsp. salt
2 cups bran	1 tsp. baking soda
3 cups mashed banana	1½ cups raisins
¼ cup orange juice	

Cream butter and sugar, then add eggs and beat until light. Stir in bran. Mix bananas with orange juice. Sift together dry ingredients. Add dry ingredients alternately with bananas to creamed mixture, beating after each addition. Fold in raisins. Pour into greased and floured loaf pans and bake at 350 degrees F for 1 hour.

Makes 2 loaves.

—Donna Jubb
Fenelon Falls, Ontario

TEN-YEAR GRANOLA

"THE TITLE REFERS TO THE 10 YEARS DURING WHICH THIS RECIPE EVOLVED, EACH BATCH BEING appraised and modified by my husband."

6 cups oatmeal
1 cup wheat flakes
1 cup rye flakes
1 cup almonds **or** cashews
1 cup sunflower seeds
½ cup sesame seeds

¼-½ cup whole wheat flour
1 cup brown sugar
salt
½ cup oil
½ cup honey
3 tsp. vanilla

Combine dry and wet ingredients separately and then mix together, stirring well to moisten. Lightly grease large roasting pan, then scoop in granola. Bake at 300 degrees F for 40 minutes, stirring frequently.

Makes approximately 10 cups.

—Susanna Barnett
Bellevue, Washington

JOHN'S BREAD

OUR VERMONT TESTER SAYS, "I'LL DEFINITELY MAKE THIS AGAIN. IT'S A HEARTY, CHEWY BROWN bread. Just great!" Serve warm with cream cheese.

5¼ cups graham flour
3 cups flour
¾ cup sugar
1½ tsp. salt

1 Tbsp. baking soda
1 Tbsp. baking powder
1 cup molasses
3 cups sour milk

Combine all ingredients and mix thoroughly. Place in 2 greased loaf pans and bake at 350 degrees F for 1 hour.

Makes 2 loaves.

—Susan Holec
Brooklyn, Wisconsin

LEMON BREAD

THIS IS A SWEET CAKELIKE BREAD, RICH WITH LEMON FLAVOUR.

1 cup butter
2 cups sugar
4 eggs
½ tsp. salt
½ tsp. baking soda
3 cups flour
1 cup buttermilk

grated rind of 1 lemon
1 cup chopped pecans

Glaze
1 cup sugar
juice of 3 lemons

Cream butter and sugar, then add eggs one at a time and mix well. Sift together salt, baking soda and flour and add to creamed mixture alternately with buttermilk. Add lemon rind and nuts and pour into 2 large greased and floured loaf pans. Bake at 350 degrees F for 1 hour.

Meanwhile, prepare glaze. Heat sugar and lemon juice slowly to dissolve sugar. Pour over loaves while cooling in pans.

Makes 2 loaves.

—Susan Robinson
Crane, Texas

FRENCH HONEY BREAD

1 cup honey
1 cup milk
½ cup sugar
2 egg yolks, beaten

2½ cups flour
1 tsp. baking soda
½ tsp. salt
¾ cup currants **or** chopped nuts

Combine honey, milk and sugar in heavy pot and heat slowly until well blended. Cool slightly, then add egg yolks. Combine flour, baking soda and salt, then stir slowly into honey mixture. Stir in currants or nuts. Pour into greased loaf pan and bake at 325 degrees F for 1 to 1½ hours.

Makes 1 loaf.

—Giedre Abromaitis
Ottawa, Ontario

CHEDDAR DILL LOAF

"WE SERVE THIS LOAF, A FAMILY FAVOURITE, VERY THINLY SLICED AND LIGHTLY BUTTERED WITH smoked turkey and ham as a pre-dinner snack."

2 cups flour
2 Tbsp. sugar
3 tsp. baking powder
1½ Tbsp. dill seed
2 Tbsp. minced onion

1 cup grated sharp Cheddar cheese
1 cup milk
1 egg
3 Tbsp. melted butter

Combine flour, sugar, baking powder and dill in large bowl. Add onion and cheese and mix well.

Combine milk, egg and butter in small bowl. Add all at once to dry ingredients and stir to moisten. Bake in greased loaf pan at 350 degrees F for 50 to 55 minutes.

Makes 1 loaf.

—Jim & Penny Wright
Roxboro, Quebec

HONEY SOUR CREAM COFFEECAKE

"I FOUND THIS COFFEECAKE AND THE RECIPE FOR IT ON MY DOORSTEP SHORTLY AFTER MY daughter's birth. What a treat!" The recipe is very versatile—add fruit or cocoa for a different taste.

¼ cup butter
½ cup honey
2 eggs, lightly beaten
1 tsp. baking soda
1 cup sour cream **or** yogurt
1½ cups flour
1½ tsp. baking powder

1 Tbsp. vanilla

Topping
¼ cup chopped nuts
½ tsp. cinnamon
2 Tbsp. butter
1 Tbsp. honey

Cream together butter, honey and eggs. Stir baking soda into sour cream, then add to butter mixture. Combine flour and baking powder, then stir into liquid ingredients. Add vanilla. Pour into greased and floured tube pan.

Combine topping ingredients and sprinkle over cake. Bake at 350 degrees F for 45 minutes, open oven door and let cool in oven.

—Leslie Pierpont
Santa Fe, New Mexico

CHRISTINE'S CORNBREAD

¾ cup sugar
½ cup butter
2 eggs, beaten
½ tsp. salt

2 tsp. baking powder
1½ cups flour
1 cup cornmeal
1½ cups milk

Cream together sugar, butter and eggs. Sift together salt, baking powder, flour and cornmeal, then add to creamed mixture alternately with milk. Bake in greased 9″ x 13″ pan at 375 degrees F for 25 to 30 minutes.

—Laine Roddick
Brockville, Ontario

BANANA OATMEAL COFFEECAKE

¾ cup flour
¾ cup whole wheat flour
¾ cup oats
1 tsp. baking powder
¾ tsp. baking soda
½ tsp. salt
½ cup butter, softened
½ cup brown sugar
½ cup white sugar
2 eggs

1 tsp. vanilla
2 ripe bananas, mashed
⅓ cup sour milk

Topping
⅓ cup brown sugar
¼ cup chopped pecans
3 Tbsp. flour
2 Tbsp. butter

Combine flours, oats, baking powder, baking soda and salt and mix well. Cream together butter and sugars, then add eggs and vanilla. Beat in bananas, then milk. Fold wet ingredients into dry.

Make topping by combining ingredients and mixing until crumbly. Pour batter into greased and floured 9″ x 13″ pan, sprinkle with topping and bake at 375 degrees F for 20 to 25 minutes.

—Ann Lutz
Black Mountain, North Carolina

APRICOT PRUNE COFFEECAKE

¾ cup prunes
¾ cup dried apricots
2 cups flour
2 tsp. baking powder
½ tsp. salt
¾ cup butter
¾ cup sugar
2 eggs

¾ cup milk
1 tsp. vanilla

Filling
⅔ cup brown sugar
1 Tbsp. flour
1 Tbsp. cinnamon
4 Tbsp. melted butter

Soak prunes and apricots in boiling water to cover for 5 minutes. Drain and set aside.

Combine flour, baking powder and salt. Cream together butter and sugar, then beat in eggs. Combine milk and vanilla. Add milk and dry ingredients alternately to butter mixture, mixing well after each addition. Stir in fruit.

Pour ⅓ of the batter into greased and floured tube pan. Combine filling ingredients and pour half of this onto batter. Repeat, ending with layer of batter. Bake at 350 degrees F for 55 minutes.

—Maureen Marcotte
Farrellton, Quebec

CRANBERRY COFFEECAKE

"My husband and I run a small seasonal marina and waterfront café. This coffeecake is a favourite among our clientele."

8 oz. cream cheese, softened
1 cup butter
1½ cups sugar
1½ tsp. vanilla
4 eggs

2¼ cups flour
1½ tsp. baking powder
2 cups fresh cranberries
½ cup chopped nuts
confectioners' sugar

Thoroughly cream together cream cheese, butter, sugar and vanilla. Add eggs one at a time, mixing well after each addition.

Gradually add 2 cups flour and baking powder. Combine remaining ¼ cup flour with cranberries and nuts and fold into batter.

Pour into greased and floured tube pan and bake at 350 degrees F for 1 hour and 15 minutes. Let stand for 5 minutes before removing from pan. Dust with confectioners' sugar.

—*Mrs. Robert Uttech*
Eagle River, Wisconsin

GERMAN FRUIT CRUMB COFFEECAKE

"I grew up with this recipe. Whenever we would go to visit my grandmother, she had one of these coffeecakes in her pantry waiting to be sliced and enjoyed by her children and grandchildren. More recently, I have made this for our local natural-food market, where it was extremely popular." Use plain water if you do not have just-boiled potatoes.

Cake
2 cups hot potato water
¼ cup honey
1 tsp. salt
2 pkgs. yeast
1 egg, beaten
½ cup melted unsalted butter
7 cups flour

Topping
4 cups flour
2 cups sugar
¼ tsp. salt
1 tsp. cinnamon
1 cup melted unsalted butter

milk
6-8 cups sliced fruit

For cake: Combine water, honey and salt and stir until honey is dissolved. When lukewarm, add yeast and let dissolve. Stir in egg, then add butter and 3½ cups flour. Beat well, then gradually add remaining flour.

Turn out on lightly floured surface and let rest for 10 minutes. Knead until smooth and elastic. Place in greased bowl, turning once to grease all sides of dough. Let rise until doubled in size – about 1 hour.

While dough is rising, make topping. Combine flour, sugar, salt and cinnamon, then stir in butter until mixture forms crumbs.

Punch down dough. (It can be covered with a damp cloth and kept refrigerated for up to 5 days, if desired, at this point.) Divide in half and pat each half out onto a greased cookie sheet. Prick with fork and brush with milk. Spread fruit out evenly over dough, then cover with crumb mixture. Let rise for 30 minutes more, then bake at 350 degrees F until lightly brown – 30 to 45 minutes.

Makes 2 cakes.

—*Nancy Wellborn*
Manitou Springs, Colorado

TARRAGON TEA WAFERS

"SESAME SEED IS THE SYMBOL OF IMMORTALITY, AND TARRAGON IS AN INGREDIENT OF THE DRINK of kings. The two herbs are brought together in these tea wafers."

½ cup butter
1 cup firmly packed brown sugar
1 tsp. vanilla
1 egg
½ cup toasted sesame seeds

½ cup crushed pecans
1½ tsp. crushed tarragon
¾ cup flour
¼ tsp. baking powder
¼ tsp. salt

Cream butter and sugar, then mix in vanilla and egg. Beat in sesame seeds, pecans and tarragon. Add dry ingredients and mix well. Drop in small mounds, about 3 inches apart, on greased baking sheet. Bake at 375 degrees F for 8 to 10 minutes. (Watch them: they burn easily.) Let cool for a minute before removing from pan.

Makes about 4 dozen wafers.

—*Cary Elizabeth Marshall*
Thunder Bay, Ontario

TARRAGON CHEESE BREAD

USE SWISS, MOZZARELLA OR MONTEREY JACK CHEESE FOR THIS RECIPE. THIS MAKES A FRAGRANT, hearty bread that is delicious warm or cold.

bread dough for 1 loaf
1½ lbs. white cheese

3 eggs, beaten
1 Tbsp. tarragon

Roll bread dough into a 22- to 24-inch circle. Grate cheese, then mix with 2 eggs and tarragon. Grease a 9"-round cake pan and line with dough, leaving a large overhang. Fill with cheese, then bring dough up and over filling, folding into pleats. Grab pleats 3 inches from end and twist to seal. Set to rise in warm place until doubled in bulk—about 1 hour.

Bake at 375 degrees F for 45 minutes. Brush with remaining egg, then bake for 15 minutes more. Let cool slightly, then cut into wedges to serve.

—*Debi Larson*
Mountain View, Missouri

CHEESY CURRY BISCUITS

2 cups flour
3 tsp. baking powder
½ tsp. salt
½ tsp. curry powder

4 Tbsp. butter
⅔ cup grated sharp Cheddar cheese
⅞ cup milk

Sift together flour, baking powder, salt and curry powder. Cut in butter until mixture is mealy. Add cheese, then make well in centre. Gradually add milk, stirring, until soft dough is formed.

Turn onto floured board and knead briefly. Roll out to ¾-inch thickness. Cut into 2-inch biscuits. Bake on ungreased cookie sheet at 450 degrees F for 12 to 15 minutes.

Makes 16 biscuits.

—*Carol Swann-Jacob*
Port McNeill, British Columbia

CINNAMON BUNS

MAKE UP THE DOUGH THE NIGHT BEFORE, AND LET THE BUNS RISE FOR THE FINAL TIME IN THE refrigerator overnight. This then becomes a quick but very special breakfast.

½ cup warm water
½ tsp. white sugar
1 pkg. yeast
2 cups milk
½ cup butter, softened
1 cup white sugar

1 tsp. salt
1 tsp. vanilla
5 cups flour
melted butter
¼ cup brown sugar
1 Tbsp. cinnamon

Combine water and ½ tsp. white sugar, then add yeast. Let sit for 10 minutes, then add milk, butter, 1 cup white sugar, salt, vanilla and flour (only enough so dough can still be mixed with a wooden spoon). Mix well, then let rise for 2 to 3 hours.

Turn out onto well-floured work surface. Punch down, then flatten into rectangular shape. Brush with melted butter, then sprinkle with brown sugar and cinnamon. Roll up and cut into 1¼-inch slices. Place in greased muffin tins and let rise until doubled in size. Bake at 375 degrees F for 30 minutes.

Makes approximately 24 buns.

—Rose Strocen
Canora, Saskatchewan

HONEY PECAN ROLLS

"WE KEEP BEES, SO THIS RECIPE HELPS US USE UP OUR PLENTIFUL SUPPLY OF HONEY."

1 Tbsp. yeast
2 tsp. honey
½ cup warm water
1 tsp. salt
¼ cup honey
2 eggs, lightly beaten
½ cup butter, melted
3-3½ cups flour
1 cup coarsely chopped pecans

Glaze
¾ cup honey
¾ cup brown sugar
6 Tbsp. butter

Filling
melted butter
½ cup brown sugar
2 tsp. cinnamon

Combine yeast, 2 tsp. honey and water and let sit for 10 minutes. Add salt, ¼ cup honey, eggs and ½ cup melted butter and mix well. Add flour to make thick dough.

Turn out onto floured board and knead for 5 minutes. Place in greased bowl, turning once. Cover and let rise until doubled – about 1 hour.

Place pecans in bottom of 9" x 13" pan. For glaze, combine honey, ¾ cup sugar and butter in heavy saucepan. Bring to a boil, remove from heat and cool slightly.

Roll dough into 15-by-13-inch rectangle. Brush with melted butter and sprinkle with ½ cup brown sugar and cinnamon. Roll up and cut into 1-inch slices. Place over pecans, pour glaze over and let rise for 1 hour. Bake at 350 degrees F for 30 minutes.

Makes 15 rolls.

—Mary Ellen Hoar
Covington, Pennsylvania

CINNAMON SOUR CREAM TWISTS

THERE ARE FEW PEOPLE WHO WILL TURN DOWN THIS BREAKFAST DELICACY. SERVED HOT FROM the oven and dripping with butter, they are irresistible. Make this dough the day before and then bake up the twists for a special breakfast.

1 pkg. yeast	2 eggs, beaten
¼ cup warm water	1 tsp. salt
4 cups flour	1 tsp. vanilla
1 cup butter, melted	1 cup sugar
1 cup sour cream	1 tsp. cinnamon

Sprinkle yeast into water and stir until dissolved. Combine flour, butter, sour cream, eggs, salt and vanilla. Stir in yeast and work until smooth. Cover with damp cloth and refrigerate for at least 2 hours or up to 2 days.

Combine sugar and cinnamon. Roll dough into 15-by-18-inch rectangle, then coat both sides with sugar-cinnamon mixture. Fold over in thirds, then roll into ¼-inch-thick rectangle. Cut into 1-inch-wide strips, twist and place on greased baking sheet. Bake at 375 degrees F for 15 minutes.

Makes approximately 18 twists.

—Marklyn A. Hallett
Spokane, Washington

CARAMEL ROLLS

THERE CAN BE FEW THINGS BETTER AT TEMPTING PEOPLE OUT OF BED IN THE MORNING THAN THE smell of sticky buns baking and coffee brewing. These are attractive, delicious and easy to make. Eat them right away, though, as they do not keep well.

2 cups flour	¾ cup milk
4 tsp. baking powder	2 Tbsp. soft butter
½ tsp. salt	1 cup brown sugar
½ cup butter	1 Tbsp. cinnamon

Combine flour, baking powder and salt. Cut in ¼ cup butter until butter is size of peas, then stir in milk. Mix this to a soft dough.

Turn onto floured board and pat into a ⅜-inch-thick rectangle. Spread dough with 2 Tbsp. soft butter and sprinkle with ½ cup brown sugar mixed with cinnamon. Roll up and cut into 1-inch slices.

Place remaining ¼ cup butter in two 9″-round pans and melt. Sprinkle with remaining ½ cup sugar. Arrange rolls on this, and bake at 450 degrees F for 15 to 20 minutes, moving to top oven shelf after 12 minutes. Turn out onto serving dish at once, scraping out any caramel that remains in pan.

Makes 12 rolls.

—Janeen Clynick
Clinton, Ontario

POTATO STICKY BUNS

"THESE STICKY BUNS ARE A FAVOURITE WITH MY FAMILY. WHENEVER WE TRAVEL TO OUR SON'S or daughter's house for a visit, I am asked to bring along a package of sticky buns. Luckily, they can be made ahead of time and frozen."

1 cup hot mashed potatoes
½ cup sugar
1½ tsp. salt
½ cup butter
1 pkg. yeast
2 eggs

1½ cups warm potato water
7 cups flour
brown sugar
chopped nuts
melted butter
cinnamon

Combine potatoes, sugar, salt and butter. When lukewarm, add yeast, eggs and potato water. Stir in flour to make a stiff dough. Knead until smooth, then let rise until doubled in size – 1 hour. Punch down, refrigerate and chill thoroughly.

Butter four 9″-round pans. Cover with ⅓-inch brown sugar, then sprinkle with nuts. Roll dough to ½-inch thickness. Brush with butter and sprinkle with brown sugar and cinnamon. Roll dough up and cut into ½-inch circles. Place in pans and let rise again until doubled – 30 minutes. Bake at 350 degrees F for 25 to 35 minutes.

Makes 2 dozen buns.

—Marilyn Vincent
Gainesville, Virginia

STICKY BUNS

AS WITH THE OTHER YEAST RECIPES IN THIS SECTION, WORK ON THESE BUNS CAN BE STARTED THE evening before they are to be eaten. Breakfast-eaters will be most appreciative and will think you rose before the sun to make them.

1 Tbsp. yeast
¼ cup lukewarm water
1 cup scalded milk
¾ cup sugar
2 Tbsp. shortening
1 tsp. salt
4 cups flour

1 egg
¼ cup melted butter
2 tsp. cinnamon
¼ cup raisins
light corn syrup
½ cup chopped pecans

Soften yeast in water and let stand for 10 minutes. Combine scalded milk, ¼ cup sugar, shortening and salt and cool to lukewarm. Stir in 1½ cups flour and egg. Stir in the yeast then add remaining flour. Mix well, let rest for 10 minutes, then knead until smooth.

Let rise until doubled – 1 hour. Punch down and roll out to ¼-inch-thick rectangle. Brush on melted butter, then sprinkle with remaining ½ cup sugar, cinnamon and raisins. Roll dough up.

Butter a 9″ x 13″ baking pan. Drizzle thin layer of corn syrup in bottom of pan, and sprinkle with nuts. Cut dough into 12 slices, and place in pan. Bake at 350 degrees F for 20 to 30 minutes.

Makes 12 buns.

—Anne Morrell
Margaree Valley, Nova Scotia

FERGOSA

½ cup chopped onion
3 Tbsp. butter
1 cup flour
1½ tsp. baking powder
salt

1½ cups grated cheese
⅓ cup milk
1 egg, lightly beaten
poppy seeds

Sauté onion in 1 Tbsp. butter until transparent, then set aside. Combine flour, baking powder, salt, 2 Tbsp. butter, ½ cup cheese and milk and beat until smooth. The dough will be sticky. Knead 10 times on floured board, working in a bit of flour if necessary.

Grease an 8-inch pie plate and your hands, then spread dough evenly in pan. Combine remaining 1 cup cheese and egg. Spread on dough. Sprinkle with onion and poppy seeds. Bake at 425 degrees F for 20 minutes.

Serves 4 to 6.

—Rosande Bellaar-Spruyt
Rupert, Quebec

CHOCOLATE PEANUT BUTTER SQUARES

A RICH, TASTY COMBINATION OF CHOCOLATE AND PEANUT BUTTER, THESE SQUARES RANKED high with the Camden East staff who tasted them.

1½ cups graham cracker crumbs
1 cup icing sugar
½ cup butter

¾ cup peanut butter
6 oz. chocolate chips

Combine cracker crumbs and icing sugar. Melt butter and peanut butter, then pour into crumbs, mix well and pat into bottom of greased 8″ x 8″ pan. Melt chocolate chips and pour over crust. Chill for 30 minutes, then cut into squares.

Makes 16 squares.

—Barbara Littlejohn
Niagara Falls, Ontario

WHITE CHOCOLATE MOCHA JAVA BARS

CUT THESE BARS BEFORE THE WHITE CHOCOLATE HARDENS COMPLETELY. THEY ARE A DELI-ciously decadent variation of Nanaimo Bars.

¾ cup butter
½ cup sugar
1 tsp. vanilla
1 egg
2 cups graham cracker crumbs
1 cup desiccated coconut
½ cup finely chopped toasted hazelnuts

2 tsp. instant coffee crystals
2 Tbsp. hot coffee
2½ cups icing sugar
¼ cup cocoa
2 Tbsp. milk
6 oz. white chocolate

Combine ½ cup butter, sugar, vanilla and egg in top of double boiler. Cook, stirring, over boiling water until slightly thickened. Blend in cracker crumbs, coconut and hazelnuts and spread evenly in greased 9″ x 9″ baking pan. Let stand 15 minutes.

Meanwhile, dissolve instant coffee crystals in hot coffee. Blend well with icing sugar, cocoa, remaining ¼ cup butter and milk. Spread over crust and chill for 10 minutes. Melt chocolate and spread over filling. Chill well.

Makes 16 to 18 squares.

—Denise Atkinson
Alcove, Quebec

POPPY SEED SQUARES

POPPY SEEDS, COCONUT AND HONEY ARE A WINNING COMBINATION. THE SQUARES ARE CHEWY and delicious.

1¾ cups flour
1 tsp. baking powder
¼ tsp. baking soda
1¼ cups sugar
½ tsp. salt
½ cup butter, melted
⅓ cup honey

2 eggs
2 Tbsp. milk
1 tsp. vanilla
1 cup coconut
½ cup poppy seeds
icing sugar

Sift flour, baking powder, baking soda, sugar and salt into mixing bowl. Add butter, honey, eggs, milk and vanilla. Beat with electric mixer until well blended, then stir in coconut and poppy seeds. Spread evenly in greased 9″ x 13″ pan. Bake at 350 degrees F for 25 to 30 minutes. Remove to wire rack and cool, then sprinkle top with icing sugar.

Makes approximately 24 squares.

—Tracy Willemsen
Prince George, British Columbia

TANTE VIVIEN'S BUTTERSCOTCH BROWNIES

NOT TOO SWEET, THESE BROWNIES ARE VERY QUICK AND EASY TO MAKE.

½ cup melted butter
1 cup brown sugar
1 egg, beaten
1 tsp. vanilla
¾ cup flour

1 tsp. baking powder
½ cup walnuts
½ cup coconut
½ cup currants

Combine all ingredients and mix well. Bake in greased 9″ x 9″ pan at 350 degrees F for 30 minutes. Cut into squares while still warm.

Makes 12 to 16 squares.

—Olga Zuyderhoff
Perth, Ontario

CHRIS WARKENTIN'S APRICOT BARS

PROBABLY JUST ABOUT ANY DRIED FRUIT COULD BE SUBSTITUTED FOR INTERESTING VARIATIONS. These are quite sweet, sticky and sinful.

⅔ cup dried apricots
½ cup butter
1¼ cups brown sugar
1⅓ cups flour

2 eggs
½ tsp. baking powder
½ cup chopped walnuts
1 tsp. almond extract

Cover apricots with water and simmer for 10 minutes. Drain, cool and chop.

Mix butter, ¼ cup sugar and 1 cup flour with fork and then fingers until crumbly. Press into 8″ x 8″ pan and bake at 350 degrees F for 20 minutes, or until lightly browned.

Meanwhile, beat eggs well. Beat in remaining 1 cup sugar, then add ⅓ cup flour and baking powder. Stir in apricots, nuts and almond extract and spread over baked crust. Bake for 20 to 30 minutes more.

Makes 12 to 16 squares.

—Andrea Stuart
Winnipeg, Manitoba

RIGO JANCSI

THESE HUNGARIAN SQUARES ARE MADE FOR CHOCOLATE FANATICS. THEY TAKE A LOT OF TIME to prepare so are definitely for special occasions.

Cake
3 oz. unsweetened chocolate
4 eggs, separated
½ cup sugar
¾ cup butter
⅔ cup flour
¼ tsp. salt
1 tsp. vanilla

Filling
10 oz. semisweet chocolate
2 cups heavy cream
2 Tbsp. coffee liqueur

Frosting
1 cup superfine sugar
½ cup hot coffee
6 oz. semisweet chocolate
2 Tbsp. light corn syrup
2 Tbsp. butter
2 Tbsp. coffee liqueur

To make cake: Melt chocolate in top of double boiler over hot water, then cool to lukewarm. Grease 15" x 10" baking pan, line with waxed paper and grease the paper.

Beat egg whites until foamy and doubled in volume in medium-sized bowl. Beat in ¼ cup sugar, 1 Tbsp. at a time, until meringue stands in soft peaks.

Beat butter in large bowl. Gradually add remaining ¼ cup sugar and continue beating until mixture is well blended. Beat in egg yolks until smooth, then cooled chocolate. Sift flour and salt into chocolate mixture. Stir to blend, then add vanilla.

Stir ⅓ of the meringue mixture into chocolate mixture, then fold in remaining meringue mixture until well blended. Spread batter evenly into prepared pan.

Bake at 350 degrees F for 15 minutes, or until top springs back when lightly touched. Cool in pan on wire rack for 5 minutes, then loosen cake around edges with sharp knife and invert onto a large cookie sheet. Peel off waxed paper, invert cake onto a large cake rack and cool completely.

Meanwhile, make filling. Cut chocolate into small pieces. Combine with cream in saucepan and heat slowly, stirring constantly, until chocolate melts. Remove from heat and stir in coffee liqueur. Pour into bowl and chill for 1½ hours, or until mixture is completely cold. Beat chilled chocolate-cream mixture until stiff and thick.

Cut cooled cake in half crosswise. Place half on small cookie sheet. Top with whipped chocolate cream, spreading to make a layer about 1½ inches thick. Top with second half of cake. Chill for at least 1 hour, or until filling is firm.

To make frosting: Heat sugar and coffee until sugar dissolves. Cut chocolate into small pieces and add to saucepan along with corn syrup. Heat to boiling, stirring constantly, then cook at a slow boil, still stirring constantly, for 5 minutes. Remove from heat and add butter and coffee liqueur. Beat for 5 minutes, or until mixture thickens. Quickly spread over cake layer about ¼-inch thick. Chill for at least 1 hour.

Makes 12 squares.

—Kristine Mattila
Quesnel, British Columbia

CARROT ZUCCHINI SQUARES

MOIST AND TASTY, THESE SQUARES ARE A GOOD WAY TO GET CHILDREN TO EAT THE OFTEN
unpopular zucchini.

⅔ cup firmly packed light brown sugar
½ cup butter
1 egg
1 tsp. vanilla
1½ cups flour

1 tsp. baking powder
salt
⅔ cup coarsely grated carrot
⅔ cup coarsely grated zucchini, drained
½ cup raisins

Beat sugar and butter together. Add egg and vanilla and beat thoroughly. Add remaining
ingredients and stir together. Spoon into greased 9″ x 9″ pan. Bake at 350 degrees F for 30
minutes, or until a toothpick inserted in the centre comes out clean.

Makes 12 to 16 squares.

—Rosalind Mechefske
Guelph, Ontario

CINNAMON CRUNCHIES

"THIS RECIPE WAS GIVEN TO ME BY MY MOTHER-IN-LAW. IT REMINDS ME OF THE 'CINNAMON PIE'
we made out of leftover pie crust as children."

1 cup flour
¼ tsp. salt
½ tsp. cinnamon
⅓ cup butter
½ cup sugar
1 egg yolk
2 Tbsp. milk

¼ tsp. vanilla

Topping
1 egg white
3 Tbsp. sugar
½ tsp. cinnamon
¼ cup chopped walnuts

Sift together flour, salt and cinnamon. Add remaining ingredients and mix well. Spread in
an ungreased 8″ x 8″ baking pan.

To make topping: Beat egg white until frothy and spread over dough. Mix sugar, cinnamon
and walnuts and sprinkle over top. Bake at 350 degrees F for 30 minutes.

Makes 12 to 16 squares.

—Marla J. Davis
Jamestown, New York

HONEY PECAN BUTTERBALLS

1 cup butter
¼ cup honey
2 cups flour

½ tsp. salt
2 tsp. vanilla
2 cups finely chopped pecans

Cream butter and honey, then stir in flour, salt and vanilla. Fold in nuts. Form into small
balls and place on greased cookie sheets. Bake at 300 degrees F for 40 to 45 minutes or
until lightly browned.

Makes 3 to 4 dozen cookies.

—Teresa Carel
Winona, Missouri

WELSH CURRANT CAKES

"These cookies take some practice to make perfectly. They should look like English muffins and be as light and flaky as biscuits." Well-cleaned empty tuna cans can be kept and used as cutters for these and similar biscuits.

3 cups flour
1 cup sugar
1½ tsp. baking powder
1¼ tsp. salt
½ tsp. baking soda

2 tsp. nutmeg
1 cup shortening
1 cup currants
2 eggs
6 Tbsp. milk

Sift together flour, sugar, baking powder, salt, baking soda and nutmeg. Cut in shortening, then add currants. Beat eggs and milk together. Add to flour mixture and mix to make a stiff dough. Chill for 1 to 2 hours.

Divide dough into thirds, then roll out to ¼-inch thickness on lightly floured board. Cut into round biscuits.

Heat griddle until water drops bounce off it. Lightly grease, then cook biscuits until tops puff and turn shiny. Flip and bake until golden.

Makes 24 biscuits.

—Mary Bacon
Middletown, Pennsylvania

SWEDISH GINGER COOKIES

"I love to make these cookies with my children, not only because they are delicious to eat, but also because the children enjoy watching the baking soda reaction in the saucepan." An enticing winter bedtime snack is ginger cookies accompanied by hot chocolate or warm milk. Ginger is the underground stem of a plant that grows in Asia, the West Indies, South America, Africa and Australia. It is equally at home in cakes, cookies and desserts as well as in curries and other savoury dishes.

⅔ cup unsulfured molasses
⅔ cup honey
1 Tbsp. ginger
1 Tbsp. cinnamon
2 tsp. baking soda

⅔ cup butter, cut into 1" chunks
1 egg, lightly beaten
2 cups whole wheat flour
2 cups white flour

In heavy 2-quart saucepan over moderate heat, bring molasses, honey, ginger and cinnamon just to a low boil, stirring occasionally. Add baking soda and stir until mixture foams to top of pan. Remove from heat, add butter and stir until melted. Mix in egg and gradually stir into flours in bowl.

Turn dough out of bowl and knead lightly until well blended. Divide dough into 2 balls. Roll out on lightly floured board to ⅛-inch thickness. Cut cookies with cutters, or freehand with sharp knife, and place on foil-lined cookie sheet. Bake at 325 degrees F for about 13 minutes.

Makes approximately 8 dozen 2½-inch cookies.

—Leslie Pierpont
Santa Fe, New Mexico

LACE COOKIES

"THIN, CRISP AND ALMOST TRANSPARENT, THESE SPLENDID COOKIES ARE EASY TO MAKE." BAKE the cookies on parchment paper – it is available in cooking supply stores, can be used over and over, and the cookies will lift off easily, thus eliminating the frustration of having a perfect cookie glued forever to the cookie sheet.

1½ cups oatmeal
1½ cups light brown sugar
2 Tbsp. flour
½ tsp. salt

⅔ cup melted butter
1 egg, lightly beaten
½ tsp. vanilla

Combine oatmeal, sugar, flour and salt and mix well. Stir in melted butter, then egg and vanilla. Line cookie sheets with parchment paper. Drop batter by half-teaspoonsful, 2 inches apart. Flatten cookies with fork dipped in water.

Bake at 350 degrees F until lightly browned – approximately 5 minutes. Cool cookies on parchment paper (just slide off cookie sheet), then lift off with spatula.

Makes approximately 40 cookies.

—Sharon McKay
Riverview, New Brunswick

KIPFEL

KIPFEL, OR BUTTERHORNS, ARE A TRADITIONAL GERMAN COOKIE, OFTEN SERVED WITH afternoon tea or coffee. These are also delicious dipped in hot chocolate as a bedtime snack. For a real treat, add a dash of chocolate or almond liqueur to the hot chocolate and top with sweetened whipped cream.

2 Tbsp. warm water
¼ tsp. sugar
1 Tbsp. yeast
2 cups flour
½ cup butter
2 egg yolks
½ cup sour cream
confectioners' sugar

Filling
1 cup finely chopped walnuts
½ cup sugar
1 tsp. vanilla
2 egg whites
pinch cream of tartar

Combine water and sugar, then stir in yeast and set aside for 10 minutes. Place flour in bowl, cut in butter, then add yeast, egg yolks and sour cream. Mix well, form into a ball and knead. Divide into 3 parts and chill for at least 1 hour.

Sprinkle pastry board with confectioners' sugar, roll dough out into circle and cut into 12 wedges.

Make filling by combining nuts, sugar and vanilla. Beat egg whites with cream of tartar until stiff, then fold into nut mixture. Fill wide end of dough with 1 tsp. filling and spread toward narrow end. Roll up from wide end to narrow. Bake at 350 degrees F for 15 minutes.

Makes 36 butterhorns.

—Gladys Sykes
Regina, Saskatchewan

GRANDMA MARION'S COCONUT-OATMEAL COOKIES

"THE TASTE AND TEXTURE OF THESE COOKIES VARY DEPENDING ON THEIR THICKNESS. IF PRESSED very thin, they are crisp, caramel-like and quick-cooking. If thicker, they are a softer, heartier cookie."

¾ cup brown sugar
¼ cup white sugar
1 cup butter
1 egg
1½ cups flour

1 tsp. baking powder
1 tsp. baking soda
1½ cups rolled oats
¾ cup coconut
¼ tsp. vanilla

Cream sugars and butter, then add egg. Sift in flour, baking powder and baking soda, then mix in rolled oats and coconut. Stir in vanilla. Shape into balls, place on greased cookie sheet and flatten with fork dipped in cold water. Bake at 375 degrees F for 5 to 10 minutes.

Makes 3 dozen cookies.

—Isabel Bradley
Gloucester, Ontario

WONDERFUL OATMEAL RAISIN COOKIES

NO EXAGGERATION — THESE ARE TRULY WONDERFUL, CHEWY AND CRISP AT THE SAME TIME.

1 cup shortening
1 cup brown sugar
½ cup white sugar
1 egg
1 tsp. vanilla
½ tsp. cinnamon
½ tsp. ginger

¼ tsp. nutmeg
1 tsp. salt
1 tsp. baking soda
2 cups rolled oats
1 cup flour
½ cup whole wheat flour
1 cup raisins

Cream shortening and sugars. Add egg, vanilla, cinnamon, ginger, nutmeg, salt and baking soda, then stir in oats, flours and raisins. Roll into small balls and place on greased cookie sheet. Flatten with floured fork. Bake at 350 degrees F for 8 to 10 minutes.

Makes 4½ dozen.

—Mary Burbidge
Bancroft, Ontario

OATMEAL COOKIES

1 cup raisins
2½ tsp. baking soda
3 eggs
1 tsp. vanilla
1 cup butter
1 cup brown sugar

1 cup white sugar
2½ cups flour
1 tsp. salt
1 tsp. cinnamon
2 cups oatmeal

Place raisins and 2 cups water in saucepan and boil for 5 minutes. Add 1 tsp. baking soda, stir, then remove raisins and drain, discarding water and baking soda. Beat eggs well, add raisins and vanilla and let stand, covered, for at least 1 hour.

Cream butter and sugars. Add flour, salt, cinnamon and remaining 1½ tsp. baking soda. Mix well, then blend in egg-raisin mixture and oatmeal. Drop by large teaspoonful on ungreased cookie sheet and bake at 350 degrees F for 10 to 12 minutes.

Makes 5 to 6 dozen cookies.

—Laurabel Miller
Denbigh, Ontario

OLD-FASHIONED CHOCOLATE CHIP OATMEAL COOKIES

"THESE COOKIES HAVE A LIGHT, CRUNCHY TEXTURE WHEN FINISHED. THEY HAVE BEEN FILLING our cookie jar for many years – a longtime family favourite!"

1 cup butter
1 cup brown sugar
¾ cup white sugar
1 egg, lightly beaten
1 tsp. vanilla
2 cups flour

½ tsp. salt
1 tsp. baking soda
1 cup rolled oats
12 oz. chocolate chips
½ cup chopped walnuts

Cream butter and sugars until creamy. Add egg, 1 Tbsp. water and vanilla and continue to beat until fluffy. Sift flour, salt and baking soda. Blend into creamed mixture. Stir in remaining ingredients. Drop by teaspoonsful onto greased cookie sheets. Bake at 350 degrees F for 8 to 10 minutes, or until lightly browned.

Makes 3 dozen cookies.

—Susan Varga
Bradford, Ontario

OLD-FASHIONED COCONUT MACAROONS

1 egg
¼ cup sugar
2 cups shredded coconut

Beat egg, then beat in sugar and stir in coconut. Drop onto greased cookie sheet to form small mounds. Bake at 350 degrees F for 12 minutes, or until golden. Cool on pan for a few minutes before transferring to cooling rack.

Makes 2 dozen macaroons.

—I. Atkins
Strathroy, Ontario

PUMPKIN COOKIES

EVEN NON-PUMPKIN FANS WILL ENJOY THIS MOIST, SPICY COOKIE. PUMPKIN CAN BE BAKED, puréed and frozen in the fall and then thawed for use during the winter and spring.

½ cup shortening
1 cup brown sugar
1 cup mashed pumpkin
1 cup raisins
½ cup nuts
1 tsp. vanilla

2 cups flour
1 tsp. baking soda
1 tsp. cinnamon
1 tsp. baking powder
icing sugar (optional)

Cream shortening and sugar, then add pumpkin, raisins, nuts and vanilla and mix well. Sift together flour, baking soda, cinnamon and baking powder and add to creamed ingredients. Mix well, then drop by teaspoonsful onto greased cookie sheet. Bake at 350 degrees F for 8 to 10 minutes. When cool, dust with icing sugar if desired.

Makes 3 dozen cookies.

—Leslie Ann Gray
Amherstview, Ontario

LINZER COOKIES

"THIS RECIPE HAS BEEN PASSED THROUGH FIVE GENERATIONS OF MY FAMILY. THE BOOK containing it is close to disintegration from so many years of use."

¾ cup lard
¾ cup butter
¾ cup sugar
2 eggs

rind & juice of 1 lemon
4 cups flour
jam
icing sugar

Cream lard and butter, then add sugar, eggs and lemon rind and juice. Mix in flour. Roll out to ¼-inch thickness and cut into 2-inch rounds. Bake at 350 degrees F for 20 minutes, or until golden. Cool on rack. Spread half the rounds with jam, then cover with remaining cookies. Dust with icing sugar.

Makes 2 dozen sandwich cookies.

—*Margaret Smit*
Acton, Ontario

PRIZE MINCEMEAT COOKIES

1 cup butter
1½ cups sugar
3 eggs
3 cups flour

1 tsp. baking soda
½ tsp. salt
1⅓ cups mincemeat

Cream butter and sugar, then beat in eggs, one at a time, until smooth. Set aside. Combine flour, baking soda and salt. Gradually add to creamed mixture, then stir in mincemeat. Drop by rounded teaspoonsful onto greased cookie sheet, spacing cookies 2 inches apart. Bake at 375 degrees F for 8 to 10 minutes.

Makes 6½ dozen cookies.

—*Fran Bakke*
Hastings, Minnesota

APRICOT PINWHEEL COOKIES

1 cup chopped dried apricots
¼ cup sugar
1 cup butter, softened
1 cup icing sugar

1 egg
1 tsp. almond extract
3 cups flour
¼ tsp. salt

Combine apricots with ½ cup boiling water in small bowl, set aside until water is absorbed, then stir in sugar. Chop in blender or food processor until consistency of thick, spreadable purée. Set aside. Cream together butter and icing sugar until fluffy. Beat in egg and almond extract. Stir together flour and salt and add, mixing until well blended and dough forms a ball. Chill dough for 30 minutes.

Roll half of dough into a 9-by-12-inch rectangle; spread with half apricot mixture. Roll up from widest side. Wrap in plastic wrap. Repeat with remaining ingredients. Refrigerate rolls for 3 hours or overnight.

Cut into ½-inch slices, then place on greased cookie sheets. Bake at 350 degrees F for 15 minutes, flip cookies over and bake for another 5 minutes.

Makes 5 dozen cookies.

—*Lynn Tobin*
Thornhill, Ontario

PERFECT PEANUT BUTTER COOKIES

A LOFTY CLAIM, PERHAPS, BUT ONE THAT OUR TESTERS ASSURE US IS VALID. USE EITHER SMOOTH or crunchy peanut butter.

½ cup butter
½ cup peanut butter
½ cup white sugar
½ cup packed brown sugar
1 egg

¾ tsp. vanilla
1¼ cups flour
¾ tsp. baking soda
¼ tsp. salt

Beat butter, peanut butter, white sugar and ¼ cup brown sugar until light and fluffy. Beat in egg and vanilla. Combine flour, baking soda and salt, then beat into butter mixture until blended. Sprinkle remaining ¼ cup brown sugar on top of dough and gently fold so sugar granules are still visible.

Roll dough into teaspoonful-sized balls and place 2 inches apart on ungreased cookie sheets. Press into ¼-inch-thick circles. Bake at 375 degrees F for 8 to 10 minutes.

Makes 3 dozen cookies.

—*Carlene T. Blankenship*
Martinsville, Virginia

CHOCOLATE SHORTBREAD COOKIES
WITH CHOCOLATE CHIPS

1 lb. butter, softened
1 cup icing sugar
1¾ cups flour
1 cup cornstarch

¼ cup cocoa
¼ tsp. vanilla
⅓ cup mini chocolate chips

Cream butter and sugar together. Sift together flour, cornstarch and cocoa. Stir into butter mixture, then fold in vanilla and chocolate chips. Drop by teaspoonsful onto ungreased cookie sheet. Bake at 275 degrees F for 30 to 35 minutes.

Makes 4 dozen cookies.

—*Patricia Forrest*
Whitfield, Ontario

COOKIE JAR GINGERSNAPS

THESE ARE LIGHT AND GINGERY — THEY WON'T LAST LONG IN YOUR COOKIE JAR.

¾ cup shortening
1 cup sugar
1 egg
¼ cup molasses
2 cups flour

1 Tbsp. ginger
2 tsp. baking soda
1 tsp. cinnamon
½ tsp. salt
granulated sugar

Cream shortening, then add sugar, egg and molasses. Mix in flour, ginger, baking soda, cinnamon and salt. Form teaspoonsful of dough into round balls, roll in granulated sugar and place 2 inches apart on ungreased cookie sheets. Bake at 350 degrees F for 10 to 15 minutes.

Makes 3 dozen cookies.

—*Hazel Schwartz*
Lumby, British Columbia

BROWN SUGAR JAM COOKIES

"THIS RECIPE CAME FROM MY GRANDMOTHER, THROUGH MY MOTHER, WITH VERY INDEFINITE quantities. It has required a certain amount of experimentation to pin down. We've all eaten a lot of these cookies over the years." Use a tart jam rather than an overly sweet one.

1 cup butter	2 tsp. vanilla
1 cup white sugar	2½ cups flour
1 cup brown sugar	¾ tsp. baking powder
2 eggs	jam

Cream butter and sugars, then add eggs and vanilla and beat well. Add dry ingredients, beating thoroughly. Roll three-quarters of the dough into balls, about 1 inch in diameter, place on greased cookie sheets, and flatten with fork. Place ¼ tsp. jam on each cookie, and top with a very small "hat" of cookie dough. Bake at 400 degrees F for 8 to 10 minutes.

Makes 3 dozen cookies.

—Muriel Doris
Calgary, Alberta

MOLASSES SUGAR COOKIES

INCREASE THE BAKING TIME IF YOU PREFER A CRISP COOKIE. THE TIME GIVEN HERE WILL RESULT in a soft, chewy cookie.

¾ cup shortening	2 tsp. baking soda
1 cup sugar	½ tsp. cloves
¼ cup molasses	½ tsp. ginger
1 egg	1 tsp. cinnamon
2 cups flour	½ tsp. salt

Melt shortening in heavy pan, remove from heat and let cool. Combine sugar, molasses and egg, beat well, then add shortening. Sift together flour, baking soda, cloves, ginger, cinnamon and salt. Add to sugar mixture and mix well. Chill, then form into 1-inch balls. Roll in granulated sugar and place on greased cookie sheets 2 inches apart. Bake at 375 degrees F for 8 minutes.

Makes 3 dozen cookies.

—Mrs. John Schobelock
Chillicothe, Ohio

CRUNCHY MAPLE COOKIES

"THIS IS MY HUSBAND'S FAVOURITE COOKIE TO TAKE ON FISHING OR HUNTING TRIPS."

1 cup shortening	4 cups flour
1 cup brown sugar	½ tsp. salt
1 egg	2 tsp. baking soda
1 cup maple syrup	granulated sugar
1 tsp. vanilla	

Cream shortening and brown sugar, then blend in egg, syrup and vanilla. Add flour, salt and soda, and beat until blended. Shape into 1-inch balls, and coat with granulated sugar. Bake on greased cookie sheets at 350 degrees F for about 10 minutes.

Makes about 5 dozen cookies.

—Helen Potts
Tilden Lake, Ontario

ALMOND ORANGE COOKIES

2 eggs
2 Tbsp. orange juice
½ tsp. almond extract
⅔ cup honey

6-7 cups ground almonds
1 cup whole wheat flour
2 tsp. dry orange peel
semisweet chocolate

Beat eggs and orange juice together until frothy. Beat in almond extract and honey, then stir in almonds, flour and peel. Knead lightly, adding more flour until dough does not stick to work surface. Roll dough into 2 cylinders, 1 inch wide. Chill for 1 to 2 hours, then cut into slices ¼ inch thick with a serrated knife.

Bake on foil-covered cookie sheets at 350 degrees F for 12 to 15 minutes. After the cookies have cooled, frost each with melted semisweet chocolate. When chocolate is solid, store cookies in airtight containers.

Makes 5 to 6 dozen cookies.

—Susan O'Neill
Bella Coola, British Columbia

CHOCOLATE-DIPPED RASPBERRY ALMOND CRISPS

THESE MAKE AN ELEGANT TREAT FOR AN AFTERNOON TEA PARTY OR A SPECIAL DESSERT.

1 cup flour
1 cup finely chopped, blanched almonds
½ cup butter, softened
6 Tbsp. sugar

1½ tsp. vanilla
¼ cup raspberry jam
2 oz. semisweet chocolate, melted

Combine flour and almonds. Cream butter, sugar and vanilla, then stir in flour mixture, using hands to work mixture into smooth dough. Shape into roll 2 inches in diameter. Wrap and chill for at least 3 hours. Cut into ¼-inch slices. Bake on ungreased cookie sheet at 350 degrees for 10 to 12 minutes. Cool.

Spread half the cookies with jam and top with remaining cookies. Dip half of each cookie into melted chocolate, then place on waxed paper until chocolate is set. Store refrigerated.

Makes 18 sandwich cookies.

—Alice M. Gibson
Yarker, Ontario

Eggs & Cheese

"Many's the long night I've dreamed of cheese—melted mostly."

—*Robert Louis Stevenson*

If quiche was the "period luncheon" of the 1970s, there is no doubt that its popularity has now plummeted in many circles, sunk in part by the richness of its own contents: bacon, butter, cream, eggs and cheese—heavyweights in the world of saturated fat and an overdose for anyone counting calories or milligrams of cholesterol.

Still, both eggs and cheese can play an important role in most balanced diets, providing goodly amounts of protein with liberal amounts of essential vitamins and minerals—most noticeably calcium in cheeses. Indeed, both of these foods are vital for growing children, older adults and people on meatless regimens.

"Cheese has always been a food that both sophisticated and simple humans love," said M.F.K. Fisher, and chunks of Cheddar in a ploughman's lunch contrast with a delectably runny Brie with fruit at the end of a gourmet dinner. Fisher's observation seems to hold equally true of eggs, whether served sunny-side up on a heavy roadside diner plate or shirred with *fines herbes* in a Wedgwood chafing dish.

Taken together, eggs and cheese can have a natural affinity, meeting agreeably in frittatas, omelettes, quiches, tarts, puffs and soufflés. For unexpected guests and impromptu meals, both eggs and cheeses can be godsends: readily available, easy and quick to prepare and almost universally greeted with pleasure.

We especially commend to your attention Frittata Fairbanks, the second recipe in this chapter. Brimming with zucchini, broccoli, Cheddar and sunflower seeds, it is a baked omelette embellished with sour cream, salsa, avocados and peppery nasturtium blossoms and is the kind of dish that brings prize ribbons at fairs and hurrahs when served to guests.

We have a definite prejudice toward fresh, locally produced eggs, preferably from free-range birds. We may have to pay a few cents more than for their supermarket counterparts, but when one knows the supplier, there is no risk of getting eggs that have been languishing in cold storage for weeks.

It's best to make omelettes in small batches. Prepare the filling first, since the eggs will take just a minute or so to cook. Have the eggs at room temperature before beginning, and beat them lightly and quickly so as to incorporate as little air as possible. Add butter or oil to a pan, and heat it just to the point of fragrance before adding the eggs. Cook quickly over high heat, lifting gently to allow the eggs to cook through.

Different cheeses can be used interchangeably in many of these dishes. Among the lower fat cheeses are unprocessed Swiss, brick and cottage cheese. Monterey Jack is an especially valuable ingredient to have on hand, combining good flavour with only traces of fat and cholesterol.

BAKED VEGETABLE FRITTATA

A FRITTATA IS LITTLE MORE THAN AN OMELETTE, THE DIFFERENCE BEING THAT THE FILLING IS usually mixed into the eggs before they are cooked. Frittatas may be baked or cooked, covered, on top of the stove.

2 Tbsp. butter
1 onion, finely chopped
1 clove garlic, minced
1 green pepper, diced
¼ cup chopped parsley
19-oz. can tomatoes, drained & chopped
4-5 eggs

½ cup bread crumbs
1 tsp. salt
¼ tsp. pepper
1 tsp. Worcestershire sauce
2 cups grated Swiss cheese
1 green pepper, cut in rings

In skillet, melt butter over medium heat and cook onion and garlic until tender. Add green pepper and parsley and cook for 1 minute longer. Remove from heat and add tomatoes.

In large bowl, beat eggs well. Stir in bread crumbs, salt, pepper, Worcestershire sauce and cheese. Gently stir in vegetables. Pour mixture into buttered 9"-round baking dish. Bake, uncovered, at 350 degrees F for 30 to 35 minutes, or until top is golden brown. Let stand for 5 minutes before serving. Garnish with green pepper rings.

Serves 4.

—Grace Neumann
Ottawa, Ontario

FRITTATA FAIRBANKS

THIS FRITTATA WAS THE TOP PRIZEWINNER IN THE EGG, BRUNCH AND PARTY CATEGORIES AT THE 1986 Tanana Valley State Fair in Alaska, as well as being declared "Grand Champion Purple Rosette in Culinary Capers." As its creator says, "This is not only the most delectable omelette I have ever eaten, it is one of the most beautiful dishes imaginable."

½ cup butter
1 Tbsp. soy sauce
1 clove garlic, diced
¼ cup sunflower seeds
3 small onions, diced
1 zucchini, sliced
1 head broccoli, sliced
12 eggs
3 Tbsp. plain yogurt

3 Tbsp. bran
1 sprig dill
3 cups grated Cheddar cheese
1 cup sour cream
1 avocado, sliced
2 cups alfalfa sprouts
½ cup salsa
nasturtiums & fuchsia to garnish

Melt butter in large, heavy, ovenproof skillet. Add soy sauce, then sauté garlic, sunflower seeds, onions, zucchini and broccoli until onions are transparent. Mix together eggs, yogurt, bran and dill. Pour over vegetables in skillet. Bake, uncovered, at 350 degrees F for 30 to 45 minutes or until cooked through. Cover with cheese, then bake for 10 minutes longer, or until cheese is melted.

Remove from oven. Cover with sour cream. Place avocado slices around omelette in spokelike fashion. Spread sprouts in centre of omelette and spoon salsa between sprouts and avocado. Garnish with nasturtiums and fuchsia.

Serves 6 to 8.

—Mark Boberick
Fairbanks, Alaska

SIMPLE POTATO OMELETTE

OMELETTES REQUIRE DELICATE HANDLING, BUT WITH A LITTLE PRACTICE CAN BE MASTERED BY anyone. They come in 2 basic varieties—plain, in which the eggs are beaten whole, and soufflé, in which the yolks and whites are beaten separately. Plain omelettes are generally savoury (like those here) while soufflé omelettes are commonly sweet and served as dessert. This is a simple, tasty omelette. Serve with spicy tomato salsa for added colour and flavour.

4 potatoes, diced	salt & pepper
2 onions, finely chopped	6 eggs
¼ cup oil	2 Tbsp. milk

Sauté potatoes and onions in oil until tender. Add salt and pepper to taste. Beat eggs and milk together. Pour over potatoes and mix evenly. Cover and cook gently until mixture is set. Cut in wedges and serve hot or cold.

Serves 4 to 6.

—Dorothy Cage
Beaverlodge, Alberta

PIZZA OMELETTE

SPECIAL OMELETTE PANS ARE AVAILABLE FOR THOSE WHO ARE REGULAR OMELETTE-MAKERS. They should be kept for omelettes only. Any heavy-bottomed skillet can be used successfully, though, especially the non-stick variety. The following makes a great pizza-flavoured meal without the heaviness of pizza.

3 Tbsp. butter	½ cup sliced cooked sausage
3 eggs	½ cup sliced mushrooms
1 Tbsp. milk	½ cup grated mozzarella cheese
½ cup thick tomato sauce	

Melt butter in skillet. Beat eggs with milk, then pour into skillet and cook until firm, lifting edges to prevent sticking. Spread tomato sauce over half the omelette, then add sausage, mushrooms and cheese. Fold omelette in half, cover skillet, reduce heat and cook for 3 to 4 minutes, or until cheese melts.

Serves 1.

—Wendy Moore-MacQueen
Petawawa, Ontario

VEGETABLE OMELETTE

10 eggs	1 Tbsp. finely chopped sweet red pepper
4 mushrooms, sliced	1 Tbsp. finely chopped celery
2 green onions, sliced	⅔ cup grated Cheddar cheese
1 Tbsp. finely chopped green pepper	salt & pepper
1 Tbsp. cooked squash	

Beat eggs until frothy. Add remaining ingredients and mix well. Pour into ungreased casserole dish and bake, uncovered, at 350 degrees F for 25 to 30 minutes.

Serves 4 to 6.

—Kelvin Mayes
Kamloops, British Columbia

EGG CURRY

SERVE THIS CURRY OVER RICE OR TOAST FOR A MILD BUT FLAVOURFUL LUNCH DISH.

6 eggs
¼ cup oil
1 large onion, chopped
3 slices gingerroot, minced **or**
   1 tsp. ground ginger
2 Tbsp. minced parsley

1 tsp. turmeric
2 tsp. curry powder
3 tomatoes, peeled, seeded & chopped
1 cup plain yogurt
¼ lb. mushrooms, sliced
2 Tbsp. lemon juice

Hard-boil eggs, drain, peel, halve and set aside. Heat oil in wok, then stir in onion and ginger. Stir-fry until onion is golden – 3 to 4 minutes – over medium heat. Add parsley, turmeric and curry powder, lower heat and simmer for 4 minutes, stirring occasionally. Add tomatoes and simmer for another 8 minutes. Add yogurt and mushrooms, mix well and cook for 10 minutes longer. Add eggs, then simmer for 3 minutes. Stir in lemon juice just before serving.

Serves 2 to 4.

—Diane & David Ladouceur
Calgary, Alberta

INDIAN EGGS

THIS MAKES A GREAT BRUNCH FOR CORN LOVERS.

8 slices bacon
1 onion, chopped
1½ cups corn

1 Tbsp. Worcestershire sauce
salt & pepper
8 eggs, lightly beaten

Fry bacon, drain, then crumble and set aside. Pour off half the bacon fat and add onion. Sauté until onion is soft. Add corn and seasonings. Heat through, then add eggs. Cook, stirring, until set. Serve with bacon sprinkled over the top.

Serves 3 to 4.

—Ann Kostendt
St. Thomas, Ontario

NEW ZEALAND-STYLE EGGS

THIS IS A QUICK AND EASY EGG DISH FOR A LATE BREAKFAST OR A LUNCH. SERVED WITH A SALAD, it makes a satisfying light meal.

4 Tbsp. butter
¼ cup minced onion
1 cup cold diced cooked potatoes
5 eggs

½ cup milk
salt & pepper
2 Tbsp. snipped parsley
4 tomatoes, quartered

In 3 Tbsp. butter, sauté onion and potatoes until golden. Beat eggs with milk, ¾ tsp. salt, pepper and parsley, until just blended, then pour over potatoes. Cook over medium heat, gently scraping the mixture from the bottom as it cooks, until it is set but still moist.

Meanwhile, sprinkle tomatoes with salt and pepper. Sauté until tender in 1 Tbsp. butter in another skillet. Arrange tomatoes around potatoes.

Serves 4.

—Alyson Service
Merrickville, Ontario

CHILIES RELLEÑOS CASSEROLE

THIS CASSEROLE IS DELICIOUS — THE FLAVOUR OF THE CHILIES PERMEATES THE CHEESY CUSTARD for a dish that is smooth in texture but has a bite to its taste. Use jalapeño peppers if your taste buds would like a real treat. Serve as a brunch, lunch or supper dish with refried beans and salad.

16-oz. can green chilies, rinsed,
  split & laid flat
1 lb. Monterey Jack cheese, grated
1 lb. sharp Cheddar cheese, grated

4 Tbsp. flour
2 13-oz. cans evaporated milk
4 large eggs

Grease bottom of 9″ x 13″ glass pan. Layer chilies and cheeses, topping with layer of chilies. Mix flour with some evaporated milk to make a paste, then mix in remaining milk. Beat in eggs. Pour over chilies and bake at 350 degrees F for 45 to 50 minutes, or until mixture is somewhat firm. Remove from oven and let stand for 10 minutes before serving.

Serves 10.

—Sandra Senchuk-Crandall
Santa Rosa, California

GOLDEN EGGS MAYONNAISE

4 Tbsp. butter
1 Tbsp. oil
2 Tbsp. curry powder
8 eggs, hard-cooked & peeled

1 cup mayonnaise
3 Tbsp. chopped chutney
1 head lettuce
½ cup chopped olives

Heat butter and oil in saucepan over medium heat. Stir in curry powder until well blended. Add eggs and cook, turning constantly, over low heat for 10 minutes. Remove to plate with slotted spoon, cover and cool, but do not refrigerate.

To serve, mix mayonnaise with chutney. Cut eggs in half. Make a nest of lettuce in salad bowl, add eggs, then pour mayonnaise over them. Sprinkle chopped olives around the mayonnaise.

Serves 4 to 6.

—Donna Jubb
Fenelon Falls, Ontario

ITALIAN CHEESE LOAF

THIS LOAF CAN BE SERVED HOT OR COLD, OR IT CAN BE CUT INTO 2-INCH SQUARES, FRIED IN butter and served with bacon. We served this with Tomato Curry (see page 97) with delicious results.

1 cup dry rice
4 eggs
6 Tbsp. oil
½ tsp. basil

¼ cup minced parsley
1 cup grated sharp Cheddar cheese
salt & pepper

Cook rice. Beat 3 eggs, add oil and beat well. Add remaining ingredients (except last egg) and cooked rice.

Grease loaf pan. Pour in mixture, spreading it evenly and spread with remaining egg, well beaten. Bake at 350 degrees F for 1 hour.

Serves 6.

—Donna Jubb
Fenelon Falls, Ontario

SNAILS

So named because they look like snails when cooked, these hors d'oeuvres can be made using any variety of fillings—we provide two here.

Pastry for a double 9-inch pie shell

Walnut Mushroom Filling

4 Tbsp. butter
3 cups finely diced mushrooms
¼ cup finely diced onion
1 cup finely chopped walnuts

¼ cup grated sharp Cheddar cheese
½ clove garlic, crushed
pepper
2 tsp. caraway seeds

Bacon Cheese Filling

5 slices bacon
1½ cups grated Monterey Jack cheese

1½ cups grated sharp Cheddar cheese
4 Tbsp. chopped chives

Roll dough into 2 large, thin rectangles.

For Walnut Mushroom Filling: Melt butter and briefly sauté mushrooms and onion. Remove from heat and add remaining ingredients. Mix well. Spread on 1 dough rectangle and roll up like a jelly roll. Wrap well and chill for 1 hour. Cut into ½-inch-thick slices and bake at 425 degrees F for 25 to 30 minutes, or until golden brown.

For Bacon Cheese Filling: Cook bacon until very crisp. Crumble. Mix with cheeses, then add chives. Spread on remaining dough and proceed as above.

Makes approximately 40.

—Diane Milan
Northfield, Minnesota

CRAB & ASPARAGUS TART

A delicious appetizer, this tart is also suitable for a lunch or supper main dish and can be frozen successfully.

Pastry for single 9-inch pie shell

1 Tbsp. butter
1 Tbsp. flour
½ cup milk
nutmeg
½ cup whipping cream
2 Tbsp. sherry

12 oz. crabmeat
salt & pepper
2 egg yolks
12 stalks asparagus, lightly steamed
¼ cup grated Gruyère cheese

Line pie plate with pastry and bake at 350 degrees F for 10 minutes.

Melt butter, stir in flour until smooth, then stir in milk and cook until thickened. Add a grating of nutmeg. Remove from heat, stir in cream and sherry. Add crab and salt and pepper. Lightly beat egg yolks, then add to crab mixture and stir gently. Pour into pastry shell. Lay asparagus decoratively on top, then sprinkle with cheese.

Bake at 350 degrees F for 20 minutes.

Serves 6.

—Sandy Campisano
Weston, Massachusetts

SHIRRED EGGS DELUXE

SERVED WITH A FRUIT SALAD AND WARM MUFFINS, THESE EGGS MAKE A DELICIOUS AND attractive brunch.

2 Tbsp. butter	6 slices bacon
12 eggs	¾ cup sliced mushrooms
salt & pepper	⅓ cup Parmesan cheese

Butter 6 individual custard dishes. Break 2 eggs into each dish and add a dash of salt and pepper. Bake at 325 degrees F for 15 minutes.

Meanwhile, cook bacon until crisp, then crumble. Sauté mushrooms in bacon drippings until golden brown. Top eggs with bacon, mushrooms and cheese. Return to oven for 5 more minutes, or until whites are set but yolks are still soft.

Serves 6.

—Jayne Simms-Dalmotas
Ottawa, Ontario

SUMMER CHEESE SOUFFLÉ

THIS SOUFFLÉ CAN BE ASSEMBLED UP TO TWO DAYS BEFORE COOKING AND SERVING. IT PUFFS UP beautifully while baking and is a very attractive dish, equally delicious for brunch or lunch, or served with ham for dinner.

5 slices crusty Italian bread	1 tsp. dry mustard
butter, softened	1 tsp. Worcestershire sauce
¾ lb. sharp Cheddar cheese, grated	½ tsp. curry powder
4 eggs, beaten	½ tsp. salt
2 cups milk	

Butter each slice of bread lightly on both sides and cut into cubes. Layer bread and cheese in ungreased 1-quart casserole dish. Combine remaining ingredients and pour over bread and cheese. Cover and refrigerate for up to 2 days.

Bake, uncovered, at 350 degrees F for 50 minutes.

Serves 6.

—Donna Jubb
Fenelon Falls, Ontario

EGG & CHEESE PUFFS

LESS TRICKY TO MAKE THAN A SOUFFLÉ, THESE INDIVIDUAL EGG PUFFS STILL RISE BEAUTIFULLY.

6 eggs	¼ tsp. salt
½ cup light cream	⅛ tsp. white pepper
3 Tbsp. flour	1½ cups grated Cheddar cheese
1½ tsp. dry mustard	

Combine all ingredients but cheese and beat well. Grease 4 10-oz. soufflé dishes or custard cups well, then sprinkle cheese in them. Pour in egg mixture.

Bake at 350 degrees F for 30 to 35 minutes, or until puffy and golden.

Serves 4.

—Elaine Darbyshire
Golden, British Columbia

EGG CASSEROLE

3 cups cubed, cooked ham
½ lb. sharp Cheddar cheese, grated
3 cups cubed rye bread
3 Tbsp. melted butter

3 Tbsp. flour
1 tsp. dry mustard
4 eggs
3 cups milk

Layer ham, cheese and bread in greased 9″ x 13″ pan. Drizzle with butter. Combine flour and mustard and sprinkle over mixture in pan. Beat eggs, add milk and mix well. Pour over pan mixture. Refrigerate for 4 to 24 hours.

Bake, uncovered, at 350 degrees F for 1 hour.

Serves 8 to 10.

—Jackie Dysart
Espanola, Ontario

EGGS IN NESTS

SIMPLER TO MAKE THAN ITS APPEARANCE WOULD LEAD YOU TO BELIEVE, THIS IS A DELICIOUS brunch dish.

2 Tbsp. butter
2 Tbsp. flour
½ tsp. salt
pepper
1 cup milk

½ cup grated sharp Cheddar cheese
4 slices toast
4 eggs
cream of tartar
16-20 asparagus spears, steamed

Melt butter, then stir in flour and cook over low heat for 1 minute. Stir in salt, pepper and milk. Bring to a boil, stirring, and cook until thickened. Stir in cheese. Set aside, keeping warm.

Place toast on cookie sheet. Separate eggs, keeping yolks whole and separate from one another. Beat whites with a pinch of cream of tartar until stiff.

Place 4 or 5 asparagus spears on each slice of toast. Pile egg whites over asparagus, then make a dent in each pile. Drop 1 yolk into each dent.

Bake at 350 degrees F for 8 to 10 minutes, or until meringue edges are golden and yolks are still runny. Serve with cheese sauce.

Serves 4.

—Cary Elizabeth Marshall
Thunder Bay, Ontario

CHILI EGG PUFF

SERVED WITH SALAD AND FRESH WHOLE-GRAIN BREAD, THIS MAKES A COMPLETE SUPPER; WITH fruit bread or muffins and fruit salad, it functions as a delicious brunch.

10 eggs
½ cup flour
2 cups cottage cheese

1 lb. Monterey Jack cheese, grated
½ cup melted butter
2 4-oz. cans California green chilies, diced

Beat eggs until light and lemon-coloured. Add flour, cottage cheese, Monterey Jack cheese and melted butter. Blend until smooth, then stir in chilies. Pour into greased 9″ x 13″ dish. Bake, uncovered, at 350 degrees F for 35 minutes. Let stand for a few minutes, then serve.

Serves 6 to 8.

—Nancy R. Franklin
San Jose, California

BACON & EGG PIE

Pastry for single 9-inch pie shell

½ lb. bacon	6 Tbsp. milk
1 tomato	salt & pepper
6 eggs	1 cup grated Cheddar cheese

Line pie plate with pastry. Fry bacon, drain well and place on pastry. Slice tomato over bacon. Beat eggs and milk together. Pour over tomato and bacon. Season with salt and pepper to taste. Top with grated cheese. Bake at 450 degrees F for 45 minutes.

Serves 4.

—Sheelagh Stone
High River, Alberta

BROCCOLI & CHEESE PIE

Crust	**Filling**
1 cup grated Cheddar cheese	1½ cups broccoli florets, steamed
¾ cup flour	1 cup evaporated milk
¼ tsp. salt	1 cup chopped onion
¼ tsp. dry mustard	1 cup sliced mushrooms
¼ cup butter, softened	½ tsp. salt
	¼ tsp. nutmeg
	pepper
	3 eggs, lightly beaten

Combine crust ingredients and press into 9-inch pie plate. Place broccoli in pie plate. Combine milk, onion, mushrooms, salt, nutmeg and pepper in saucepan and simmer for a few minutes. Stir a bit of this into the eggs, then stir eggs into remaining hot mixture. Pour over broccoli.

Bake at 400 degrees F for 15 minutes, reduce heat to 375 degrees and bake for another 30 to 35 minutes, or until firm. Let stand for 5 minutes before serving.

Serves 4 to 6.

—Ingrid Magnuson
Winnipeg, Manitoba

CHILIES RELLEÑOS QUICHE

Pastry for single 9-inch pie shell

2 cups grated Monterey Jack cheese	¼ tsp. pepper
4-oz. can whole green chilies	2 eggs, separated
4 eggs	taco sauce
1 cup light cream	

Bake crust at 425 degrees F for 5 minutes. Sprinkle 1 cup cheese on crust, then layer with ½ the chilies. Repeat. Beat together 4 whole eggs, cream and pepper and pour over cheese and chilies. Bake at 375 degrees for 30 minutes.

In a small bowl, beat egg whites until stiff. Fold in lightly beaten yolks carefully. Spoon mixture over hot filling to edge of crust. Return to oven and bake for 5 minutes longer, or until golden brown. Serve with taco sauce.

Serves 6 to 8.

—Linda Stanier
Lacombe, Alberta

ROSS'S BETTERAVE PIE

USING STAR ANISE SEED CLUSTERS RATHER THAN GROUND ANISE RESULTS IN A FRESHER TASTE. The clusters really do look like stars and have a musty licorice smell. Betterave is another word for beet.

2 star anise seed clusters
1 tsp. fenugreek
3 dried chili peppers
1 Tbsp. brandy
¾ lb. side bacon, chopped
1 onion, chopped
6 large eggs
⅛ tsp. white pepper
juice of 1 lemon

¼ cup chopped parsley
1 tsp. soy sauce
1 tsp. Worcestershire sauce
olive oil
filo pastry
1 lb. beet greens, washed & stems removed
1 lb. brick cheese, thinly sliced
1 cup sliced pitted black olives

Grind star anise, fenugreek and chili peppers to a powder with mortar and pestle. Add to brandy and let sit for 1 hour. Force through cheesecloth; keep the liquid and discard the rest.

Meanwhile, fry bacon until almost crisp, then drain off fat. Add onion to bacon and sauté for 5 minutes, or until onion is transparent. Combine eggs, pepper, lemon juice, parsley, soy sauce and Worcestershire sauce. Mix well, then stir in bacon and onion.

Brush 9″ x 13″ dish with olive oil. Place 4 layers of filo pastry in dish, brushing each layer with olive oil. Smooth on ½ the beet greens, then the egg mixture. Place cheese over this, then the olives. Add remaining beet greens, then top with 4 layers of filo brushed with oil. Bake at 350 degrees F for ½ hour, or until golden brown.

Serves 4 to 6.

—Steve D. Ross
Lacombe, Alberta

TAMALE PIE

THIS APPEALING DISH, TOGETHER WITH A GREEN SALAD, MAKES A SATISFYING VEGETARIAN MEAL.

2 onions, chopped
3 cloves garlic, crushed
¼ cup oil
1 green pepper, chopped
2 cups tomatoes, chopped
1½ cups corn
1 cup pitted black olives
½ Tbsp. chopped thyme

½ Tbsp. chopped oregano
½ Tbsp. chopped basil
1 tsp. chili powder
¾ cup yellow cornmeal
2 cups milk
3 eggs
2 cups shredded Cheddar cheese

Fry onions and garlic in oil until transparent. Add green pepper and cook 5 minutes longer. Add tomatoes, corn and olives. Cook, stirring, until heated through. Add herbs and chili powder, then set aside.

Cook cornmeal in milk over medium heat until thickened—about 8 to 10 minutes—stirring frequently. Remove from heat, beat in eggs, then add to vegetable mixture. Stir well. Place in greased casserole dish and bake, uncovered, at 350 degrees F for 30 minutes. Sprinkle with cheese and bake for 20 minutes longer.

Serves 6.

—Terri d'Aoust
Rossland, British Columbia

FRENCH CANADIAN ONION CHEESE QUICHE

Crust
¾ cup flour
½ tsp. salt
¼ tsp. dry mustard
1 cup grated Cheddar cheese
¼ cup melted butter

Filling
2 cups finely chopped onion
2 Tbsp. butter
1 cup cooked noodles
2 eggs
1 cup hot milk
½ tsp. salt
pepper
1 cup grated Cheddar cheese

For crust: Combine flour, salt, mustard and cheese. Add melted butter and mix well. Pat into bottom and sides of 9-inch pie plate.

For filling: Cook onions in butter until transparent, then add noodles. Mix, then pour into pie plate. Beat together eggs, hot milk, salt, pepper and cheese. Pour over noodles.

Bake at 325 degrees F for 35 to 40 minutes.

Serves 6.

—Jeannine Bélanger
Vankleek Hill, Ontario

LIPTAUER CHEESE SPREAD

PREPARE IN ADVANCE TO ALLOW THE FLAVOURS TO BLEND THOROUGHLY. THE PAPRIKA GIVES this Viennese cheese spread its beautiful colour. All ingredients should be at room temperature.

8 oz. cream cheese
½ cup butter
1 Tbsp. finely minced onion
1 Tbsp. dry mustard
2 anchovies

1 tsp. capers
1 Tbsp. caraway seeds
¼ tsp. paprika
1 clove garlic, crushed

Combine all ingredients and blend until smooth.

Makes approximately 1½ cups.

—Lillian Steinfeld
Halcott Center, New York

HERB GARDEN CHEESE BALL

THE HERBS CAN BE VARIED IN THIS RECIPE — USE WHATEVER YOUR GARDEN PRODUCES.

1 cup ricotta cheese
¼ cup chopped basil
1 Tbsp. chopped chives
2 cloves garlic, crushed

1 Tbsp. Parmesan cheese
1 tsp. kelp powder
3 Tbsp. minced parsley

Combine all ingredients except parsley, blend well and form into a ball. Roll in parsley. Chill.

Makes approximately 1½ cups.

—Helen Shepherd
Lyndhurst, Ontario

PARMESAN CHEESE BALL

EVERY COOK HAS HIS OR HER OWN FAVOURITE CHEESE BALL RECIPES. THEY ARE GOOD FOR A nutritious, relatively unfattening accompaniment to raw vegetables, crackers or potato chips, and make ideal potluck fare. They can also be made well ahead of time, wrapped carefully, and kept refrigerated until needed. The following recipe makes a very mild cheese ball that is well complemented by raw vegetables.

8 oz. cream cheese, softened
⅓ cup Parmesan cheese
1 small onion, finely chopped
1 clove garlic, crushed

2 tsp. soy sauce
1 Tbsp. finely chopped parsley
¼ tsp. white pepper
½ cup finely chopped dill **or** parsley

Combine cream cheese, Parmesan cheese, onion, garlic, soy sauce, 1 Tbsp. parsley and white pepper. Blend well and form into ball. Roll in chopped dill or parsley. Chill.

Makes approximately 2 cups.

—Trudi Keillor
Berwyn, Alberta

DILLY CHEESE BALL

THE COMBINATION OF THE DILL AND THE CHEESES CREATES A VERY PLEASANT TASTE. GARNISH with (or roll in) fresh dill when it is in season for added dill flavour.

8 oz. cream cheese, softened
1½ cups grated sharp Cheddar cheese
½ cup chopped dill pickles
¼ cup finely chopped green onion

2 Tbsp. mayonnaise
1 tsp. Worcestershire sauce
½ cup finely chopped walnuts
2 Tbsp. finely chopped parsley

Combine cream cheese, Cheddar cheese, dill pickles, green onion, mayonnaise and Worcestershire sauce. Beat until smooth. Cover and chill until firm. Shape into a ball and roll in mixture of nuts and parsley.

Makes approximately 3 cups.

—Virginia Grant
Stouffville, Ontario

POTTED CHEDDAR

THIS IS A NEW YEAR'S TRADITION WITH THE CONTRIBUTOR'S FAMILY. IT MAKES A FLAVOURFUL addition to a holiday feast and, pressed into small crockery pots, is a wonderful gift. Serve at room temperature to appreciate the full cheese flavour.

1 lb. sharp Cheddar cheese, grated
1 onion, chopped
¼ cup chopped parsley
¼ tsp. salt
¾ tsp. dry mustard

⅛ tsp. Tabasco sauce
½ tsp. Worcestershire sauce
¼ cup tomato sauce
⅓ cup sherry

Combine all ingredients and blend well. Chill.

Makes approximately 4 cups.

—Kathryn MacDonald
Yarker, Ontario

BLUE-CHEESE SPREAD

THIS CHEESE SPREAD HAS A DELICATE BLUE-CHEESE FLAVOUR AND A CREAMY CONSISTENCY. IT IS equally delicious served with crackers or vegetables.

12 oz. cream cheese, softened
4 oz. blue cheese
juice of ½ lemon
½ tsp. Worcestershire sauce

Combine all ingredients and blend until smooth. Chill.

Makes approximately 2 cups.

—*Kathryn MacDonald*
Yarker, Ontario

SPICY CHEDDAR BEER DIP

AS WELL AS MAKING A TANGY DIP FOR VEGETABLES OR CRACKERS, THIS MAKES A FINE TOPPING for soyburgers and hamburgers.

2½ cups grated sharp Cheddar cheese
½ cup beer
¼ cup mayonnaise
1 tsp. caraway seeds
1 tsp. Worcestershire sauce
¼ tsp. salt
¼ tsp. cayenne

In a blender, at medium speed, combine all ingredients until smooth. Cover and refrigerate for at least 20 minutes.

Makes approximately 3 cups.

—*Kristine Mattila*
Quesnel, British Columbia

Soups & Chowders

"Of soups and love, the first is best."

—*Spanish Proverb*

Although it may sound more than a bit contrived, one of the less orthodox but more successful academic dinner parties we've attended was a Stone Soup Supper given by a university president. After drinks had been served, she circulated among the crowd with two baskets, asking each guest to take a card from one or the other. We were instructed to find our dinner partner for the evening by seeking out the guest with a card that matched our own. In the bemused search to find someone else with "Two Spuds" or "Bouquet Garni," we were forced to meet and mingle, rather than stake out a corner and talk only with friends.

The trick worked admirably, and the president later retold the venerable folktale of the old woman who, lacking the ingredients to make a soup, set up her cauldron by the side of a well-travelled road. Into it, she placed water and a stone, and she heated and stirred with such enthusiasm that passersby inevitably stopped and inquired what she was making. "Why, stone soup," she exclaimed, "but a bit of carrot (or onion or turnip or potato or chicken) wouldn't hurt. Those who contributed were invited to stay and taste the result, and soon the woman had a thick, meaty soup, started from nothing but water and stone.

Although one of the great pleasures of making soup comes from the act of creating a good meal from almost nothing, its chief appeal is more tangible. There is nothing like the sight of a pot of soup simmering on the wood stove, steaming the windows on a cold day and filling the air with moist, savoury smells.

A good soup is only as good as its stock, in which long, slow cooking is more important than prime ingredients. Stock making is a good rainy day activity – save scraps in a bag in the freezer, prepare the stock in bulk, and freeze in 2-cup quantities. Old vegetables and tough meats actually provide more flavour than tender ones. Beware of strong-tasting vegetables and meats: cabbage, turnip, broccoli, lamb and ham can be overpowering at the stock-making stage. Start with a disjointed poultry carcass or 4 to 5 pounds of meat and bones. Chop two of each: onions, carrots, celery stalks (leaves intact). Parsley, cloves, bouquet garni and a bay leaf are optional. Place everything in lightly salted cold water, and simmer with the lid partially off. Never boil, and if clear stock is desired, remove the scum as it forms, especially in the first half hour or so. Cook for 4 to 6 hours, cool slightly, and strain through cheesecloth. Cool to room temperature, and refrigerate. Remove the top layer of fat just prior to use.

As the old folktale suggests, soup begs for improvisation, and the following recipes show just how rich the possibilities can be.

FRESH TOMATO & CABBAGE SOUP

2 Tbsp. butter
1 clove garlic, crushed
2 cups coarsely chopped cabbage
1 tsp. salt
2 Tbsp. flour
4 tomatoes, peeled, seeded & chopped

2 Tbsp. parsley
½ tsp. basil
⅛ tsp. celery seed
⅛ tsp. pepper
2 cups milk

Melt butter and sauté garlic and cabbage for 3 to 4 minutes. Add 2 cups water and salt, bring to a boil, reduce heat and simmer for 5 minutes. Dissolve flour in ¼ cup water, then stir into soup, cooking until thickened. Add tomatoes, parsley, basil, celery seed and pepper. Simmer for 5 to 10 minutes, stirring often. Stir in milk and heat through.

Serves 4 to 6.

—Norma Somers
Boissevain, Manitoba

BEET VEGETABLE SOUP

"AN EXCEPTIONALLY PRETTY SOUP—PINK WITH LOTS OF COLOURFUL VEGETABLES. GARNISH WITH fresh dill," says our Vermont tester.

1 cup cubed potatoes
1 cup cubed carrots
1 cup cubed beets

¼ tsp. salt
pepper
1 cup sour cream

Cook potatoes, carrots and beets in 1 cup water until just done. Add salt and pepper, remove from heat and stir in sour cream.

Serves 4.

—Deborah Elmer
Delisle, Saskatchewan

FRESH PEA SOUP

4 cups peas
5 Tbsp. oil
1 tsp. salt
1 cup chopped celery heart
1 bunch parsley
2 Tbsp. flour

1 Tbsp. sweet paprika
1 tsp. pepper

Soft Noodles
1 egg
1 cup flour

Braise peas in 3 Tbsp. oil, stirring gently, for 5 minutes. Add salt, celery heart, parsley and 4 cups water. Cover and cook over low heat for 20 minutes, or until peas are tender.

Meanwhile, in small pot, heat remaining 2 Tbsp. oil. Stir in flour, paprika and pepper and cook gently for 2 minutes. Slowly add 1 cup water. When thickened, stir into soup and boil for 5 minutes.

Prepare noodles: Mix egg and ¼ cup cold water, adding enough flour to make a very soft dough.

Remove cover from soup, and drizzle dough into soup with a fork. Cook for 5 to 10 minutes.

Serves 4 to 6.

—Julie Herr
Acton Vale, Quebec

CREAMY CELERY SOUP

OUR VERMONT TESTER REPORTS, "LOVELY GREEN COLOUR—ESPECIALLY APPROPRIATE FOR spring. The cream stock and crunchy celery make for a very pleasant combination of textures."

4 stalks celery with leaves, chopped
¼ tsp. crushed garlic
⅛ tsp. thyme
3 leaves parsley, minced
2 Tbsp. butter

1 Tbsp. flour
2 cups milk
½ cup chicken stock
salt & pepper

Cover celery with water in heavy pot. Bring to a boil and cook until celery is just tender. Reduce heat to simmer and add garlic, thyme and parsley. Continue cooking until most of juice is absorbed. Remove from heat, cover and set aside.

Melt 1 Tbsp. butter and stir in flour. Remove from heat and slowly stir in milk, then stock, then remaining 1 Tbsp. butter. Return to heat and cook, stirring, until almost boiling. Remove from heat.

Return celery to heat. Slowly add cream sauce, stirring constantly. Cook for 5 minutes over low heat. Season with salt and pepper.

Serves 2.

—Deborah Elmer
Delisle, Saskatchewan

CAULIFLOWER SOUP

THE PARSLEY ROOTS AND GREENS IN THIS RECIPE AID DIGESTION. THE SOUP HAS A DELICATE flavour and makes a very attractive beginning to a meal.

1 cauliflower, broken into florets
1 tsp. salt
3 Tbsp. oil
1 clove garlic, chopped
2 parsley roots, sliced

1 bunch parsley, chopped
2 Tbsp. flour
1 Tbsp. sweet paprika
1 cup cooked rice **or** small noodles
½ cup sour cream

Cook cauliflower in 5 cups water with salt until tender—20 minutes. Meanwhile, heat oil in skillet and sauté garlic, parsley roots and parsley for 5 minutes. Stir in flour and paprika, then add 1 cup water. Cook, stirring, until thickened, then stir into cauliflower and water. Boil for 5 minutes, then add rice or noodles and sour cream.

Serves 4.

—Julie Herr
Acton Vale, Quebec

EGG LEMON SOUP

3-4 cups chicken stock
½ cup white wine
¾ cup cooked rice **or** fine egg noodles

3 eggs
3 Tbsp. lemon juice
pepper

Heat stock and wine to rolling boil. Add rice or pasta. Whisk eggs and lemon juice together until frothy, then quickly whisk into boiling stock. Pepper generously and serve immediately.

Serves 4 to 6.

—Elizabeth Templeman
Heffley Creek, British Columbia

CREAMED ARTICHOKE SOUP

A RICH AND MILD-TASTING CREAM SOUP THAT IS BEST MADE WITH HOMEMADE CHICKEN BROTH.

4 cups chicken stock
20 oz. frozen **or** canned artichoke hearts,
   defrosted & drained
3 Tbsp. butter
3 Tbsp. flour

1½ cups light cream
¼ tsp. ground thyme
¼ tsp. white pepper
salt
½ cup dry long-grain rice, cooked
   (optional)

Bring stock to a boil in a saucepan; add artichoke hearts, cover and simmer over low heat for 10 minutes. Purée the artichokes with some of the stock in a blender or food processor. Return to saucepan with remaining stock.

Melt butter in a small saucepan, add flour, stir to blend well; stir in cream and thyme. Add pepper and salt to taste. Simmer over low heat for 5 minutes, stirring constantly. Pour cream mixture into the saucepan with stock and artichokes; stir and simmer for 5 minutes. If you add rice, simmer for 10 minutes.

Serves 6 to 8.

—Nancy R. Franklin
San Jose, California

CREAM OF TOMATO SOUP

SERVE THIS SOUP TOPPED WITH GRATED CHEESE AND GARLIC CROUTONS FOR A DRESSIER DISH.

4 cups canned tomatoes
1 bay leaf
2 carrots, chopped
2 onions, chopped
2 stalks celery, chopped

5 Tbsp. butter
5 Tbsp. flour
3 cups milk
salt & pepper

Cook tomatoes, bay leaf, carrots, onions and celery until tender — 35 to 40 minutes. Discard bay leaf. Purée soup.

Melt butter and stir in flour. Stir in milk and cook, stirring, until thickened. Slowly add puréed mixture. Add salt and pepper to taste.

Serves 4.

—Caren Barry
Windsor, Connecticut

SHARON'S CREAM OF EGGPLANT SOUP

1 cup butter
1½ cups chopped onion
1½ cups chopped celery
1½ cups chopped potato
2 eggplants, peeled & chopped
½ tsp. curry

¼ tsp. thyme
¼ tsp. basil
4 cups chicken stock
2 cups heavy cream
parsley

Melt butter in heavy skillet. Sauté onion, celery, potato, eggplants, curry, thyme and basil for 15 minutes, stirring constantly. Add stock and bring to a boil. Reduce heat, cover and simmer for 25 to 30 minutes. Remove from heat, stir in cream and garnish with parsley.

Serves 4 to 6.

—Mary Matear
London, Ontario

CREAM OF MUSHROOM & WILD RICE SOUP

½ cup dry wild rice
⅓ cup butter
3 stalks celery, finely chopped
1 bunch green onions, including tops, chopped
1½ lbs. mushrooms, sliced

¼ cup chopped fresh parsley
⅓ cup flour
3 cups chicken broth
2 13-oz. cans evaporated milk
salt & pepper

Rinse wild rice thoroughly. Cook, covered, in 1¼ cups water until tender – about 40 minutes. Melt butter in soup pot and add celery and onions. Sauté for a few minutes. Add mushrooms and parsley. Cook over high heat, stirring, until juices start to evaporate. Stir in flour and cook at least one more minute. Gradually stir in broth until smooth. Add evaporated milk, wild rice and salt and pepper to taste.

Serves 4.

—Sandy Lance
Cos Cob, Connecticut

SPINACH & DANDELION SOUP

IF DANDELION GREENS ARE NOT AVAILABLE, THIS SOUP CAN BE MADE WITH ALL SPINACH OR WITH spinach and escarole. The nutmeg adds a different taste.

6 cups chicken stock
3 cups chopped dandelion greens
3 cups chopped spinach
3 green onions, chopped

1 clove garlic, crushed
salt & pepper
nutmeg
2 hard-cooked eggs, chopped

Heat chicken stock and add dandelion greens. Cook for 3 minutes, then add spinach, onions, garlic and salt and pepper. Cook until greens are tender – 5 minutes. Serve with nutmeg and eggs.

Serves 6.

—Cary Elizabeth Marshall
Thunder Bay, Ontario

CILANTRO SOUP

"YOU MAY SUBSTITUTE WATERCRESS FOR THE CILANTRO, BUT THE TASTE WILL BE LESS SPICY."
This soup has a lovely, delicate "green" taste.

4½ Tbsp. butter
1½ cups chopped onions
4½ cups sliced leeks
¾ cup chopped celery
3 cups peeled, sliced potatoes
5½ cups chicken stock

1½ tsp. salt
½ tsp. white pepper
3 cups cilantro **or** watercress, leaves & fine stems only
1½ cups light cream
sour cream & chopped cilantro for garnish

Melt butter and sauté onions, leeks and celery until tender but not brown. Cover and cook over low heat for 15 minutes. Add potatoes, stock, salt, pepper and cilantro. Simmer, covered, for 15 to 20 minutes. Purée until smooth in blender or food processor.

Return mixture to clean pot, add cream and heat but do not boil. Serve, hot or cold, garnished with a dollop of sour cream and some chopped cilantro.

Serves 8 to 10.

—Louise Routledge
Port Coquitlam, British Columbia

ALMOND SOUP

"A SWEETISH, SUMMER SOUP, THIS WOULD MAKE A SIMPLE BUT TASTY WAY TO BEGIN A MEAL.
It can be served hot or cold."

3 Tbsp. almond paste
⅔ cup finely chopped blanched almonds
5 cups chicken stock
3 egg yolks, beaten

2 cups light cream
½ tsp. sugar
½ tsp. salt
¼ tsp. almond extract

Combine almond paste, almonds and chicken stock in saucepan. Cover and bring to a gentle boil. Reduce heat and simmer for 30 minutes.

In bowl, combine egg yolks, cream, sugar and salt. Beat ½ cup hot stock into egg mixture, then beat back into stock. Cook until slightly thickened. Stir in almond extract.

Serves 6 to 8.

—Sandra K. Bennett
Greenville, South Carolina

MUSHROOM & LEEK SOUP

WHETHER GARNISHED AND SERVED FORMALLY OR EATEN FROM MUGS BY THE FIREPLACE, THIS
soup is sure to satisfy.

6 leeks
½ cup butter
½ lb. mushrooms, sliced
¼ cup flour
1 tsp. salt

1 tsp. pepper
1 cup chicken stock
3 cups milk
1 Tbsp. sherry
lemon slices & fresh parsley

Wash white part of leeks thoroughly and slice thinly. Sauté leeks in ¼ cup butter until soft but not brown. Remove leeks. In remaining butter, sauté mushrooms until soft. Blend in flour, salt and pepper. Gradually add stock and milk and stir until mixture is thick and creamy. Add leeks and simmer for 10 minutes. Stir in sherry just before serving. Garnish with thin slices of lemon and chopped fresh parsley.

Serves 6.

—Denise Ford
Burlington, Ontario

POTATO SOUP

"A PERFECT IDAHO SOUP WHERE WE HAVE PLENTY OF SPUDS AND COLD WEATHER. WE SERVE IT
 with bread, hot and fresh out of the oven."

¼ cup oil
1 cup chopped onion
1 cup diced carrots
1 cup chopped celery
5 potatoes, diced
1 tsp. oregano

1 tsp. salt
1½ tsp. dill weed
½ tsp. paprika
6 cups chicken **or** vegetable stock
½ cup beer
½ cup evaporated milk

Heat oil in large heavy pot and sauté onion, carrots, celery and potatoes until onions are transparent. Add oregano, salt, dill weed, paprika, stock and beer and bring to a boil. Reduce heat and simmer for 30 minutes, or until potatoes are tender. Add milk and heat for 2 minutes.

Serves 4.

—Christine Leazer
Twin Falls, Idaho

SWISS POTATO SOUP

"This recipe has been in my family for years — it's a favourite with us after a winter day spent hiking in the woods. Creamy, but not too rich, this is a homey soup with surprising sophistication."

4 medium potatoes, pared
2 slices bacon, diced
¼ cup minced onion
2 Tbsp. butter
1 Tbsp. snipped parsley
2 tsp. salt

½ tsp. nutmeg
cayenne
¼ tsp. dry mustard
1 tsp. Worcestershire sauce
3 cups milk
½ cup grated Swiss cheese

Cook potatoes in boiling water until tender; drain. Meanwhile, sauté bacon and onion over low heat, stirring, until brown and tender. Mash potatoes; add bacon, onion, butter, parsley, salt, nutmeg, cayenne, mustard and Worcestershire sauce. Stir in milk. Cook over low heat, stirring. Sprinkle with cheese and serve at once.

Serves 4.

—Alyson Service
Merrickville, Ontario

LATIN SOUP WITH GARNISHES

Soup
3½-lb. chicken
2 stalks celery with leaves, halved
2 onions, peeled & quartered
3 bay leaves
2 sprigs parsley
¼ tsp. coriander
3½ tsp. salt
¼ tsp. pepper
2 carrots, peeled & sliced
8 potatoes, peeled & quartered
2 Tbsp. dry rice
7 ears corn

Aji Sauce
6 Tbsp. chopped coriander
½ cup olive oil
3 Tbsp. minced onion
1 Tbsp. lemon juice
2 tsp. parsley
1 Tbsp. wine vinegar
¾ tsp. crushed hot red pepper
½ tsp. salt
¼ tsp. pepper

Garnishes
1 cup heavy cream
3 avocados, diced
½ cup capers
5 hard-cooked eggs, chopped

Bring chicken and water to cover to boil in large heavy pot. Simmer for 5 minutes, drain liquid and rinse chicken. Return chicken to pot with 8 cups water, celery, onions, bay leaves, parsley, coriander, salt, pepper, carrots and 5 potatoes. Cover, bring to a boil, then simmer for 1 hour, or until chicken is tender.

Remove chicken and potatoes from stock. Strain stock and return to pot. Mash potatoes and stir into stock. Add 3 uncooked potatoes and rice and cook until just tender — about 15 minutes. Skin and bone chicken, then cut into large chunks. Cut kernels from 3 ears of corn and cut remaining ears into 2-inch pieces. Add chicken and corn to stock and cook until corn is tender — about 7 minutes.

Meanwhile, prepare sauce: Combine all sauce ingredients and mix well. Serve soup with pitcher of cream, platter of garnishes and sauce.

Serves 10.

—Kristine Mattila
Quesnel, British Columbia

SAMBAR

"THIS IS A SOUTH INDIAN dhal-based soup usually served with plain boiled rice. It is hot and delicious." If you can't find tamarind in an Oriental grocery store, substitute lemon juice.

2 Tbsp. tamarind
¾ cup yellow split peas
½ tsp. turmeric
¼ tsp. salt
4 tomatoes, chopped
½ tsp. cumin seed
5 dried hot red peppers
½ tsp. peppercorns
¼ tsp. fenugreek seeds
1 tsp. ground coriander

2 Tbsp. dry-roasted coconut
6 Tbsp. butter
1 small eggplant, cubed
1 potato, peeled & cubed
1 onion, sliced
½ tsp. sugar (optional)
salt
½ tsp. mustard seed
½ cup coriander
asafoetida

Soak tamarind in ½ cup water. Bring 5 cups water to boil in large pot. Add peas, turmeric and salt. Boil for a few minutes, then cook over low heat until most of the liquid evaporates—30 minutes. Mash. Add 5 cups water and bring to a boil. Reduce heat, add tomatoes, then simmer.

Roast cumin seed, peppers, peppercorns and fenugreek separately. Cool, then grind together along with coriander and coconut. Add to soup. Melt 2 Tbsp. butter in skillet and sauté eggplant for 2 to 3 minutes. Add potato and cook for 2 minutes, then add eggplant and potato to soup.

Melt another 2 Tbsp. butter in skillet. Sauté onion until translucent, then add to soup along with sugar and salt to taste and simmer for 15 to 20 minutes. Strain tamarind juice and discard pulp. Add juice to soup and simmer for 5 minutes.

Melt remaining 2 Tbsp. butter and add mustard seed and coriander. When mustard seeds stop crackling, add a pinch of asafoetida. Stir into dhal.

Serves 8 to 10.

—Ingrid Birker
Montreal, Quebec

WILD RICE SOUP

"THIS SOUP HAS A SUBTLE SAVOURY FLAVOUR AND IT IS AN INNOVATIVE WAY TO SERVE WILD RICE to a crowd without going broke!"

1½ Tbsp. cornstarch
10 cups beef stock
3 Tbsp. butter
2 cups diced celery
1½ cups diced carrot
1½ cups diced onion

½ lb. mushrooms, sliced
1¼ cups wild rice
1 Tbsp. chopped thyme
1 bay leaf
pepper
parsley sprigs

Mix cornstarch with 1 cup stock and set aside. Melt butter in large heavy pot and sauté celery, carrot and onion until soft. Add mushrooms and sauté for 5 minutes more. Add remaining 9 cups stock, rice, thyme and bay leaf and bring to a boil. Reduce heat, cover and simmer for 45 minutes, or until rice is tender. Stir in cornstarch mixture and cook until slightly thickened. Add pepper to taste. Remove bay leaf and garnish with parsley.

Serves 12.

—Pam Collacott
North Gower, Ontario

WORLD'S BEST FRENCH ONION SOUP

"THIS RECIPE, GENEROUSLY SHARED BY A LOCAL FRENCH RESTAURANT, HAS INGREDIENTS THAT are deceptively simple and inexpensive."

2 large sweet onions (Spanish or Bermuda)
½ cup butter
1 clove garlic, crushed
3 Tbsp. flour

1 tsp. salt
seasoned croutons (large, garlicky,
   homemade ones are best)
1 lb. Swiss Emmentaler cheese, shredded

Peel and thinly slice onions. Separate slices into rings. In large saucepan or 4-quart Dutch oven, melt ¼ cup butter. Add onions. Over high heat, stirring frequently, sauté onions until they appear almost burnt: quite brown with the odd black bit.

Reduce heat to low and add garlic. Sauté until garlic is soft. Do not allow garlic to brown. Add 10 cups hot water and return to boil, then simmer slowly, uncovered, until liquid is reduced by half – 5 to 7 hours.

In a small skillet, melt remaining butter and stir in flour. Stir constantly over low heat to produce a caramel-coloured roux. Add a couple of tablespoonsful of the hot stock, stirring constantly. Then add this to stock in pot, stirring constantly. Allow to boil for about 5 minutes to thicken slightly and eliminate any raw flour taste. Add salt.

In 4 ramekins or onion-soup bowls, place a couple of tablespoonsful of shredded cheese. Then ladle in the soup to within a half inch of the top of each bowl. Cover soup with seasoned croutons, then carefully divide the cheese over each bowl, taking care that the croutons and cheese don't sink. Place under broiler, or in a 450 degree F oven, until cheese is melted and begins to brown.

Serves 4.

—Sandy Robertson
Port Robinson, Ontario

MEXICAN BEAN SOUP

OUR VERMONT TESTER SAYS, "I WHOLEHEARTEDLY RECOMMEND THIS RECIPE. IT HAS JUST THE right amount of spice, is very well balanced and is the right consistency for a soup."

7 oz. dry pinto beans, soaked overnight
   & drained
½ lb. ham, cubed (optional)
2½ cups water
1½ cups tomato juice
2½ cups chicken stock
2 onions, chopped
1½-2 cloves garlic, minced
1½ Tbsp. chopped parsley
2 Tbsp. chopped green pepper
2 Tbsp. dark brown sugar
2 tsp. chili powder
½ tsp. salt

1 bay leaf
½ tsp. oregano
¼ tsp. cumin
¼ tsp. rosemary
¼ tsp. celery seed
¼ tsp. thyme
¼ tsp. basil
⅛ tsp. marjoram
⅛ tsp. curry
⅛ tsp. cloves
½ cup dry sherry
chopped scallions

Combine all ingredients except sherry and scallions in large heavy pot. Simmer, partially covered, for 3 hours, or until beans are tender. Remove bay leaf.

Add sherry just before serving, then sprinkle with scallions.

Serves 6.

—Beazie Larned
Stamford, Connecticut

BLUE CHEESE SOUP

1½ Tbsp. butter
½ cup chopped onion
3 Tbsp. flour
3 cups chicken stock

1 cup milk
⅛ lb. blue cheese
¼ lb. spinach, chopped
¼ cup heavy cream

Melt butter and sauté onion for 3 minutes. Stir in flour, then slowly add chicken stock and milk. Cook, stirring, for 5 minutes. Crumble blue cheese and add. Cook until melted, then add spinach and cream and heat through.

Serves 2 to 4.

—Rhonda Barnes
Fulford Harbour, British Columbia

CREAMY CHEDDAR CHEESE SOUP

"THIS MAKES A RICH AND DELICIOUS SOUP. THE FLAVOURS BLEND WELL, AND IT IS QUICK AND easy to make. Add fresh-baked bread and butter, and you have a hearty winter meal that will delight everyone."

½ cup butter
½ cup diced carrot
¾ cup diced onion
½ cup diced celery
½ cup flour
2 Tbsp. cornstarch
4 cups rich chicken stock

4 cups milk
⅛ tsp. baking soda
1½ cups grated sharp Cheddar cheese
½ tsp. salt
pepper
finely chopped parsley

Melt butter in large heavy pot. Add carrot, onion and celery and sauté until they are soft. Add flour and cornstarch and mix well, then add chicken stock and milk, mixing well. Cook, stirring constantly, until mixture has a smooth texture and thickens. Add baking soda and cheese and stir until smooth and blended. Season with salt and pepper. Sprinkle with parsley just before serving.

Serves 8 to 10.

—James Mottern
Knoxville, Tennessee

CARROT SOUP

"A FAVOURITE SATURDAY SUPPER IN OUR HOUSEHOLD IS A LARGE BOWL OF THIS SOUP WITH A slice of homemade bread." If you like a *really* thick soup, thicken with a paste of 3 Tbsp. flour and ¼ cup milk just before serving.

2 Tbsp. butter
1 onion, chopped
5 cups chicken stock
1 lb. carrots, grated
3 potatoes, grated
½ tsp. thyme

¼ tsp. Tabasco sauce
1 tsp. Worcestershire sauce
1½ cups milk
2 cups grated Cheddar cheese
salt

Melt butter and sauté onion until tender. Add chicken stock and bring to a boil. Add carrots, potatoes, thyme, Tabasco sauce and Worcestershire sauce and simmer until vegetables are tender – 30 to 40 minutes. Add milk and cheese and cook until cheese is melted. Salt to taste.

Serves 6 to 8.

—Lois B. Demerich
Etters, Pennsylvania

CRÈME SENEGALESE SOUP

4 Tbsp. butter
6 leeks, chopped
1 large green apple, peeled, cored
  & chopped
¾ cup chopped onion
1 clove garlic, minced
2 Tbsp. curry

1 lb. potatoes, peeled & diced
6 cups chicken stock
salt & pepper
1 cup heavy cream
Tabasco sauce
½ cup diced cooked chicken

Melt butter, then add leeks, apple, onion and garlic. Cook until leeks are limp — 10 to 15 minutes. Sprinkle with curry and cook for 5 minutes more. Add potatoes, cook for 3 minutes, then add stock. Simmer for 45 minutes. Add salt and pepper to taste.

Blend soup in batches. Add cream, Tabasco sauce to taste and chicken just before serving. Serve hot or cold.

Serves 8.

—Colleen Suche
Winnipeg, Manitoba

GOLDEN SQUASH SOUP

COOK AND FREEZE SQUASH IN THE FALL, THEN USE IT TO MAKE THIS SOUP IN THE WINTER. IF YOU prefer a completely smooth soup, the potatoes can be puréed as well.

4 Tbsp. butter
⅓ cup diced onions
1 large potato, finely diced
1 cup chicken stock
2 cups cooked squash

¼ tsp. salt
¾ tsp. curry
white pepper
¾ cup milk
paprika

Melt butter and sauté onions until softened. Add potato, stock, squash, salt, curry and pepper. Heat through over medium heat, then simmer for 10 minutes, or until potatoes are tender. Stir in milk. Sprinkle with paprika.

Serves 4.

—Linda Russell
Exeter, Ontario

WINE & CHEESE MUSHROOM SOUP

2 Tbsp. olive oil
1 cup chopped onions
1 clove garlic, chopped
1 lb. mushrooms, sliced
2 Tbsp. tomato paste
4 cups chicken stock

5 egg yolks
⅓ cup Parmesan cheese
2 Tbsp. chopped parsley
¼ cup port
4 slices French bread, toasted & buttered

Heat oil in heavy pot and cook onion and garlic for 6 minutes over moderate heat. Add mushrooms and cook, stirring, for 10 minutes. Stir in tomato paste, then stock, and bring to a boil. Reduce heat and simmer for 15 minutes.

In a small bowl, combine egg yolks, cheese and parsley. Add 1 cup hot stock in a stream, beating well, then stir this back into pot. Add port and simmer for 15 minutes. Place bread in 4 bowls and ladle soup over.

Serves 4.

—James W. Houston
Willowdale, Ontario

BROCCOLI SOUP

MADE WITH FRESH-FROM-THE-GARDEN BROCCOLI, THIS SOUP IS A LOVELY EARLY-SUMMER LUNCH dish. Serve with sliced tomatoes and garlic mayonnaise.

6 cups chicken stock
1 head broccoli, cut into florets
1 cup chopped onion
1 Tbsp. chopped tarragon

salt & pepper
nutmeg
1 cup sour cream **or** yogurt

Bring stock to a boil. Add broccoli and onion and cook for 6 to 8 minutes, or until broccoli is tender. Purée soup. Reheat, then add tarragon, salt and pepper and nutmeg. Add sour cream or yogurt, whisking thoroughly. Do not allow soup to boil.

Serves 4 to 6.

CABBAGE SOUP

A ZESTY, SPICY SOUP WITH AN ITALIAN FLAVOUR, THIS WOULD BE GREAT FOR A HEARTY after-ski repast. Add crusty bread and bowls of marinated olives to round out the meal.

4 hot Italian sausages
3 Tbsp. olive oil
2-3 cloves garlic, crushed
1 onion, chopped
1 carrot, sliced
2 stalks celery, chopped
2 28-oz. cans crushed tomatoes
2 potatoes, peeled & cubed

2 cups cooked navy beans
2 cups coarsely chopped cabbage
½ cup white wine
½ tsp. pepper
1 Tbsp. oregano
2 tsp. basil
salt
Parmesan cheese

Cook sausages in large heavy pot. Discard fat and slice sausages; set aside. Heat oil and sauté garlic and onion until transparent. Add carrot and celery and sauté briefly. Stir in tomatoes and raise heat. Add potatoes, beans, cabbage, wine, pepper, oregano, basil, salt and sausages. Boil for 10 to 15 minutes, reduce heat, cover and simmer until potato and cabbage are tender. Sprinkle with Parmesan cheese and serve.

Serves 6 to 8.

—Elizabeth Templeman
Heffley Creek, British Columbia

CARROT, CASHEW & CURRY SOUP

"I TASTED A SOUP LIKE THIS IN A LITTLE PLACE CALLED THE SOUP KITCHEN IN CALGARY, Alberta. I liked it so much that I developed this version of it for my own use."

¼ cup butter
5-6 carrots, sliced
1 onion, halved & sliced
1 green pepper, chopped
4 cloves garlic, crushed

1 cup cashews
4 cups soup stock
2 tsp. curry
1 bay leaf
salt & pepper

Melt butter and sauté carrots, onion, green pepper, garlic and cashews until onion is transparent. Add remaining ingredients and simmer until carrots are tender but not mushy—30 minutes. Remove bay leaf before serving.

Serves 4.

—Bonnie Lawson
Medicine Hat, Alberta

MUSSEL CHOWDER WITH CORN

"This recipe was created a few summers ago while my husband and I were vacationing on a remote island in Maine. Mussels were free for the picking; other ingredients depended on the limited supplies of the island's general store."

4 slices bacon, diced
2 onions, diced
2 potatoes, diced
strained stock from steaming mussels
3 cups mussel meat

2 cups milk
12-oz. can evaporated milk
1½ cups corn
salt & pepper

Fry bacon until crisp, then drain. Sauté onions until translucent in bacon fat, then place in large pot with potatoes. Add stock and water to cover. Simmer until potatoes are tender. Add remaining ingredients, including bacon, and heat through.

Serves 2 to 4.

—Wendy Gwathmey
Wilmington, North Carolina

HARVEST-TIME PUMPKIN SOUP

1 small pie pumpkin, cleaned out
2 potatoes
2 carrots
1 onion, finely chopped
2 cloves garlic, crushed
olive oil
fresh parsley, basil & thyme, chopped

salt & pepper
4 Tbsp. cream
2 Tbsp. butter
2 Tbsp. soy sauce (optional)
sour cream
chopped chives

Cut pumpkin, potatoes and carrots into pieces and steam until tender. Remove peel from pumpkin. Save steaming water. Sauté onion and garlic in a little olive oil until transparent. Purée onion, garlic and vegetables in a food processor, adding reserved water. Return the purée to a saucepan and add spices, salt and pepper, cream, butter and soy sauce. If soup is too thick, thin with a little water, milk or chicken stock. Heat but do not boil. Garnish with a dollop of sour cream and chopped chives.

Serves 4 to 6.

—Robin Mello
Buckfield, Maine

LAMB SOUP

1 leftover meaty lamb leg
2 cups chopped spinach
2 tomatoes, cubed
½ cup peas
½ cup corn
3 potatoes, cubed

¾ cup sliced mushrooms
salt & pepper
Worcestershire sauce
1 onion, diced
¼ cup dry barley

Simmer lamb leg in 6 to 8 cups water for 4 hours. Strain, reserving liquid. Chop meat.

Combine meat, reserved stock and remaining ingredients in large heavy pot. Simmer for 1 hour, or until vegetables are tender, adding liquid if necessary.

Serves 6.

—Patricia E. Wilson
Belleville, Ontario

OXTAIL SOUP

"THIS IS A RICH AND HEARTY SOUP FOR A MEAN FEBRUARY DAY. START EARLY TO MAKE THE stock so it can cool and the fat can be removed. My grandmother's secret was to add whatever root vegetables were available."

2 Tbsp. butter **or** oil
2-3 lbs. disjointed oxtails
½ cup chopped onion
3 cloves garlic, chopped
1 bay leaf
8 cups water
1½-2 cups chopped tomatoes
1½ tsp. salt
4-6 peppercorns

2 cups diced potatoes
1 cup sliced carrots
1 cup sliced celery
1 turnip **or** parsnip **or** celeriac **or**
   combination, chopped
¼ cup chopped parsley
1 tsp. basil
½ tsp. thyme
⅓-½ cup dry barley

Heat butter or oil and brown oxtails. Add onion and garlic and sauté for 2 to 3 minutes. Add bay leaf, water, tomatoes, salt and peppercorns. Bring to a boil, reduce heat, cover and simmer for 2 to 4 hours.

Strain stock and chill to remove fat. Set oxtails aside. When cool, remove meat from bones and chop. Bring defatted stock to a boil and add chopped meat and remaining ingredients. Simmer for 30 to 40 minutes, or until vegetables are tender.

Serves 8 to 10.

—Lynne Roe
Orangeville, Ontario

LANDLUBBER'S GUMBO

BUY FILÉ POWDER AT A SPECIALTY FOOD STORE—BE SURE NOT TO LET THE SOUP BOIL AFTER IT has been added.

3-4-lb. chicken
1 Tbsp. salt
1 stalk celery
1 carrot
1 onion
2 Tbsp. butter
2 cups diced smoked pork shoulder,
   bone reserved
2 lbs. okra, stems removed
1 green pepper, diced
4 onions, sliced
2 cloves garlic, crushed

28-oz. can plum tomatoes
4 cups fish stock
⅓ cup chopped parsley
4 dashes Tabasco sauce
4 Tbsp. Worcestershire sauce
juice of ½ lemon
2 bay leaves
½ tsp. thyme
12 oz. crabmeat
2 lbs. shrimp, shelled
1 tsp. filé powder

Cook chicken, salt, celery, carrot and onion in 4 cups water (or to cover) for 30 minutes. Cool, then remove chicken and vegetables, skim fat from stock, and reserve stock. Discard vegetables. Chop chicken.

Melt butter in large pot. Sauté chicken and pork for 2 minutes. Add okra, green pepper and onions and cook for 5 minutes. Add garlic, tomatoes, chicken and fish stocks, parsley, Tabasco sauce, Worcestershire sauce, lemon juice, bay leaves, thyme, pork bone and crabmeat. Simmer for 2½ to 3½ hours. Add shrimp and cook for 5 minutes. Remove bay leaves and add filé powder just before serving.

Serves 12.

—Elizabeth Alexander
Kingston, Ontario

ASPARAGUS & CRAB SOUP

VIETNAMESE IN ORIGIN, THIS SOUP IS ELEGANT ENOUGH TO BEGIN A DINNER PARTY, BUT SIMPLE to prepare.

1 Tbsp. oil
1 clove garlic, minced
2 Tbsp. minced shallots
¾ lb. flaked crabmeat
8 cups chicken stock
2 Tbsp. fish sauce **or** 1 tsp. anchovy paste

3 Tbsp. cornstarch, mixed with 3 Tbsp. water
1 lb. asparagus, steamed & cut in 1″ lengths
salt & pepper
toasted croutons for garnish

Heat oil in a large skillet and sauté garlic and shallots until tender, about 6 minutes. Stir in the crabmeat and cook for 4 to 5 minutes, stirring constantly. In the soup pot, heat the chicken stock to a gentle boil. Stir in fish sauce, if available, or anchovy paste. Add the crab mixture and return to simmer. Stir cornstarch mixture into soup. Simmer and stir until thickened, about 5 minutes. Add asparagus. Add salt and pepper to taste. Ladle into heated bowls and garnish with croutons.

Serves 8 to 10.

HAM-LENTIL SOUP WITH CHEESE TORTELLINI

"A RICHLY FLAVOURED, CHILL-CHASING SOUP — ESPECIALLY FAVOURED BY THE HARVEST CREW after a cold day of combine repairs. Serve in pre-warmed bowls and garnish with chives. Good accompanied by warm garlic toast and a platter of sliced fresh fruits and vegetables."

2 Tbsp. butter
⅓ cup chopped onion
1 clove garlic, minced
1⅓ cups dry lentils, rinsed & drained
1 cup cubed ham
1 stalk celery, sliced
1 cup peeled, seeded & chopped tomatoes

3″ sprig thyme
1 tsp. salt
1 large bay leaf
Tabasco sauce
¾ cup dry cheese-filled tortellini
snipped chives for garnish

Melt butter in large, heavy pot over moderate heat. Add onion and garlic and cook, stirring frequently, until onion is limp. Add lentils, ham and celery. Cook, stirring frequently, until lentils just start to brown. Add 8 cups water, tomatoes, thyme, salt, bay leaf and Tabasco sauce and stir to blend. Cook, covered, for 1 hour. Add tortellini and cook for another 30 minutes. Garnish with chives.

Serves 4.

—Ellen Ross
Underwood, Iowa

BORSCHT

8 whole fresh beets
1 small onion, diced
2 Tbsp. butter
4 cups chicken stock

2 medium-sized potatoes
1½ cups sour cream
salt & pepper

Boil unpeeled beets for 30 minutes, or until tender. Peel and set aside. In large pot, sauté onion in butter for 5 minutes or until transparent. Add chicken stock, potatoes and beets and simmer for 20 minutes, or until potatoes are soft. Purée and chill for at least 3 hours. Whisk sour cream into soup just before serving and season to taste with salt and pepper. Garnish each bowl with a dollop of sour cream.

Serves 6.

SPINACH SOUP WITH DILL & LEMON

SERVE THIS SOUP HOT OR CHILLED – IT IS DELICIOUS EITHER WAY.

3 Tbsp. butter
2 onions, chopped
1 lb. spinach, washed & stems removed
3 Tbsp. dry rice
2 cups peas
2 Tbsp. chopped dill
4 cups chicken stock

salt & pepper
nutmeg
grated peel of ½ lemon
1 cup heavy cream
½ cup sour cream
chopped dill

Melt butter and sauté onions until tender. Add spinach and cook, stirring, until it wilts. Add rice and peas and toss, then add dill and chicken stock. Bring to a boil, stir in salt and pepper, nutmeg and lemon peel. Reduce heat, cover and simmer for 20 minutes, or until rice is tender.

Purée, in batches, in blender or food processor. Stir in cream just before serving. Serve with a dollop of sour cream and chopped dill in each bowl.

Serves 6 to 8.

—G. Rogne & F. Goodwin-Rogne
Sherwood Park, Alberta

MEAL-IN-A-SOUP

1 Tbsp. butter
¾ lb. ground beef
2 onions, sliced
3 stalks celery, sliced
2 large carrots, sliced
1 potato, diced

1½ cups cauliflower florets
19-oz. can tomatoes
1½ tsp. salt
⅛ tsp. pepper
¾ cup dry macaroni

Melt butter, add ground beef and brown slightly, stirring. Add remaining ingredients, except pasta. Cover and bring to a boil. Reduce heat and simmer for 30 minutes. Add macaroni about 7 to 9 minutes before the end of cooking time.

Serves 4 to 6.

—Eileen Caldwell
Newburgh, Ontario

TUNISIAN SOURBA

THE COOK CONTROLS THE HEAT PRODUCED BY THE CHILIES, FROM MILDLY FLAVOURFUL TO tongue-searing. Serve with dunkers of crusty bread.

1½ lbs. beef, cut into 1″ cubes
3 carrots, cut into discs
1 large onion, chopped
4 Tbsp. olive oil
2 Tbsp. tomato paste

1-3 tsp. finely chopped red chilies, seeds
  removed
6 cups beef stock **or** consommé
salt & pepper
1 cup dry pasta shells
1½ tsp. lemon juice

In a heavy pot, sauté meat, carrots and onion in olive oil, stirring frequently until meat is browned and onions are tender. Add tomato paste, 1 tsp. chilies, stock and salt and pepper. Simmer for 30 minutes. Taste liquid and add more chilies if desired. Simmer until meat is tender. Add pasta and cook until tender. Stir frequently. Just before serving, stir in lemon juice.

Serves 6 to 8.

MANDARIN HOT & SOUR SOUP

"I DEVELOPED THIS RECIPE AFTER LIVING IN CHINA FOR TWO YEARS AND GROWING TO LOVE hot and sour soup." Hotness and sourness can be adjusted by adding to or subtracting from the amount of vinegar and chili oil.

6-8 cups chicken stock
¼ lb. lean pork, shredded
2-3 dried black mushrooms, soaked & shredded
3-4 dried tree ears, soaked & shredded (optional)
½-1 square tofu, diced
¼ cup shredded bamboo shoots
½ cup sliced mushrooms
2 green onions, chopped

1 slice cooked ham, shredded
4 Tbsp. vinegar
1 tsp. chili oil
¼ tsp. white pepper
¾ tsp. salt
½ tsp. sesame oil
½ tsp. sugar
1 Tbsp. soy sauce
3 Tbsp. cornstarch dissolved in 3 Tbsp. water
2 eggs, lightly beaten

Bring stock to a boil, add pork, black mushrooms and tree ears. Cook for 2 to 3 minutes. Add remaining ingredients except for cornstarch and eggs, reduce heat, and simmer for 2 minutes more. Slowly stir cornstarch mixture into soup and continue cooking until stock is thickened. Turn off heat. Slowly pour in eggs in a thin stream while stirring.

Serves 6 to 8.

—Barb McDonald
Stella, Ontario

SMOKY POTATO & BACON SOUP WITH CHEDDAR CROUTONS

THIS IS A MEAL-IN-A-BOWL SOUP, ESPECIALLY GOOD ON A COLD WINTER'S DAY. THE CROUTONS would be tasty in other soups as well—double or triple the recipe, and freeze the rest for later use.

1 thick strip bacon, with rind
¼ cup butter
1 cup chopped onion
½ cup chopped celery
½ cup chopped leek
5 cups chicken stock
½ tsp. salt
½ tsp. white pepper
2 cups peeled, cubed potatoes
½ cup heavy cream

Croutons
1 cup grated sharp Cheddar cheese
1 egg, lightly beaten
½ tsp. Dijon mustard
1 green onion, chopped
cayenne
4 slices bread

Remove rind from bacon and reserve. Chop bacon. Melt butter, then add rind, onion, celery and leek and cook for 10 minutes over medium heat, stirring. Add stock, salt and pepper and bring to a boil. Add potatoes and simmer for 25 minutes. Remove rind and discard. Purée soup, then return to pot and add cream. Fry bacon until crisp and add to soup.

To make croutons: Combine cheese, egg, mustard, onion and cayenne. Spread onto bread. Bake at 375 degrees F for 10 to 15 minutes or until dry. Cool, then cut into cubes. Sprinkle on soup.

Serves 6 to 8.

—Terry Seed
Toronto, Ontario

FRIDAY NIGHT CHICKEN SOUP & MATZO BALLS

1 stewing hen
4 lbs. chicken necks & backs
1 onion, studded with 5-6 cloves
1 clove garlic, peeled
1 tsp. salt
6 peppercorns
½ tsp. thyme
1 bay leaf
2 leeks
2 carrots
2-3 stalks celery with leaves
1 turnip
1-2 parsley roots
¼ cup chopped parsley

Matzo Balls
3 eggs, separated
1 tsp. salt
¾ cup matzo meal
2 Tbsp. oil
¼ tsp. pepper

In large stockpot, combine hen, necks and backs, onion, garlic, salt, peppercorns, thyme, bay leaf and 12 cups water. Bring to a boil, reduce heat, cover and simmer for 1½ hours. Remove hen, bones, garlic, onion and bay leaf. Add remaining ingredients and return to boil. Simmer for 1 hour, then strain.

Meanwhile, prepare matzo balls: Beat together egg yolks, salt, matzo meal, oil and pepper. Beat egg whites until stiff and fold into egg yolk mixture. Chill for 1 hour, then form into balls, using 2 Tbsp. per ball. Cook, covered, for 20 minutes in simmering soup.

Serves 8 to 10.

—Lynne Roe
Orangeville, Ontario

MARY'S POZOLE (Pah-zó-lay)

"IN AN EFFORT TO REPRODUCE A SOUP I ENJOYED IN MEXICO, I DEVISED THIS VERSION OF pozole. The basic soup is made, then each person adds the vegetables he likes at the table. The bracing heat provided by the chilies is balanced by the crunch of raw vegetables."

1 stewing hen
2 onions, chopped
2 carrots, chopped
3 stalks celery & leaves, chopped
1 tsp. thyme
1 tsp. sage
1 tsp. rosemary
1 tsp. salt

1 tsp. pepper
2 red chilies
1 cup cooked chickpeas
any combination of radishes, cabbage,
    zucchini, green onions, tomatoes, Swiss
    chard, chopped or sliced finely & placed
    in separate bowls
1 lemon **or** lime, thinly sliced

Place hen, onions, carrots, celery, thyme, sage, rosemary, salt and pepper in a stockpot. Cover with water and simmer until hen is tender – 1 to 2 hours. Remove chicken, strain stock and reserve 8 cups. Strip meat from bones, removing skin; chop and place in soup pot. Add stock. Simmer chilies in about 1 cup water for 10 minutes. Place chilies and water in blender and purée. Add to soup, a few teaspoonsful at a time, until desired level of spiciness is reached. Add chickpeas and simmer soup for 10 minutes.

To serve: Fill soup bowls about half full of chicken soup. Add desired vegetables and complete with a squeeze of lemon or lime juice. Extra hot sauce can be passed.

Serves 10 to 12.

—Mary McCollam
Stella, Ontario

DAVID'S CREAM OF CRAB SOUP

A RICH, CREAMY BROTH UNDERLIES THE CRAB FLAVOUR OF THIS SOUP. TASTE IMPROVES IF THE soup is made ahead of time, chilled and then reheated over very low heat.

¼ cup butter
¼ cup minced onion
2 Tbsp. flour
¼ tsp. celery seed
1 tsp. salt
⅛ tsp. pepper

Tabasco sauce
1 cup chicken **or** vegetable stock
¼ cup dry sherry
2½ cups milk
2½ cups light cream
1 lb. crabmeat

Melt butter in heavy pot, then sauté onion until tender. Slowly blend in flour, celery seed, salt, pepper and Tabasco sauce to taste, stirring constantly. Add stock, sherry, milk and cream and cook over medium heat, stirring constantly, until thick enough to coat a spoon.

Stir in crabmeat and heat through.

Serves 4 to 6.

—David G. Weifenbach
Reisterstown, Maryland

SCALLOP CHOWDER

"WHEN I LIVED IN THE TROPICS, MY FAVOURITE DISH WAS CONCH CHOWDER. THIS IS MY WEST Coast adaptation of that soup."

¼ cup oil
½ cup chopped bacon
½ cup chopped onion
½ cup chopped celery
½ cup chopped carrot
½ cup chopped green pepper
1 cup diced potato

1 bay leaf
1½ tsp. thyme
⅓ cup tomato paste
1 cup scallops, halved
salt
Tabasco sauce

Heat oil and cook bacon until crisp. Add onion, celery, carrot, green pepper, potato, bay leaf and thyme and sauté for 3 minutes. Add tomato paste and cook, stirring, for 6 minutes. Add 4 cups water, bring to a boil, reduce heat and simmer for 1 hour.

Stir in scallops, salt and Tabasco sauce to taste and cook for 5 minutes, or until scallops are cooked.

Serves 4.

—Barbara Brennan
Sidney, British Columbia

AVOCADO CORIANDER SOUP

NO VEGETABLE IS AS CREAMY AS AN AVOCADO, AND IT IS SHOWN OFF AT ITS BEST IN THIS delicate, pale green soup.

2 ripe avocados, peeled & halved
2 scallions, roughly chopped
2 cups light cream
juice of ½ lime
½ cup chicken stock

¼ tsp. salt
¼ tsp. cayenne
¼ cup fresh coriander leaves
salt & pepper
fresh coriander leaves for garnish

Put all ingredients except garnish in food processor or blender, and process until smooth. Refrigerate for 3 hours until completely chilled. Thin with more chicken stock if necessary, and season to taste with salt and pepper. Garnish with fresh coriander leaves.

Serves 4.

CHILLED CURRIED ZUCCHINI SOUP

"I SERVED THIS TO A FRIEND WHO INSISTED HE HATED ZUCCHINI, ONIONS, CURRY POWDER AND buttermilk and didn't know what cumin was. He was most enthusiastic about all of them combined in this soup, however!"

2 lbs. zucchini	1 Tbsp. cumin
6 Tbsp. butter	2 cups chicken stock
1 cup minced green onions	3 cups buttermilk
1 Tbsp. curry	salt & pepper

Scrub, trim and chop zucchini. Melt butter and slowly cook zucchini and onions, covered tightly, over medium-low heat, for 15 minutes, or until zucchini is soft. Add curry and cumin and cook for 2 minutes. Stir in stock. Purée soup in blender or food processor in batches. Place puréed soup in large bowl, then stir in buttermilk and salt and pepper. Chill for at least 4 hours.

Serves 6.

—Sandy MacLennan
Millgrove, Ontario

GREEN VICHYSSOISE

A GREEN-FLECKED COOL SOUP WITH A HEARTY TEXTURE, THIS IS IDEAL FOR A LIGHT MEAL in itself. Serve with a green salad and fresh bread.

2 Tbsp. butter	4 bunches watercress, leaves & tender
5 small leeks, white part only	stems **or** 4 cups fresh spinach leaves
6 cups chicken stock	1 cup heavy cream
2 medium baking potatoes, peeled & diced	salt & pepper

Heat butter and gently sauté leeks for 10 minutes, then add chicken stock and potatoes and simmer until potatoes are tender—about 20 minutes. Add watercress or spinach and simmer 5 minutes longer. Purée soup, leaving flecks of green, and chill for at least 3 hours. Add cream and season to taste with salt and pepper. Garnish with sprigs of watercress or parsley, and serve.

Serves 6.

GRANDMA GESINE'S CLAM CHOWDER

"MY GREAT-GRANDPARENTS CAME TO THE UNITED STATES FROM GERMANY IN THE LATE 1800S. They settled in New York City, where they opened a bar and restaurant. This chowder was always on the menu, and it has stayed in the family ever since."

18 clams	¼ tsp. pepper
1 small piece salt pork **or** ½ lb. bacon, diced	2 lbs. potatoes, diced
	6 carrots, diced
28-oz. can crushed tomatoes	3 stalks celery, diced
2-4 tsp. thyme	2 onions, diced
2 bay leaves	¼ head cabbage, diced

Steam clams until shells open. Chop clams and set aside, reserving cooking liquid. Fry pork until crisp in large heavy pot. Add 8 cups water, strained clam juice, tomatoes, thyme, bay leaves, pepper and clams. Add vegetables, bring to a boil, reduce heat, cover and simmer for at least 3 hours. Remove bay leaves before serving.

Serves 4 to 6.

—Barbara Tanzosh
Cedar Grove, New Jersey

FISH & WILD RICE CHOWDER

THIS IS A CREAMY, DELICATE CHOWDER BUT WITH CONSIDERABLE DEPTH. IT TAKES ONLY A SHORT time to prepare, which adds to its freshness of flavour.

½ cup dry wild rice
½ tsp. salt
½ cup butter
1 cup chopped onion
½ cup chopped green pepper
1 cup sliced celery
1 cup sliced mushrooms

¾ cup flour
7 cups chicken stock
1 tsp. salt
½ tsp. white pepper
1 lb. orange roughy **or** scrod, cubed
1 cup light cream
2 Tbsp. white wine

Cook rice with salt in 2 cups water for 35 minutes. Drain and set aside.

Melt butter and sauté onion, green pepper, celery and mushrooms over low heat for 5 to 7 minutes. Stir in flour and cook for 3 to 4 minutes longer. Add chicken stock and bring to a boil. Add salt, pepper and fish and simmer for 5 to 10 minutes, or until fish is tender. Add rice, cream and wine.

Serves 6 to 8.

—Jerald G. Riessen
Mendota Heights, Minnesota

CONSOMMÉ MADRILÈNE

THE TOMATO GIVES THIS CLEAR, SHIMMERING SOUP A SLIGHTLY ROSY TINGE. IT IS LIGHTLY gelatinous, elegant and refreshing.

3 quarts chicken stock
1½ lbs. lean beef chuck, cut into small
　chunks
2 carrots, finely diced

1 leek, white part only, finely diced
6 tomatoes, seeded & chopped
1 tsp. coarse salt
chives for garnish

Put everything into stockpot and bring to a gentle boil. Skim scum off surface and lower heat to keep soup at a gentle simmer, uncovered, for 1½ hours. You should have about 3 cups of liquid when finished. Strain through a double thickness of dampened cheesecloth, then chill consommé until lightly set – about 2 hours. Serve garnished with chives.

Serves 2.

AVGOLEMONO SOUP

GOLDEN YELLOW AND ZINGY WITH LEMON, THIS SOUP IS AN IDEAL SUMMER ADDITION TO YOUR cold-soup repertoire.

6 cups chicken stock
1 cup uncooked rice
juice of 2 lemons

3 egg yolks
salt & pepper
chopped parsley for garnish

Bring stock to a boil and add rice; half cover pot and cook rice until tender, about 20 minutes. Meanwhile, beat lemon juice and egg yolks together until smooth. Whisk 1 cup of hot broth into yolk mixture, then slowly add this mixture back to stock and rice in the pot. Stir soup gently over low heat for 3 to 5 minutes until the soup thickens slightly. Be careful not to curdle the egg yolks. Chill for 3 hours; stir well to circulate the rice, and season to taste with salt and pepper. Garnish with chopped parsley.

Serves 4.

AFRICAN LENTIL SOUP

"I FIRST MADE THIS SOUP WITH SPICES MY SISTER BROUGHT FROM KENYA. NOW I MAKE MY OWN blend to create a flavourful and spicy meal that is perfect for vegetarians." This is not a soup for the fainthearted—it is *hot*.

Spice Paste
½ tsp. cayenne
1½ tsp. paprika
½ tsp. ginger
½ tsp. cardamom
1½ tsp. turmeric
¼ tsp. coriander
¼ tsp. cinnamon
2 tsp. red wine vinegar

Soup
4 cloves garlic, crushed
3 carrots, sliced
1 onion, chopped
4 green onions, chopped
¼ cup oil
½ cup tomato paste
2 cups dry lentils
1 small chili, chopped

Make a paste of the spices by combining cayenne, paprika, ginger, cardamom, turmeric, coriander and cinnamon. Mix in vinegar and 1 Tbsp. water to make a smooth paste.

Sauté garlic, carrots and onions in oil over medium heat until soft. Stir in tomato paste, spice paste and ½ cup water. Simmer over low heat, stirring, for 5 minutes. Add remaining ingredients and 5 cups water, bring to a boil, reduce heat and simmer for 45 minutes.

Serves 6.

—Judith Christensen
Los Angeles, California

CLAM CHOWDER

THIS IS A HEARTY SOUP WITH A VELVETY-SMOOTH, NICELY COLOURED BROTH. REAL CLAM aficionados could easily increase the amount of clams. This chowder combines the cream of a New England clam chowder with the tomatoes of a Manhattan chowder.

2 oz. salt pork **or** bacon, chopped
1 clove garlic, chopped
½ cup chopped onion
3 cups diced potatoes
1½ tsp. thyme
1 bay leaf
4 cloves
2 tsp. salt
½ tsp. pepper
10-oz. can clams

½ cup chopped green pepper
½ carrot, diced
¼ cup chopped celery
3 cups diced tomatoes
2 Tbsp. flour
4 cups scalded milk
2 cups cream
3 Tbsp. butter
¼ cup chopped parsley

In large heavy pot, sauté pork. Add garlic and onion and sauté until onion is golden.

Add 3 cups water, potatoes, thyme, bay leaf, cloves, salt and pepper and simmer for 15 minutes. Add clams and their juice, green pepper, carrot, celery and tomatoes. Simmer for 10 minutes.

Mix flour with ½ cup milk. Stir into soup with remaining milk and cream and simmer for 10 minutes more. Stir in butter and parsley.

Serves 8 to 10.

—Xenia von Rosen
Mission, British Columbia

ANDALUSIAN GAZPACHO

AN AUTHENTIC AND SIMPLY MADE VERSION OF THE ZESTY SPANISH CLASSIC. MOST NORTH American vegetable gardens will be able to supply all the fresh ingredients.

2½ cups chicken stock
1½ cups cubed white bread,
   crust removed
4 cups crushed & drained tomatoes,
   strained to remove seeds
1 small white onion, quartered
1 green pepper, quartered
½ large cucumber, peeled,
   seeded & diced
1 clove garlic

¼ cup red wine vinegar
2 Tbsp. mayonnaise
1 cup light cream
salt & pepper

Garnishes
1 cup each diced white onion,
   diced green pepper,
   diced cucumber &
   toasted croutons

Pour ½ cup chicken stock over bread cubes and let soak while you put all other ingredients, except mayonnaise and cream, in a food processor or blender and purée until smooth. Add soaked bread cubes and continue puréeing. Put mixture through food mill to remove remaining tomato seeds and green pepper skins. Chill for at least 3 hours until flavours blend and soup is well chilled. Whisk in mayonnaise and cream. Season to taste with salt and pepper. Serve with garnishes.

Serves 6 to 8.

Salads & Vegetables

" . . . piles of white and green fennel, sea-dust-coloured artichokes, great radishes, carrots, scarlet large peppers—a great mass of colours and vegetable freshnesses."

—D.H. Lawrence

We are probably as guilty as any of having preconceived notions of what life and sustenance must be like for trappers in the Far North, and thus it was with pleasure that we received Beth Hunt's recipe submission from Mayo in the Yukon Territory. "We live on a trapline for most of the year, quite a distance from town," she wrote, "so we can only take in vegetables that store well in the root cellar—carrots and potatoes. The special appeal of this Carrot Sprout Salad to us is that we can have it fresh year-round."

While we still can't quite envisage Sergeant Preston hunkering down by a campfire with a plateful of Alfalfa Sprouts Vinaigrette, the last decade's shift in vegetable tastes has obviously made its way into the Land of the Midnight Sun.

Industry analysts tell us that the produce section is now the fastest-growing and most profitable area in the modern supermarket. For a generation that grew up with canned peas and iceberg lettuce, the option of feeding our children fresh Chinese snow peas and flavourful romaine and Boston lettuce even in the dead of winter is a revolutionary luxury.

Alas, as recently reported in the U.S. edition of *Harrowsmith*, the seductive availability of year-round fresh produce comes with a price: diminished nutritional content and chemical contaminants in the form of pesticides, fungicides and preservatives—many of these embedded in a film of beautifying wax that simply does not rinse off. Flash-frozen produce, we are told, is often a much better choice than vegetables and fruits subjected to vitamin-sapping shipping from Florida, California and other points south.

The best solution, of course, is to grow one's own or to buy locally from farmers and vendors we trust. Some nutritionists say we need to cook seasonally, accepting the natural succession of ripening dates of different fruits and vegetables throughout the year. "Savour fresh asparagus in the early spring and tomatoes in the heat of summer," they say. "Resist the inferior cello-wrapped supermarket versions of winter."

Good advice, perhaps, but not always an attractive option for those of us in cold regions with short growing seasons. Home canning and freezing offer season-extending alternatives, as do an increasing number of new-age northern market gardeners who are now able to supply organically grown lettuce almost until Christmas and very respectable solar greenhouse tomatoes as early as March. May their numbers increase.

In the meantime, whatever approach one takes to procuring wholesome produce—up to and including sprouting one's own by a wood stove in a trapline cabin—there is no doubt that most of us will find inspiration in the highly recommended recipes that follow. Robert Service, if you could only see us now.

BUTTERED GREEN BEANS WITH CASHEWS

1½ lbs. green beans
3 Tbsp. butter
¼ tsp. salt

½ tsp. pepper
¼ cup chopped parsley
1 cup roasted unsalted cashews

Trim beans and blanch in boiling water. Meanwhile, melt butter and stir in salt, pepper and parsley. Drain beans and place in warm bowl. Sprinkle with cashews and then pour butter over. Toss well.

Serves 6 to 8.

—Kristine Mattila
Quesnel, British Columbia

TAMARI ALMOND GREEN BEANS

2-3 cups French-cut green beans
1 small onion, chopped
1 clove garlic, minced

4 Tbsp. butter
½ cup slivered almonds
3 Tbsp. tamari

Cook beans, drain and set aside. In large saucepan, fry onion and garlic in butter until almost transparent. Add almonds and stir-fry for a minute or two longer. Stir in green beans and add tamari. Mix well and serve when heated through.

Serves 4.

—Mikell Billoki
Gore Bay, Ontario

FRIED STRING BEANS

"DURING A RATHER HARD WINTER, WE LIVED MOSTLY ON OUR CANNED FOOD, FROZEN FRUITS, vegetables and meats, plus potatoes, carrots and onions. We made many interesting and different dishes. This was one we really liked."

¼ lb. bacon
½ cup chopped onion

1 quart canned beans
salt & pepper

Fry bacon until crisp, then set aside. Drain most of bacon fat off, leaving about 4 Tbsp. in pan. Cook onion in bacon fat until soft. Add drained beans and fry until lightly browned – about 20 minutes. Add bacon and salt and pepper. Heat and serve.

Serves 4.

—Irene Whetson
Rock Creek, Ohio

LEMON-BUTTERED CABBAGE

SERVE THIS FRESH-TASTING CABBAGE WITH ROAST PORK FOR FLAVOURS THAT COMPLEMENT ONE another well.

¼ cup butter
1 head cabbage, shredded
½ tsp. grated lemon rind
2 Tbsp. lemon juice

½ tsp. celery seed
½ tsp. salt
¼ tsp. pepper

Melt butter in large skillet. Add shredded cabbage, cover and cook over medium heat, stirring occasionally, for 8 to 10 minutes, or until just tender. Add remaining ingredients. Stir to combine and serve at once.

Serves 6 to 8.

—Holly Andrews
Puslinch, Ontario

BRUSSELS SPROUTS WITH BACON SAUCE

"TOP BRUSSELS SPROUTS WITH THIS CREAMY BACON SAUCE AND YOU WILL ELEVATE THEM TO gourmet status."

1 lb. Brussels sprouts
4 slices bacon
1 small onion, chopped
½ cup sour cream

1 Tbsp. flour
⅛ tsp. salt
pepper

Trim stems and outer leaves from sprouts and cut an X in base. Boil or steam, covered, for 10 minutes, or until crispy-tender. Cook bacon until crisp, remove from pan and drain. Remove all but 1 Tbsp. of fat from pan, then add onion and sauté until tender – about 5 minutes. Combine sour cream, flour, salt and pepper. Stir sour cream mixture into onion; add crumbled bacon and heat sauce through. When sprouts are done, drain well, top with sauce and serve.

Serves 4 to 5.

—Donna Jubb
Fenelon Falls, Ontario

SCALLOPED CABBAGE

"THIS RECIPE HAS BEEN HANDED DOWN THROUGH THE FAMILY, ALTHOUGH I AM UNAWARE OF anyone ever writing it down. My mother made it on the farm, and her mother before her. My children continue to make it in their own homes, and so, I suppose, in that sense it has become a traditional dish for us."

3½ cups coarsely chopped cabbage
1-2 onions, chopped
¼ cup butter
¼ cup flour

1 cup milk
½ cup grated Cheddar cheese
dry bread crumbs
Parmesan cheese

Steam cabbage and onions for 5 to 8 minutes over boiling water. Melt butter, stir in flour and blend to make a smooth paste. Add milk gradually, stirring constantly. Remove from heat when thickened. Add Cheddar cheese and cabbage mixture, blending thoroughly. Pour into greased casserole dish and top with bread crumbs and Parmesan cheese. Bake, uncovered, at 350 degrees F for 25 minutes.

Serves 4 to 6.

—Shirley Fulton
Chesterville, Ontario

MAPLE-GLAZED CARROTS

1½ lbs. whole baby carrots
3 Tbsp. butter
½ cup maple syrup

½ tsp. salt
2 Tbsp. chopped parsley **or** mint

Cook carrots in boiling, salted water until almost tender. Drain, reserving ¼ cup liquid. Melt butter and roll carrots in it. Add reserved liquid, maple syrup and salt. Cook, uncovered, until liquid is thickened and carrots are tender – about 10 minutes. Sprinkle with parsley or mint.

Serves 6.

—Lynn Tobin
Thornhill, Ontario

ALMOND BUTTER CARROTS

CARROTS DESERVE BETTER TREATMENT THAN THE SLICING AND BOILING THEY GENERALLY GET. This is a simple but tasty method of dressing up the nutritious, inexpensive vegetable.

6 carrots, scraped & julienned
3 Tbsp. butter
⅓ cup slivered almonds

¼ tsp. curry powder
1 Tbsp. lemon juice

Steam carrots until crispy-tender. Melt butter until lightly browned, add almonds and sauté until golden brown, stirring constantly. Stir in curry powder and lemon juice, and cook over low heat for 1 to 2 minutes. Pour over carrots and serve.

Serves 4 to 6.

—Jayne Simms-Dalmotas
Ottawa, Ontario

SPICY CARROTS

"THIS VEGETABLE DISH CAN BE SERVED HOT OR COLD AND IS ESPECIALLY GOOD WITH LAMB. THE carrots are aromatic and full of flavour."

2 lbs. carrots, scraped & cut into ½" slices
5 Tbsp. olive oil
½ tsp. salt
½ tsp. pepper
½ tsp. cinnamon

½ tsp. cumin seed
3 cloves garlic, finely chopped
½ tsp. thyme
1 bay leaf
1 Tbsp. lemon juice

Cook carrots until firm but tender—about 15 minutes. Drain, reserving ½ cup liquid, and keep warm. Meanwhile, in large frying pan combine oil and all other ingredients except reserved liquid and lemon juice. Simmer for 10 minutes, then add carrot liquid and carrots, turning carrots frequently to coat well. Cook for 3 to 5 minutes to heat thoroughly. Sprinkle with lemon juice, remove bay leaf and serve.

Serves 6.

—Judith Almond-Best
Madoc, Ontario

CORN OYSTERS

⅓ cup cornmeal
⅓ cup flour
2 tsp. salt
¼ tsp. pepper
3 egg yolks, beaten

½ cup melted butter **or** oil
2 cups corn
3 egg whites, beaten until stiff
oil for cooking

Combine cornmeal, flour, salt and pepper and mix well. Stir in egg yolks and butter or oil. Add corn, then gently fold in egg whites. Drop by spoonfuls into hot oil and fry until golden brown.

Serves 4.

—Darlene Abraham
Ailsa Craig, Ontario

CORN & EGGPLANT CASSEROLE

IF YOUR GARDEN PROVIDES YOU WITH AN OVERABUNDANCE OF EGGPLANT IN THE FALL, BAKE extras at 350 degrees F until soft, then peel, purée and freeze in plastic bags. To use, thaw and squeeze out excess moisture.

1 eggplant, cubed	2 slices bread
3 Tbsp. oil	¼ cup milk
3 Tbsp. chopped onion	1 cup cooked corn
½ cup diced green pepper	1 cup grated Cheddar **or** Swiss cheese
¼ cup diced sweet red pepper	salt & pepper
¼ cup chopped mushrooms	2 large eggs
1 Tbsp. chopped parsley	2 Tbsp. bread crumbs
½ tsp. basil	3 Tbsp. grated Cheddar **or** Swiss cheese
thyme, oregano, marjoram, tarragon **or** savory	1 Tbsp. melted butter

Place eggplant in saucepan and cover with boiling water; cover and simmer for 15 minutes. Drain, squeezing out liquid gently, then mash.

Heat oil in skillet and sauté onion until clear. Add peppers, mushrooms, parsley, basil and herbs. Sauté for 1 minute, then blend into eggplant. Soak bread in milk for 5 minutes. Squeeze out excess milk, tear bread into small pieces and add to eggplant with corn and 1 cup cheese. Season with salt and pepper. Beat eggs until thick and fold into vegetable mixture.

Pour into greased casserole dish. Combine bread crumbs and 3 Tbsp. cheese and sprinkle over top. Drizzle with melted butter. Bake, uncovered, at 350 degrees F for 1 hour.

Serves 4.

—Ingrid Birker
Montreal, Quebec

FRESH CORN PUDDING

FREEZING FRESH-FROM-THE-COB CORN IS TIME CONSUMING, BUT THE TASTE IN MIDWINTER MAKES the work well worthwhile. Blanch the corn on the cob, immerse immediately in ice-cold water, then cut the kernels from the cob with a small, very sharp knife. Bag and freeze.

2½ cups corn	1 tsp. salt
3 eggs, beaten	⅛ tsp. pepper
3 Tbsp. chopped onion	1 Tbsp. sugar
2 Tbsp. melted butter	¼ cup dry bread crumbs
¼ cup flour	¼ cup Parmesan cheese
2 cups milk	

Combine corn, eggs, onion, butter, flour, milk, salt, pepper and sugar, and spoon into greased casserole dish. Combine bread crumbs and cheese and sprinkle over corn mixture. Place casserole in pan containing 1 inch hot water and bake, uncovered, at 325 degrees F for 1 hour or until firm.

Serves 6.

—Terry Braatz
Mooresville, North Carolina

VINNY'S EGGPLANT ITALIANO

1 eggplant	1¼ cups bread crumbs
6 eggs	1 lb. spinach
1¼ cups Parmesan cheese	salt & pepper

Peel eggplant carefully from top to bottom, reserving the peels, and cube. Boil eggplant and peels for 15 to 20 minutes in water to cover.

Meanwhile, beat eggs, add cheese and bread crumbs and mix well. Cook spinach for 3 to 4 minutes, drain well and chop. Drain eggplant and peels. Mash eggplant, add spinach and mix well. Add to egg mixture and mix well. Season with salt and pepper.

Grease a 9″ x 9″ baking pan and spread peels shiny side down on bottom. Fill with eggplant mixture and bake, uncovered, at 350 degrees F for 40 to 45 minutes.

Serves 10 to 12.

—Lisa Caggiula-Duke
Rainbow Lake, New York

GREEK EGGPLANT & CHEESE

1 large eggplant, sliced ¼″ thick	⅛ tsp. cinnamon
olive oil	⅛ tsp. pepper
1 onion, chopped	1½ cups cottage cheese
1 large clove garlic, minced	¼ cup Parmesan cheese
28-oz. can tomatoes, drained	1 egg
2 Tbsp. parsley	1 cup grated Cheddar or mozzarella cheese

Brown eggplant in olive oil and set aside. Sauté onion and garlic in more olive oil. Add tomatoes, parsley, cinnamon and pepper. Simmer, uncovered, for 5 minutes. Spread half the tomatoes in a greased 9″ x 13″ baking pan. Mix cottage and Parmesan cheeses together and beat in egg. Spread this over the layer of tomatoes.

Arrange eggplant slices, overlapping, on top of cheese, then spread remaining tomatoes over eggplant. Top with grated Cheddar or mozzarella. Cover tightly and bake at 375 degrees F for 30 minutes. Uncover and bake for another 10 to 15 minutes. Let stand for 10 minutes before serving.

Serves 4 to 6.

—Susan O'Neill
Bella Coola, British Columbia

SOUTH-OF-THE-BORDER EGGPLANT CASSEROLE

1 large eggplant, sliced	2 cloves garlic, crushed
¾ cup olive oil	½ tsp. cumin
28-oz. can tomato sauce	1 cup pitted black olives
4-oz. can green chilies	1½ cups grated Cheddar cheese
½ cup sliced green onions	½ cup sour cream

Brush eggplant with oil and place on baking sheet. Bake at 450 degrees F for 10 to 20 minutes, or until soft. Combine tomato sauce, chilies, onions, garlic, cumin and olives in saucepan and simmer for 10 minutes.

Grease shallow casserole dish and layer eggplant, sauce and cheese, ending with cheese. Bake, uncovered, at 350 degrees F for 25 minutes. Serve with sour cream.

Serves 6 to 8.

—Sybil D. Hendricks
Plymouth, California

Sweet & Sour Pork with Peaches, page 212

Chicken & Bell Peppers, page 165

82

Green Bean & Potato Salad, page 109

Dutch Cherry Cake, page 277; White Chocolate Mocha Java Bars, page 24; Kipfel, page 29; Lace Cookies, page 29

Orange Waffles, page 14

Carrot Mincemeat, page 270

Malpeque Oyster Stew, page 153

Oriental Rice Salad, page 117

POTATO PANCAKES (LATKES)

3 eggs, separated
4½ cups grated potatoes, well drained
6 Tbsp. grated onion
1-1½ tsp. salt

¼ tsp. pepper
3 Tbsp. matzo meal **or** potato flour
   or dry bread crumbs
oil

Beat together everything but egg whites and oil. Beat whites until stiff, then fold into potato mixture. Fry in about ½ inch hot oil, using a heaping tablespoonful of batter for each pancake. Turn when edges are golden brown. Keep pancakes hot until all are fried.

Makes 14 to 16 pancakes.

—Lynne Roe
Orangeville, Ontario

STUFFED ONIONS "AU FOUR"

"ON SUNDAYS, WHEN MY FATHER TOOK OVER COOKING DUTIES, HE LOVED TO CREATE THIS special dish. In my European family, onions were always an integral part of a meal."

8 large onions
1 Tbsp. butter
5 Tbsp. dry rice
4 oz. ham, chopped
½ red pepper, chopped
4 oz. mushrooms, chopped

1 cup white wine
1 cup chicken stock
4 oz. mozzarella cheese, cubed
1 bundle chives, chopped
salt & pepper
1 cup heavy cream

Peel onions and cut off crowns. Cook in boiling salted water for 10 minutes, then rinse until cold. Hollow out onions, then chop removed centre parts. Melt butter and sauté chopped onions, rice, ham, red pepper and mushrooms. Add ½ cup wine and chicken stock, cover and simmer for 20 minutes, or until all liquid is absorbed. Add cheese, chives and salt and pepper.

Stuff hollowed onions with rice mixture, place in greased casserole dish and bake, uncovered, at 450 degrees F for 10 minutes. Pour remaining ½ cup wine over onions and bake for 15 to 20 minutes more. When onions are crisp and light brown, add cream and heat through.

Serves 4 to 6.

—Inge Benda
Bridgetown, Nova Scotia

MINTED NEW PEAS

"MY GRANDMOTHER WAS FROM ENGLAND, AND SHE KEPT A BIG, SPRAWLING PATCH OF MINT tucked behind her beloved roses. Her peas with fresh mint was one of my favourite dishes as a child – to this day, the odour of a rose or of a sprig of mint reminds me of her garden."

½ cup chopped green onions
3 Tbsp. butter
2 cups fresh peas
1 Tbsp. finely chopped mint

1 tsp. sugar
1 tsp. lemon juice
¼ tsp. salt
¼ tsp. rosemary

Cook onions in butter until tender. Add remaining ingredients and 2 Tbsp. water. Cover and cook until peas are tender. Garnish with lemon twist and fresh mint leaves, if desired.

Serves 4.

—Alyson Service
Merrickville, Ontario

CHAMP

"CHAMP IS A VERY OLD AND VERY POPULAR IRISH DISH. I DON'T THINK A WEEK PASSED THAT WE didn't have this for our main course at dinnertime at least one day when I was a child. It's economical and was a favourite Friday dish for those who kept Lent. My father's book of *Irish Country Recipes* says, 'In a farmhouse, 2 stones (28 lbs.) or more of potatoes were peeled and boiled for dinner. Then the man of the house was summoned when all was ready, and while he pounded this enormous potful of potatoes with a sturdy wooden beetle, his wife added the potful of milk and nettles or scallions or chives or parsley, and he beetled it till it was smooth as butter, not a lump anywhere. Everyone got a large plateful, made a hole in the centre and into this put a large lump of butter. Then the champ was eaten from the outside with a spoon or fork, dipping it into the melting butter in the centre. All was washed down with new milk or freshly churned buttermilk.'"

9 potatoes
6 green onions, chopped

1¼ cups milk
salt & pepper

Peel potatoes and boil in salted water until tender. Drain and mash. When free from lumps, beat in green onions and milk. Season with salt and pepper and beat until creamy. Champ must be kept very hot and be served on hot plates.

Serves 6 to 8.

—*Hazel R. Baker*
Coombs, British Columbia

INDIAN SPICED NEW POTATO FRY

3 Tbsp. oil
1 tsp. mustard seed
1 lb. small, even-sized new potatoes,
    boiled & peeled
1 tsp. chili powder

1½ tsp. coriander
¼ tsp. turmeric
½ tsp. salt
3 sprigs coriander, chopped
lemon juice

Heat oil in wok and add mustard seed and potatoes. Stir-fry over low heat until lightly browned. Sprinkle with chili powder, coriander, turmeric and salt and continue to stir-fry for 5 to 6 minutes. Remove from heat and sprinkle with coriander and lemon juice.

Serves 2 to 4.

—*Lynn Andersen*
Lumsden, Saskatchewan

BAKED HASH BROWNS

"THIS IS AN EASY WAY TO MAKE DELICIOUS, CRISPY HASH BROWNS. I SERVE IT FOR SPECIAL breakfasts or brunch with eggs and broiled tomatoes. It is also good for supper with smoked pork chops."

4 slices bacon
4 potatoes, grated
1 onion, grated
⅓ cup bread crumbs

1 egg
⅛ tsp. pepper
⅛ tsp. salt

Cook bacon lightly, so that fat is cooked out but bacon is not yet crisp. Drain, reserving fat. Dice bacon. Put bacon fat into a 9″ x 9″ baking pan. Heat at 400 degrees F.

Combine remaining ingredients, including bacon, and spread in the hot dish. Bake at 400 degrees, uncovered, for about 45 minutes.

Serves 2.

—*Ruth Ellis Haworth*
Toronto, Ontario

SPINACH WITH PEANUT SAUCE

Even children liked spinach cooked this way when we tested this recipe, so it must be good. See page 175 for directions to make coconut milk.

2 lbs. spinach
2 Tbsp. butter
1 large onion, chopped
crushed hot red peppers

1 Tbsp. whiskey
1 tsp. soy sauce
½ cup coconut milk
½ cup crushed unsalted peanuts

Cook spinach without water until limp. Cool, then squeeze to remove all moisture. Melt butter and sauté onion and pepper until onion is soft. Stir in remaining ingredients and cook, stirring, for 2 to 3 minutes. Add spinach, stir and heat through.

Serves 6.

—Ingrid Birker
Montreal, Quebec

ITALIAN SPINACH DUMPLINGS

1 pkg. spinach
4 tsp. salt
½ tsp. ground nutmeg
¼ tsp. pepper

1 egg, lightly beaten
½ cup ricotta cheese
6 Tbsp. flour
1 Tbsp. butter

Cook spinach and drain thoroughly, pressing with spoon to squeeze out all liquid. Chop finely or purée. Combine spinach, 1 tsp. salt, nutmeg, pepper, egg and ricotta cheese in large bowl. Gradually add flour, using enough to make a firm mixture. Shape into 1-inch balls. Place on a plate and chill for at least 30 minutes.

Combine 8 cups water, butter and remaining 3 tsp. salt in large saucepan. Bring to a boil. Drop balls gently into water, several at a time, and cook, uncovered, for 8 minutes, or until balls rise to top and are tender. Lift out with a slotted spoon and keep warm.

Serves 4.

—Ingrid Birker
Montreal, Quebec

SPINACH MOULD

This vegetable dish can be cooked ahead of time. It freezes well and holds its shape when sliced.

½ cup flour
1 tsp. salt
1 tsp. baking powder
3 eggs

1 cup milk
1 lb. mild Cheddar cheese, grated
2 pkgs. spinach, chopped
½ cup finely chopped onion

Combine flour, salt and baking powder and mix well. Beat eggs. Add flour mixture and milk to eggs, beating well. Add cheese, spinach and onion and mix well. Pour into greased, small tube pan and bake, uncovered, at 350 degrees F for 35 minutes. Leave in pan to cool and set. Serve warm or cool.

Serves 4 to 6.

—Evelyn M. Grieve
Toronto, Ontario

SWISS CHARD ROLLS

THERE ARE MANY VARIATIONS TO THIS RECIPE. ADD WALNUTS TO THE FILLING, OR USE OTHER vegetables. Sprinkle the casserole with grated cheese and then bake.

1 cup dry brown rice
4 Tbsp. oil
2 stalks celery, chopped
12 large mushrooms, sliced

2 onions, chopped
12 large Swiss chard leaves
4 cups spicy tomato sauce

Cook rice and set aside until cool. Heat oil and sauté celery, mushrooms and onions. Mix with rice.

Fill leaves with vegetable mixture and roll up, folding in ends. Place in 9″ × 13″ baking pan and pour tomato sauce over. Bake, covered, at 350 degrees F for 15 to 20 minutes.

Serves 12 as a side dish, 4 as a main dish.

—Arlene Pervin
Moyie, British Columbia

STUFFED PUMPKIN

THIS IS AN IDEAL HOLIDAY DISH FOR NON MEAT-EATERS. TASTY AND COLOURFUL, NO ONE WILL miss the turkey.

1 pumpkin
6 Tbsp. oil
2 onions, chopped
2 cloves garlic, chopped
2 stalks celery, chopped
1 green pepper, chopped
1 lb. mushrooms, chopped
1 cup cooked, chopped spinach

4 cups cooked rice
salt & pepper
1 tsp. sage
¾ tsp. thyme
½ tsp. rosemary
½ tsp. basil
½ tsp. oregano

Wash pumpkin and slice off top as you would for a jack-o'-lantern. Scoop out seeds and rinse inside of pumpkin.

Heat oil and sauté onions, garlic, celery, green pepper and mushrooms for 10 minutes. Combine with remaining ingredients and place in pumpkin. Replace lid so it is not tightly sealed.

Bake at 350 degrees F in baking dish with 1 inch water for approximately 1½ hours, or until pumpkin flesh is soft.

Serves 6.

ORANGE SQUASH

1-2 Tbsp. grated gingerroot
juice and grated rind of 2 oranges
1 Tbsp. coriander

¼ cup butter, softened
salt
3 small squash, halved & seeded

Combine ginger, orange rind, juice of 1 orange, coriander, butter and salt and mix well. Place in squash halves. Bake in covered casserole dish with juice of other orange at 350 degrees F for 45 minutes.

Serves 6.

—Wendy Vine
Ganges, British Columbia

SQUASH WITH GARLIC, GOAT CHEESE & WALNUTS

"THIS IS A GREAT FALL RECIPE. IT SMELLS WONDERFUL WHEN BAKING. USE ANY KIND OF SQUASH, and while firm goat cheese is preferable, a creamy variety will do."

1 medium squash, peeled & halved
3 Tbsp. butter
2 cloves garlic, crushed
2 Tbsp. flour
1 cup light cream
½ cup whipping cream
salt & pepper
nutmeg
½ cup crumbled goat cheese

Topping
2 Tbsp. Parmesan cheese
2 Tbsp. bread crumbs
1 Tbsp. butter, softened
¼ cup chopped walnuts

Seed squash and cut into ¾-inch cubes. Cook in boiling water until tender – 6 to 8 minutes – then drain and keep warm in a bowl.

Melt butter over medium heat, sauté garlic for 1 minute, then stir in flour and cook for 2 minutes. Remove from heat and gradually whisk in creams, salt and pepper and nutmeg. Return to heat and cook, stirring, until thickened. Remove from heat and stir in cheese until it melts. Pour over squash, toss, then turn into greased casserole dish.

Combine topping ingredients and sprinkle over squash. Bake, uncovered, at 425 degrees F for 10 to 12 minutes or until brown and bubbling.

Serves 4 to 6.

—Terry Seed
Toronto, Ontario

STUFFED SUNBURST SQUASH

8-10 'Sunburst' squash
3 eggs, beaten
½ cup Parmesan cheese
½ cup ricotta cheese

½ cup grated mozzarella cheese
4 Tbsp. chopped basil
½ lb. Italian sausage, browned &
   crumbled

Parboil whole squash for 8 minutes. Drain, then cut off tops of squash and scoop out seeds. Combine remaining ingredients and mix well. Stuff into squash and replace tops. Place in shallow pan with ½ inch water and bake, uncovered, at 350 degrees F for 30 minutes, or until filling is set.

Serves 4 to 5.

—Laurie D. Glaspey
Oakridge, Oregon

SWEET POTATOES À L'ORANGE

4 sweet potatoes
2 cups orange juice
2 oranges, peeled & sliced,
   rind reserved

1 tsp. cinnamon
2 tsp. cornstarch

Peel sweet potatoes, cut into quarters and place in greased casserole dish.

In saucepan, heat orange juice, rind from oranges, cinnamon and cornstarch until thick, stirring often. Pour sauce over potatoes and top with orange slices. Bake, covered, at 350 degrees F for 45 minutes to 1 hour.

Serves 4 to 6.

—Beth Armstrong-Bewick
Fredericton, New Brunswick

VERY DIFFERENT TURNIPS

THE USE OF MILK AND CHEESE SOFTENS THE BITTER TASTE OFTEN ASSOCIATED WITH TURNIPS.
of turnips.

2 lbs. turnips, peeled & cubed
1 onion, minced
½ cup butter

1½ cups grated sharp Cheddar cheese
½ cup milk
salt & pepper

Cook turnips for 20 to 30 minutes, or until tender, then mash. Cook onion in 4 Tbsp.
butter until soft. Add turnip, remaining butter, cheese and milk. Heat until cheese melts,
then season with salt and pepper.

Serves 6.

—Mary M. Loucks
Godfrey, Ontario

TURNIPS & APPLES

1 large turnip
1 Tbsp. butter
2 apples
¼ cup brown sugar
½ tsp. cinnamon

Crust
⅓ cup flour
⅓ cup brown sugar
2 Tbsp. butter

Cook turnip, then mash with butter. Peel and thinly slice apples. Toss with sugar and
cinnamon. In greased casserole dish, arrange turnip and apples in layers, beginning and
ending with turnip.

Combine crust ingredients until texture is crumbly. Pat on top of turnip. Bake, uncovered,
at 350 degrees F for 45 minutes.

Serves 4.

—Pat de la Ronde
Terrace, British Columbia

RUTABAGA BHARTA

"RUTABAGAS ARE ONE OF OUR FAVOURITE VEGETABLES, SO WE ALWAYS GROW A LOT. WE ARE
constantly looking for new things to do with them. This recipe came from a small East
Indian store in Edmonton."

1 lb. rutabagas
2 Tbsp. oil
½-inch piece gingerroot, finely chopped
1 onion, finely chopped
2 tsp. aniseed **or** fennel
1 tsp. fenugreek

½ tsp. pepper
½ tsp. paprika **or** chili powder
½ tsp. garam masala
1 tsp. salt
1 tsp. brown sugar

Peel rutabagas and cut into small pieces. Boil in minimum water until soft, then mash.
Heat oil and sauté gingerroot and onion. Add spices, mashed rutabagas, salt and sugar.
Mix well and cook gently until excess moisture has evaporated.

Serves 6.

—Barbara Prescott
Edson, Alberta

ZUCCHINI PANCAKES

FREEZE SHREDDED ZUCCHINI WHEN YOU THINK YOU CANNOT POSSIBLY EAT ANOTHER ONE, AND use through the winter for this recipe, soups, breads, et cetera. Just be sure to drain well before using. Small amounts of grated zucchini can be added to almost any soup, stew or casserole recipe without altering the flavour or texture. It is a good way to allow zucchini haters the benefit of eating this nutritious vegetable.

2 cups grated zucchini	½ tsp. baking powder
2 eggs, beaten	½ tsp. salt
¼ cup chopped onion	savory
½ cup flour	oil

Drain zucchini in strainer, pressing out as much liquid as possible, then combine with eggs and onion. Mix remaining ingredients, except for oil, in separate bowl. Stir dry ingredients into zucchini mixture, then drop by spoonsful into hot oil and fry until lightly brown.

Serves 4.

—Darlene Abraham
Ailsa Craig, Ontario

ZUCCHINI ENCHILADAS

THE VERMONT STAFF GAVE THESE ENCHILADAS A RESOUNDING "YES" WHEN THEY TASTED THEM — a wonderful way to use up zucchini. They were definitely one of the most popular test lunches and were surprisingly easy to make. The ambitious cook could make his or her own tortillas, although there are many good commercial varieties available – the frozen ones are generally fresher-tasting than those in cans. Increase the chilies to suit personal taste buds – the amount listed gives a delicate hot taste.

1 zucchini, grated	8 oz. sour cream
1 onion, chopped	½ lb. Monterey Jack cheese, grated
2 canned green chilies, drained & chopped	2 cups tomato sauce
12 corn tortillas	

Combine zucchini, onion and chilies and mix well. Heat tortillas a minute on each side to soften in hot, dry skillet. Keep warm.

To assemble, spread each tortilla with sour cream. Place 2 to 3 Tbsp. zucchini mixture in middle, 2 Tbsp. cheese on this and roll up. Place seam side down in greased 9" x 9" casserole dish. Pour tomato sauce over the enchiladas and top with remaining cheese. Bake, uncovered, at 350 degrees F for 30 minutes.

Serves 4.

—Leslie Pierpont
Santa Fe, New Mexico

ZUCCHINI CHEESE CASSEROLE

"VERY QUICK AND EASY, THIS IS A TASTY WAY TO SUBDUE THE ALWAYS OVERPOPULATED zucchini patch."

4 medium zucchini, sliced
½ cup chopped onion
2 Tbsp. oil

1 lb. cottage cheese
1 tsp. basil
⅓ cup Parmesan cheese

Sauté zucchini and onion in oil. Whip cottage cheese with basil in blender. Place alternating layers of zucchini and cheese in 1½-quart casserole dish; top with Parmesan cheese. Bake, uncovered, at 350 degrees F for 25 to 30 minutes.

Serves 6.

—Sandra K. Bennett
Greenville, South Carolina

ZUCCHINI CUSTARD

"LIGHT AND FLUFFY — ALMOST LIKE A SOUFFLÉ," RAVED OUR VERMONT TESTERS.

2 lbs. zucchini, coarsely grated
1 onion, minced
1 clove garlic, crushed
3 Tbsp. olive oil
⅓ cup minced parsley
⅛ tsp. thyme

⅛ tsp. rosemary
1 tsp. salt
⅛ tsp. pepper
5 eggs
½ cup flour
¾ cup Parmesan cheese

Stir-fry zucchini, onion and garlic in oil in large, heavy skillet over medium heat for 10 to 12 minutes, or until zucchini is tender. Mix in parsley, thyme, rosemary, salt and pepper. Beat eggs until frothy, then mix in flour and Parmesan cheese. Stir zucchini mixture into eggs, spoon into greased 1½-quart casserole dish, and bake, uncovered, at 300 degrees F for 1 to 1¼ hours, or until knife inserted in centre comes out clean.

Serves 4 to 6.

—Doreen Deacur
Pefferlaw, Ontario

HERBED TOMATOES

4 ripe tomatoes
salt
¼ cup butter
⅛ tsp. pepper
1 tsp. brown sugar
1 Tbsp. lemon juice

½ cup diced celery
3 Tbsp. finely chopped chives **or**
    green onion
3 Tbsp. chopped parsley
½ tsp. oregano

Core tomatoes and sprinkle with salt. Melt butter in frying pan, add pepper and brown sugar, then place tomatoes in pan, cored side down. Cover and simmer slowly for 5 minutes. Turn tomatoes over and spoon butter mixture into hollow. Add remaining ingredients to pan and sauté for 2 minutes. Cover and simmer until tomatoes are just tender – 8 minutes. Spoon mixture into tomatoes and lift carefully from pan. Pour any remaining pan liquids over tomatoes and serve.

Serves 4.

—Lynn Tobin
Thornhill, Ontario

TOMATO CURRY

This curry can also be made with half ripe and half unripe tomatoes, although the result will not be as smooth. Serve with rice, noodles, meatloaf, fish or hard-cooked eggs.

2 Tbsp. oil
2 onions, chopped
1 Tbsp. chopped coriander
1 tsp. toasted cumin seed

2 cloves garlic, crushed
2 lbs. ripe tomatoes, peeled & chopped
1 Tbsp. brown sugar
salt

Heat oil and sauté onions until golden. Add coriander and cook, stirring, for 1 minute, then add remaining ingredients. Cook for 30 minutes over medium heat.

Serves 6 as a sauce.

—Ethel Hunter
Warkworth, Ontario

TOFU WITH MUSTARD & TAMARI SAUCE

Beautiful to look at and full of flavour, this is a good dish for people unfamiliar with tofu.

⅓ cup peanut oil
¼-½ cup dark mustard
¼ cup tamari
1 lb. firm tofu, rinsed & drained

4 cups chopped vegetables (peppers,
  bok choy, mushrooms, snow peas)
3 cups cooked brown rice, kept warm

Heat oil, stir in mustard and tamari and mix well. Quarter tofu and carefully place in sauce. Cook, turning frequently, for 10 to 15 minutes. Cover and set aside.

Meanwhile, steam vegetables until crispy-tender. Place rice on serving platter, surround with vegetables and top with tofu and sauce.

Serves 4.

—Janice Baldrate & Anne Kress
West Acton, Massachusetts

TOFU RATATOUILLE

This makes a tasty side dish, or it can be served over pasta as the main meal.

3 cloves garlic, crushed
⅓ cup olive oil
1 onion, chopped
1½ green peppers, chopped
2 zucchini, sliced
1 eggplant, cubed

1 cup sliced mushrooms
1 block tofu
1 tsp. basil
1 tsp. oregano
1 tsp. salt
1½ cups tomato juice

Sauté garlic in oil. Add onion, peppers, zucchini, eggplant and mushrooms, one vegetable at a time, and stir after each addition. Sauté for 10 minutes, then add tofu and sauté for 5 minutes more. Add basil, oregano, salt and tomato juice, and simmer for 10 minutes.

Serves 4.

—Shiela Alexandrovich
Whitehorse, Yukon

SPICED CAULIFLOWER & POTATOES

1 cauliflower
6 potatoes, peeled
5 Tbsp. oil
1 tsp. fennel seed
1 tsp. cumin seed
¼ tsp. mustard seed
¼ tsp. fenugreek

1 dried red chili pepper, crushed
1 tsp. salt
1 tsp. cumin
1 tsp. coriander
2 tsp. turmeric
pepper
1 tsp. garam masala

Break cauliflower into florets and dice potatoes. Heat oil in large heavy skillet until oil is smoking. Add fennel seed, cumin seed, mustard seed and fenugreek and cook, shaking skillet, until seeds begin to pop. Add chili pepper, then stir in cauliflower and potatoes.

Reduce heat to medium and add salt, cumin, coriander, turmeric and pepper. Sauté for 10 minutes, stirring and adding oil if needed. Stir in garam masala and 3 Tbsp. water. Cook, covered, over low heat for 15 minutes. Stir. Add water (just a bit) if needed and cook for 20 minutes more, or until vegetables are tender.

Serves 6.

—Cynthia R. Topliss
Montreal, Quebec

RUSSIAN VEGETABLE PIE

Pastry for double-crust 9-inch pie
1 onion, chopped
3 cups grated cabbage
3 Tbsp. butter
⅛ tsp. basil
⅛ tsp. marjoram

⅛ tsp. tarragon
salt & pepper
⅛ tsp. dill
½ lb. mushrooms, sliced
4 oz. cream cheese, softened
4-5 hard-cooked eggs

Line pie plate with pastry. Sauté onion and cabbage in 2 Tbsp. butter. Add basil, marjoram, tarragon, salt and pepper and dill and cook until onion and cabbage are soft. Set aside.

Melt remaining 1 Tbsp. butter and sauté mushrooms. Spread cream cheese on pastry, then slice eggs over this. Add vegetable mixture and mushrooms and top with pie crust. Bake at 400 degrees F for 15 minutes; reduce heat to 350 degrees F and cook for 20 to 25 minutes more.

Serves 4 to 6.

—Lyette Sausoucy
Bonshaw, Prince Edward Island

VEGETABLES PARMIGIANA

2 Tbsp. oil
1 Tbsp. butter
1 lb. eggplant, peeled & sliced ½" thick
1 lb. zucchini, sliced ½" thick
1 onion, halved & sliced
1 tsp. salt

1 tsp. oregano
½ tsp. pepper
1½ cups tomato sauce
2 cloves garlic, crushed
½ lb. mozzarella cheese, sliced
2 Tbsp. Parmesan cheese

Heat oil and butter and sauté eggplant, zucchini and onion for 10 minutes. Stir in salt, oregano and pepper, then spoon into greased 2-quart baking dish. Mix tomato sauce with garlic and pour over vegetables. Tuck mozzarella cheese slices into vegetables so half of each slice is on surface. Sprinkle with Parmesan cheese and bake, uncovered, at 375 degrees F for 25 minutes.

Serves 4.

—Nancy R. Franklin
San Jose, California

CALZONE

CALZONE IS BASICALLY A PIZZA TURNOVER. IT CAN BE MADE AS ONE LARGE TURNOVER OR as individual turnovers. The filling possibilities are limited only by the cook's imagination – try pesto, chicken cacciatore, seafood, a meat spaghetti sauce, ricotta cheese and spinach and so on. For this version, we suggest a combination of onion, mushrooms, olives and zucchini. Calzone can also be eaten cold, without the sauce, as picnic fare.

Sauce
8-oz. can tomato sauce
6½-oz. can tomato paste
¼ cup minced onion
3 cloves garlic, crushed
¼ tsp. pepper
¼ tsp. oregano
¼ tsp. basil
10 fennel seeds, crushed

Crust
½ tsp. sugar
½ tsp. pepper

½ tsp. parsley
1½ tsp. yeast
1 egg, beaten
2-3 cups flour

Filling
4 cups partially cooked vegetables
1 tsp. parsley
1 tsp. basil
1 tsp. oregano
1 cup grated mozzarella cheese

1 egg, beaten

Combine sauce ingredients in saucepan and simmer for 45 minutes.

For crust: Mix ⅔ cup hot water with sugar, pepper and parsley. Add yeast and beaten egg. Stir in flour to make a soft dough and set in warm place to rise.

Toss vegetables in lightly oiled skillet with parsley, basil and oregano for 10 minutes. Stir in cheese.

Shape dough into oval the thickness of pizza crust. Lay half on and half off a greased cookie sheet. Mix filling ingredients together and arrange on half of dough that is on cookie sheet. Trickle ¼ cup sauce over filling. Fold dough over and pinch edges closed. Bake calzone at 350 degrees F for 3 minutes. Remove from oven and glaze with beaten egg. Cut steam vents and bake for 30 minutes, then broil until golden. Serve with sauce.

Serves 4 to 6.

—E. K. Molitor
Winnipeg, Manitoba

GREEN SALAD WITH MUSTARD VINAIGRETTE

1 head Romaine lettuce
1 head Boston lettuce
2 heads endive

Dressing
⅓ cup olive oil
¼ cup cider vinegar

¾ tsp. marjoram
2 tsp. minced green onion
1 clove garlic, minced
1 tsp. snipped parsley
2 tsp. Dijon mustard
salt & pepper

Tear up lettuces and slice endive thinly. Toss together and chill.

Place oil, vinegar, marjoram, green onion, garlic, parsley and mustard in jar with lid and shake well to mix. Season with salt and pepper. Toss greens with dressing just before serving.

Serves 12.

—Pam Collacott
North Gower, Ontario

GREENS WITH DEEP-FRIED CHÈVRE

"ABSOLUTELY FANTASTIC! THIS IS EASY TO MAKE AND IT TASTES DELICIOUS. IF YOU PREFER A LESS robust cheese, use brie," says our Camden East tester.

½ lb. chèvre
½ cup fine dry bread crumbs
salt & pepper
1 egg
½ head radicchio
1 head Belgian endive
1 head Boston lettuce
¼ cup olive oil

⅛ cup lemon juice
½ tsp. basil
½ tsp. thyme
¼ tsp. pepper
1 clove garlic, crushed
1 tsp. dry mustard
oil for cooking

Form cheese into 4 flattened balls. Mix bread crumbs with salt and pepper in flat bowl. Beat egg in another bowl. Dip cheese rounds in bread crumbs, then egg, then crumbs again, coating well. Refrigerate for several hours.

Wash and dry greens and assemble on 4 plates, keeping leaves whole. Combine remaining ingredients, except cooking oil, for dressing. Heat ½ inch of oil in skillet until hot, then fry each cheese round until golden brown, turning frequently to prevent burning. Dress salad, top with cheese rounds and serve.

Serves 4.

—Lynn Tobin
Thornhill, Ontario

SPINACH, WATERCRESS & MUSHROOM SALAD

"MY AUNT AND UNCLE OPERATE A RESTAURANT IN PENNSYLVANIA DUTCH COUNTRY. THEY serve this salad there – it has been in our family for three generations."

2 bunches spinach, washed & torn
1 bunch watercress, washed & torn
½ lb. mushrooms, sliced
½ lb. lean bacon, diced

2 eggs
1 Tbsp. sugar
6 Tbsp. dill vinegar
2 Tbsp. chopped dill

Toss spinach and watercress with mushrooms. Fry bacon until crisp. Whip eggs lightly and stir in sugar, vinegar and dill. Pour off all but 2 Tbsp. bacon drippings, then pour egg mixture into skillet. Cook, stirring, until it thickens. Pour over greens and serve warm.

Serves 4 to 6.

—Sandy Lance
Cos Cob, Connecticut

FANTASTIC SPINACH SALAD

1 lb. spinach, washed & torn
½ cup diced, cooked bacon
1 cup sliced green onions
½ lb. mushrooms, sliced
2 cloves garlic, crushed
1½ tsp. salt

¼ cup lemon juice
½ cup olive oil
¼ tsp. pepper
¼ tsp. dry mustard
¼ tsp. Tabasco sauce
2 egg yolks

Mix spinach with bacon, onions and mushrooms. Combine remaining ingredients and shake in jar to make a creamy dressing. Toss with salad and serve.

Serves 6 to 8.

—Trudy McCallum
Oshawa, Ontario

SPINACH SALAD WITH TANGY CREAMY DRESSING

THIS RECIPE WAS A SALAD CATEGORY WINNER IN A LOCAL COOKING CONTEST. INSPIRED BY THE contributor's love of quiche, it combines ingredients available year-round.

6 cups spinach
4 slices bacon, chopped & cooked until
 crisp
1 hard-cooked egg, chopped
1 small red onion, sliced
½ cup sliced mushrooms
1 orange, peeled, seeded & chopped
⅔ cup grated Swiss cheese

Dressing
½ cup light cream
4 Tbsp. vinegar
1 tsp. dry mustard
1 Tbsp. chopped parsley
½ tsp. sugar (optional)
salt & pepper

Wash spinach and pat dry. Tear into bite-sized pieces and toss with remaining salad ingredients. Shake all dressing ingredients together. Toss lightly with salad.

Serves 6 to 8.

—Sandy Robertson
Port Robinson, Ontario

SPINACH GOUDA SALAD

THIS WAS SUBMITTED TO US WITH THE FOLLOWING REPRIMAND: "I SENT THIS RECIPE TO YOU FOR the second edition of your cookbook. It must have gone astray or you must have been suffering from sensory overload when you tasted it, because it's one of the tastiest salads around. I'm giving you one more chance!" It did, indeed, go astray last time. Now, tested and tasted, we agree with the contributor.

Dressing
⅓ cup oil
1 Tbsp. cider vinegar
1 clove garlic, minced
½ tsp. salt
¼ tsp. pepper
1 tsp. dill weed

10 oz. spinach, washed & torn
8-10 mushrooms, sliced
6 pieces bacon, chopped & cooked until
 crisp
¼ cup chopped green onion
1 cup grated Gouda cheese

Combine dressing ingredients and mix well. Toss remaining ingredients in a bowl with dressing.

Serves 6 to 8.

—Colleen Suche
Winnipeg, Manitoba

SPINACH SALAD WITH SOUR CREAM DRESSING

1 pkg. fresh spinach, washed & dried
1 small onion, sliced into thin rings
6 slices bacon, cooked crisp & crumbled
1 cup sliced mushrooms
2 eggs, hard-cooked & chopped
1 cup sour cream

2 Tbsp. lemon juice
1 Tbsp. grated onion
white pepper
1 tsp. Worcestershire sauce
¼ tsp. salt
1 tsp. sugar

Tear spinach and toss with onion, bacon, mushrooms and eggs. Combine remaining ingredients, blend well and chill for 30 minutes. Toss with salad.

Serves 4 to 6.

—Donna Parker
Pictou, Nova Scotia

KALE SALAD

"THIS RECIPE MAKES USE OF A VEGETABLE MANY PEOPLE OVERLOOK, YET KALE IS AVAILABLE IN most markets and can be grown easily. It lasts long into the winter, even under the snow, and in spring it sprouts new green top growth for early salads."

4 slices bacon, chopped
⅓ cup sugar
½ tsp. salt
1 Tbsp. cornstarch
1 egg, beaten

¼ cup cider vinegar
1 head kale
1 onion, chopped
3 hard-cooked eggs, chopped
pepper

Fry bacon slowly until crisp. Mix together sugar, salt and cornstarch, then add egg, vinegar and 1 cup water and stir until smooth. Remove all but 1 to 2 Tbsp. drippings from pan, then stir liquid ingredients into pan and cook over medium heat, stirring, until thickened. Cool slightly.

Wash kale, remove heavy centre rib and tear leaves into bite-sized pieces. Place in large bowl, add onion, eggs and pepper and toss with dressing. Serve warm or chilled.
Serves 6.

—*Harriet Felguieras*
Slatington, Pennsylvania

CARROT SPROUT SALAD

"WE LIVE ON A TRAPLINE FOR MOST OF THE YEAR, QUITE A DISTANCE FROM TOWN, SO WE CAN only take in vegetables that store well in the root cellar, such as carrots and potatoes. The special appeal of this salad to us is that we can have fresh salad all year round."

2 cups grated carrots
2 cups alfalfa sprouts
⅓ cup raisins
2 Tbsp. toasted sunflower seeds
½ tsp. salt

pepper
1 clove garlic, crushed
1 Tbsp. vinegar
1 Tbsp. oil

Combine carrots, sprouts, raisins and sunflower seeds. Combine salt, pepper, garlic, vinegar and oil and pour over salad. Mix well and serve immediately.

Serves 4.

—*Beth Hunt*
Mayo, Yukon

CELERIAC, PEPPER & CHICKEN SALAD

CELERIAC, A TURNIP-ROOTED CELERY, ABSORBS A LOT OF LIQUID. IF MORE THAN INDICATED IS required, use some of the water in which the celeriac was cooked. Strain well before using, however, as celeriac has a lot of soil in it.

¼ cup raisins
1 celeriac
2 chicken breasts, cooked & chopped
½ red pepper, diced
½ green pepper, diced

2 Tbsp. apple cider vinegar
2 Tbsp. olive oil
chopped parsley
salt & pepper

Soak raisins in ½ cup water for 2 hours. Drain and reserve liquid. Cook celeriac (in skin) in water until tender. Save cooking liquid. Peel and dice celeriac.

Toss all ingredients, including raisin liquid, adding cooking liquid if needed.

Serves 4.

—*Gabriele Klein*
Montreal, Quebec

SNOW PEA & RED PEPPER SALAD

"THIS IS A COLOURFUL SALAD, SUITABLE FOR ANY FESTIVE OCCASION BUT A GREAT FAVOURITE with our family anytime. Quick and easy to make too."

1½ lbs. snow peas
1 lb. mushrooms
2 sweet red peppers
2 cloves garlic, finely chopped
3 Tbsp. white wine vinegar
3 Tbsp. lemon juice

1 Tbsp. sugar
1 tsp. salt
pepper
1 cup oil
⅓ cup toasted sesame seeds

Remove tops and strings from snow peas. Blanch for 1 minute in large pot of boiling water. Drain immediately and plunge into iced water to chill quickly. Drain again and dry on paper towels. Slice mushrooms. Cut peppers into ½-inch dice. Using a food processor or bowl and whisk, combine garlic, vinegar, lemon juice, sugar, salt and pepper. While beating, slowly add oil to make a smooth dressing. In salad bowl, toss vegetables together; just before serving, add dressing and sesame seeds and toss well.

Serves 12.

—Margaret Brister
Fonthill, Ontario

GINGER SALAD DRESSING

½ cup coarsely chopped onion
¼ cup coarsely chopped carrot
2 tsp. coarsely chopped celery
1½ tsp. minced gingerroot
1¼ cups oil
¾ cup soy sauce

½ cup vinegar
¼ cup lemon juice
1½ tsp. tomato paste
salt & pepper
Tabasco sauce

Purée onion, carrot, celery and gingerroot in blender or food processor. Add remaining ingredients.

Makes 2 cups.

—Mary Hewson
Fort Smith, Northwest Territories

CREAMY CAESAR SALAD DRESSING

IT IS IMPORTANT TO USE FRESHLY GRATED PARMESAN CHEESE IN THIS DRESSING TO FULLY appreciate its flavour.

3 oz. olive oil
1 large clove garlic, minced
1 Tbsp. wine vinegar
½ tsp. salt
½ tsp. pepper

8 drops Worcestershire sauce
3 drops Tabasco sauce
½ tsp. anchovy paste
1 egg
¼ cup Parmesan cheese

Place all ingredients except egg and Parmesan cheese in blender. Cook egg in boiling water for 1 minute, add to blender and blend for 1 minute at high speed. Add Parmesan cheese and blend again.

Makes approximately 1 cup.

—Colleen Suche
Winnipeg, Manitoba

LUXEMBOURG SALAD DRESSING

4 cloves garlic, minced
⅓ cup vinegar
2 Tbsp. lemon juice
1½ Tbsp. Dijon mustard

1½ Tbsp. mixed salad herbs (parsley,
    chives, tarragon, chervil)
1 cup olive oil
salt & pepper

Whisk garlic, vinegar, lemon juice and mustard together. Whisk in herbs, then gradually whisk in oil. Season with salt and pepper.

Makes about 1½ cups.

—Kristine Mattila
Quesnel, British Columbia

SWEET & SOUR ONION SALAD DRESSING

⅓ cup cider vinegar
1 tsp. dry mustard
½ tsp. salt
1 tsp. celery seed

1 Tbsp. sugar
1 onion, chopped
1 cup oil

In blender, mix together vinegar, mustard, salt, celery seed and sugar. Add onion, then add oil in steady trickle.

Makes 2 cups.

—Linda Fritz
Brighton, Colorado

J.B.'S COLESLAW

THE PINEAPPLE JUICE AND SOUR CREAM GIVE THIS COLESLAW A LIGHT CREAMY TASTE.

¼ cup sour cream
¼ cup mayonnaise
¼ cup pineapple juice
1 Tbsp. lemon juice
1 Tbsp. sugar

½ tsp. salt
⅛ tsp. pepper
5 cups shredded cabbage
1 apple, diced
1 stalk celery, diced

Combine sour cream, mayonnaise, pineapple and lemon juices, sugar, salt and pepper and mix well. Toss together cabbage, apple and celery and then toss with dressing.

Serves 6 to 8.

—June Plamondon
Moisie, Quebec

TOMATO GREEN PEPPER SALAD

1 large onion, finely chopped
2-3 green peppers, thinly sliced
½ tsp. basil
pepper

3 Tbsp. red wine vinegar
3-4 Tbsp. olive oil
4-5 tomatoes, sliced

Toss together onion and peppers. Combine basil, pepper, vinegar and oil and pour over onion and peppers. Toss, then chill for 1 to 2 hours. Stir in tomatoes just before serving.

Serves 6.

—Trudi Keillor
Berwyn, Alberta

VIETNAMESE COLESLAW

"BECAUSE OF THE QUANTITY OF GARLIC, THIS SALAD IS NOT FOR THE FAINT OF HEART, BUT IT'S the garlic that makes it authentic." Dress this salad only when you are ready to serve – it does not keep well once dressed.

1 head Napa cabbage
3 large carrots, peeled & grated
1 large red onion, finely chopped
1 chicken, cooked, meat removed from
  bone & chopped
1 cup rice wine vinegar

⅓ cup fish sauce
½-1 tsp. pepper
10 cloves garlic, minced
1 tsp. sugar
½ cup peanuts

Slice cabbage finely (do not grate). Mix with carrots, onion and chicken. Chill. Meanwhile, prepare dressing. Combine vinegar, fish sauce, pepper, garlic and sugar and mix well. Toss with salad when ready to serve. Garnish with peanuts.

Serves 6.

—Donna J. Torres
Santa Barbara, California

GREEN COLESLAW

"WONDERFUL COLOUR, LIGHT AND TASTY – ONE OF THE BEST COLESLAWS I'VE TASTED," SAYS OUR Vermont tester.

12 cups slivered cabbage
1 large green pepper, chopped
1 onion, chopped
1 cup sugar
1 cup vinegar

¾ cup oil
1 Tbsp. dry mustard
1 Tbsp. celery seed
1 Tbsp. salt

Toss together cabbage, pepper and onion. Sprinkle with sugar and toss. Combine remaining ingredients in saucepan and bring to a boil. Pour over slaw and toss. Chill.

Makes 14 cups.

—Shirley Morrish
Devlin, Ontario

ONION & OLIVE SALAD

SERVE THIS AS A SPICY SIDE DISH IN SMALL QUANTITIES.

1 bunch green onions, coarsely chopped
1 Spanish onion, sliced paper-thin
½ cup wine vinegar
1 tsp. salt
1 cup sliced green olives with pimiento

1½ cups sliced black olives
1 clove garlic, minced
1 cup olive oil
pepper

Place onions in bowl, pour vinegar over, sprinkle with salt and place in refrigerator for at least 1 hour. Add olives and garlic, then toss with olive oil and grind black pepper over to taste. Allow to marinate for at least ½ hour.

Serves 8.

—Ingrid Birker
Montreal, Quebec

MUSHROOM CHEESE SALAD

1 small red onion, thinly sliced
1 lb. fresh mushrooms, sliced
⅓ cup olive oil
¼ cup red wine vinegar
½ tsp. salt
½ tsp. sugar

½ tsp. chervil
tarragon
cayenne
¼ lb. sharp Cheddar cheese, cubed
½ cup watercress leaves & top sprigs
lettuce

Separate onion into rings. Toss with mushrooms in medium bowl. Shake oil, vinegar, salt, sugar, chervil, tarragon and cayenne together in jar. Pour over mushroom mixture and toss to blend. Cover and chill for several hours.

Add cheese cubes and watercress to salad at serving time and toss to blend. Serve on lettuce.

Serves 6.

—Mary Hewson
Fort Smith, Northwest Territories

DANISH VEGETABLE SALAD

THE DRESSING FOR THIS SALAD WOULD ALSO WORK WELL ON ANY LEFTOVER, LIGHTLY COOKED vegetable.

½ lb. asparagus, sliced into ½" lengths &
    cooked
2 carrots, pared, sliced ¼" thick & cooked
1 cup snow peas, snapped in half &
    steamed
10-12 mushrooms, quartered & steamed
2 Tbsp. capers

3 Tbsp. mayonnaise
3 Tbsp. sour cream
2 tsp. lemon juice
½ tsp. Dijon mustard
salt & pepper
2 cups halved cherry tomatoes

Toss vegetables, except tomatoes, together. Mix remaining ingredients, except tomatoes, for dressing. Pour over vegetables and stir gently to coat evenly. Garnish with tomatoes and chill for 2 to 4 hours.

Serves 6 to 8.

—Lynne Roe
Orangeville, Ontario

ZESTY RUTABAGA SALAD

1 rutabaga, thinly sliced
3 carrots, cut into ¼" slices
½ small head cauliflower, broken into
    florets
1 small green pepper, cut into strips
1 tsp. salt

Dressing
½ cup vinegar
¼ cup oil
⅓ cup sugar
¼ tsp. curry powder
1 tsp. salt
¼ tsp. pepper

Cut rutabaga slices in wedges. Drop all vegetables into boiling salted water in large saucepan. Boil, uncovered, for 5 minutes or until crispy-tender. Drain. Chill in cold water, then drain again. In screw-top jar, combine dressing ingredients. Cover and shake. Pour over vegetables and toss lightly. Refrigerate, covered, for several hours or overnight, tossing occasionally.

Serves 6.

—Donna Jubb
Fenelon Falls, Ontario

GREEK CUCUMBER YOGURT SALAD

FOR THOSE NOT TROUBLED BY THE DIGESTIVE DIFFICULTIES OFTEN ASSOCIATED WITH NORTH American cucumbers, substitute them for a fresher, less expensive salad.

1 large English cucumber
¼ cup plain yogurt
1 green onion, sliced
1 large clove garlic, minced

½ tsp. dried mint
1½ tsp. cider vinegar
¼ tsp. salt
white pepper

Slice cucumber as thinly as possible. Mix together remaining ingredients and add cucumber slices. Refrigerate for at least 1 hour before serving.

Serves 2 to 4.

—Susan O'Neill
Bella Coola, British Columbia

CURRIED APPLE, BEET & CABBAGE SALAD

THIS SALAD HAS A TANGY SWEET AND SOUR FLAVOUR WITH A MILD, PLEASANT CURRY TASTE.

4 cups shredded red cabbage
2 cups julienned cooked beets
3 large green apples, grated
⅔ cup mayonnaise

1 tsp. Dijon mustard
1 tsp. curry
salt & pepper
¼ cup chopped parsley

Toss cabbage, beets and apples in large bowl. Combine mayonnaise, mustard and curry and toss with salad. Add salt and pepper to taste. Chill for 1 hour. Garnish with parsley.

Serves 8 to 10.

—Ingrid Birker
Montreal, Quebec

GREEN BEAN & ARTICHOKE SALAD

PREPARE THE DRESSING AND KEEP AT ROOM TEMPERATURE; COOK THE BEANS AHEAD OF TIME, so they are chilled when it is time to assemble the salad. Serve immediately once it is assembled.

¾ cup light olive oil
⅓ cup red wine vinegar
3 Tbsp. chopped chives
½ tsp. salt
2 tsp. basil
2 tsp. oregano
¾ tsp. dry mustard
¾ tsp. pepper

¼ tsp. cayenne
¼ cup chopped parsley
3 cups sliced green beans, cooked
2 cups quartered artichoke hearts
1 lb. mushrooms, sliced
2 green peppers, chopped
4 stalks celery, sliced
4 green onions, chopped

Combine oil, vinegar, chives, salt, basil, oregano, mustard, pepper, cayenne and parsley. Whisk well and set aside. Toss vegetables with dressing and serve.

Serves 10 to 12.

—Judith Christensen
Los Angeles, California

ANTIPASTO SALAD

10 leaves Romaine lettuce
8 slices Genoa salami, julienned
1 carrot, shredded
1 Tbsp. chopped capers
2 Tbsp. chopped pitted black olives
1 red onion, sliced in rings

1 stalk celery, sliced
½ green pepper, julienned
1 Tbsp. Romano cheese
salt & pepper
1 Tbsp. olive oil
1 Tbsp. red wine vinegar

Tear lettuce into bite-sized pieces. Toss with salami, carrot, capers, olives, onion, celery and green pepper. Sprinkle with cheese and salt and pepper. Drizzle oil, then vinegar over all and toss lightly.

Serves 4.

—Sandy Robertson
Port Robinson, Ontario

LIMA BEAN & TUNA SALAD

"THIS RECIPE WAS GIVEN TO ME BY A CLOSE FRIEND IN 1976. SHE KNEW THAT I DID NOT LIKE lima beans and assured me that I would like this recipe. To my surprise, she was right."

1 lb. dry baby lima beans
2 Tbsp. olive oil
2 7-oz. cans tuna
½ green pepper, chopped
1 onion, minced
2 cups diced celery

½ tsp. salt
⅛ tsp. pepper
2 Tbsp. lemon juice
2 Tbsp. chopped parsley
mayonnaise

Cover washed beans with water, bring to a boil and boil for 2 minutes. Cover and let stand for 1 hour, then cook until tender. Drain and cool.

Add remaining ingredients and toss. Chill well.

Serves 8.

—Judy Sheppard-Segal
Falmouth, Maine

SUMMER BEAN SALAD

A WELL-ROUNDED AND APPEALING SALAD—THE BEANS COMPLEMENT EACH OTHER IN COLOUR and flavour without compromising texture.

2 cups cooked sliced green beans
2 cups cooked sliced wax beans
2 cups cooked kidney beans
2 cups cooked chickpeas
½ red onion, chopped
2 Tbsp. chopped parsley

1 stalk celery, chopped
1 cup quartered artichoke hearts
6 Tbsp. peanut oil
3 Tbsp. cider vinegar
1 clove garlic, minced
salt & pepper

Combine beans, chickpeas, onion, parsley, celery and artichoke hearts in large bowl. Combine remaining ingredients and toss with salad. Chill for at least 2 hours to blend flavours.

Serves 6 to 8.

—Lynne Roe
Orangeville, Ontario

GREEN BEAN & POTATO SALAD

4 large russet potatoes
¾ lb. green beans, snapped in half
⅓ cup olive oil
¼ cup cider vinegar
1 clove garlic, crushed

½ tsp. basil
¼ tsp. thyme
salt & pepper
½ tsp. dry mustard
⅓ cup Parmesan cheese

Scrub and dice potatoes. Cook in boiling water. Steam green beans until bright green and crispy-tender. Combine potatoes and beans. Mix together oil, vinegar, garlic, basil, thyme, salt and pepper and mustard. Toss with vegetables. Sprinkle with cheese. Serve warm or at room temperature.

Serves 4 to 6.

—Nancy R. Franklin
San Jose, California

MOM'S POTATO SALAD

"OUR FAMILY OF 11 CHILDREN GREW UP ON THIS. WITH SO MANY PEOPLE, IT WAS EASIEST TO have buffet-style meals. This dish is easy to enlarge."

Dressing
¼ cup sugar
¼ cup flour
2 tsp. salt
1½ tsp. dry mustard
¾-1 tsp. cayenne
4 egg yolks, lightly beaten
1½ cups milk
½ cup vinegar
1 Tbsp. butter

6 potatoes, cooked & diced
5 hard-cooked eggs, diced
1 cup chopped parsley
2 stalks celery, chopped
½ cup chopped chives
½ cup chopped radishes
¼ cup chopped red onion

To make dressing: In top of double boiler, mix sugar, flour, salt, mustard and cayenne. Stir in yolks and milk and cook, stirring, until thickened. Add vinegar and butter, mix well, then cool. Combine remaining ingredients and toss with cooled dressing. Chill.

Serves 8 to 10.

—Penny Tognet
Brooks, Alberta

PENNSYLVANIA GERMAN POTATO SALAD

THIS PIQUANT SWEET AND SOUR DRESSING MAKES A TASTY CHANGE FROM MORE COMMON mayonnaise-based dressings for potato salad.

Dressing
½ cup sugar
1 Tbsp. flour
1 tsp. Dijon mustard
1 Tbsp. salt
2 eggs, lightly beaten
⅔ cup vinegar

6 large potatoes, cooked & diced
1 cup chopped celery
½ cup minced onion
3 hard-cooked eggs, diced
chopped chives

To make dressing: In top of double boiler, mix sugar, flour, mustard and salt. Add eggs, vinegar and 2 Tbsp. water and cook, stirring, over boiling water until thickened. Combine potatoes, celery, onion and eggs and toss with dressing. Garnish liberally with chives.

Serves 4 to 6.

—Janet Jokinen
Cobourg, Ontario

MARINATED MUSHROOMS

"Pungent mushrooms, great garlic flavour and nice texture. This makes a wonderful addition to a relish or pickle platter." If small button mushrooms are available, they can be left whole.

1½ lbs. mushrooms, halved
¼ onion, chopped
2 cloves garlic, crushed
2 sprigs parsley
½ cup olive oil

¼ cup dry white wine
¼ cup cider vinegar
1 Tbsp. lemon juice
½ tsp. salt
pepper

Boil mushrooms for 5 minutes. Meanwhile, combine remaining ingredients in large jar. Add drained mushrooms and marinate for 24 hours. Mushrooms will keep for 1 week.

—Mary Rogers
Hastings, Ontario

RICE & VEGETABLE SALAD

"An a-1 salad!" says our Vermont tester. "It has a wonderful fresh taste, good texture and tangy flavour."

1 cup dry rice
2 cups peas
1½ cups chopped celery
½ cup minced green onions
½ cup toasted almonds
½ cup oil

2 Tbsp. vinegar
2 Tbsp. soy sauce
2 tsp. curry
½ tsp. salt
½ tsp. sugar
½ tsp. celery salt

Cook rice, then mix with peas, celery, onions and almonds. Combine remaining ingredients, pour over salad and toss. Chill before serving.

Serves 4 to 6.

—Greta Bacher
Dorset, Ontario

MILLET VEGETABLE SALAD

This makes a colourful, tasty, nutritious summer vegetarian salad.

2½ cups cooked millet
4 tomatoes, chopped
½ cup diced green pepper
¾ cup sliced zucchini
½ cup chopped scallions
2 Tbsp. chopped parsley

1 tsp. basil
¼ cup mayonnaise
1 tsp. Dijon mustard
¼ tsp. pepper
2 Tbsp. lemon juice

Combine millet, tomatoes, pepper, zucchini, scallions and parsley. Whisk remaining ingredients together until smooth, then toss with salad.

Serves 4 to 6.

—Ingrid Birker
Montreal, Quebec

TOWN HALL SUPPER SALAD

"A MUCH-REQUESTED SALAD FAVOURITE AT OUR COMMUNITY SUPPERS AND LUNCHEONS, THIS IS a nutritious as well as a tasty salad."

¼ cup dry wild rice
4 cups broccoli florets
4 cups cauliflower florets
2 cups raisins
1⅓ cups roasted, salted peanuts
½ lb. bacon, fried crisp & crumbled

¼ cup toasted wheat germ
4 green onions, thinly sliced
2 cups mayonnaise
¼ cup sugar
1½ Tbsp. raspberry vinegar
pepper

Cook rice until tender, drain well and set aside. Blanch broccoli and cauliflower, drain, then rinse in cold running water. Combine with rice, raisins, peanuts, bacon, wheat germ and onions. Beat together mayonnaise, sugar, vinegar and pepper until smooth. Toss with salad ingredients. Chill well.

Serves 12.

—*Ellen Ross*
Underwood, Iowa

Beans & Grains

*"If pale beans bubble for you in a red earthenware pot,
You can oft decline the dinners of sumptuous hosts."*

—*Marcus Valerius Martialis*

We have little anticipation of being invited to dinner by *New York Times* columnist Russell Baker, but based on the following account of his approach to bean cookery, the thought of declining might come to mind:

"At this point in the meal," Baker once wrote, "the stomach was ready for serious eating, and I prepared beans with bacon grease, a dish I perfected in 1937 while developing my *cuisine du depression*. The dish starts by placing a pan over a very high flame until it becomes dangerously hot. A can of Heinz pork and beans is then emptied into the pan and allowed to char until it reaches the consistency of hardened concrete. Three strips of bacon are fried to crisps, and when the beans have formed huge, dense clots firmly welded to the pan, the bacon grease is poured in and stirred vigorously with a large screwdriver. The correct drink with this dish is a straight shot of room-temperature gin."

Unfortunately, Baker's idea of beans is alive and well—many North Americans still think of beans and cooked grains as unimaginative staples associated with a fast meal from a can. There is little doubt that we would be much healthier if beans and grains made up a greater portion of our daily diet.

Globe-hoppers can attest that beans and grains appear much more prominently in the classic dishes of other lands. Gourmets in France sigh over the golden, crusty bean dish known as Cassoulet, while in Rio de Janeiro, Brazilians line up in front of restaurants on Sunday for *feijoada completa*, the spicy national dish of black beans and meats served from big, steaming kettles. Middle Easterners have been known to raise their voices over the best way to make tabouli, a refreshing grain salad.

The recipes in this chapter attest to the rich repertoire of culinary uses for beans and grains, which never need be bland and boring. In truth, however, a noteworthy proportion of the least edible recipes evaluated by our testers came from submissions for this chapter—dry baked beans that stuck in one's throat, nutburgers that disintegrated at the slightest touch and other agglomerations of virtuous ingredients. One particularly loathsome lunch moved an editor to recall a conversation overheard years ago between two earnest young parents on the wonders of grain "hot dogs." The advocate claimed the nutritional value was extraordinarily high and superior in every way to commercial wieners. The other pointed out that this was undoubtedly true but that if her child refused to eat them, they were of no value whatsoever.

To which we say Amen and present to you a selection of dishes which sacrifice neither nutrition nor taste and which will be eaten with relish—not guilt. No warm gin required.

ALMOND BUTTER RICE

"THIS IS ESPECIALLY GOOD SERVED WITH SHISH KEBABS AND GREEK SALAD. IT IS, TO THOSE IN our house, the best way to cook rice."

½ tsp. salt
1 cup dry basmati rice
½ cup butter
1 onion, finely chopped
1 clove garlic, crushed

½-1 tsp. turmeric
2 cups strong chicken stock
½ cup chopped parsley
½ cup slivered almonds, toasted

Combine salt with 2 cups water. Bring to a boil, then pour over rice. Let stand for 30 minutes, then rinse rice with cold water and drain well. Meanwhile, melt butter and sauté onion and garlic for 2 minutes. Stir in turmeric and rice. Cook, stirring, over medium heat until butter is absorbed – 5 minutes.

Place in greased casserole dish and stir in stock. Bake, covered, at 325 degrees F for 45 minutes. Stir in parsley, sprinkle with almonds and bake, uncovered, for 15 more minutes.

Serves 4.

VEGETABLE PAELLA

THERE ARE AS MANY PAELLA RECIPES AS THERE ARE SPANISH COOKS. THE ESSENTIAL INGREDIENTS are rice and saffron – after that, it is up to the imagination of the cook and the ingredients that are available. Almost all paellas include chicken and seafood (we include such a recipe on page 155); we present this as a tasty vegetarian alternative.

2 cups dry basmati rice
4 Tbsp. olive oil
2 onions, sliced fine
4 cloves garlic, crushed
3 green peppers, sliced
2 tomatoes, sliced

1 bay leaf
½ tsp. saffron threads
salt
2 cups snow peas, steamed just until
  colour changes
2 pimientos, diced

Boil rice until tender but firm. Meanwhile, heat oil in large heavy pot, then sauté onions, garlic, peppers and tomatoes. Combine rice with vegetables, add 2½ cups water, bay leaf, saffron and salt. Cover and cook over low heat until water is almost absorbed. Add peas and pimientos and heat through.

Serves 4.

PERSIAN RICE

4 cups dry basmati rice
4 potatoes, peeled & thinly sliced
6 Tbsp. butter

½ cup currants
⅛ tsp. saffron, soaked in ¼ cup hot water
salt & pepper

Cook rice until tender but firm. Rinse while still warm with cold water to remove starchiness. Place potato slices in bottom of greased casserole dish. Dot with 2 Tbsp. butter. Spread rice over potatoes, then sprinkle with currants and saffron water. Melt remaining butter and pour over casserole. Add salt and pepper.

Cover and bake at 350 degrees F for 15 minutes. Remove from oven, shake gently and let stand, uncovered, for 10 minutes. Discard potatoes when serving.

Serves 8.

VEGETABLE RICE PILAF

THIS PILAF IS FOOLPROOF, ATTRACTIVE AND FLAVOURFUL.

½ cup butter
½ cup chopped onion
½ cup chopped celery
½ cup thinly sliced green pepper
½ cup grated carrot

salt & pepper
1 cup dry basmati rice
1 cup water
1 cup chicken stock
¼ cup chopped parsley

Melt ¼ cup butter in skillet and sauté onion, celery, green pepper and carrot until tender. Add salt and pepper. Place in greased casserole dish. Melt remaining butter and cook rice, stirring, until brown. Add rice to casserole along with water, stock and parsley. Cover and bake at 375 degrees for 30 minutes. Stir, replace cover and bake for 30 minutes longer.

Serves 4.

—Evelyn M. Grieve
Toronto, Ontario

BROWN BASMATI RICE
WITH FRUITS, FLOWERS & VEGETABLES

BROWN BASMATI RICE, READILY AVAILABLE IN MOST HEALTH-FOOD STORES, HAS A NUTTY flavour. The calendula petals add flavour and colour. Serve this rice with fish, poultry or meat.

½ cup dry brown basmati rice
1 Tbsp. oil
1 Tbsp. butter
¼ cup thinly sliced green beans
¼ cup grated carrot

3 Tbsp. drained crushed pineapple
1 Tbsp. calendula petals
½ Tbsp. snipped chives
pepper

Bring 1 cup water to a boil in heavy saucepan. Add rice, stir, reduce heat and simmer, covered, for 45 minutes, or until water is absorbed and rice is tender. Remove from heat and set aside.

Put oil, butter and 1 Tbsp. water in small skillet. Heat over medium heat, then add beans and carrot. Cook just until beans turn bright green. Add rice, pineapple, calendula petals, chives and pepper. Heat through, stirring gently.

Serves 2 to 3.

—Ellen Ross
Underwood, Iowa

SWISS CHARD & RICE CASSEROLE

INCREDIBLY QUICK AND EASY TO PREPARE, THIS CASSEROLE HELPS USE UP THAT EVER BOUNTIFUL Swiss chard.

3 cups cooked rice
2 eggs, beaten
salt

19-oz. can tomatoes, drained & diced
1 lb. Swiss chard leaves, torn up
½ lb. mild Cheddar cheese, grated

Combine rice, eggs, salt, tomatoes and chard in greased casserole dish and mix well. Stir in half the cheese. Sprinkle remaining cheese over top. Cover and bake at 350 degrees F for 30 minutes.

Serves 4 to 6.

—Julie Herr
Acton Vale, Quebec

CABBAGE & RICE

THIS WAS A BIG HIT — EVEN WITH THE DOUBTERS IN THE CROWD — WHEN WE TESTED IT IN OUR Vermont office. It is easy to prepare and has a subtle sweetness.

3 Tbsp. oil **or** butter
6 cups chopped cabbage
1 onion, chopped
1½ cups cooked brown rice
¾ cup grated Swiss cheese

¾ cup sliced mushrooms, sautéed
½ tsp. savory
1 egg
½ cup wheat germ
2 Tbsp. butter, melted

Heat oil or butter in heavy pot and sauté cabbage and onion until cabbage is tender. Keep covered with the heat low. Combine remaining ingredients except wheat germ and melted butter. Layer half cabbage mixture in greased casserole dish. Spread rice mixture over this. Top with remaining cabbage.

Combine wheat germ and melted butter and drizzle over casserole. Bake, uncovered, at 350 degrees F for 30 to 40 minutes.

Serves 3 to 4.

—Susan O'Neill
Bella Coola, British Columbia

WILD RICE

6 Tbsp. butter
½ cup chopped parsley
½ cup chopped onion
1 cup sliced celery
1½ cups dry wild rice

3 cups hot chicken stock
1 tsp. salt
½ tsp. marjoram
½ cup sherry

Combine butter, parsley, onion and celery in heavy skillet and cook for 10 minutes, or until soft but not brown. Add remaining ingredients except sherry. Bring to a boil, reduce heat, cover and cook for approximately 45 minutes, stirring occasionally. Add hot water if mixture gets too dry. When rice is tender, stir in sherry and cook, uncovered, for 5 more minutes.

Serves 6 to 8.

—Rose Strocen
Canora, Saskatchewan

WILD RICE BARON

2 lbs. ground beef
1 lb. mushrooms, sliced
½ cup chopped celery
1 cup chopped onion
½ cup butter
2 cups sour cream

¼ cup soy sauce
¼ tsp. pepper
1 cup dry wild rice, cooked
1 cup dry basmati rice, cooked
½ cup slivered almonds, browned
  in butter

Brown ground beef. Sauté mushrooms, celery and onion in butter until limp. Combine sour cream, soy sauce and pepper. Add rice, beef, vegetables and ¼ cup almonds. Toss lightly. Place in greased casserole dish and bake, uncovered, at 350 degrees F for 1 hour, stirring occasionally and adding water if necessary. Garnish with remaining almonds.

Serves 12.

—Ingrid Magnuson
Winnipeg, Manitoba

CASHEW NUT FRIED RICE

THIS IS A WONDERFUL DISH — BEAUTIFUL TO LOOK AT, FULL OF DIFFERENT TEXTURES AND VERY tasty. It does not take long to prepare once the rice is cooked.

6 Tbsp. peanut oil
8 eggs
½ head cabbage, shredded
6 green onions, sliced
½ lb. bacon, fried & crumbled
1½ cups roasted cashews
2 slices gingerroot

3 Tbsp. sesame oil
3 Tbsp. soy sauce
3 Tbsp. sherry
2 cups cooked brown rice
2 cups cooked basmati rice
2 cups cooked wild rice

Heat wok, then add peanut oil. Add eggs, stir quickly to scramble, then remove and keep warm. Stir-fry remaining ingredients until crispy-tender and heated through. Remove ginger slices and add eggs.

Serves 10.

—Sandra K. Bennett
Greenville, South Carolina

ORIENTAL RICE SALAD

⅓ cup oil
2 Tbsp. orange juice
1 Tbsp. brown sugar
2 tsp. soy sauce
½ tsp. dry mustard
salt & pepper

1 cup dry rice, cooked
4 green onions, sliced
1 cup chopped water chestnuts
2 cups sliced celery
1 tomato, chopped

Combine oil, orange juice, sugar, soy sauce, mustard and salt and pepper in large bowl and mix well. Stir in warm rice. Add onions, water chestnuts, celery and tomato and toss lightly. Chill well.

Serves 4 to 6.

—Rose Strocen
Canora, Saskatchewan

FESTIVE RICE RING

SERVE THIS AS AN EDIBLE CENTREPIECE FOR A SPECIAL BUFFET. WHEN THE CENTRE OF THE RING is filled with colourful vegetables, it is very attractive. If desired, a combination of wild, basmati and brown rices can be substituted for the brown rice.

6 Tbsp. butter
3 large onions, diced
3 cloves garlic, crushed
1½ cups sliced mushrooms
½ lb. spinach, chopped
½ lb. watercress, chopped

2 cups dry brown rice, cooked
1 cup milk
3 eggs, beaten
2 cups grated sharp Cheddar cheese
soy sauce
cayenne

Heat butter in heavy skillet and sauté onions, garlic and mushrooms. Stir in spinach and watercress and cook until spinach is wilted.

Combine rice with milk, eggs, cheese, soy sauce and cayenne. Stir in vegetables. Place in greased tube pan and bake at 350 degrees F for 1 to 1½ hours. Let stand for 10 minutes, then invert onto platter and garnish with colourful vegetables if desired.

Serves 12 to 15.

—Michael & Dyan Walters
Kitchener, Ontario

BROCCOLI & BROWN RICE CASSEROLE

2 lbs. broccoli
3 Tbsp. butter
½ lb. mushrooms, sliced
3 Tbsp. flour
1 cup milk
½ cup chicken stock

1 tsp. thyme
2 Tbsp. soy sauce
salt & pepper
¾ cup grated Cheddar cheese
9-oz. can tuna
2 cups dry brown rice, cooked

Cut broccoli into spears, lightly steam, then set aside. Melt butter in heavy skillet and sauté mushrooms until limp. Stir in flour until smooth. Gradually add milk and chicken stock, stirring well. Add thyme, soy sauce and salt and pepper. Cook over medium heat, stirring, until thickened. Stir in ½ cup cheese and the tuna and continue cooking until cheese melts.

Assemble casserole by layering rice, broccoli and tuna mixture in greased casserole dish. Top with remaining cheese. Bake, covered, at 350 degrees F for 30 minutes.

Serves 6.

BROCCOLI NUT CASSEROLE

1½ cups dry brown rice
2-3 Tbsp. oil
1 large onion, chopped
2 cloves garlic, crushed
½ tsp. dill
1 tsp. thyme
1 tsp. oregano

½ bunch parsley, chopped
½ lb. mushrooms, sliced
1 green pepper, sliced
1 head broccoli, cut into florets
½ cup cashews
½ lb. Swiss **or** Gruyère cheese, grated
2 Tbsp. Parmesan cheese

In heavy pan with tight-fitting lid, combine rice, 3 cups water and dash of salt. Bring to a boil, reduce heat and simmer, covered, until water is absorbed – about 45 minutes. Heat oil in large skillet. Add onion, garlic, dill, thyme and oregano and cook until onions are limp. Add parsley, mushrooms, green pepper and broccoli and cook, stirring often. When broccoli becomes deep green but is still crisp, toss in nuts and remove from heat. Spread rice in greased casserole dish. Cover with vegetable-nut mixture, mix well and sprinkle with cheeses. Bake, uncovered, at 350 degrees F for 15 minutes, or until bubbly.

Serves 8.

—Sandra K. Bennett
Greenville, South Carolina

FIESTA PILAF

¼ cup butter
3 cloves garlic, finely chopped
1 cup finely chopped green onions
1 cup sliced mushrooms
½ cup diced red pepper
½ cup diced green pepper

1 cup dry wild rice
¼ tsp. thyme
⅛ tsp. cloves
4 cups chicken stock
pepper

Melt butter and add garlic, onions and half the mushrooms. Cook over low heat for about 3 minutes. Add peppers and remaining mushrooms. Increase heat and cook for 2 to 3 minutes. Stir in wild rice, coating well with buttery mixture. Season with thyme and cloves. Pour in stock and bring to a boil; cover and simmer over low heat for 45 to 50 minutes. Season with pepper.

Serves 4.

—Mo'e Howard-Samstag
Bramalea, Ontario

MUSHROOM RICE

EQUALLY DELICIOUS AS A SIDE DISH OR AS A POULTRY STUFFING, THIS WILL KEEP YOU FROM ever using commercially prepared rice dishes. For a 12-to-14-lb. turkey, double the recipe.

2 Tbsp. butter
1 onion, chopped
6 mushrooms, sliced
⅔ cup dry brown rice
⅓ cup dry wild rice

2 cups hot chicken stock
1 Tbsp. chopped parsley
¼ tsp. thyme
pepper to taste

In heavy pot with tight-fitting lid, melt butter over medium heat. Sauté onion and mushrooms until limp. Add rice. Cook, stirring, until rice browns. Pour in stock. Stir in parsley, thyme and pepper. Cover pot and bring to a boil. Reduce heat and simmer for 35 to 45 minutes. Turn off heat and let stand, covered, for 10 minutes.

Serves 4 to 5.

—Lynne Roe
Orangeville, Ontario

WILD & FRUITY DRESSING

½ cup sliced celery
¼ cup minced onion
2 Tbsp. butter
½ cup chopped dried apricots
1 cup orange juice
1 cup dry wild rice, soaked overnight &
    drained

2 tsp. grated orange peel
½ tsp. sage
1 cup chicken **or** vegetable stock
salt & pepper

Sauté celery and onion in butter until crispy-tender. Soak apricots in orange juice, then add to celery-onion mixture. Add remaining ingredients and bring to a boil. Reduce heat, cover and simmer for 25 minutes, or until rice is tender and all liquid is absorbed. Season to taste with salt and pepper.

Stuffs 1 large chicken or 8 pork chops, with enough left for a side dish.

—Mo'e Howard-Samstag
Bramalea, Ontario

INDONESIAN RICE SALAD

2 cups cooked rice (basmati, brown, wild
    or a combination)
¼ cup raisins
3 green onions, chopped
¾ cup sliced water chestnuts
1 cup bean sprouts

1 green pepper, chopped
2 stalks celery, chopped
1 cucumber, chopped
⅓ cup sliced radishes
⅓ cup sesame seeds, toasted
⅓ cup cashews, toasted

Dressing
¾ cup oil
⅓ cup lemon juice
2 Tbsp. soy sauce
1 Tbsp. sherry

2 cloves garlic, crushed
1 slice gingerroot
salt & pepper

Combine salad ingredients and toss gently. Place dressing ingredients in jar with lid and shake until blended. Pour over salad and toss. Chill well.

Serves 6.

WILD RICE CAKE

"MY FRIEND GRACE MILASHENKO OF SASKATOON PRESENTED ME WITH A GIFT OF Saskatchewan wild rice, and I set forth to experiment. The wild rice cake was daring in that, if it didn't work, I would have wasted many expensive ingredients. Fortunately, it produced a moist, delightful cake with a curious tang of the outdoors."

1 cup dry wild rice, washed, soaked in
   cold water overnight & drained
2-3 strips orange zest
1 tsp. sugar
1 pkg. yeast
¼ cup melted butter
½ cup maple syrup
1 tsp. salt

½ tsp. cinnamon
2 eggs
½ cup brown sugar
1½ cups whole wheat flour
2 cups unbleached white flour
¼ cup wheat germ
⅓ cup buttermilk **or** sour milk
handful crushed walnuts

Praline Topping
¼ cup brown sugar
½ cup chopped walnuts
¼ tsp. nutmeg

1 Tbsp. melted butter
2 Tbsp. cream

Cook drained rice in 2½ cups water, adding zest strips when water comes to a boil. Reduce heat to medium and cook for 45 minutes to 1 hour, or until rice is fluffy.

Mix sugar with ½ cup warm water. Stir in yeast and set aside for 10 minutes. Meanwhile, combine melted butter, maple syrup, salt and cinnamon with cooked rice. Beat in eggs, then add brown sugar. Stir in flours, wheat germ and buttermilk. Add walnuts. Stir in yeast mixture. Mix well and let rise for 1 hour.

Stir down dough. Grease tube pan and pour in dough. Let rise for another hour. Bake at 400 degrees F for 15 minutes, lower heat to 375 degrees and bake for an additional 45 minutes, or until done.

Meanwhile, prepare praline topping: Mix all ingredients together. Pour over hot or cooled cake. Broil about 3 inches from direct heat for 2 to 3 minutes, or until amber-brown.

— Mo'e Howard-Samstag
Bramalea, Ontario

HERBED LENTIL & RICE CASSEROLE

"THE AROMA OF THIS CASSEROLE IS JUST AS SATISFYING AS THE ACTUAL TASTE."

2⅔ cups chicken stock
¾ cup dry lentils
¾ cup chopped onions
½ cup dry brown rice
¼ cup dry white wine
½ tsp. basil

¼ tsp. salt
¼ tsp. oregano
¼ tsp. thyme
1 clove garlic, crushed
pepper
¼ lb. Cheddar cheese, grated

Combine all ingredients except cheese. Stir in half the cheese. Mix well, then place in ungreased casserole dish and bake, covered, at 350 degrees F for 1½ to 2 hours, or until lentils and rice are cooked, stirring twice during cooking. Uncover, top with remaining cheese and bake 3 to 5 minutes longer.

Serves 4 to 6.

—Connie Holck
River Falls, Wisconsin

SWISS CHEESE, RICE & BULGUR

½ cup butter
½ cup chopped onions
½ cup dry white wine
1½ cups strong chicken stock

½ tsp. salt
¾ cup dry brown rice
½ cup bulgur
¼ lb. Swiss cheese, grated

Melt butter in heavy pot, then sauté onions until limp. Add wine, stock, salt and rice, then cover. Bring to a boil, reduce heat and simmer until rice is almost tender – about 20 minutes. Add bulgur and cook until it is tender – 5 to 10 minutes. Stir in cheese and let stand for 5 minutes. Stir and serve.

Serves 4 to 6.

—Linda Giesecke
Philadelphia, Pennsylvania

COUSCOUS WITH VEGETABLES

1½ lbs. couscous
1½ lbs. pumpkin, cut into chunks
4 green peppers, quartered
4 stalks celery, sliced
1 turnip, chopped
2 onions, chopped
2 cups cooked chickpeas

1 tsp. salt
1 tsp. hot paprika
1 tsp. cumin
½ tsp. dry mustard
½ tsp. chili peppers
1 tsp. curry powder
2 cloves

Soak couscous in hot water to cover for 10 minutes. Put 3 quarts liquid (water, stock or bean liquid) in cooking pot, bring to a boil and add remaining ingredients. Add couscous, cover and cook for 15 minutes. Stir well, cover and cook for 15 minutes more.

Serves 6.

VEGETARIAN COUSCOUS

COOK COUSCOUS BY POURING 4 CUPS BOILING WATER OVER 2 CUPS DRY COUSCOUS. COVER AND let stand for 5 minutes. Mix in 4 tablespoons butter and fluff up with a fork.

3 Tbsp. oil
1 onion, chopped
1 red pepper, chopped
1 green pepper, chopped
1 tsp. allspice
2 sweet potatoes, peeled & cubed
2 tomatoes, peeled & chopped
1 Tbsp. lemon juice

½ tsp. saffron threads
4-5 cumin seeds
2 cups cooked chickpeas
salt
2 zucchini, chopped
4 cups hot cooked couscous
hot pepper sauce

Heat oil over medium heat. Add onion, peppers and allspice and cook until onion is soft – 5 minutes. Stir in sweet potatoes and cook, stirring often, for 2 minutes. Add tomatoes, ¼ cup water, lemon juice, saffron, cumin and chickpeas. Season with salt, cover, reduce heat and simmer for 15 minutes. Mix in zucchini and cook for 5 minutes more.

To serve, spread couscous around edge of deep platter and spoon vegetables into centre. Serve with hot pepper sauce.

Serves 6

—Helene Gauvreau
Victoria, British Columbia

POTATOES & FARINA

FARINA IS MORE COMMONLY KNOWN AS CREAM OF WHEAT. THIS DISH, HOWEVER, RESEMBLES not breakfast cereal but a fine barley. It makes a tasty side dish to either a meat or a vegetarian entrée.

2 potatoes, peeled & diced
½ cup oil

2 cups dry farina
salt & pepper

Boil potatoes in 1 cup salted water. Do not drain. Heat oil, add farina and sauté over medium-low heat until farina is golden brown. Mash potatoes in cooking water, adding salt and pepper. Add farina, mix, cover and cook over low heat until farina is tender – 10 to 15 minutes.

Serves 4.

MILLET CASSEROLE

"WE FIRST SERVED THIS AS PART OF A VEGETARIAN THANKSGIVING MEAL WITH FRIENDS. IT WAS one of the favourite dishes and elicited many requests for its recipe. Yeast flakes, often identified as 'good-tasting' or 'delicious nutritious' yeast, can be bought at natural-food stores."

1 cup dry millet
4 Tbsp. oil
1 tsp. basil
1 tsp. cumin
1 tsp. curry
2 cloves garlic, crushed
3 onions, chopped

2 stalks celery, chopped
½ green pepper, chopped
1 cup wheat germ
1 cup yeast flakes
28-oz. can tomatoes
6½-oz. can tomato paste
1 cup grated Cheddar cheese

Cook millet in 4 cups water until tender – 30 minutes. Meanwhile, heat oil and sauté basil, cumin, curry, garlic, onions, celery and green pepper for 2 to 3 minutes. Remove from heat. Stir in wheat germ, yeast, tomatoes and tomato paste. Combine with cooked millet. Place in greased casserole dish and bake, covered, at 350 degrees F for 45 minutes, then sprinkle with cheese and cook, uncovered, for a further 15 minutes.

Serves 6 to 8.

TABOULI

THIS IS A DELICIOUS VERSION OF TABOULI. WE HAD NOT TRIED ONE BEFORE THAT DID NOT COOK the bulgur, but our concern was unnecessary. The bulgur "cooks" by soaking overnight in the dressing.

½ cup dry bulgur
3 cups packed, chopped parsley
6 4" mint tops (leaves only), chopped
½ cucumber, chopped
1 onion, chopped
2-3 tomatoes, chopped

½ green pepper, chopped
juice of 2 lemons
1 shallot, chopped
½ cup oil
salt & pepper

Combine all ingredients and mix well. Let stand, refrigerated, overnight. Toss gently before serving.

Serves 6 to 8.

—Penny Tognet
Brooks, Alberta

KIBBEH

SERVE THIS WARM OR COLD, AS A MAIN DISH OR AS A SANDWICH FILLING IN PITA BREAD. IT IS delicious dipped in yogurt. The filling can be omitted and the kibbeh baked plain.

Filling
2 Tbsp. butter
2 onions, finely chopped
½ cup pine nuts

Kibbeh
4½ cups dry bulgur
3 lbs. ground lamb or beef
3 onions, finely chopped
1 Tbsp. salt
1 tsp. pepper

¾ tsp. cinnamon
½ tsp. allspice
¼ cup ice water
oil

Prepare filling by melting butter, then sautéing onions until limp. Add pine nuts, mix well and set aside.

For kibbeh: Wash bulgur in cold water. Drain well by squeezing out excess water. Combine meat, onions, salt, pepper, cinnamon and allspice. Mix well. Add bulgur and knead well, adding ice water by the tablespoonful to keep mixture cold.

Grease a 9" x 12" baking dish. Smooth half the meat mixture evenly in the pan. Spread filling over meat, then smooth remaining meat mixture over this. Make deep lines through kibbee to form diamond shapes. Dribble oil over top. Bake, uncovered, at 350 degrees F for 30 minutes, or until brown.

Serves 8 to 10.

—Katherine S. Jones
Kalamazoo, Michigan

SOYBEAN BAKED BEANS

CHILI SAUCE IS THE UNUSUAL INGREDIENT HERE. THIS IS A DELICIOUS WAY TO EAT THE nutritious, but often disliked, soybean. For vegetarians, the bacon can be omitted and the beans will still have a rich flavour.

3 cups dry soybeans
1 tsp. salt
2 Tbsp. oil
1 tsp. dry mustard
½ cup brown sugar
¼ cup molasses
⅓ cup maple syrup

1 onion, chopped
½ cup chopped celery
½ cup tomato paste
¼ cup chili sauce
¼ lb. bacon, chopped
1½ tsp. salt

Wash soybeans. Soak overnight in 9 cups cold water. Drain. Place in heavy pot with salt, oil and enough water to cover beans generously. Bring to a boil, reduce heat, cover and simmer for 3 hours.

Place drained beans in greased casserole dish and add remaining ingredients. Mix well. Cover and bake at 300 degrees F for 3 hours, stirring occasionally and adding liquid if necessary.

Serves 10.

—Barbara Curtis
Coe Hill, Ontario

MANY-BEAN BAKED BEANS

THE DIFFERENT TASTES AND TEXTURES OF FIVE KINDS OF BEANS ARE WHAT MAKE THIS BEAN DISH special. Beans can be cooked ahead of time and frozen, making the assembly of this dish much quicker.

2 cups cooked black turtle beans,
　　cooking liquid reserved
2 cups cooked pinto beans,
　　cooking liquid reserved
2 cups cooked navy beans,
　　cooking liquid reserved
2 cups cooked lima beans,
　　cooking liquid reserved
2 cups cooked kidney beans,
　　cooking liquid reserved

8 slices bacon, diced
2 cups chopped onions
½ cup brown sugar
1 tsp. salt
1½ tsp. dry mustard
2 cloves garlic, minced
½ cup vinegar
½ cup tomato paste

Combine beans, reserving cooking liquid separately, in large greased casserole dish. Fry bacon until crisp. Set aside. Fry onions in bacon fat, then add bacon and remaining ingredients. Cook for 5 minutes and pour over beans. Add reserved bean liquid to just cover beans.

Bake, uncovered, at 325 degrees F for 1½ to 2 hours, adding liquid if necessary.

Serves 10.

BLACK BEAN SOUP WITH HAM

3 cups dry black turtle beans
2 large onions, chopped
5 stalks celery, chopped
1 bay leaf
4 ham hocks

3 Tbsp. butter
3 Tbsp. flour
3 Tbsp. red wine vinegar
salt & pepper

Place beans, onions, celery, bay leaf and ham in large heavy pot. Add 10 to 12 cups water. Bring to a boil, reduce heat, cover and simmer until beans are tender – 3 hours.

Remove ham and set aside. Discard bay leaf. Purée soup. If too thick, add liquid. Cut meat from bone, dice and return to soup. Mash together butter and flour, adding a little water if needed. Stir into soup. Add vinegar and salt and pepper.

Serves 10 to 12.

BLACK BEAN & TOMATO SALAD

1 cup cooked black turtle beans
1 Tbsp. cider vinegar **or** lemon juice
2 Tbsp. olive oil
salt & pepper

1 large onion, chopped
2 large tomatoes, chopped,
　　or 1½ cups cherry tomatoes
2 cloves garlic, chopped

While beans are still warm, mix with vinegar, oil and salt and pepper. Chill, then add onion, tomatoes and garlic, combining well. Chill overnight.

Serves 4.

—Judith Almond-Best
Madoc, Ontario

CARIBBEAN BEANS & RICE

2 cups dry kidney beans
1 Tbsp. salt
3 Tbsp. butter
2 cloves garlic, crushed
4 green onions, chopped
1 tomato, chopped

⅛ tsp. cloves
2 Tbsp. chopped parsley
salt & pepper
1 tsp. chili powder
2 cups dry rice

Soak beans overnight. Add salt and 6 cups water. Bring to a boil, reduce heat, cover and simmer until tender – 40 to 60 minutes. Drain, reserving liquid.

Heat butter in heavy covered skillet. Add garlic, onions, tomato, cloves, parsley, salt and pepper and chili powder and sauté for 5 minutes. Add beans, rice and 4 cups liquid reserved from cooking beans (add water if necessary). Bring to a boil, reduce heat, cover and simmer, without stirring, for 20 to 25 minutes.

Serves 8.

BAKED BEANS WITH PIZZAZZ

2 cups dry navy beans
4 Tbsp. butter
2 large onions, chopped
4 cloves garlic, crushed
½ tsp. salt
1 tsp. allspice
pepper
2 tsp. dill

5 Tbsp. light molasses
5 Tbsp. Poupon mustard
4 cups tomato juice
2 Tbsp. lemon juice
1 Tbsp. soy sauce
1 green pepper, chopped
1 stalk celery, chopped
2 carrots, diced

Cover beans with water. Bring to a boil, reduce heat, cover and simmer for 1 to 2 hours, or until beans are tender. Add water during cooking if necessary. When cooked, drain.

Meanwhile, melt butter and sauté onions and garlic until limp. Add salt, allspice, pepper, dill, molasses, mustard, tomato juice, lemon juice and soy sauce. Bring to a boil, reduce heat and simmer, covered, for 45 minutes.

In large, greased casserole dish, combine beans, sauce and vegetables. Bake, covered, at 325 degrees F for 1 to 2 hours, or until liquid is absorbed.

Serves 6 to 8.

SOYBEAN NUT LOAF

4 cups cooked soybeans
1 cup ground almonds
½ cup sesame seeds
3 Tbsp. butter
2 stalks celery, chopped
2 cloves garlic, chopped
2 onions, chopped

½ green pepper, chopped
1 tsp. cayenne
1 tsp. oregano
1 tsp. basil
1 tsp. cumin
3 Tbsp. peanut butter

Purée soybeans, almonds and sesame seeds. Melt butter and sauté celery, garlic, onions and green pepper. Stir into soybean-nut mixture. Add spices and peanut butter and mix well. Place in greased loaf pan and bake at 350 degrees F for approximately 1 hour.

Serves 6.

TERESITA'S BEANS

"THIS RECIPE CAME TO ME FROM A MEXICAN friend. IT IS A FAVOURITE AT OUTDOOR SUMMER parties. Leftover beans may be mashed and thinned with water and red wine to make an excellent soup."

2¼ cups dry black beans
1 lb. boneless pork, cut into bite-sized
   pieces
4 Tbsp. oil
1 large green pepper, chopped
1 large onion, chopped
4-oz. can jalapeño peppers, chopped

⅓ cup sherry
1 Tbsp. cumin
salt & pepper
6-oz. can tomato sauce
1 bay leaf
4 cloves garlic, crushed

Soak beans in cold water overnight. Drain, then cover with cold water and cook over low heat until crispy-tender—about 3 hours.

Meanwhile, brown pork in oil. Add green pepper and onion and cook until soft. Add to cooked, drained beans along with remaining ingredients. Cook over low heat—1 hour for chewy beans, 2 hours for very soft beans.

Serves 8.

—Rebecca Quanrud
Bismarck, North Dakota

MEXICAN BEAN DIP

1½ cups dry pinto beans, cooked, drained
   & mashed
3 cloves garlic, minced
1 cup minced onion
1 tsp. salt

pepper
½ tsp. crushed hot red peppers
⅓ tsp. cumin
¼ tsp. dry mustard

Combine all ingredients and mix well. Chill.

Makes approximately 3 to 4 cups.

PESTO BEAN SALAD

"PESTO ADDS A WONDERFUL FLAVOUR TO ALMOST EVERYTHING. IT IS MOST COMMONLY associated with pasta, but I developed this easy salad one summer day, when confronted with leftover pesto and beans."

3 cups cooked navy beans
2 cups cooked white kidney beans
¾ cup garlic mayonnaise

Pesto
1 cup fresh basil
1 clove garlic
¼ cup parsley
¼ tsp. salt

¼ cup olive oil
¼ cup Parmesan cheese
2 Tbsp. pine nuts
salt & pepper

Combine beans and mayonnaise and toss to coat beans completely.

Make pesto by placing first seven ingredients in blender or food processor and processing to make a chunky paste. Toss into salad. Add salt and pepper and chill thoroughly.

Serves 6 as a side dish.

BEAN TORTILLA CASSEROLE

IF COOKED BEANS ARE KEPT ON HAND, THIS DISH CAN BE ASSEMBLED QUICKLY AS A TASTY vegetarian casserole.

½ cup dry pinto beans
½ cup dry kidney beans
2 cups chopped onion
2 cloves garlic, crushed
1 cup chopped red **or** green pepper
4-6 Tbsp. oil
6-oz. can tomato sauce

12-oz. can tomatoes
¾ tsp. salt
1 tsp. oregano
1 tsp. basil
¼ tsp. cayenne
4 corn tortillas
2 cups grated Cheddar cheese

Cook beans until tender, and reserve cooking liquid. Sauté onion, garlic and pepper in oil until limp. Stir in tomato sauce, tomatoes, salt, oregano, basil and cayenne, and simmer for 30 minutes.

Mash beans with ¼ cup cooking liquid and 1 cup tomato-vegetable sauce, but do not purée. Assemble casserole in greased 9″ x 9″ baking pan. Place one-third of sauce in bottom of pan, then 2 tortillas, then half the mashed beans, then one-third of the cheese. Repeat. Place remaining sauce and cheese over top.

Bake, uncovered, at 350 degrees F for 30 to 40 minutes.

Serves 6.

—Rhoda Mozorosky
Roseburg, Oregon

HARICOTS BRETONNE

SURPASSED ONLY BY SOYBEANS AND CHICKPEAS, LIMA BEANS RANK HIGH IN THE BIOLOGICAL value of legumes. Biological value is a measure of the proportion of absorbed protein that is retained by the body.

1 lb. dry lima beans
2 carrots, quartered
1 onion, studded with 2 cloves
1 bay leaf
salt & pepper
2 cups chopped onions

1 clove garlic, minced
1 tsp. thyme
4 Tbsp. butter
4 tomatoes, chopped
4 Tbsp. tomato paste
¼ cup chopped parsley

Sort and rinse lima beans. Place in soup pot with 8 cups water, bring to a boil and cook for 10 minutes. Remove from heat and let stand for 30 minutes. Drain, then return to pot with 8 cups fresh water. Add carrots, whole onion, bay leaf and salt and pepper. Bring to a boil, reduce heat, cover and simmer for 30 minutes. Remove bay leaf and set mixture aside.

Sauté chopped onions, garlic and thyme in butter until limp—about 5 minutes. Add tomatoes and cook for 10 minutes, stirring occasionally. Add tomato paste and salt and pepper to taste. Cover and simmer for 20 minutes.

Remove carrots and whole onion from beans. Chop and add to tomato mixture. Drain beans and reserve liquid. Add beans to tomato mixture with 1 cup liquid and parsley. Simmer, uncovered, for 15 minutes.

Serves 8 to 10.

—Ingrid Birker
Montreal, Quebec

TOFU IN PEANUT SAUCE

PIQUANT AND CRUNCHY, THIS IS A WONDERFUL WAY TO PRESENT TOFU TO THOSE WHO DO NOT like its texture. Rich in protein, tofu is soybean curd. It is soft and bland in its basic form, so lends itself to all kinds of cooking. It has no cholesterol, is low in calories and is very inexpensive. Add it anonymously to soups or salad dressings, or feature it by spicing it up as we have done in this recipe.

½ cup hot vegetable stock
½ cup peanut butter
½ tsp. crushed hot red peppers
2 Tbsp. honey
5 Tbsp. soy sauce
¼ cup red wine vinegar
¾ lb. snow peas

4 Tbsp. oil
4 slices gingerroot, chopped
4 cloves garlic, crushed
1 lb. tofu, drained & cubed
6-8 green onions, sliced
1 cup chopped peanuts

Prepare sauce by mixing together stock and peanut butter until smooth. Stir in crushed peppers, honey, 2 Tbsp. soy sauce and vinegar and set aside. Snap ends off snow peas and set aside.

Heat 2 Tbsp. oil in wok. Add half the ginger and garlic and sauté for 30 seconds. Add tofu and stir-fry for approximately 5 minutes. Add it to peanut sauce, mix gently and set aside.

Return wok to stove. Add remaining oil and sauté remaining ginger and garlic. Add onions, peanuts and snow peas, and sauté for 2 to 3 minutes, stirring frequently. Add remaining 3 Tbsp. soy sauce.

Meanwhile, gently heat tofu-peanut butter mixture. Pour sauce over snow peas and mix gently to coat well. Serve over rice.

Serves 6.

CURRIED LENTILS

THE AROMA GIVEN OFF WHILE THESE LENTILS ARE COOKING IS MOST ENTICING. SERVE THIS DISH hot as a main course or cold as a sandwich spread in pita bread. We suggest that it be served with raita – a cooling yogurt, cucumber, sweet pepper and tomato salad.

3 Tbsp. oil
1 onion, quartered & sliced
2 cloves garlic, minced
2 Tbsp. chopped gingerroot
2 bay leaves, crumbled
8 cloves
2 tomatoes, chopped

4 Tbsp. hot curry powder
1 tsp. cinnamon
crushed chilies
1 tsp. turmeric
3 cups dry green lentils
salt & pepper
fresh coriander for garnish

Heat oil in soup pot and sauté onion. Add garlic, ginger, bay leaves and cloves. Cook, stirring, for 1 minute. Add tomatoes and continue cooking.

Mix curry powder, cinnamon, chilies and turmeric with ¼ cup water. Add to pot and cook, stirring, for 2 to 3 minutes. Add lentils and salt and pepper and cook for 2 more minutes. Add 6 cups water, bring to a boil, reduce heat, cover and simmer for 45 minutes to 1 hour, adding water if needed. Serve garnished with fresh coriander.

Serves 6.

—Wendy Vine
Ganges, British Columbia

CURRIED LENTIL SPAGHETTI SAUCE

Despite our initial hesitation about this recipe – primarily because it does not call for browning the beef and vegetables – this spaghetti sauce was delicious and the hit of the Camden East lunchroom. It can be assembled first thing in the morning and left to simmer all day, with only an occasional stir.

2 28-oz. cans tomatoes	1 onion, chopped
1 cup dry lentils	1½ Tbsp. curry
1 lb. ground beef	2 tsp. cumin
½ cup tomato paste	1 tsp. oregano
1 clove garlic, crushed	1 tsp. basil
½ cup chopped green pepper	1 Tbsp. parsley
½ cup chopped mushrooms	salt & pepper

Combine all ingredients in heavy pot. Bring to a boil, stir thoroughly, reduce heat to lowest setting, cover and simmer for 1½ to 2 hours.

Serves 6 to 8.

—Judie Wright
West Brome, Quebec

SWEET & SOUR LENTIL BAKE

What a wonderful combination of flavours – the zest of curry, zing of cayenne and sweetness/pungency of apple and sausage.

½ lb. pork sausage	1 tart apple, chopped
4 cups cooked lentils	2 cloves garlic, chopped
2 Tbsp. butter	1 Tbsp. cornstarch
1 tsp. curry	¼ cup brown sugar
cayenne	¼ cup cider vinegar
1 onion, chopped	2 tsp. Worcestershire sauce
1 carrot, chopped	½ cup chicken stock

Brown pork sausage, breaking it up as it cooks. Drain and add to lentils. Melt butter and sauté curry and cayenne for 2 minutes. Add onion, carrot, apple and garlic and sauté for 5 minutes.

Combine cornstarch and brown sugar. Slowly pour in vinegar, mixing until smooth, then add Worcestershire sauce and stock. Combine all ingredients in greased casserole dish and mix well. Bake, uncovered, at 350 degrees F for 45 minutes, or until bubbly.

Serves 4.

—Gretchen Sonju
Armstrong, British Columbia

Pasta

"Ticker tape ain't spaghetti."

—*Mayor Fiorello LaGuardia*

We recently reviewed a new and much-bally-hooed pasta restaurant, heading off with empty stomachs and filled with eager anticipation. Returning home some hours later, we had been reminded why we like to make our own noodles and sauces. The restaurant erred, in typical North American fashion, in its excesses—too many noodles, cooked for too long, in too much sauce, with too many tastes.

Pasta should not and need not be treated solely as an edible undercushion for other foods. Fresh pasta, made with good flour, fresh eggs and any judicious amendments the cook wishes to make, can be a taste experience in its own right. To be sure, it lends itself to dressing up well, but too many people overdress.

In fact, it is the North American heavy hand with the ladle and sauces bogged down with animal fats and salt that have earned pasta an undeservedly bad reputation in the popular mind. Ounce for ounce, pasta has fewer calories than lean turkey meat, and it is high time we lay to rest the myth that pasta is fattening. Low in sodium and fat and high in complex carbohydrates, pasta is daily fare in certain regions of Italy that have been found to have lower rates of both heart disease and cancer.

Flat noodles can be made entirely by hand but not without difficulty, and most modern-day pasta makers quickly invest in a mechanical pasta machine. The hand-powered models work very nicely for flat noodles and are quite reasonably priced. For those willing to spend more, electric machines are available that handily deal with the heavy mixing and extrusion processes, turning out flat and round noodles of various types. Both machines eliminate the heavy physical labour of rolling out the stiff dough and ensure uniformity of thickness and width.

Beyond the basics, your imagination can take over: vegetables (tomatoes, spinach, peppers), herbs, cheeses and nuts can all be blended into the dough to produce pastas rich in colour and taste.

When cooking fresh pasta, treat it with respect, and do not even consider leaving the room. Use plenty of water, 4 to 5 quarts per pound of noodles, and bring it to a full boil before adding the pasta. You may wish to add a tablespoon each of oil and salt at this point. Add all the pasta at once, and never attempt to cook more than two pounds at a time. Watch closely, and sample often. Some thinner noodles will cook almost instantly, while others may take up to three minutes. When done, remove from the heat, and drain immediately. You may wish to rinse with hot water to eliminate starch. Some cooks like to toss lightly with butter or oil to keep the individual strands well separated.

Buon appetito!

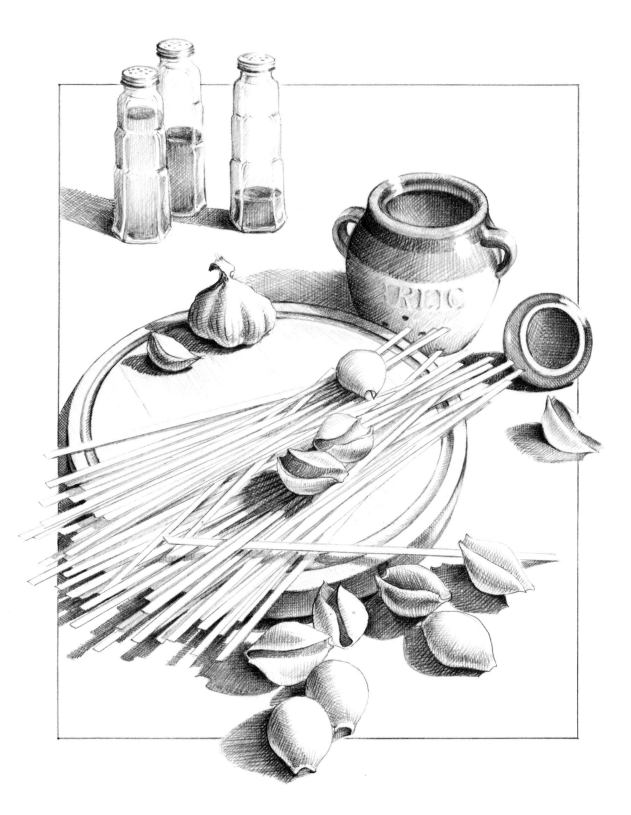

PASTA

WE USED THIS RECIPE IN *The Harrowsmith Pasta Cookbook*, BUT AS MORE PEOPLE ARE beginning to make their own pasta, we felt we should run it once more for those who do not have that book.

2 cups flour	2 tsp. oil
3 eggs	2 Tbsp. water

To make dough by hand, mound flour on work surface, and make a well in the centre. Combine eggs, oil and water, and pour into well. Mix together, using a fork at first and then working by hand. Knead dough for 5 to 8 minutes, or until smooth and elastic. Cover and let stand for 10 minutes.

If using a food processor, place all ingredients in machine and process until a ball forms. Knead for 2 to 4 minutes, or until smooth and elastic. Cover and let stand for 2 minutes.

In either case, if dough is too wet, add flour; if too dry, add an egg.

To roll pasta by hand, divide dough into thirds, and roll on floured board until it reaches desired thinness. Cut as desired. If using a pasta machine, divide dough into thirds, and begin with rollers at first setting, rolling twice through each setting, until desired thinness is attained. Cut by machine or by hand.

PASTA VARIATIONS

Vegetable: Almost any cooked, puréed vegetable can be used. For green pasta, use spinach, broccoli or peas. Tomatoes or carrots result in an orange noodle. For a bright red colour, use beets. Cook vegetables until tender, then purée, leaving vegetables coarse enough that the pasta will have texture as well as flavour.

For the above pasta recipe, use ½ cup cooked, puréed vegetables and one less egg. Prepare dough as directed above.

Herbs: Wash, dry and chop finely 4 Tbsp. of herb desired (or a combination). Mix with flour before adding remaining ingredients. For a beautiful yellow dough, dissolve a small amount of saffron in 2 Tbsp. boiling water, and use in place of the cold water.

Other Flours: To make whole wheat pasta, use 1½ cups whole wheat flour and ½ cup unbleached white flour. Other flour options include semolina, buckwheat and triticale.

CREAMY PASTA SAUCE WITH FRESH HERBS

1½ cups heavy cream	¼ cup Parmesan cheese
4 Tbsp. butter	¼ cup chopped mixed herbs (basil, mint,
½ tsp. salt	parsley, chives)
⅛ tsp. nutmeg	1 lb. angel hair pasta, cooked, drained &
cayenne	rinsed

Combine cream, butter, salt, nutmeg and cayenne in heavy saucepan. Simmer for 15 minutes, or until slightly reduced and thickened. Whisk in cheese and herbs and simmer for 5 minutes. Serve over cooked pasta.

Serves 4.

—*Barb McDonald*
Stella, Ontario

PORK & MUSHROOM SPAGHETTI SAUCE

4 lbs. coarsely ground Boston butt
2 lbs. mushrooms, sliced
1½ cups chopped celery
1 cup chopped onion
1½ cups chopped green pepper
2 Tbsp. salt

3 Tbsp. oregano
3 Tbsp. paprika
1 tsp. pepper
13-oz. can tomato paste
28-oz. can tomatoes

Brown pork in heavy saucepan. Add mushrooms, celery, onion, green pepper, salt, oregano, paprika, pepper and 1 cup water. Bring to a boil. Add tomato paste and tomatoes. Simmer for 1½ hours. Serve over cooked pasta.

Serves 10 to 12.

—Fran Pytko
Syracuse, New York

WHITE CLAM SAUCE

SERVE THIS DELICATE SAUCE OVER A SPINACH OR TOMATO PASTA TO PROVIDE CONTRAST. A thick, flat noodle such as linguine is best to absorb the sauce.

2 Tbsp. oil
1 onion, chopped
1 13-oz. can clams, drained, juice reserved
1½ Tbsp. butter
1½ Tbsp. flour

1½ cups light cream
¼ cup white wine
salt & pepper
parsley

Heat oil and sauté onion until translucent. Add water to clam juice, if necessary, to make ¾ cup. Pour into pot and cook until onion is soft.

Melt butter, stir in flour, then add cream and wine, and cook, stirring, over medium-low heat until thickened and smooth. Pour into onion mixture. Season with salt and pepper and parsley. Add clams and simmer for 20 minutes. Serve over cooked pasta.

Serves 2 to 3.

—Sharon Moroso
Sault Ste. Marie, Ontario

SMOOTH SPAGHETTI SAUCE

THIS RECIPE IS FOR THOSE WHO PREFER A SMOOTH SAUCE FOR SPAGHETTI, LASAGNE OR manicotti. Quick to assemble, it can be left to simmer for hours. The vinegar adds an unusual taste.

2 Tbsp. olive oil
½ cup chopped onion
1 large clove garlic, minced
⅓ cup red wine vinegar
¼ tsp. thyme
½ tsp. basil
½ tsp. oregano

1½ tsp. salt
2 Tbsp. parsley
½ tsp. Worcestershire sauce
¼ tsp. pepper
2 Tbsp. honey
28-oz. can tomatoes
3 6½-oz. cans tomato paste

Heat olive oil and sauté onion and garlic. Add remaining ingredients. Bring to a boil, reduce heat to low, cover and simmer for several hours, stirring occasionally.

Makes 7 cups.

—Susan O'Neill
Bella Coola, British Columbia

MUSHROOM SAUCE FOR PASTA

Top this sauce with Olivade (recipe follows). The mild sweetness of the mushroom sauce complements the olive flavour of Olivade. Either is also delicious served alone with pasta.

3 Tbsp. butter
¼ cup chopped green onion
⅓ cup diced red pepper

1½ cups sliced mushrooms
1 cup heavy cream
salt & pepper

Melt butter, then sauté onion and red pepper for 1 minute. Add mushrooms and sauté for 3 to 4 minutes. Stir in cream and salt and pepper. Heat through.

Serves 3 to 4.

—Sandra K. Bennett
Greenville, South Carolina

OLIVADE

2 lbs. large Kalamata olives, pitted
½ cup olive oil
1¼ cups chopped walnuts
2 cloves garlic, minced

2 tsp. chopped basil
½ tsp. pepper
1 cup Parmesan cheese
2-4 tsp. red wine vinegar

Combine olives, oil, walnuts, garlic, basil and pepper. Mix well. Add cheese and vinegar to taste. This mixture may be stored, refrigerated, for up to 2 months.

—Sandra K. Bennett
Greenville, South Carolina

PASTA CARBONARA

We offer here two carbonara recipes. Although both retain the basic concept of a carbonara, they differ considerably from each other.

1 lb. thickly sliced bacon, diced
1 lb. linguine
3 eggs

⅓ cup chopped Italian parsley
½ cup Parmesan cheese
pepper

Fry bacon until crisp. Drain well on paper towels. Cook linguine until just tender. While this is cooking, beat eggs, then stir in parsley and cheese. Drain and rinse linguine, then mix with egg mixture. Add bacon and pepper and toss again.

Serves 4 to 6.

—Barb McDonald
Stella, Ontario

SPAGHETTI ALLA CARBONARA

1 lb. spaghetti
1 clove garlic, minced
2 Tbsp. olive oil
½ lb. mushrooms, sliced

2 cups diced ham
4 eggs
¼ cup minced parsley
¾ cup Parmesan cheese

Cook spaghetti until just tender. Drain and rinse. Meanwhile, sauté garlic in olive oil for 2 minutes. Add mushrooms and ham and sauté until ham is slightly crisp. Beat eggs lightly, add parsley and cheese and mix with spaghetti. Pour ham mixture over and mix well.

Serves 4 to 6.

—Diane Pearse
Stella, Ontario

CREAMY GARLIC SAUCE

THE CREAMINESS OF THIS SAUCE COMPLEMENTS ITS TANGY GARLIC FLAVOUR – COTTAGE CHEESE may be substituted if ricotta is unavailable.

½ cup milk
2 Tbsp. butter
3-4 cloves garlic, crushed
1 lb. ricotta cheese

pasta of your choice, cooked, drained & rinsed
½ cup Parmesan cheese
pepper

Heat milk and butter in heavy pot. Add garlic and simmer for 5 minutes, then remove garlic. Add ricotta cheese and cook, stirring, over low heat until ricotta has melted. Remove from heat and cover. Toss pasta with ricotta mixture, and sprinkle with Parmesan cheese and pepper.

Serves 2 to 3.

—Irene Louden
Port Coquitlam, British Columbia

ARTICHOKE HEART SPAGHETTI SAUCE

THIS IS A VERY SPICY TOPPING, PARTICULARLY GOOD WITH FRESH FETTUCCINE. SERVED AS AN appetizer, it provides a tangy beginning to a meal.

1 large can artichoke hearts, sliced
½ cup olive oil
2 tsp. crushed hot red pepper
1 tsp. salt

3 cloves garlic, minced
4 Tbsp. chopped parsley
juice of 1 lemon

Combine artichoke hearts, oil, red pepper, salt and garlic in heavy pot. Cook over medium heat, stirring, until hot. Add parsley and lemon juice. Serve over cooked noodles, topped with pepper and Parmesan cheese.

Serves 4.

HUNGARIAN STEW & NOODLES

"I DEVELOPED THIS RECIPE FOR MY DAUGHTER'S FIRST BIRTHDAY PARTY, WHEN I WAS STILL AN inexperienced cook. I wanted something that was tasty but would appeal to people from 1 year old to 80 years old, something I could make ahead of time and something that could be made easily in a large quantity. This was the result, and I've used it for many family gatherings since."

½ cup oil
1 clove garlic, crushed
5 lbs. stewing beef, cut into 1″ cubes
4 onions, sliced
18-oz. can tomato paste
2½ cups water
1 Tbsp. paprika

2 tsp. salt
1 tsp. pepper
1 bay leaf
16 oz. noodles
2 Tbsp. butter
1 Tbsp. parsley

Heat oil. Cook garlic for 1 minute, then discard. Add beef and onions, and cook over medium-high heat until meat is lightly browned. Stir in tomato paste, water, paprika, salt, pepper and bay leaf. Bring to a boil, reduce heat to low, cover and simmer for 3 hours.

When stew is nearly done, cook noodles. Toss with butter and parsley. To serve, heap noodles in middle of serving plate and surround with stew.

Serves 10.

BASILED NOODLES

1 lb. curly noodles
4 Tbsp. butter
¾ cup chopped walnuts

⅓ cup chopped basil
salt & pepper

Cook noodles in boiling water. Meanwhile, melt butter in small saucepan over medium heat and add nuts. Cook for 3 to 4 minutes. Add basil and cook for 1 minute to soften and to release flavour. Mix with drained noodles and add salt and pepper to taste.

Serves 8 as a side dish.

—Diane M. Johnson
Westfir, Oregon

CRAB PASTA CASSEROLE

"In northern California, Dungeness crabs come on the market between Christmas and New Year's. This casserole provides welcome relief from heavy holiday meals."

3 Tbsp. butter
½ cup chopped onion
1 clove garlic, minced
2½ Tbsp. flour
1½ cups chicken stock
⅓ cup dry white wine
1 Tbsp. chopped basil

1 jar marinated artichoke hearts,
   drained & chopped
⅛ tsp. cayenne
1 lb. fusilli, cooked, drained & rinsed
1 Tbsp. butter
2 Tbsp. Parmesan cheese
1 lb. crabmeat
1 cup grated Monterey Jack cheese

Melt butter, then sauté onion and garlic until golden. Sprinkle with flour, mix, then add chicken stock and simmer until thickened. Add wine, basil, artichokes and cayenne. Set aside.

Toss pasta with butter and Parmesan cheese. Layer pasta, crabmeat and sauce in greased casserole dish. Top with grated cheese. Bake, uncovered, at 350 degrees F for 30 minutes.

Serves 4.

—Noreen Braithwaite
Redding, California

NOODLES CZARINA CASSEROLE

Pasta is one of the world's best "comfort foods"—it always makes the eater feel full, warm and cared-for. This dish is a pleasant combination of tastes and textures.

½ cup chopped onion
2 Tbsp. butter
2 Tbsp. flour
1 tsp. salt
pepper
⅔ cup powdered milk
1 cup water

1 tsp. Dijon mustard
1 cup cottage cheese
½ cup grated Cheddar cheese
2 Tbsp. lemon juice
¾ lb. dry egg noodles, cooked
parsley

Sauté onion in butter until tender. Stir in flour, salt and pepper until smooth. Combine powdered milk with water, then add to roux with mustard. Cook, stirring, until thickened. Stir in cheeses and lemon juice, then noodles. Pour into greased casserole dish and bake, uncovered, at 350 degrees F for 40 to 45 minutes. Sprinkle with parsley.

Serves 4.

SPAGHETTI BALLS & SAUCE

DELICIOUS NONMEAT "MEATBALLS," THESE ARE BASED ON CREAM CHEESE AND WALNUTS. THE spaghetti balls are simmered in the tomato sauce and then poured over cooked pasta.

Balls
2 eggs
¾ cup cracker crumbs
¼ cup wheat germ
½ cup ground walnuts
4 oz. cream cheese
1 clove garlic, chopped
oil **or** butter

Sauce
3 Tbsp. oil
¼ green pepper, chopped
¼ lb. mushrooms, sliced
1 onion, chopped
salt
¼ tsp. sage
½ tsp. oregano
½ bay leaf
28-oz. can tomatoes
6½-oz. can tomato sauce

Lightly beat eggs, then combine with cracker crumbs, wheat germ, walnuts, cream cheese and garlic. Mix well. Shape into small balls. Chill for 1 hour, then brown in oil or butter.

Meanwhile, make sauce. Heat oil and sauté green pepper, mushrooms and onion. Add salt, herbs, tomatoes and tomato sauce. Add browned spaghetti balls, and simmer for 1 hour.

Serve over spaghetti.

Serves 6.

—Vicky Chandler
London, Ontario

GREEN SPAGHETTI WITH CHEESE & TOMATO SAUCES

THE CONTRIBUTOR TASTED THIS WHILE VACATIONING IN ITALY AND SUCCESSFULLY RE-CREATED it upon her return home. This is an attractive dish because of the combination of colours.

Tomato Sauce
4 Tbsp. butter
1 large onion, chopped
½ lb. bacon
4 large tomatoes, peeled, seeded
 & cubed
1 Tbsp. basil
salt & pepper

Cheese Sauce
3 cups sour cream
½ lb. sharp Cheddar cheese, grated
1 Tbsp. oregano
salt & pepper
paprika

1 lb. dry spaghetti, cooked, drained
 & rinsed

For tomato sauce: Melt butter, then sauté onion and bacon. Add tomatoes and basil and cook for 5 minutes. Add salt and pepper and keep hot.

For cheese sauce: Heat sour cream slowly. Add cheese and cook, stirring, until melted. Stir in remaining ingredients.

Place spaghetti on plates. Pour tomato sauce over spaghetti and top with cheese sauce.

Serves 4.

—Inge Benda
Bridgetown, Nova Scotia

RIGATONI WITH MEATBALLS

MANY OF US GREW UP WITH CANNED RIGATONI AS A LUNCHTIME RITUAL. HOMEMADE RIGATONI provides a tastier, more nutritious alternative and does not take long to make.

Meatballs
1 lb. ground beef
salt & pepper
2-3 eggs
bread crumbs
basil, thyme, oregano, rosemary,
   marjoram, summer savory
1-2 cloves garlic, crushed
½ cup oil or less

Sauce
1 onion, chopped
28-oz. can tomatoes
13-oz. can tomato paste
1 cup sliced mushrooms
basil
oregano

1 lb. rigatoni, cooked & drained

Combine ground beef, salt and pepper, eggs, a pinch of bread crumbs, a small pinch each of desired herbs and garlic. Mix well and form into small meatballs. Brown in oil. Remove from pot and set aside.

Brown onion for sauce in meatball drippings. Add tomatoes, tomato paste, mushrooms, basil and oregano. Bring to a boil, then reduce heat. Return meatballs to pot and simmer for 1 to 1½ hours. Serve over cooked rigatoni.

Serves 4.

—Cary Elizabeth Marshall
Thunder Bay, Ontario

RAVIOLI

IF YOU MAKE RAVIOLI OFTEN, YOU MAY WISH TO INVEST IN A RAVIOLI CUTTER. THIS LOOKS LIKE a wooden rolling pin with small square indentations. The serrated edges on the squares cut easily through the dough. If you use this, roll the dough out in sheets and then fill, rather than rolling out in strips.

pasta
1 egg, lightly beaten

Filling
1½ lbs. ground beef
¼ cup Parmesan cheese
1¼ cups chopped raw spinach
2 Tbsp. chopped parsley

½ cup bread crumbs
¼ lb. dry Italian salami, chopped
2 eggs, lightly beaten
salt & pepper

Make pasta using basic pasta recipe (page 132); set aside.

Cook beef until well browned. Drain off fat, then mix with remaining filling ingredients. Cool.

Flour a large work surface. Roll out dough until it is very thin. Brush with lightly beaten egg. Cut dough into 1½-inch strips. Place filling on alternate strips of dough by teaspoonfuls, about 2 inches apart. Place empty dough strips on top of filled ones. Pinch down sides well with a fork, cut between hills of filling and pinch edges closed.

Cook a few at a time in boiling water for 15 minutes, remove and drain. Serve with tomato sauce, if desired.

Makes approximately 4 dozen.

—Diane Capelazo
Alvinston, Ontario

CAPPELLETTINI IN BRODO

Pasta
1 egg
1 egg yolk
1 cup flour
1 tsp. salt
1 Tbsp. water

Filling
2 chicken breasts, boned
2 green onions, chopped
2 Tbsp. oil

fresh thyme, oregano, sage & parsley
1 clove garlic, crushed
1 egg yolk
Parmesan cheese
salt & pepper
bread crumbs
salt & pepper
bread crumbs

20 cups rich chicken broth

Combine pasta ingredients. Mix well, cover and set aside.

Sauté chicken breasts and onions in oil until chicken is cooked through but not browned. Grind chicken.

Mix herbs to taste in order given. Blend in garlic, egg yolk, 2 Tbsp. Parmesan cheese, cooked chicken and salt and pepper. Add bread crumbs if necessary to hold mixture together. Roll into pencil-thick coil.

Put pasta through pasta machine at thinnest setting, or roll out until paper-thin. Cut into 1-inch squares.

Pinch off a small piece of the chicken coil, and place in the middle of the pasta square. Press 2 opposite corners of pasta firmly together, making a triangle. Wrap around a finger, press smallest corners together and turn down middle point of triangle. Repeat for remaining pasta.

Poach cappellettini in broth for 15 minutes. Serve garnished with parsley and Parmesan cheese.

Serves 8 to 10.

—Mirella Guidi
Kingston, Ontario

CURRIED PASTA SALAD

16 oz. dry spiral pasta
¼ cup olive oil
1 green pepper, sliced
1 red pepper, sliced
3-4 stalks celery, chopped
2 cups broccoli florets
1 13-oz. can pitted black olives, drained
1 4-oz. can water chestnuts, drained
  & sliced

2 cups chopped purple cabbage

Dressing
⅔ cup olive oil
3 Tbsp. wine vinegar
1 large clove garlic, crushed
1-1½ Tbsp. curry powder
1 tsp. coriander
⅓ cup Parmesan cheese

Cook pasta in boiling water until soft but not soggy. Rinse in cold water and then toss with olive oil. Add remaining salad ingredients and set aside.

Combine dressing ingredients, except Parmesan cheese. Toss with salad, then allow to sit for 5 to 10 minutes. Add Parmesan cheese, toss and serve.

Serves 8 to 10.

—Colleen Suche
Winnipeg, Manitoba

PASTA PATRICIA

A VARIATION OF THE CLASSIC CREAM SAUCE FOR PASTA, THIS DISH HAS A SOMEWHAT THINNER result. The addition of cottage cheese makes it an especially good source of calcium and protein. Any pasta is acceptable, but we recommend a thick, flat noodle or a round one to better absorb the sauce.

¼ cup butter
1 onion, chopped
2 cloves garlic, minced
salt
¼ tsp. pepper
¾ tsp. nutmeg
¼ tsp. sweet paprika

1 Tbsp. chopped basil
¾ cup chopped green pepper
1 cup sour cream
¼ cup Parmesan **or** Romano cheese
¾ cup fine-curd cottage cheese
¼ lb. ham, julienned
cooked pasta

Melt butter and sauté onion and garlic until onion is translucent. Add salt, pepper, nutmeg, paprika, basil and green pepper and sauté for 2 more minutes. Stir in sour cream and cheeses, then add ham and heat through. Serve over cooked pasta.

Serves 4.

—Patricia Pryde
Toronto, Ontario

BRADFORD CARROT ALFREDO

6 carrots, peeled
12 oz. dry fettuccine **or** 1 lb. fresh
  fettuccine
½ cup butter
1 cup heavy cream

1 cup Parmesan cheese
½ lb. sliced ham, cut into thin strips
½ tsp. nutmeg
pepper

Cut carrots lengthwise into strips the same size as the fettuccine. Cook fettuccine, drain and keep hot. Cook carrot strips for 3 minutes, or until crispy-tender. Drain.

Melt butter in large pot over low heat. Whisk in cream and Parmesan cheese. Stir in ham and carrots and heat gently. Add fettuccine, nutmeg and pepper. Toss together well. Cook, stirring, until heated through.

Serves 6 to 8.

—Evelyn Hall
Scarborough, Ontario

TURKEY-STUFFED PASTA SHELLS

1 lb. ground raw turkey
1 onion, chopped
2 Tbsp. butter
1 egg, slightly beaten
2 cups cottage cheese
1½ cups grated Cheddar cheese
½ tsp. oregano

½ tsp. sage
¼ tsp. pepper
1 lb. spinach, chopped & steamed
1 lb. large pasta shells
2-3 cups rich tomato sauce
Parmesan cheese

Brown turkey and onion in butter. Combine egg with cottage cheese, Cheddar cheese, oregano, sage and pepper. Squeeze excess liquid from spinach and stir into cheese mixture along with turkey and onion. Mix well.

Stuff pasta shells with filling. Place 3 to 4 Tbsp. tomato sauce in bottom of greased 9" x 13" baking pan. Arrange shells in pan, then pour tomato sauce over. Sprinkle with Parmesan cheese and bake at 350 degrees F for 50 to 60 minutes.

Serves 6 to 8.

—Lois B. Demerich
Etters, Pennsylvania

SEAFOOD LINGUINE

2 cups sliced mushrooms
4 shallots **or** green onions, finely chopped
½ cup butter
1½ cups Madeira
1 Tbsp. tomato paste
1 Tbsp. snipped tarragon
¼ tsp. salt

pepper
10 oz. linguine
1½ lbs. shrimp, shelled
1½ cups heavy cream
4 egg yolks, beaten
salt & pepper

Cook mushrooms and shallots in butter, uncovered, over medium-high heat for 4 to 5 minutes, or until vegetables are tender. Remove with slotted spoon and set aside.

Stir Madeira, tomato paste, tarragon, ¼ tsp. salt and pepper into butter in skillet. Bring to a boil, and cook vigorously for 10 minutes, or until mixture is reduced to ½ cup.

Meanwhile, cook pasta. Drain and keep warm. Drop shrimp into boiling water and cook for 1 to 3 minutes, or until shrimp turn pink. Drain and keep warm.

In small bowl, stir together cream and egg yolks. Add Madeira mixture. Return to skillet. Cook and stir until thickened. Stir in shrimp and mushroom mixture and heat through. Season with salt and pepper. Toss with pasta.

Serves 6.

—Kristine Mattila
Quesnel, British Columbia

SEAFOOD PASTA SALAD WITH PESTO DRESSING

This dressing, with or without pesto, is also excellent with potato salad. This is a good picnic salad.

Dressing
2 eggs
½ cup sugar
1 Tbsp. dry mustard
paprika
2 tsp. flour
¾ cup vinegar
1 Tbsp. pesto

Salad
½ lb. corkscrew pasta
1 lb. shrimp, shelled & deveined
1 lb. scallops, rinsed
1 cup cooked peas
½ cup diced red pepper
½ cup minced green onion
½ cup chopped celery
1 cup black olives
salt & pepper

For dressing: Beat eggs well. Add sugar, mustard, paprika and flour and beat well. Then add vinegar and ¼ cup water. Cook in double boiler until thickened. Set aside. When cool, stir in pesto.

Meanwhile, prepare salad. Cook pasta, drain and rinse. Cook shrimp and scallops in boiling water for 1 minute. Drain immediately.

Toss all salad ingredients in large bowl, then mix in enough dressing to coat. Chill well, then allow salad to return to room temperature before serving.

Serves 6.

—Diane Pearse
Stella, Ontario

FRIED JAO-TZE

Originating in northern China, these are essentially fried dumplings, which may also be steamed or boiled. When they are fried, offer a variety of dips as accompaniment – honey-mustard sauce or soy sauce with ginger, to mention just two.

Dough
1½ cups flour
8 Tbsp. water

Filling

6 Chinese mushrooms	1½ Tbsp. soy sauce
⅓ lb. ground pork	1 Tbsp. cornstarch
½ cup diced bamboo shoots	salt
⅓ cup chopped shrimp	½ egg, beaten
1½ Tbsp. Chinese sherry	⅓ cup oil

For dough: Place flour in bowl and add water, mixing until well blended. Knead, cover and let stand for 45 minutes.

For filling: Cover mushrooms with boiling water and let stand for 20 minutes. Drain, then squeeze. Cut off stems, discard, then chop mushroom caps. Combine mushrooms with pork, bamboo shoots, shrimp, sherry, soy sauce, cornstarch, salt and egg and mix well. Refrigerate for several hours.

Place dough on lightly floured board and knead for 5 minutes, or until smooth and elastic. Stretch into sausage shape, then pull off 25 to 30 pieces. Roll into balls, flatten, then roll out into 3-inch circles, covering with damp towel as you make them.

Place 2 teaspoons filling on centre of each circle. Bring edges of dough up and pinch together firmly in the centre, forming a crescent. Seal with water and leave each end open. Make a pleat in one end, then gather up remaining dough on end, making 3 or 4 pleats. Repeat at other end. Keep finished crescents covered.

Heat oil. Cook dumplings until golden brown on bottom – 2 minutes. Pour 1 cup water around dumplings. Cover pot tightly and cook on high heat until water is almost gone – 5 minutes – then reduce heat to low for 5 minutes. Return heat to high just to brown dumplings on bottom. Serve bottom-side up.

Serves 6 as an appetizer.

MACARONI & CHEESE CASSEROLE

Tomatoes give this macaroni and cheese casserole an added zing. It was developed by the adopted grandmother of the contributor and can be frozen successfully.

3 cups dry elbow macaroni, cooked & drained	pepper
1 lb. sharp Cheddar cheese, grated	1 cup chopped onion, sautéed in butter
28-oz. can tomatoes, including juice	Parmesan cheese

Combine all ingredients except Parmesan cheese and mix well. Top with Parmesan cheese. Bake, uncovered, at 350 degrees F for 1 hour.

Serves 8.

—Anna J. Lee
Sault Ste. Marie, Ontario

BRAISED SHRIMP IN PASTA SHELLS
WITH PIQUANT MUSHROOM TOMATO SAUCE

"THIS IS A DISH TO MAKE WHEN THE URGE TO CREATE AND TO FILL YOUR HOME WITH A HEADY aroma calls you into the kitchen for a few hours of satisfying cooking. I developed this particular recipe to combine a love of pasta-making with the intriguing notion of mingling zesty Italian and pungent Indian flavours." When we tested this in our Camden East office, there were many loud cries of "More, please!"

Braised Shrimp
½ tsp. cumin seed
½ lb. large shrimp, shelled & deveined
2 Tbsp. oil
1 tsp. crushed hot red peppers
1 clove garlic, crushed
½ tsp. crushed black pepper
1 Tbsp. lemon juice

Mushroom Tomato Sauce
¼ tsp. cumin seed
¼ tsp. coriander seed
1 tsp. butter
1 tsp. olive oil
1 clove garlic, crushed

2 shallots **or** 1 onion, chopped
½ lb. mushrooms, coarsely chopped
1 Tbsp. capers
1 green chili, roasted, peeled & pounded,
   or ½ tsp. crushed hot red peppers
½ tsp. turmeric
½ tsp. basil
½ tsp. thyme
½ tsp. oregano
salt & pepper
1 cup finely chopped tomatoes & juice

1 pound fresh pasta (uncut)
2 Tbsp. Parmesan cheese

For shrimp: Roast cumin seed in dry, heavy pot until it crackles. Remove from pot. Braise shrimp in oil until they turn pink. When cool, combine with cumin and remaining ingredients. Marinate for at least 2 hours.

Meanwhile, prepare sauce. Roast cumin and coriander seeds in dry, heavy pot until they crackle. Remove from heat, crush finely and set aside. Melt butter in oil, then sauté garlic and shallots or onion over medium heat until pale gold. Turn heat to high, add mushrooms, and cook until soft. Add capers, chili, turmeric, basil, thyme, oregano, salt and pepper, cumin and coriander. Cook for 30 seconds, then add tomatoes and juice. Reduce heat and simmer for 15 to 20 minutes, stirring occasionally.

Now, prepare the pasta. Roll out one half very thinly, then cut into 6-to-8-inch discs. Boil disks in water, 2 at a time, then place in a bowl of ice water with oil. Drain and place between damp towels. Cut remaining pasta dough into fettuccine and cook. Set aside 1 fettuccine for each disc, then stir remaining noodles into tomato sauce. Gently mix in shrimp.

For assembly: Butter individual au gratin dishes (one for each pasta disc). Lightly coat each disc with tomato sauce on both sides, then centre in dish with edges hanging over sides. Place one portion of filling in centre, then sprinkle with Parmesan cheese. Fold edges of disc toward centre, crimping together. Fasten with toothpick, then wind single strand of fettuccine around top.

Bake at 450 degrees F for 5 to 8 minutes, or until a pale golden crust forms. Remove toothpick before serving.

Serves 6, approximately.

—Lesley-Anne Paveling
Mozart, Saskatchewan

NOODLE CASSEROLE DELUXE

AVAILABLE IN MOST ORIENTAL SUPPLY STORES, DRIED TREE EARS HAVE A DISTINCTIVE TASTE AND texture. They are somewhat similar to black Chinese mushrooms, which can be substituted if tree ears are not available.

1 oz. tree ears
1 oz. black Chinese mushrooms
1 lb. mushrooms, quartered
2 Tbsp. lemon juice
3 Tbsp. butter
1 onion, finely chopped
1 bunch parsley, chopped
salt & pepper

¼ tsp. thyme
3 eggs, beaten
1 cup heavy cream
½ cup milk
nutmeg
3 cups dry egg noodles, cooked
5 Tbsp. Parmesan cheese
1 cup buttered bread crumbs

Soak tree ears in warm water for 30 minutes and the Chinese mushrooms for 15 minutes. Drain, then chop. Mix regular mushrooms with lemon juice.

Melt butter and sauté onion for 5 minutes. Add all mushrooms and sauté for 2 minutes longer. Add parsley, salt and pepper and thyme and sauté for 10 minutes.

Mix together eggs, cream, milk, nutmeg and salt and pepper. Place cooked noodles and mushroom mixture in greased 9" x 9" casserole dish. Pour egg mixture over and mix well. Sprinkle with cheese and bread crumbs.

Bake, uncovered, at 400 degrees F for 25 to 30 minutes.

Serves 4.

—Inge Benda
Bridgetown, Nova Scotia

CHEESY BROCCOLI CASSEROLE

THIS IS A RICH, TASTY CASSEROLE. IT FEEDS A CROWD AND CAN BE PREPARED AND ASSEMBLED a day ahead.

3 eggs
2½ cups ricotta cheese
¾ cup sour cream
¼ cup butter
1 lb. mushrooms, sliced
2 heads broccoli, cut into florets
2 onions, chopped

salt & pepper
1 lb. dry egg noodles, cooked, drained
  & rinsed
2 Tbsp. yeast
½ cup bread crumbs
1 cup grated Swiss cheese

Combine eggs, ricotta cheese and sour cream; mix well. Set aside.

Melt butter in heavy skillet. Sauté mushrooms, broccoli and onions until onions are transparent—5 to 10 minutes. Sprinkle with salt and pepper.

In greased 9" x 13" pan, combine cooked noodles, egg mixture and vegetables. Add yeast and mix well. Sprinkle with bread crumbs and grated cheese.

Bake, covered, at 350 degrees F for 30 minutes, then uncovered for 15 minutes.

Serves 8.

LASAGNE STUFFED WITH TINY MEATBALLS

A LOT OF WORK BUT WELL WORTH THE EFFORT, THIS RECIPE MAKES ENOUGH LASAGNE TO SERVE
16 people. It can also be frozen and used for a last-minute meal.

1 lb. lasagne noodles

Sauce
3 Tbsp. oil
2 onions, chopped
½ green pepper, diced
10 mushrooms, sliced
1-2 cloves garlic, minced
3 28-oz. cans tomato sauce
1 Tbsp. chopped parsley
1 tsp. basil
½ tsp. oregano

Cheese Filling
2 cups cottage **or** ricotta cheese, puréed
2 eggs, lightly beaten
1 lb. mozzarella cheese, grated

½ cup Parmesan cheese

Meatballs
1½ lbs. ground meat (beef, veal **or** pork)
¼ cup Parmesan cheese
1 clove garlic, minced
1½ Tbsp. chopped parsley
⅛ tsp. nutmeg
1 tsp. basil
½ tsp. grated lemon rind
¼ tsp. salt
¼ tsp. pepper
⅔ cup dry bread crumbs
1 Tbsp. milk
1 egg

Cook noodles in boiling water, drain, rinse and set aside.

Prepare sauce. Heat oil in large pot. Add onions and sauté until soft. Add green pepper,
mushrooms and garlic and cook, stirring, for 3 minutes. Stir in tomato sauce and herbs.
Bring to a boil, reduce heat, and simmer while preparing rest of dish.

For meatballs: Combine meat, cheese, garlic, parsley, nutmeg, basil, lemon rind, salt and
pepper and mix well. In another bowl, combine bread crumbs, milk and egg. Work this
into meat, then chill mixture for 1 hour. Shape into tiny meatballs, keeping your hands
damp with cold water. Cook meatballs by steaming over low heat in enough water to
prevent sticking. Drop cooked meatballs into tomato sauce, setting aside a small amount
of sauce to spread on bottom of lasagne pans.

For filling: Combine cottage or ricotta cheese with eggs and mozzarella cheese.

To assemble, grease two 9″ x 13″ pans. Spread bottom of pans with very thin layer of
tomato sauce. On top of this, place a layer of noodles, then half the cheese mixture, then
one third of the meatballs and tomato sauce. Sprinkle with Parmesan cheese. Repeat.
Top with layer of noodles, remaining meatballs and sauce and Parmesan cheese.

Bake, uncovered, at 375 degrees F for 30 minutes, or until bubbling and golden. Let stand
for 10 minutes before serving.

Serves 16.

—Lynne Roe
Orangeville, Ontario

Fish & Seafood

"Give me a platter of choice finnan haddie . . . and you may tell the butler to dispense with the caviar, truffles and nightingales' tongues."

—*Craig Claiborne*

The vegetarian life, we've recently noted, no longer involves the same degree of self-denial it once demanded. It is a spicier world in which we live today, with a variety of fruits, vegetables, ethnic ingredients and flavourings unheard of in most North American communities a decade ago. More significant, for those who do not draw a philosophical line at cold-blooded creatures, is the growing choice and abundance of fresh and flash-frozen fish and seafoods.

The dilemma facing those of a vegetarian persuasion is not a new one, however, as noted in the memoirs of Benjamin Franklin: "Being becalm'd off Block Island, our people set about catching cod and hauled up a great many. Hitherto, I had stuck to my resolution of not eating animal food and on this occasion consider'd . . . the taking of every fish as a kind of unprovoked murder. . . . But I had formerly been a great lover of fish, and when this came hot out of the frying pan, it smelt admirably well. I balanc'd some time between principle and inclination, till I recollected that when the fish were opened, I saw smaller fish taken out of their stomachs; then I thought, 'If you eat one another, I don't see why we mayn't eat you.' So I din'd upon cod very heartily. . . . So convenient a thing it is to be a reasonable creature, since it enables one to find or make a reason for everything one has a mind to do."

Like Franklin, we would be hard-pressed to pass up a freshly caught filleted fish, especially if sautéed in butter or a bit of oil and lemon. Escoffier's pronouncement that "the greatest dishes are very simple dishes," holds especially true with fish, and this chapter boasts many recipes that rely on simplicity and speed for their success – Salmon Barbecue and Tarragon Mussels among others.

Two simple rules prevail if one is to be successful in cooking any type of fish or seafood: start with fresh specimens, and do not overcook. With cardiovascular fitness experts now advocating at least two fish meals a week, the availability of fresh fish is increasing, but high-quality frozen fish can also be very good indeed – better, in fact, than the goods of a questionable fresh-fish-monger.

Unhappily, for those of us who love fish and seafood, the combined effects of acid rain, industrial pollution and lax sanitation regulations in coastal areas is right now promising a crisis in the quality of our once impeccably clean supply. Unless action is taken, ours may be one of the last generations to savour the healthy products of our oceans, streams and lakes. With some areas of North America already condemned as fishing grounds, it is surely one of the great environmental issues of our lifetime and one we can ill afford to ignore.

STEAMED RED SNAPPER WITH GINGER SAUCE

2-3 lbs. red snapper, cleaned & scaled but left whole

Sauce
2 Tbsp. vinegar
1 Tbsp. sugar
1 Tbsp. soy sauce
4 tsp. sesame oil
½ tsp. pepper
1 Tbsp. cornstarch
1 cup chicken stock

Vegetable Garnish
1 cup sliced green pepper
1 cup sliced red pepper
⅓ cup grated gingerroot
1 cup sliced green onions
1 Tbsp. oil

Steam fish for 15 to 25 minutes until flaky.

Meanwhile, combine sauce ingredients and cook over medium heat until thickened. Sauté all but a bit of each vegetable in oil until slightly soft. Add sauce and pour over fish. Garnish with remaining vegetables.

Serves 4 to 6.

—Billie Sheffield
North Gower, Ontario

SCALLOPED SALMON

"FAST AND SIMPLE BUT WITH AN OUTSTANDING FLAVOUR, THIS IS FIRM AND SLICES WELL, HOT OR cold," comments our Camden East tester.

½ cup chicken stock
2 eggs, beaten
½ cup milk
2 Tbsp. chopped parsley
1 Tbsp. minced onion

½ tsp. dry mustard
16-oz. can salmon
2 cups bread crumbs
1 tsp. sage
1 cup grated Cheddar cheese

Combine all ingredients and mix well. Pour into greased 9-inch pie pan. Bake, uncovered, at 350 degrees F for 35 to 40 minutes.

Serves 4.

—Ingrid Magnuson
Winnipeg, Manitoba

SALMON SEVICHE

"THIS COLD FISH DISH MAKES A WONDERFULLY REFRESHING APPETIZER." THE CONTRIBUTOR SERVES it on a bed of Boston lettuce with pickled cucumber.

3 lemons
3 oranges
3 cloves garlic
3 green onions
2 Tbsp. sugar

½ tsp. salt
1 Tbsp. red peppercorns (optional)
⅛ tsp. white pepper
1½ lbs. fresh red salmon

Squeeze juice of lemons and oranges into medium-sized bowl. Slice garlic and onions and add to juices. Add remaining ingredients except fish and stir to dissolve sugar. Thinly slice salmon into marinade. Marinate for at least 4 hours before serving. The fish will be opaque and look cooked when it is ready to eat.

Serves 6 to 8 as an appetizer.

—Janet Jokinen
Cobourg, Ontario

FRESH SALMON PÂTÉ

"MY RECIPE WAS INSPIRED BY A SALMON PÂTÉ I HAD AT THE PILGRIM'S INN, DEER ISLE, MAINE. Their version was coated with finely chopped pistachios." This pâté has a delicate flavour – be sure to serve with a light, mild cracker.

⅔-lb. salmon steak
salt
4 oz. cream cheese
1 Tbsp. heavy cream
1 tsp. lime juice

¼-½ tsp. dill
pepper
⅓ cup whole almonds
⅓ cup parsley

Poach salmon in 2 Tbsp. water with dash of salt until just done – pink through. Cool slightly, then remove bones and skin. Crumble salmon into bowl. Add cream cheese and mix thoroughly. Add cream, stirring until smooth. Add lime juice, dill and pepper and mix well. Chill for 1 to 2 hours.

To serve, finely chop almonds and parsley in shallow bowl. Spoon chilled pâté into centre. Pat into ball, then turn to coat with almonds and parsley.

Serves 8 to 10 as an appetizer.

—Jane Crosen
Brooklin, Maine

SALMON BARBECUE

1 cup dry vermouth
¾ cup oil
⅓ cup lemon juice
2 Tbsp. chopped chives
½ tsp. celery salt

½ tsp. thyme
1½ tsp. salt
½ tsp. pepper
4 salmon steaks

Combine all ingredients except salmon steaks and mix well. Pour over salmon and marinate, refrigerated, for 4 hours. Barbecue for approximately 10 minutes on each side, depending on thickness of steaks.

Serves 4.

—Debra Gaudreau
Jackson, Michigan

SEVICHE

THIS IS A CENTRAL/SOUTH AMERICAN DISH. THE CITRIC ACID IN THE LIME OR LEMON JUICE "cooks" the fish.

1½ lbs. fresh firm white fish fillets
1 cup lime **or** lemon juice
½ cup olive oil
2-3 cloves garlic, crushed
½ tsp. thyme
1 tsp. oregano

¼ tsp. coriander
1 small hot pepper, chopped
1 red pepper, cut in strips
1 green pepper, cut in strips
2 green onions, chopped
1 tomato, chopped

Cut fish into thin strips. Cover with juice and chill for at least 1½ hours.

Meanwhile, combine olive oil, garlic, thyme, oregano, coriander and hot pepper. Once fish has turned white, pour this mixture over it. Add red and green peppers, onions and tomato. Mix gently. Chill 1 hour more before serving.

Serves 6 to 8 as an appetizer.

—Cary Elizabeth Marshall
Thunder Bay, Ontario

SALMON MOUSSE

Although somewhat time-consuming to prepare, this mousse is well worth the effort. For a beautiful presentation, pipe the mousse into artichoke hearts. Garnish with a dollop of mayonnaise and a caper.

1 lb. fresh salmon
¼ cup chopped celery with leaves
1½ tsp. chopped onion
¾ tsp. salt
⅛ tsp. pepper
small piece bay leaf
¼ cup butter, softened
1 Tbsp. egg white

2 tsp. lemon juice
½ tsp. salt
white pepper
cayenne
tarragon
1 tsp. unflavoured gelatin
¼ cup whipping cream
¼ cup mayonnaise

Place salmon on large piece of foil. Sprinkle with celery, onion, ¾ tsp. salt, ⅛ tsp. pepper and bay leaf. Wrap foil securely around fish and place in boiling water. Boil for 10 minutes per inch of thickness of fish. Remove from water and cool. Remove skin and bones. Discard bay leaf. Grind fine.

Add butter and egg white and blend well. Add lemon juice, ½ tsp. salt, white pepper, cayenne and tarragon.

Soak gelatin in ¼ cup cold water for 5 minutes, then set in small pan of hot water and heat until gelatin dissolves – 5 minutes. Cool but do not chill. Whip cream until stiff. Beat gelatin into mayonnaise, then beat into salmon. Fold in whipped cream. Pipe into artichoke hearts, if desired.

Serves 8 as an appetizer.

POACHED FISH JAPANESE STYLE

1 cup soy sauce
sugar
1 tsp. grated gingerroot

½ cup sherry
1 clove garlic, slashed
1 trout, cleaned but left whole

Combine soy sauce, sugar, gingerroot, sherry, garlic and 2 cups water in a skillet and bring to a boil. Add trout and poach for 3 minutes on each side, turning only once.

Serves 1.

—Jan Iwanik
Cranbrook, British Columbia

BAKED WHITEFISH

½ cup milk
2 tsp. Dijon mustard
4 tsp. mayonnaise
1¼ lbs. whitefish fillets
1 clove garlic, crushed

¼ tsp. salt
⅛ tsp. thyme
white pepper
½ tsp. tarragon
½ tsp. chopped chives

Pour milk into bottom of greased casserole dish. Combine mustard and mayonnaise and spread over fish. Sprinkle with garlic, salt, thyme, pepper, tarragon and chives. Place fillets in casserole and bake, covered, at 400 degrees F for 20 to 25 minutes, or until fish flakes easily.

Serves 4.

—Linda Humphrey
St. Albans, Maine

HADDOCK IN FENNEL & YOGURT

FRIED COCONUT FLAKES ARE AVAILABLE IN CANS IN MANY ETHNIC FOOD STORES. IF NOT available, simply dry-roast coconut flakes in a heavy saucepan.

3 Tbsp. olive oil
2 onions, chopped
2 cloves garlic, minced
1 small hot green chili, chopped
1 Tbsp. fennel seeds, crushed

2 Tbsp. fried coconut flakes
1 cup plain yogurt
½ tsp. salt
2 lbs. haddock fillets, cut into 2"-3" pieces
2 sprigs coriander, chopped

Heat oil in heavy pot and sauté onions, garlic and chili until mixture turns light brown. Add crushed fennel and coconut and sauté for 3 minutes more.

Lightly beat together yogurt with 1 cup water. Add to pot and stir. Add salt and simmer for 5 minutes. Add fish and simmer for 5 to 7 minutes, or until fish is tender and flaky. Garnish with coriander.

Serves 4.

—Ingrid Birker
Montreal, Quebec

STEAMED SOLE WITH TOMATO COULIS

2 carrots
2 zucchini
3 purple & white turnips
3 Tbsp. butter
1 large tomato

3 sprigs lemon thyme **or**
  ½ tsp. thyme & ½ tsp. sage
salt & pepper
4 fillets sole
juice of 1 lemon

Grate or julienne into 2-inch strips, carrots, zucchini and turnips. Melt 1 Tbsp. butter with 3 Tbsp. water in skillet. Toss vegetables in skillet to coat and mix. Remove from heat.

Purée tomato, including skin, with herbs and remaining 2 Tbsp. butter. Season with salt and pepper.

Arrange sole on top of vegetables, brush with lemon juice and season lightly with salt and pepper. Cover skillet tightly, place over medium heat and steam for 6 minutes, or until fish is white.

Place one quarter of the vegetables on each of 4 plates and top with a fillet of sole. Pour tomato purée into skillet, boil over high heat for 1 minute, then pour in a ribbon around each mound of vegetables.

Serves 4.

—The Art of Cooking School
Kingston, Ontario

BROILED LEMON SOLE WITH CUCUMBER DILL TOPPING

2 lbs. lemon sole
1 cup mayonnaise
½ cup chopped cucumber
1 Tbsp. chopped dill

3 green onions, sliced
Tabasco sauce
salt & pepper

Arrange fish in single layer on greased tray. Combine remaining ingredients and spread evenly over fish. Broil 3 to 5 inches from heat for 5 to 7 minutes.

Serves 4.

FISH DUET RING MOULD

OUR CAMDEN EAST TESTER COMMENTS, "THE SUBTLE FLAVOURS OF SALMON, SOLE AND broccoli come together extremely well in this dish."

3 Tbsp. butter
1 small onion, finely chopped
5 Tbsp. flour
1 cup milk
1 tsp. salt
½ tsp. white pepper
4 eggs, separated

6 sole fillets
1 lb. salmon, ground
½ tsp. paprika
½ tsp. chervil
1 head broccoli, cooked & chopped
½ tsp. nutmeg

Melt butter and sauté onion until golden. Stir in flour, then add milk gradually and cook over medium-low heat, stirring, until sauce thickens. Add salt and pepper.

Beat egg yolks and blend in a little cream sauce. Stir in remaining sauce and set aside to cool.

Grease a 2-quart ring mould. Line bottom and sides with sole fillets, skin side up, with tips of fillets draped over edge of mould. Place salmon, paprika and chervil in one bowl and broccoli and nutmeg in another. Divide cream sauce evenly between them. Mix well and season to taste.

Beat egg whites until stiff. Add half to salmon and half to broccoli. Fold in gently.

Spread broccoli mixture onto fillets, then salmon mixture. Fold fillet tips over. Place buttered round of waxed paper on top. Bake in a water bath at 375 degrees F for 45 minutes. Siphon off excess juices, unmould and serve hot or cold.

Serves 10 to 12 as an appetizer.

—Lillian Steinfeld
Halcott Center, New York

SHRIMP-STUFFED SOLE

1 clove garlic, minced
1 large shallot, diced
3 Tbsp. butter
⅔ cup chopped parsley
⅛ tsp. dill
3 large basil leaves, chopped
juice of ½ lemon
salt & pepper

¼ cup bread crumbs
1 cup cooked, chopped shrimp
1 tomato, peeled, seeded & diced
4 sole fillets
2 tsp. butter
6 thin slices lemon
3 Tbsp. chicken stock
2 Tbsp. white wine

Sauté garlic and shallot in 3 Tbsp. butter, but do not brown. Add ⅓ cup parsley, dill, basil, lemon juice and salt and pepper, and cook gently for 2 minutes. Stir in bread crumbs and shrimp and let stand for 2 minutes. Stir in tomato.

Place sole in greased shallow casserole dish, with half of each fillet lining pan edge. Place ⅓ to ½ cup stuffing on each fillet. Fold other half of fillet over stuffing and tuck end under. Dot fish with 2 tsp. butter, lay lemon slices on top and sprinkle with remaining ⅓ cup parsley. Combine stock and wine and pour over fillets.

Bake, covered, at 350 degrees F for 20 minutes, or until flaky but still moist.

Serves 4.

—Laurie D. Glaspey
Oakridge, Oregon

SZECHUAN SHRIMP

1 lb. small shrimp, peeled & deveined
1½ Tbsp. cornstarch
1 egg white
¼ cup diced bamboo shoots
¼ cup chopped green onions
¼ cup chopped green pepper
½ tsp. crushed hot red pepper
1 clove garlic, minced

1 Tbsp. grated gingerroot
½ cup chicken stock
5 Tbsp. tomato paste
½ tsp. soy sauce
2 Tbsp. dry sherry
½ tsp. sesame oil
2 cups plus 2 Tbsp. peanut oil
salt

Rinse shrimp in cold water and pat dry. Combine cornstarch and egg white and mix well. Add shrimp and stir to coat. Let stand for 5 hours. Combine bamboo shoots, green onions, green pepper, hot red pepper, garlic and gingerroot. Set aside.

Blend together stock, tomato paste, soy sauce, sherry and sesame oil. Set aside. Heat 2 cups peanut oil in wok. Cook shrimp for 1 minute, then remove shrimp from oil. Drain oil from wok. Heat remaining 2 Tbsp. oil in wok. Cook shrimp and vegetable mixture quickly over high heat. Add tomato-paste mixture, and cook until shrimp are coated and mixture is heated through. Add salt to taste.

Serves 2.

—Trudy McCallum
Oshawa, Ontario

MALPEQUE OYSTER STEW

¾ cup unsalted butter
1 cup finely chopped celery
1 cup thinly sliced leeks
1 cup finely grated carrots
1 onion, finely chopped
½ cup whole wheat flour
2 cups light cream

2 cups milk
1 cup minced clams with liquor
  (about 5 large clams)
2 cups shucked oysters with liquor
  (about 30 oysters)
pepper
fresh coriander or parsley

Melt ½ cup butter in saucepan, stir in vegetables, cover tightly and cook over low heat for 30 minutes, stirring occasionally.

Meanwhile, in medium saucepan, melt remaining butter, whisk in flour and cook over medium heat for 2 to 3 minutes, but do not brown. Remove from heat and gradually whisk in cream and milk. Return to heat, and cook until sauce is smooth and thickened, whisking constantly. Stir sauce into vegetables.

In another saucepan, combine clams and oysters with liquors. Cook, uncovered, over low heat for 10 minutes or until oysters just start to curl. Stir seafood into vegetable mixture and heat through gently. Season with pepper to taste and garnish each serving with a sprig of coriander or parsley.

Serves 8.

—Tyne Valley Tea Room
Tyne Valley, Prince Edward Island

STEAMED OYSTERS ON THE HALF SHELL

Shuck oysters, saving the juice. Place oysters in half shell on baking dish. To each oyster add salt, small piece of minced garlic and a dab of butter. Cover with ½ slice bacon. Bake at 350 degrees F for 15 minutes, or until bacon is cooked.

—John Isenhower
Seaford, Delaware

SESAME SHRIMP & ASPARAGUS

SERVE THIS DISH OVER RICE ACCOMPANIED BY A SALAD OF MIXED GREENS.

1 Tbsp. sesame seeds
⅓ cup oil
1½ lbs. asparagus, cut into 2″ pieces

2 small onions, sliced
1½ lbs. shrimp
4 Tbsp. soy sauce

Toast sesame seeds until golden in dry skillet over medium heat. Set aside.

Heat oil and cook asparagus, onions and shrimp for 5 minutes over medium-high heat. Stir in sesame seeds and soy sauce.

Serves 4.

SEAFOOD-STUFFED AVOCADOS

THIS WAS A BIG HIT WITH OUR TESTERS. THE TEXTURES AND FLAVOURS COMPLEMENT EACH other perfectly.

2 Tbsp. butter
1 onion **or** 3 green onions, chopped
1 stalk celery, finely chopped
6-8 large mushrooms, chopped
6 oz. light cream
2 Tbsp. flour
4 oz. dry white wine

4 oz. lobster, cooked & chopped
4 oz. shrimp, cooked & chopped
4 oz. crabmeat, cooked & chopped
2 large avocados, halved
salt & pepper
sweet paprika

In large skillet, melt butter and sauté onions, celery and mushrooms. When just limp, blend cream and flour together and add to vegetables. Cook slowly, stirring, and add wine. When hot, add seafood and remove from heat. Mound in avocado halves and sprinkle with salt and pepper and paprika.

Serves 4.

—Linda Powidajko
Oakville, Ontario

SEAFOOD CASSEROLE

½ lb. crabmeat
½ lb. shrimp
½ lb. scallops
⅓ cup butter
½ lb. mushrooms, sliced
2 onions, chopped
½ cup flour

1 tsp. dry mustard
2 cups milk
1 cup heavy cream
salt & pepper
2 Tbsp. sherry
1 cup grated Swiss cheese

Boil crabmeat, shrimp and scallops together for 5 minutes. Drain and set aside.

Melt butter, then sauté mushrooms and onions until tender. Stir in flour and mustard, and cook for 1 to 2 minutes. Slowly stir in milk and cream and cook until thickened. Add salt and pepper, seafood and sherry. Remove from heat and allow to cool. Spoon into greased casserole dish and cover with grated cheese.

Bake, uncovered, at 300 degrees F until browned – 30 minutes.

Serves 4.

PAELLA

LIKE MOST REGIONAL DISHES, PAELLA VARIES IN INGREDIENTS FROM COOK TO COOK. THIS version combines meat and seafood in a colourful, festive presentation. Other possible ingredients include sausage, octopus, clams and crayfish or lobsters.

2 cups fresh peas **or** green beans
2 lbs. halibut, cut into chunks
1 lb. mussels, scrubbed
1 lb. shrimp, shelled & deveined
½ lb. squid, cleaned & cut into rings
1 tsp. saffron threads
½ cup olive oil
½ lb. ham, cubed

1 whole chicken breast, boned & cut into chunks
2 tomatoes, sliced
1 large clove garlic, sliced
2 Tbsp. sweet paprika
3 cups dry rice
2 red peppers, roasted, peeled & cut into strips

Cook peas or beans in water until just tender. Drain, saving water. Add enough water to vegetable water to make 5 cups, bring to a boil, add fish, mussels, shrimp and squid and simmer for 5 minutes. Remove mussels and set aside.

Lift out remaining seafood and set aside. Add saffron to cooking water and let stand. In large oven-proof skillet, heat olive oil. Sauté ham and chicken until just done and set aside. In same oil, sauté tomatoes and garlic. Add paprika and cook gently for a couple of minutes. Sprinkle rice into pan, cover with peas or beans, halibut, shrimp, squid, ham and chicken. Pour water with saffron over top and bring to a boil. Continue boiling while arranging mussels and strips of pepper on top.

Bake, uncovered, at 400 degrees F for 15 minutes. Remove from oven and cook on top of stove for 1 to 2 minutes.

Serves 8.

CHEESY CRAB IN FILO

MADE AS DIRECTED, IN TWO LONG ROLLS, THIS WORKS WELL AS A MAIN COURSE. TO SERVE AS an appetizer, cut the filo and roll individually. Leftover filo dough can be well wrapped and frozen.

½ cup chopped green onions
½ cup butter
1 cup dry white wine
12 oz. crabmeat
4 oz. cream cheese
¼ cup chopped parsley

4 egg yolks, lightly beaten
1 tsp. salt
½ tsp. pepper
1 pkg. filo dough
melted butter
1 egg, beaten

Sauté onions in butter for 3 to 4 minutes. Add wine and bring to a boil. Boil for 3 to 5 minutes until liquid is reduced by half, then remove from heat. Stir in crabmeat, cheese, parsley, egg yolks, salt and pepper. Stir until cheese is melted, then set aside to cool.

Place 1 filo leaf on waxed paper. Brush with melted butter. Repeat 3 more times. Place half the crab mixture on the filo, close to the bottom, leaving a 2-inch border. Roll up, folding in ends. Repeat with more filo and remaining crab mixture.

Place on greased cookie sheet. Brush with beaten egg. Bake at 350 degrees F for 15 minutes, then at 450 degrees F for 10 minutes.

Serves 4 to 6.

—Nancy Blenkinsop
Burlington, Ontario

SCALLOPS PROVENÇALE

Since sea scallops are larger than bay scallops, the cooking time will need to be adjusted accordingly if one is substituted for the other.

2 Tbsp. peanut oil
1 lb. Atlantic scallops
1 tsp. butter
1 Tbsp. finely chopped shallots
1 clove garlic, crushed
1 cup sliced mushrooms

½ cup diced tomato
sesame oil
1 tsp. Pernod
½ tsp. paprika
juice of ½ lemon
garnish of chopped green onion & dill

Heat oil until very hot. Add scallops and sauté for 1 minute. Drain off all liquid, then add butter, shallots and garlic. Sauté for 1 minute more, then add mushrooms and tomato. Season with sesame oil, Pernod, paprika and lemon juice and cook until liquid is reduced. Serve in scallop shells with garnish.

Serves 2.

—A. Camm
Teeswater, Ontario

CRABMEAT & WATERCRESS SALAD WITH KIWI VINAIGRETTE

This is a very quick salad to assemble, but it looks and tastes exotic.

2 bunches watercress, stemmed
6 oz. crabmeat, cooked
6 Tbsp. oil
4 Tbsp. white wine vinegar

2 tsp. Dijon mustard
4 tsp. puréed kiwi fruit
salt & pepper
1 kiwi, chopped

Arrange watercress on 2 plates. Place crabmeat on top. Combine oil, vinegar, mustard, puréed kiwi and salt and pepper and mix thoroughly. Pour over salad. Garnish with chopped kiwi.

Serves 2.

—Lynn Tobin
Thornhill, Ontario

AVOCADO FILLED WITH CRAB & ALMONDS

The differing textures of crunchy apple, toasted almonds and smooth avocados combine with the crabmeat to create an unusual and special dish.

2 avocados
lemon juice
2 Tbsp. mayonnaise
½ cup heavy cream, whipped
2 drops Tabasco sauce

½ tsp. anchovy paste
2 Tbsp. almonds, toasted
3 oz. crabmeat
salt & pepper
½ apple, finely chopped

Halve and pit the avocados and sprinkle with lemon juice. Combine mayonnaise, whipped cream, Tabasco sauce, anchovy paste, almonds, crabmeat and salt and pepper. Mix well, then fold in apple. Spoon into avocado halves.

Serves 4.

—Sandy Campisano
Weston, Massachusetts

CRAB HORS D'OEUVRES

2 Tbsp. butter
2 Tbsp. flour
½ cup milk
½ lb. crabmeat, cooked & chopped
cayenne

3 green onions, chopped
4 Tbsp. chopped parsley
1 cup cracker crumbs
2 eggs, beaten with 1 Tbsp. water
oil for frying

Melt butter, stir in flour, then milk and cook over low heat until thickened – 3 to 5 minutes. Add crabmeat, cayenne, green onions and parsley. Chill for 2 hours, then roll into balls, using 1 Tbsp. for each ball. Roll in crumbs, eggs, then crumbs again. Fry in oil until browned, turning once.

Makes approximately 20 balls.

—Billie Sheffield
North Gower, Ontario

TARRAGON MUSSELS

FOR TARRAGON LOVERS ONLY, THIS DISH MAKES A TASTY APPETIZER. "I AM A POTTER AND I MADE some pots to serve this dish in. Just an ordinary pot with a lid, but the lid serves as a bowl in which to discard the shells."

4 Tbsp. butter
4-5 green onions, chopped
4 dozen mussels, scrubbed
2 tsp. flour

½ cup white wine
2 tsp. tarragon
cayenne

Melt butter and sauté green onions. Add mussels, then stir in flour, wine, tarragon and cayenne. Cover and cook over medium heat for 6 minutes.

Serves 8 as an appetizer.

—Doris McIlroy
Kanata, Ontario

PRAWNS IN COCONUT MILK

"MY HUSBAND AND I WORK AT A LARGE OPEN-PIT COAL MINE. THIS RECIPE CAME FROM A FIJIAN family working at the mine. We serve it with basmati rice, raita and chutney. Coconut milk can be bought at specialty food marts and ethnic food stores. It can also be made by pouring hot milk over grated coconut."

½ cup butter
1 onion, chopped
3 large cloves garlic, crushed
2 tsp. coriander
2 tsp. turmeric
½ tsp. cayenne

1 tsp. chili powder
½ tsp. ginger
salt & pepper
2 Tbsp. white vinegar
1 cup coconut milk
1½ lbs. large prawns, shelled & deveined

Melt butter in a wok and add the onion and garlic. Sauté over low heat until soft. Mix spices and vinegar into a paste with mortar and pestle. Add to mixture in pan and sauté for another few minutes, stirring constantly. Add coconut milk and turn up heat. Cook until thickened – 5 minutes. Add prawns and stir until coated. Simmer for a few minutes until prawns are just cooked.

Serves 4 to 5.

—Tracy Carroll
Sparwood, British Columbia

Poultry & Game

*"Poultry is for the cook what canvas is
for the painter."*

—Brillat-Savarin

If we admit that eating can be a pretty sensuous business, there are a few contributors who come instantly to mind as practitioners of the art of what might be called lusty cooking. In a previous volume, George Belcher would have taken the prize for George's Aphrodisiac Oyster Soup, which recipe came complete with the warning that it "not be eaten until the children are asleep in bed." This year's nominee has to be Barbara Sharp of Burlington, Ontario, who describes her Whiskey Chicken in these words: "Golden pieces of chicken surrounded by green peas, all glistening with buttery sauce and the delicate aroma of whiskey, are seductive enough to bring strong people to their knees."

We're not sure that this is quite what President Herbert Hoover had in mind when he promised "a chicken in every pot, a car in every driveway," but there is little doubt that poultry is now an easily affordable commodity and still one of the favourite "canvases" of the serious—and sensuous—cook.

Long a symbol of affluence and plenty (it is still so regarded in many developing countries), chicken combines excellent taste with economy, low fat and an unfettered versatility in the kitchen. Broiled or fricasseed, skewered or stir-fried, chicken marries well with sauces, glazes and condiments that range from raspberries to maple syrup and curry powder.

The same, of course, can be said for turkey, which is being marketed very successfully as an everyday meat, not something saved for one or two big meals a year. Domesticated turkeys now range in weight from small birds, 4 to 6 pounds, to giants tipping the scales at 40 pounds or more. (We presume that the experimental new behemoth turkeys in the 75-pound range are going to feed the growing demand for turkey franks, turkey burgers and turkey cold cuts.)

The introduction of these and other new products makes it clear that the poultry business is booming—at the expense of pork and beef. In addition to chicken and turkey, the availability of good fresh duck, goose, Cornish hens and even pheasant is on the rise.

So, too, is the supply of fresh and frozen rabbit, all white meat, very low in fat and cholesterol and a more frequent offering on trendy gourmet dinner menus these days. Duck also deserves a try, even if you may have had unhappy experiences with this bird in the past. Properly prepared, a nice duck can make a fine meal; keep the servings small, out of respect for the richness of the meat, and accompany with a sweet sauce, or try one of the tantalizing glazing recipes in this chapter: apple-cinnamon or blueberry-orange, for example.

We can't promise that your guests will be brought to their knees, but it may be worth a try.

WOLFE ISLAND BUTTERMILK CHICKEN

"MY HUSBAND DEVELOPED THIS RECIPE — IT IS THE CRISPIEST CHICKEN YOU'LL EVER TASTE, EVEN when reheated."

6 chicken breasts, halved
salt & pepper
2 cups flour

2 cups buttermilk
oil for frying

Season breasts with salt and pepper (and any other desired herbs). Coat with flour, dip in buttermilk, then coat again with flour.

Heat oil in deep skillet to 350 degrees F, then reduce heat to keep oil at 325 degrees. Cook chicken, a few pieces at a time, for 10 minutes, turning once.

Serves 6.

—*Lorraine Smythe*
Wolfe Island, Ontario

MADEIRA CHICKEN

SIMPLE BUT ELEGANT, WITH A RICH, CREAMY FLAVOUR.

flour for dredging
2 chicken breasts, skinned & boned
2 Tbsp. butter
2 Tbsp. minced shallots

½ cup Madeira
½ cup heavy cream
parsley
sautéed mushrooms (optional)

Lightly flour chicken, then sauté in butter for about 5 to 10 minutes per side. When done, remove and keep warm. Add shallots and sauté, stirring constantly, for 2 to 3 minutes. Add Madeira and bring to a hard boil. Add cream slowly and, stirring occasionally, reduce until thick. Serve over chicken, garnishing with fresh parsley and sautéed mushrooms.

Serves 2.

—*Lori Messer*
Sooke, British Columbia

CHICKEN GISMONDA

⅛ cup bread crumbs
⅛ cup Parmesan cheese
¼ cup melted butter
¼ cup dry sherry
2 chicken breasts, skinned & boned
1 egg, beaten with 1 Tbsp. milk

1 lb. fresh spinach
nutmeg
½ lb. mushrooms, sliced
1 clove garlic, minced
1 cup grated Cheddar cheese

Combine bread crumbs with Parmesan cheese. Set aside. Combine butter with sherry and set aside.

Dip chicken in egg-milk mixture, then coat with bread crumbs and Parmesan cheese. Sauté in one-half of the butter and sherry until brown on both sides. Rinse and trim spinach. Sprinkle lightly with nutmeg. Cover and steam until limp. Sauté mushrooms and garlic in remaining butter-sherry mixture.

To serve: Place chicken breasts on a bed of spinach, top with mushrooms, sprinkle with Cheddar cheese and bake, uncovered, for 20 minutes at 350 degrees F.

Serves 2.

—*Barbara Denz*
Baltimore, Maryland

WHISKEY CHICKEN

"GOLDEN PIECES OF CHICKEN SURROUNDED BY GREEN PEAS, ALL GLISTENING WITH BUTTERY sauce, and the delicate aroma of whiskey are seductive enough to bring strong people to their knees."

4 boneless chicken breasts	salt & pepper
juice of one lemon	2 oz. (or more) whiskey
flour for dredging	1 cup peas
4 Tbsp. butter	

Pound chicken breasts flat and thin between sheets of waxed paper. Pour lemon juice over meat in shallow glass container. Marinate for at least 1 hour, turning once or twice. Remove from juice and dredge with flour. Melt butter in large skillet and allow butter to foam. Add chicken and cook over medium heat for 2 minutes. Turn chicken over and sprinkle with salt and pepper. Pour 1 oz. whiskey over and slosh it around chicken pieces by shaking pan. Add 1 oz. more whiskey and flame it. Stand back. When flames die down, add peas and shake pan so peas heat in sauce. Cook a minute or so longer, until thoroughly heated.

Serves 3 to 4.

—Barbara Sharp
Burlington, Ontario

CHICKEN WITH TARRAGON & PEARS

2 whole chicken breasts, split, skinned & boned	**Sauce**
2-4 Tbsp. butter	¼ cup butter
1 small onion, diced	1 clove garlic, minced
brandy **or** white wine	1 Tbsp. tarragon
1 cup heavy cream	1-2 Tbsp. lemon juice
2 pears, sliced thickly	1 tsp. parsley

Brown chicken in butter. Remove from pan and keep warm. Sauté onion, adding butter if needed. Remove and place with chicken. Deglaze pan with brandy or wine. Return chicken and onion to pan, then stir in cream and pears. Simmer until chicken is cooked.

Meanwhile, prepare sauce: Melt butter and briefly sauté garlic. Stir in tarragon, lemon juice and parsley and cook for 1 minute. Set aside, then add to chicken 5 to 10 minutes before serving.

Serves 4.

—Kathy Payette
Kitchener, Ontario

STUFFED CHICKEN BREASTS

2 whole chicken breasts, halved, skinned & boned	1 egg, beaten with ¼ cup milk
4 slices ham	⅔ cup fine dry bread crumbs
4 oz. Swiss **or** Gruyère cheese, grated	¼ cup butter
flour	1 clove garlic, minced
	2 Tbsp. oil

Pound chicken breasts between sheets of waxed paper to ¼" thickness. In centre of each chicken piece, place 1 slice ham and ¼ of the cheese. Fold chicken over to make a flat rectangle and coat with flour. Dip each piece in egg-milk mixture, then roll in bread crumbs. Place pieces gently on rack and let coating set for at least 30 minutes. Melt butter, then add garlic and oil. Add chicken and cook over medium heat for about 10 minutes on each side, or until done.

Serves 4.

—Pamela Swainson
Vernon Bridge, Prince Edward Island

VEGETABLE & HAM STUFFED CHICKEN BREASTS

THIS MAKES A TASTY AND ELEGANT "COMPANY" DISH AND, SINCE IT FREEZES SUCCESSFULLY, can be made ahead of time. The concept is similar to a "cordon bleu" recipe, but the addition of hazelnuts and vegetables makes this dish much richer.

1 onion, finely chopped
2 carrots, finely chopped
1 stalk celery, finely chopped
4 slices bacon, chopped
4 Tbsp. butter
1 head broccoli, chopped
1 cup chopped hazelnuts
8 oz. cream cheese

4 whole chicken breasts, halved, skinned, boned & pounded flat
8 thin slices ham
1 cup chicken stock
1 cup dry white wine
2 Tbsp. flour
1 cup light cream
parsley

Sauté onion, carrots, celery and bacon in 2 Tbsp. butter until onions are transparent and vegetables are cooked. Add broccoli, ¾ cup hazelnuts and cream cheese and sauté until blended. Line inside of each chicken breast with slice of ham. Spoon stuffing into centre of ham and fold meat over. Lay breast with fold underneath in glass baking dish.

Combine chicken stock and wine, pour over chicken, cover and bake for 1 hour at 350 degrees F. Remove liquid, strain and reserve. Melt remaining 2 Tbsp. butter and mix in flour. Add cream and 1 cup reserved cooking liquid, whisking constantly until it thickens. Do not boil.

Place chicken breasts on serving platter and pour sauce over them. Sprinkle with remaining hazelnuts and parsley.

Serves 8.

—Linda Powidajko
Oakville, Ontario

CHICKEN WITH TOMATOES & CREAM

WHEN MADE WITH HOMEGROWN TOMATOES AND BASIL, THIS IS ESPECIALLY GOOD AS A LIGHT summer supper. Home-frozen tomatoes and basil (just wash, dry thoroughly, chop the basil and freeze in plastic bags) will also result in a fresh summery taste in midwinter.

2 whole chicken breasts, halved
3 Tbsp. butter
1 clove garlic, minced
1 small onion, minced
3 Tbsp. flour

¼ cup white wine
1 cup chopped tomatoes
½ cup light cream
¼ cup chopped fresh basil & parsley, mixed
salt & pepper

Poach chicken breasts in enough salted water to cover, until tender—about 20 minutes. Remove, reserving liquid. Skin and bone chicken and set aside. In large pan, melt butter and sauté garlic and onion. Add flour and stir well. Whisk in ½ cup stock and wine and cook over high heat until sauce is reduced, stirring constantly. Reduce heat to medium, add tomatoes, cream and basil-parsley mixture and cook for 4 to 5 minutes. Fold in chicken. Add salt and pepper. Serve on toast, over rice or in pita pockets.

Serves 4.

—Susan S. Hubbard
Syracuse, New York

CHICKEN BREASTS WITH SPINACH STUFFING & ASIAGO CHEESE SAUCE

ASIAGO IS A HARD COW'S-MILK CHEESE THAT IS SHARPER AND SALTIER THAN PARMESAN. Look for it in specialty cheese displays.

Stuffing
⅓ cup butter
¾ cup chopped green onions
½ pkg. fresh spinach
¼ lb. Black Forest ham
salt & pepper
½ tsp. fennel
¾ cup bread crumbs
½ cup Parmesan cheese
1 tsp. tarragon
nutmeg
1 egg yolk
2 whole chicken breasts, halved, skinned
  & boned
1 tsp. thyme

Asiago Sauce
1½ cups milk
2 Tbsp. butter
2 Tbsp. flour
salt & pepper
1 cup grated Asiago cheese
¼ cup dry white wine
1 Tbsp. chopped parsley
lovage (optional)

In heavy pot, melt ¼ cup butter, add onions and cook until soft. Wash, trim and coarsely chop spinach. Add to butter and onions and cook until leaves are limp, 2 to 3 minutes. Chop ham finely, add to pot and cook for 30 seconds. Remove pan from heat. Mix in salt and pepper, fennel, bread crumbs, Parmesan cheese, tarragon and nutmeg. Set aside to cool, then blend in egg yolk.

Cut a pocket on the thick breastbone side of each chicken breast. Spoon in stuffing, skewer opening shut and press gently to flatten breast. Set in single layer in ovenproof dish. Melt remaining butter, brush over breasts and season with salt and pepper and thyme. Cover with foil and bake at 400 degrees F for 40 minutes or until firm to the touch. Uncover and brown for 5 minutes.

For sauce: Scald milk. Melt butter, stir in flour and cook for 2 to 3 minutes. Pour in hot milk and beat vigorously to make a smooth sauce. Season with salt and pepper and blend in cheese. Just before serving, add wine and parsley. Add lovage if available. To serve, place chicken breasts on hot plate and top with sauce.

Serves 4.

—*Tracy Cane*
Hardwood, Ontario

LEMON MAPLE CHICKEN

THE EXCEPTIONAL FLAVOUR BELIES THE SPEED AND EASE OF ASSEMBLING THIS DISH.

4 chicken legs
½ cup maple syrup
½ cup Dijon mustard

¼ cup fresh lemon juice
1 Tbsp. grated lemon rind
1 tsp. cinnamon

Cut chicken legs at the joint but do not separate. Place in casserole dish. Combine remaining ingredients and pour over chicken. Bake at 375 degrees F for 30 minutes. Baste with pan drippings, then cook for 20 minutes longer or until done. Serve over rice using the degreased pan juices as sauce.

Serves 4.

—*Gail Driscoll*
Dutton, Ontario

HEARTY HARVEST CASSEROLE

Garlicky chicken combined with readily available winter vegetables produce a substantial, tasty, yet low-fat meal.

8 chicken thighs, skin removed
12 cloves garlic, halved
2 large potatoes, cubed
6 oz. mushrooms, sliced
3 onions, quartered
1 tsp. tarragon

1 tsp. basil
1 small acorn squash, cut into eighths
4 canned tomatoes, halved, liquid reserved
½ cup apple cider
⅓ cup red wine
salt & pepper

Make 3 cuts in each thigh and insert a garlic half in each slit. Place one-third of potatoes, one-third of mushrooms and one-third of onions in large casserole dish. Lay 4 thighs on this and sprinkle with half the tarragon and basil. Next, layer half the squash, one-third of each of potatoes, mushrooms and onions, remaining chicken and remaining tarragon and basil. Cover with remaining squash, potatoes, mushrooms and onions. Arrange tomatoes over this.

Combine ½ cup tomato liquid with cider and wine and pour over everything. Sprinkle with salt and pepper. Cover and bake at 375 degrees F for 1 hour. Let rest out of oven, still covered, for 10 to 15 minutes before serving.

Serves 4.

—*Dayna Lee Burnett*
New York, New York

DOWN-HOME CHICKEN & DUMPLINGS

Exquisitely light dumplings and a flavourful sauce make this a special treat.

1 cup flour
1 tsp. paprika
1 frying chicken, cut up
3 Tbsp. oil
1 cup chicken stock
½ cup white wine
1 tsp. curry powder
½ tsp. tarragon

Dumplings
1½ cups flour
1 Tbsp. baking powder
½ tsp. salt
1 cup milk

Place flour and paprika in plastic bag. Add chicken pieces and shake to coat. Heat oil in heavy pan with tight-fitting lid. Fry chicken pieces until golden, removing to platter as they brown.

To liquid in pan, add stock, wine, curry powder and tarragon. Add chicken and simmer, covered, until tender—about 1½ hours.

For dumplings: Sift flour and measure, then resift with baking powder and salt. Add milk and stir just until dry ingredients are dampened. Batter will be slightly lumpy. Dip a tablespoon into the hot chicken liquid to keep batter from sticking to the spoon. Drop by spoonfuls on top of chicken pieces. Cover and cook for 12 minutes, turning heat up slightly. Do not raise cover.

Put dumplings on a heated platter and surround them with chicken pieces. Serve gravy separately.

Serves 4.

—*Edie Spring*
Licking, Missouri

SESAME BAKED CHICKEN

"THE SESAME COATING ON THIS CHICKEN DELIGHTS EVERYONE'S TASTE BUDS. MY DAD AND I USED to race to see who could scrape out the most leftover 'crispies' from the bottom of the pan."

½ cup butter
1⅓ cups fine cracker crumbs
½ cup toasted sesame seeds

2-3-lb. fryer chicken, cut up
⅓ cup evaporated milk

Melt butter in 9" x 13" baking pan in the oven. Combine cracker crumbs and sesame seeds. Dip chicken pieces in evaporated milk, then roll in cracker mixture to cover. Dip skin side of chicken pieces in butter, turn over, and arrange in baking dish. Bake, uncovered, at 350 degrees F for 1½ hours.

Serves 4.

—LaRae DuFresne Bergo
Grove City, Minnesota

CHICKEN & BELL PEPPERS

MAKE THIS WITH AS MANY COLOURS OF BELL PEPPERS AS ARE AVAILABLE TO PRODUCE A colourful dish.

4 chicken breasts, skinned & boned
2 Tbsp. seasoned flour
2 Tbsp. butter
2 Tbsp. oil
2 cloves garlic, crushed
1 onion, sliced
12 large mushrooms, sliced

1 cup sliced artichoke hearts
1½-2 cups sliced bell peppers
2 oz. white wine
2 oz. white rum
2-3 tomatoes, peeled & chopped
½ tsp. dried basil

Dredge chicken breasts in seasoned flour. Heat butter and oil in skillet and sauté chicken breasts for 2 to 3 minutes on each side. Add garlic, onion, mushrooms and artichoke hearts and cook for 5 minutes. Add peppers, wine, rum and tomatoes, simmer for 6 minutes, then sprinkle with basil and simmer for about 2 minutes more. Serve over fresh noodles or rice.

Serves 4.

—Jim & Penny Wright
Roxboro, Quebec

RASPBERRY CHICKEN

4 chicken breasts or legs
¼ tsp. salt
⅛ tsp. pepper
2 Tbsp. butter
2 Tbsp. oil
1 pint fresh raspberries
3 Tbsp. white or rosé wine

1 small clove garlic, crushed
1 Tbsp. minced parsley
¼ cup chicken stock
1 tsp. crushed green peppercorns
2 Tbsp. butter, cut into pieces
sliced, sautéed mushrooms (optional)

Sprinkle chicken with salt and pepper. Heat butter and oil in large frying pan and brown chicken on all sides. Mash half the berries through a sieve to remove seeds. Refrigerate the remainder. In small bowl, combine mashed berries, wine, garlic, parsley and stock. Pour over chicken, cover and cook for 15 minutes, or until chicken is tender. Remove chicken to serving dish and keep warm. Stir crushed peppercorns into sauce. Remove pan from heat and stir in butter pieces until they melt and sauce is well blended. Pour sauce over hot chicken and garnish with reserved raspberries and mushrooms.

Serves 4 to 6.

—Mr. & Mrs. Dale Brooks
New Berlin, Illinois

CHICKEN CACCIATORE

Spicy and highly flavourful, this chicken cacciatore is an interesting departure from traditional cacciatore recipes.

2-3 lbs. chicken pieces
28-oz. can tomatoes
7-oz. can tomato sauce
1 cup chopped onions
½ cup chopped green pepper
2 stalks celery, chopped
2 carrots, chopped
4 cloves garlic, minced

½ cup dry red wine
1 tsp. salt
½ tsp. allspice
2 bay leaves
½ tsp. thyme
pepper
cayenne

Remove skin from chicken pieces, then cut meat into serving-sized pieces. Combine remaining ingredients in large pot and bring to a boil. Add chicken, cover, reduce heat and simmer for about 2 hours, or until chicken and carrots are tender. Remove bay leaves. The cover may be removed for the last half hour of cooking to reduce and thicken sauce slightly. Serve with rice or noodles.

Serves 4.

—Judith Asbil
Beaconsfield, Quebec

BELGIAN CHICKEN

3-4 lbs. chicken pieces
flour
salt & pepper
3 Tbsp. butter
½ cup chopped onion

1 cup dry white wine
1 cup chopped mushrooms
½ cup golden raisins
¾ cup light cream
chopped parsley

Coat chicken pieces in flour seasoned with salt and pepper. Sauté in butter until light brown. Add onion and cook until tender. Add wine and mushrooms, cover and simmer for 30 to 35 minutes. Add raisins and cook for 5 minutes. Remove chicken pieces and place in a warmed dish. Add cream to the gravy, reheat and pour over chicken. Sprinkle chicken with chopped parsley and serve over rice or noodles.

Serves 4.

—Joanne Avelar
Atwater, California

CHICKEN MANDARIN

2½-3 lbs. chicken, cut up
flour, seasoned with salt & pepper
1 Tbsp. oil
1 cup chicken stock
2 Tbsp. Worcestershire sauce

⅓ cup orange juice
2 tsp. cornstarch
1 can mandarin orange segments, drained
2-3 cups 'Sugar Snap' or edible pod peas

Coat chicken with flour and brown in oil in large skillet. Add chicken stock, Worcestershire sauce and orange juice. Cover and simmer for 1 hour or until tender. Remove chicken and cut meat from bones. Blend cornstarch with 2 tsp. cold water; stir into pan liquids. Bring to a boil, stirring until thickened. Add oranges, peas and boneless chicken. Cover and heat until peas have just changed colour—3 to 5 minutes. Serve over rice or noodles.

Serves 4.

—Roseann LaPlace
Colinton, Alberta

CHICKEN FRICASSEE

½ cup flour
1 tsp. salt
½ tsp. freshly ground pepper
¼ tsp. mace
¼ tsp. nutmeg
5-lb. frying chicken, cut up
⅓ cup oil

½ lb. mushrooms, sliced
1 large onion, sliced
3 cups chicken stock
¼ cup sour cream
¼ cup white wine
¼ tsp. prepared mustard
1 tsp. tomato paste

Mix flour, salt, pepper, mace and nutmeg. Roll dampened pieces of chicken in flour mixture to coat on all sides. Heat oil in large skillet over high heat. Brown chicken, then remove to a plate. Reduce heat, add mushrooms and onion and cook until soft. Add chicken and stock and bring to a boil. Reduce heat, cover, and simmer until very tender – 1 to 2 hours.

Just before serving, skim off fat and stir in a mixture of sour cream, wine, mustard and tomato paste.

Serves 4.

—Norma Somers
Boissevain, Manitoba

CHICKEN & APRICOTS

3 lbs. chicken pieces, skin removed
4 Tbsp. butter
2 large onions, sliced
2 Tbsp. flour
¼ tsp. nutmeg
paprika

salt & pepper
1 cup apricot juice
1 cup chicken stock
1 green pepper, sliced
1 lb. dried apricots, soaked overnight

Lightly brown chicken pieces in butter and remove from pan. In same pan, sauté onions until soft. Add flour, nutmeg, paprika and salt and pepper. Cook for one minute. Add apricot juice and chicken stock and bring to a boil, stirring constantly. Return chicken pieces to pan. Lower heat, cover and simmer for 30 minutes. Add green pepper and apricots. Simmer for another 15 minutes. Serve over brown rice.

Serves 6 to 8.

—Patricia Daine
Dartmouth, Nova Scotia

AFRICAN CHICKEN

¼ cup butter
1 small onion, diced
1 Tbsp. ground coriander
1½ tsp. salt
3-lb. chicken, cut up

½ cup chicken stock
1 Tbsp. lemon juice
2 Tbsp. flour
1 cup yogurt

Combine butter, onion, coriander and salt. Roll chicken in this mixture. Place in slow cooker, then pour chicken stock and lemon juice over. Cover and cook on low setting for 8 hours or less. Stir flour into yogurt, then stir into chicken just before serving.

Serves 4.

—Midge Denault
Lee Valley, Ontario

POULE AU POT (FRENCH STEWED CHICKEN)

1 cup bread crumbs
2 cloves garlic, chopped
½ onion, chopped
2 slices ham, chopped
giblets, chopped
1 tsp. thyme
½ tsp. basil
½ tsp. sage
2 eggs, beaten
4-6-lb. stewing chicken

10 cups seasoned chicken stock
2 leeks
1 Spanish onion studded with 2 cloves
3 carrots, halved
2 turnips, halved
4 potatoes, quartered
1 small cabbage, quartered
½ cup barley
flour

Combine bread crumbs, garlic, onion, ham, giblets, thyme, basil and sage. Mix well, then stir in eggs. Place stuffing in chicken. Place chicken and chicken stock in large heavy pot. Bring to a boil, reduce heat, cover and simmer for 1 hour. Add vegetables and barley and simmer for 40 minutes more.

Remove chicken and vegetables to serving dish and keep warm. Thicken gravy with flour (mix a bit of gravy with flour, then stir into pot) and pour over chicken and vegetables.

Serves 6.

—Malcolm Flowerday
Brossard, Quebec

BAKED CHICKEN ROSEMARY

THE TANGY BARBECUE-STYLE SAUCE WORKS WELL OVER PORK, LAMB OR CHICKEN.

1 frying chicken, cut up
salt & pepper
1 clove garlic, minced
1 tsp. paprika
1 Tbsp. onion, finely minced
½ cup vinegar

½ cup tomato sauce
½ cup water
1 tsp. rosemary leaves
1 Tbsp. prepared mustard
2 Tbsp. brown sugar **or** honey
1 tsp. soy sauce

Arrange chicken pieces one layer deep in 9" x 13" baking pan. Sprinkle with salt and pepper, garlic, paprika and onion. Combine remaining ingredients and pour over chicken. Bake at 325 degrees F until fork-tender – about 1 hour. Serve with rice.

Serves 3 to 4.

—Mary Irwin-Gibson
Dunham, Quebec

CHICKEN IN MUSTARD SAUCE

1½ lbs. chicken pieces
¼ cup flour
½ tsp. salt
1 clove garlic, crushed
2 Tbsp. grated onion

2 Tbsp. butter
½ Tbsp. lemon juice
¾ tsp. dry mustard
1 tsp. sugar
½ Tbsp. cornstarch

Coat chicken pieces in mixture of flour, salt, garlic and onion. Fry in butter until lightly browned. Add ½ cup water, cover and cook for 30 minutes. Combine remaining ingredients and add to liquid in pan. Turn pieces to coat with sauce, cover and cook for an additional 30 minutes or until tender. Uncover and place under hot broiler for a few minutes before serving.

Serves 2.

—Rose Strocen
Canora, Saskatchewan

MEXICAN SPICED CHICKEN

THIS IS A SPICY, HOT CHICKEN DISH WITH LOTS OF SAUCE.

4 Tbsp. olive oil
3 lbs. chicken, cut up
2 cloves garlic, chopped
1 thin slice white bread
1 onion, chopped
2 or more canned serrano chilies

⅛ tsp. cloves
⅛ tsp. cinnamon
3 large tomatoes **or** 1 cup canned tomatoes
1 cup chicken stock
salt & pepper
½ cup dry sherry (optional)

Heat oil in skillet and sauté chicken until golden. Remove and keep warm. In same skillet, sauté garlic and bread, then onion. Break up bread and place with onion, garlic, chilies, cloves, cinnamon, tomatoes and a little chicken stock in blender or food processor and purée. Pour sauce into nonferrous skillet with a lid. Simmer for a few minutes, adding remaining stock. Add chicken pieces, cover and simmer until chicken is tender – about 1 hour. Salt and pepper to taste and add sherry just before serving.

Serves 3 to 4.

—Beth Toron
Cross Creek, New Brunswick

CHICKEN STROGANOFF

3 Tbsp. oil
4 chicken breasts, skinned, boned & cut
  into thin strips
½ tsp. salt
1 tsp. pepper
1 clove garlic, minced
3 onions, sliced

1 cup sliced mushrooms
3 Tbsp. flour
6 Tbsp. white wine
2 cups chicken stock, heated
⅔ cup sour cream
1 Tbsp. tomato paste

Heat oil in heavy pan. Sear chicken pieces, season with salt and pepper and remove. Mix chicken with garlic and keep warm. Cook onions and mushrooms in pan until onions are transparent. Add extra oil if needed. Stir in flour to make a roux. Add wine, hot stock, sour cream and tomato paste, stirring it into a smooth mixture. Add chicken and garlic. Simmer gently for 20 minutes, or until chicken is tender. Serve in a ring of hot buttered noodles.

Serves 4.

—Ann Coyle
Fergus, Ontario

OVEN-CRISP CHICKEN

OUR VERMONT TESTER SAYS, "HURRAH! THIS CHICKEN HAS AN UNUSUAL AND FLAVOURFUL coating; it is very tender and moist and not at all greasy."

¾ cup cracker crumbs
½ cup Parmesan cheese
½ cup ground pecans
2 eggs

1 cup buttermilk
3-4-lb. broiler chicken, cut up
melted butter

Combine cracker crumbs, cheese and pecans. Beat together eggs and buttermilk. Roll chicken pieces in crumb mixture until evenly coated, dip in egg mixture, then roll in crumbs again. Place a single layer in lightly oiled 9" x 13" baking dish. Brush lightly with melted butter.

Bake, brushing occasionally with more butter, at 400 degrees F for 1 hour.

Serves 4.

—Nancy R. Franklin
San Jose, California

CHICKEN WITH BROCCOLI

"THIS IS A FAMILY FAVOURITE. BAKED IN A 'RAW COOKWARE' CLAY POT, IT HAS A WONDERFUL, almost smoky flavour. It's good served with buttered noodles or baked potatoes to soak up the extra sauce."

2 Tbsp. flour
1½ tsp. salt
pepper
½ tsp. tarragon
3-lb. chicken, cut into serving pieces

2 Tbsp. olive oil
juice of ½ lemon
1 cup sour cream
2 oz. grated Cheddar cheese
1 head broccoli, broken into florets

Presoak clay pot in water for 15 minutes.

Combine flour, salt, pepper and tarragon in plastic bag. Add chicken pieces two at a time and shake to coat. Brown chicken quickly in oil, then arrange in pot. Squeeze lemon juice on top of chicken.

Add sour cream and rest of flour mixture to drippings in frying pan. Stir, then pour over chicken. Sprinkle cheese over top. Place covered pot in cold oven, then set temperature at 450 degrees F and cook for 35 minutes. Add broccoli, then cook for an additional 10 minutes.

Serves 4.

—Susan Holec
Brooklyn, Wisconsin

LEMON CHICKEN

4 chicken breasts, skinned & boned
1 egg
flour
2 Tbsp. peanut oil
2½ Tbsp. cornstarch

¼ cup lemon juice
grated rind of 1 lemon
⅓ cup sugar
¼ tsp. ginger
rind of ½ lemon, cut into thin strips

Cut chicken into 1-inch strips. Beat egg with 2 Tbsp. water. Dip chicken in this, then dredge in flour. Heat peanut oil in skillet or wok and fry chicken, removing pieces once they are cooked. Mix remaining ingredients except strips of lemon rind. Bring to a boil in skillet. Add chicken and lemon rind to the mixture and heat for 5 minutes.

Serves 4.

—Mary-Lee Judah
Hinton, Alberta

STIR-FRY CHICKEN & SNOW PEAS

1 cup boned, cubed, raw chicken
2 Tbsp. oil
3 Tbsp. soy sauce
¼ tsp. pepper
1 cup snow peas

6 scallions, sliced diagonally
2 carrots, grated
2 Tbsp. cornstarch
1 cup chicken stock

Stir-fry chicken in hot oil in wok or skillet until almost done—about 2 minutes. Add soy sauce and pepper and stir. Add snow peas and stir-fry for about 2 minutes. Add scallions and carrots, stir, cover, and cook for another 3 minutes, stirring frequently. Mix the cornstarch and chicken stock and add to wok, stirring until the sauce thickens. Serve over hot rice.

Serves 4.

—Barry LeClair
Brooklyn, New York

TROPICAL CHICKEN

2 whole chicken breasts, skinned & boned
2 Tbsp. oil
¼ cup soy sauce
2 cloves garlic, crushed
1 tsp. finely chopped fresh gingerroot
pepper
1 cup peeled, ripe papaya slices
1 large green pepper, sliced
cooked rice

Cut chicken into 1-inch pieces. Heat oil in large frying pan. Add chicken pieces and brown on all sides. Pour off fat and add soy sauce. Add garlic, ginger and pepper to taste.

Cover and cook over low heat until almost tender. Add papaya and pepper slices and cook just until heated through – about 5 minutes. Serve over hot rice.

Serves 4.

—Irene Louden
Port Coquitlam, British Columbia

CHICKEN IN PARMESAN SAUCE

"EASY TO MAKE AND VERY GOOD," REPORTS THE VERMONT TEST KITCHEN.

3 lbs. chicken breasts, skinned & boned
salt & pepper
3 Tbsp. oil
3 Tbsp. butter
3 Tbsp. flour
1½ cups milk
¼ cup dry white wine
1½ Tbsp. lemon juice
½ cup Parmesan cheese
3 egg yolks, beaten
½ cup bread crumbs
½ tsp. rosemary

Cut chicken into strips, sprinkle with salt and pepper and brown in oil in hot skillet. Remove chicken and set aside. Melt butter in same skillet and blend in flour. Add milk and whisk over low heat until smooth and thickened. Add wine and lemon juice, and increase heat to medium-high. When mixture begins to boil, reduce heat to low and add ¼ cup cheese. Once cheese has melted, add egg yolks and stir well.

Place ⅛ cup cheese and ¼ cup bread crumbs in bottom of flat casserole dish. Arrange chicken on top followed by sauce, then remaining bread crumbs and cheese. Sprinkle with rosemary. Bake at 375 degrees F for 20 minutes, covered, and 10 minutes uncovered.

Serves 4 to 6.

—Mary-Lee Judah
Hinton, Alberta

CHINESE-STYLE ASPARAGUS CHICKEN

4 chicken breasts, boned & cut into
  1" cubes
¼ cup cornstarch
4 Tbsp. oil
1 Tbsp. chopped onion
1 lb. fresh asparagus, cut into 1" pieces
4 large mushrooms, sliced
¼ cup slivered almonds
2 Tbsp. soy sauce
1 Tbsp. freshly grated gingerroot
1 cup chicken stock

Shake chicken in cornstarch to coat. In wok or heavy frying pan, brown chicken in oil. Add vegetables, almonds, soy sauce and ginger. Cook, stirring, for 2 minutes. Add chicken stock and stir for an additional 2 minutes. Spoon over rice.

Serves 4.

—Ingrid Magnuson
Winnipeg, Manitoba

ALMOND GAI DING

"I enjoyed this dish so much when I had it in a restaurant that I developed my own recipe for it at home. Its success depends upon fresh vegetables."

1 egg white	1 onion, chopped
1 Tbsp. light soy sauce	2 stalks celery, sliced diagonally
sesame oil	1-2 carrots, sliced diagonally
2 chicken breasts, skinned, boned and cut into bite-sized pieces	1 cup cauliflower florets
3 Tbsp. oil	1 cup sliced mushrooms
½ cup slivered almonds	½ can water chestnuts, sliced
1 clove garlic, minced	1 Tbsp. cornstarch
2 thin slices gingerroot	

Combine egg white, soy sauce and a few drops of sesame oil. Marinate chicken in this while continuing with recipe.

Heat 1 Tbsp. oil in wok and brown almonds. Remove almonds and set aside. Add another tablespoon of oil to wok and sauté garlic and ginger for a few seconds. Add chicken. Stir-fry until just cooked – 2 to 3 minutes – then remove from wok.

Add remaining 1 Tbsp. oil to wok. Stir-fry onion, celery and carrots until carrots are just crispy-tender – 5 to 8 minutes. Add cauliflower, mushrooms and water chestnuts.

Continue cooking, stirring frequently, until vegetables reach desired doneness. Stir in chicken. Dissolve cornstarch in 2 Tbsp. water, and stir in. Cook until thickened.

Serves 4.

—Adele Dueck
Lucky Lake, Saskatchewan

CASHEW CHICKEN

This dish, often with almonds replacing the cashews, is a standard in Cantonese Chinese restaurants. It is quick and simple to prepare at home.

2 Tbsp. plus 2 tsp. cornstarch	2 cups sliced mushrooms
1 cup chicken stock	½ lb. snow peas
5 Tbsp. soy sauce	1 onion, sliced
2 lbs. chicken breasts, skinned & boned	1 clove garlic, minced
4 Tbsp. oil	1 cup cashews
4 stalks celery, sliced	cooked rice

Combine 2 tsp. cornstarch with chicken stock and 1 Tbsp. soy sauce. Set aside.

Slice chicken into strips. Blend remaining 2 Tbsp. cornstarch with remaining 4 Tbsp. soy sauce in a bowl and stir in chicken. Heat 2 Tbsp. oil in large frying pan or wok, add chicken and stir over medium heat for 3 minutes. Remove chicken. Add remaining 2 Tbsp. oil and reheat pan. Add remaining ingredients, except cashews and rice, cover and cook over medium heat for 1 minute, shaking the pan several times. Uncover and cook for another 2 to 4 minutes, stirring occasionally. Add chicken-cornstarch mixture, and stir over medium heat until the sauce thickens – about 3 minutes. Stir in most of the cashews just before serving, reserving a few for garnish. Serve over rice.

Serves 6.

—Diane Milan
Northfield, Minnesota

MILLIONAIRE CHICKEN

IT IS ALMOST IMPOSSIBLE TO DESCRIBE HOW GOOD THIS DISH IS. SERVE IT AS IS, OVER RICE, OR dress it up by also stir-frying snow peas, baby corn and mushrooms. It makes a sensational company meal when served over fried noodle cakes. (Take small bunches of fresh vermicelli noodles and place in wok with a generous amount of hot peanut oil. Pat down to form a pancake and fry, turning once, long enough to stick noodles together and until both sides are golden brown. Drain well before serving.) Tofu can be substituted for the chicken in this dish with an equally tasty result.

4 Tbsp. soy sauce	3 Tbsp. oil
2 Tbsp. honey	2 scallions, chopped
1 clove garlic, crushed	4 slices gingerroot, minced
2 whole chicken breasts, skinned, boned	½-1 tsp. crushed Szechuan pepper
& cut into bite-sized pieces	¼-½ tsp. crushed hot red pepper

Combine soy sauce, honey and garlic and pour over chicken. Let marinate for at least 1 hour.

Heat oil in wok and rapidly sauté scallions, ginger and peppers for 2 to 3 minutes. Reduce heat slightly and add chicken and marinade. Cook, stirring, until chicken is done – 5 minutes. The sauce may be thickened with cornstarch.

Serves 4.

—Evelyn Gervan
Seeley's Bay, Ontario

WRONG WONG'S CHICKEN

"A FAMILY FAVOURITE FOR YEARS, THIS MARINADE AND SAUCE RECIPE CAN ALSO BE USED WITH firm-fleshed fish."

2 chicken breasts, skinned & boned

Marinade
1 egg white
2 tsp. cornstarch
1 Tbsp. cold water

Sauce

1 Tbsp. soy sauce	2 whole dried red peppers
1 Tbsp. cold water	3 scallions, minced
1 Tbsp. white wine vinegar	1 large clove garlic, crushed
1 Tbsp. white sugar	½" gingerroot, chopped
1 Tbsp. cornstarch	2½ Tbsp. peanut oil

Slice chicken into 2-by-¼-inch strips. Mix marinade ingredients, add chicken, stir to coat and set aside for 30 minutes. Combine sauce ingredients in small bowl and set aside. Assemble peppers, scallions, garlic and ginger.

Heat 1½ Tbsp. oil in wok until smoking hot. Add chicken and stir quickly. Chicken will separate and turn white within a few minutes. Remove chicken and drain on towelling. Add 1 Tbsp. oil to wok, heat, then add peppers, scallions, garlic and ginger. Stir-fry for 30 seconds. Add chicken and toss well. Stir sauce and pour over chicken. Stir-fry over high heat until sauce thickens. Serve immediately.

Serves 2.

—Keith McLaren
Victoria, British Columbia

FESTIVE STIR-FRY

QUICK, SIMPLE AND HEALTHY, THIS DISH LOOKS REALLY PRETTY WITH THE BRIGHT RED AND green of the pepper and broccoli.

3 Tbsp. oil
1 large clove garlic, minced
2 chicken breasts, skinned, boned & cubed
1 small head broccoli, cut into florets
1 sweet red pepper, diced
1 small onion, diced
½ lb. mushrooms, sliced

¼ cup sherry
¼ cup soy sauce
2 Tbsp. vinegar
2 Tbsp. brown sugar
1 tsp. ground ginger
1 Tbsp. cornstarch
½ cup water

Heat oil in wok or heavy skillet. Add garlic and chicken. Cook, stirring, over high heat for 3 to 5 minutes. Remove chicken and reheat oil if necessary. Add vegetables and stir-fry for another 3 to 5 minutes. Combine all remaining ingredients, mixing well, and stir into wok. Add chicken, stir until hot and sauce has thickened. Serve over rice.

Serves 2 to 3.

—Penny Rioux
Blue Hill, Maine

DEBBI'S CHICKEN CURRY WITH SAFFRON RICE

AN EXCELLENT CURRY WITH MULTILEVELED SEASONINGS AND JUST A TOUCH OF STING.

Curry
1 lb. chicken breasts, cut into 1" cubes
¼ cup oil
1 cup finely chopped onion
1 clove garlic, crushed
1 tsp. freshly grated gingerroot
½ tsp. ground cumin
½ tsp. turmeric
1 tsp. ground coriander
½ tsp. hot red pepper
¼ tsp. fennel
1 tsp. garam masala
1 cup tomatoes, peeled & chopped
½ cup plain yogurt
1½ tsp. lemon juice

Saffron Rice
1 cup dry basmati rice
½ tsp. saffron threads
1 cinnamon stick
2 whole cloves
½ cup finely chopped onion
3 Tbsp. butter
½ tsp. brown sugar
½ tsp. salt
2 cardamom pods, ground

For curry: Sauté chicken in oil until just cooked. Remove and keep warm. In same pan, sauté onion, garlic and ginger. Reduce heat and add spices. Sauté for 1 minute. Add tomatoes and ¼ cup water and bring to a boil. Reduce heat and simmer for 30 minutes. Add meat and heat through. Add yogurt and lemon juice.

For saffron rice: Wash rice in cold water. Soak saffron in 2 Tbsp. boiling water for 10 minutes, reserving liquid. Fry cinnamon, cloves and onion in butter for 8 minutes. Add rice and fry for an additional 5 minutes. Add 2 cups boiling water, sugar, salt, cardamom, saffron and soaking liquid. Cover and remove from heat. Let sit undisturbed for 30 to 40 minutes, or until rice is cooked.

Serves 4.

—Heidi Juul
North Battleford, Saskatchewan

CHICKEN CURRY

NOT A CURRY YOU WOULD FIND IN A SMALL, RURAL INDIAN VILLAGE, THIS IS A VERY RICH DISH. Serve the delicately flavoured curry with an assortment of condiments — roasted cashews, diced green pepper and celery, mandarin oranges, bananas, coconut, raisins and plain yogurt.

5-6-lb. chicken	2 cloves garlic, chopped
1 onion	1½ cups chopped onion
3 celery tops	¼ tsp. ginger
1 Tbsp. salt	1½-3 Tbsp. curry powder
1 bay leaf	½ cup flour
4 cloves	1 tsp. salt
2½ cups hot milk	1 Tbsp. lemon juice
3 cups coconut	1 cup light cream
½ cup butter	

Place chicken, whole onion, celery tops, salt, bay leaf and cloves in large stockpot with 12 cups water. Bring to a boil, reduce heat and simmer, covered, for 2 hours. Remove chicken and set aside to cool, then remove meat from bones and chop. Strain stock and reserve 2 cups for use in curry.

Pour hot milk over coconut, and let stand for 45 minutes. Melt ¼ cup butter in heavy skillet, then sauté garlic, chopped onion, ginger and curry powder for 3 to 5 minutes. Stir in 2 cups stock, then coconut and milk. Reduce heat and simmer for 1 hour, stirring occasionally. Strain and press, reserving liquid and discarding coconut.

Melt remaining ¼ cup butter, stir in flour, salt and lemon juice. Gradually stir in cream and simmer for 5 minutes. Add chicken and curry sauce and gently heat through.

Serves 8.

A SIMPLE CHICKEN CURRY

"WHEN I WAS LIVING IN BOMBAY, I WAS PART OF A CULTURE-SHARING ORGANIZATION comprising American, Canadian, British and Indian women. This is one of the many interesting recipes that were exchanged." Either buy commercial canned coconut milk, or make it by pouring 2 cups hot milk over 2 cups dried coconut. Let stand for 1 hour, then strain, pressing the coconut hard to release all the milk. Feed the coconut to the birds and use the milk.

2 Tbsp. butter	1 tsp. turmeric
1 onion, chopped	½ tsp. ground ginger
2 cloves garlic, chopped	½ tsp. dry crushed chilies
1 Tbsp. ground coriander	1 frying chicken, cut up
1 tsp. mustard seed	2 cups coconut milk
1 tsp. cumin seed	2 tsp. lime juice

Melt butter, then sauté onion and garlic until golden. Add coriander, mustard, cumin, turmeric, ginger and chilies and cook gently, stirring, for 3 minutes. Add chicken and cook until lightly browned. Add coconut milk and simmer until chicken is cooked through. Season with a little salt and lime juice and serve over rice.

Serves 4 to 5.

—Ethel Hunter
Warkworth, Ontario

DRUMSTICKS BERNARD

CHICKEN WINGS HAVE BECOME A NORTH AMERICAN INSTITUTION OVER THE PAST FEW YEARS, often appearing on bar snack menus. We offer here a number of wing and sauce recipes for at-home use. Cut chicken wings into two sections to make mini drumsticks if this is to be served as a finger food. Otherwise, use regular drumsticks, allowing 2 to 3 (6 to 8 minis) per person. This glaze will do approximately 36 drumsticks.

36 drumsticks **or** 48 wings cut in half
1 cup honey
⅔ cup soy sauce
2 Tbsp. whiskey

2 cloves garlic, crushed
1" gingerroot, slivered
sesame seeds

Arrange drumsticks in deep saucepan, 12 at a time. Combine honey, soy sauce, whiskey, garlic, ginger and 1 cup water and pour over chicken. Simmer for 20 to 30 minutes, remove legs and repeat with same marinade until all legs are cooked.

Refrigerate overnight. Sprinkle with sesame seeds and reheat at 325 degrees F. Reheat and reduce marinade for dipping sauce.

Serves 12 as an appetizer.

—Patricia Daine
Dartmouth, Nova Scotia

SWEET & SOUR CHICKEN WINGS

WHEN WE TESTED THESE WINGS IN OUR VERMONT KITCHEN, THEY WERE VERY POPULAR. The meat was falling-off-the-bone tender, and the sauce adhered well to the wings.

16-20 chicken wings
2 cups brown sugar
2 Tbsp. vinegar

4 Tbsp. soy sauce
1 tsp. chopped garlic

Cut tips off wings. (Freeze tips and add to soup stock the next time you make it.) Place wings in large shallow baking dish. Mix remaining ingredients together and pour over wings. Cover and bake at 350 degrees F for 1 hour, remove cover, turn wings and bake for 40 to 60 minutes more.

Serves 4 to 6.

—Jan Higenbottam
Colgan, Ontario

SESAME CHICKEN WINGS

GOOD, CRUNCHY WINGS. SERVE WITH ANY OF THE THREE DIPS THAT FOLLOW FOR A DELICIOUS snack to have with drinks on a summer afternoon or evening.

3-4 lbs. chicken wings
2 cups flour
½ cup sesame seeds

1 tsp. ginger
1-1½ cups melted butter

Wash and dry wings and cut off tips. Combine flour, sesame seeds and ginger and mix well. Dip wings in butter and shake off excess, then roll in flour mixture. Place on cookie sheet and bake for 45 to 60 minutes at 350 degrees F. Place under broiler briefly to brown.

Serves 12 as an appetizer.

—Gail Driscoll
Dutton, Ontario

CURRIED LEMON DIP

THIS RECIPE AND THE TWO THAT FOLLOW MAKE GOOD DIPS FOR CHICKEN WINGS. THEY CAN also be used as basting sauces.

2 Tbsp. butter
4 cloves garlic, minced
½ tsp. salt
½ tsp. pepper

1 tsp. hot curry powder
2 Tbsp. freshly grated lemon peel
½ cup lemon juice

Melt butter and sauté garlic for 3 minutes. Stir in all other ingredients and simmer for 5 minutes.

SPICY WING SAUCE

1 onion, finely chopped
2 Tbsp. olive oil
2 tsp. coriander
1 tsp. cumin
1 tsp. cinnamon
1 tsp. ground cardamom

¼ tsp. cloves
¼ tsp. cayenne
2 Tbsp. white wine vinegar
1 Tbsp. tomato paste
1 tsp. salt
¼ cup water

Sauté onion in olive oil until transparent. Add remaining ingredients and stir well.

SATAY SAUCE

½ cup smooth peanut butter
⅓ cup soy sauce
⅓ cup lemon juice
⅓ cup sherry

2 Tbsp. brown sugar
1 tsp. Tabasco sauce
2 cloves garlic, finely minced

Combine all ingredients and mix well. Serve warm or at room temperature.

BEST EVER BARBECUE SAUCE

"WE USE THIS SAUCE ON ALMOST EVERYTHING: BEEF, PORK, POULTRY. IT'S GREAT ON CHICKEN wings."

2 Tbsp. butter
1 onion, finely chopped
2 cloves garlic, minced
juice of 1 orange
1 Tbsp. raisins
2 Tbsp. cider vinegar
2 Tbsp. oil
grated zest of 1 orange

1 cup molasses
1 cup tomato sauce
2 tsp. chili powder
⅛ tsp. allspice
1 tsp. prepared mustard
1 tsp. Worcestershire sauce
2 tsp. crushed hot red pepper
½ tsp. salt

Melt butter and add onion and garlic. Cook for 5 minutes. Combine orange juice, raisins, vinegar and oil in food processor or blender until smooth. Add processed ingredients and remaining ingredients to onion-garlic mixture. Heat until boiling, reduce heat and simmer, uncovered, for 15 minutes.

Makes enough sauce for 36 wings.

—Mary Eileen Clear
Baden, Ontario

CREAMED HORSERADISH SAUCE

2 Tbsp. butter
2 Tbsp. flour
1¼ cups light cream
salt

white pepper
3 Tbsp. vinegar
2 Tbsp. sugar
2-3 Tbsp. freshly shredded horseradish

Melt butter in small saucepan. Add flour and stir for a few minutes. Add cream, a little at a time, while stirring. Add salt, white pepper, vinegar, sugar and horseradish. Stir until thickened.

Serve over boiled, boned chicken meat.

—Erik Panum
Quesnel, British Columbia

COLD CHICKEN LOAF

4-lb. chicken
2 onions, halved
2 stalks celery, chopped
1 carrot, chopped
10 peppercorns
2 tsp. salt
¼ cup parsley

2 cups bread crumbs
1 cup milk
2 large eggs, lightly beaten
1 onion, finely chopped
1¼ tsp. salt
¼ tsp. pepper
½ cup chicken stock

Place chicken, onions, celery, carrot, peppercorns, salt and parsley in stockpot. Add water to cover chicken and simmer until tender. Remove chicken from bones and grind or chop in food processor. Strain stock, reserving ½ cup.

In large bowl, combine bread crumbs, milk, eggs, onion, salt and pepper. Add ground chicken and stock and mix well. Line bottom of loaf pan with waxed paper. Butter paper and sides of pan. Fill with chicken mixture. Press mixture down and smooth top. Cover with foil. Poach in a larger pan with 1 inch of water at 375 degrees F for 1 hour. Remove foil and cook an additional 10 minutes. Cool and chill thoroughly before turning out. Tastes best made a day ahead.

Serves 6.

—Kathryn MacDonald
Yarker, Ontario

BITOCHKI (RUSSIAN CHICKEN BURGERS)

1½ lbs. chicken breasts, skinned & boned
1 cup fine bread crumbs
⅓ cup heavy cream
cayenne

½ tsp. salt
½ tsp. pepper
⅛ tsp. nutmeg
2 Tbsp. oil

Cut chicken into chunks and grind in food processor or blender until it is slightly coarse in texture. Put meat into mixing bowl and add ½ cup bread crumbs, cream, cayenne, salt, pepper and nutmeg. Blend thoroughly with hands.

Divide mixture into 6 equal portions. Shape into balls. Roll each ball in remaining crumbs. Press down on balls to form flat patties. Heat oil in frying pan and brown patties on both sides—10 to 12 minutes. Serve in hamburger buns with tartar sauce or mayonnaise and shredded lettuce.

Serves 4 to 6.

—Barbara J. Kirkland
Athens, Ontario

HICKORY HOLLOW GIBLET STEW

LIGHT, AND A GOOD SOURCE OF IRON, THIS STEW IS A TASTY WAY TO GET GIBLETS INTO THE mouths of giblet-haters.

4 Tbsp. olive oil
1 lb. chicken giblets, diced
1 onion, chopped
1 stalk celery, chopped
4 Tbsp. flour
1 tsp. salt
pepper
1 bay leaf

2 Tbsp. parsley
1 tsp. dill
4 cups chicken stock
8-10 potatoes, diced
4 carrots, julienned
1 parsnip, julienned
1 cup puréed zucchini

Heat olive oil and brown giblets, onion and celery. Remove from pot and set aside. Stir flour, salt and pepper into oil until smooth. Add bay leaf, parsley, dill and chicken stock and bring to a boil. Return giblet mixture to pot and add vegetables. Bring to a boil, reduce heat, cover, and simmer for 1 hour. Remove bay leaf. Thicken gravy with flour, if desired.

Serves 4 to 6.

—Helen Shepherd
Lyndhurst, Ontario

CHICKEN OR TURKEY DIVAN

A STANDBY TO USE UP LEFTOVER POULTRY, THIS IS A GOOD HOT SUPPER — A BISCUIT-TOPPED meal in one dish. It is also a recipe that an inexperienced cook would be able to prepare with confidence and serve with pride.

Filling
1 onion, chopped
2 stalks celery, chopped
1 clove garlic, minced
2 Tbsp. butter
1 cup chicken stock
3-4 carrots, diced
½ small turnip, diced
4 potatoes, diced
parsley
savory
2 cups chopped cooked chicken **or** turkey
2 Tbsp. cornstarch mixed with
    ½ cup water

Crust
2 cups flour
4 tsp. baking powder
1 tsp. salt
¼ cup cold shortening
¼ cup cold butter
2 Tbsp. Parmesan cheese
1 cup milk

Brown onion, celery and garlic in butter. Add stock and simmer until vegetables are transparent. Add carrots, turnip, potatoes and water to cover. Bring to a boil and cook until crispy-tender. Add parsley, savory, chicken and cornstarch mixture and cook, stirring, until thickened. Pour into greased casserole dish and set aside.

For crust: Sift together flour, baking powder and salt. Cut in shortening and butter, then add cheese and milk. Mix lightly, then knead 6 to 8 times on floured surface. Roll out and cut into 2-inch biscuits. Place on chicken.

Bake, uncovered, at 375 degrees F for 18 to 20 minutes or until bubbly and browned.

Serves 6.

—Donna Parker
Pictou, Nova Scotia

POJARSKIS

CROQUETTES, AS THE NAME IMPLIES, SHOULD BE CRUNCHY ON THE OUTSIDE BUT HAVE A creamy interior texture. The chilling time before cooking is very important to bind the filling so that it does not fall apart in the frying process. These turkey croquettes are distinctive due to the use of nutmeg and the large proportion of onion.

Croquettes
1 cup soft bread crumbs
½ cup milk
2 cups ground, cooked turkey
½ cup chopped onion
½ tsp. salt
¼ tsp. pepper
1 tsp. nutmeg
flour
¼ cup butter

White Sauce
2 Tbsp. butter
2 cups sliced mushrooms
2 Tbsp. flour
salt & pepper
1 cup milk

Knead bread crumbs with milk, then add ground turkey, onion, salt, pepper and nutmeg. Shape into 4 patties, roll in flour and refrigerate for 1 hour to set shape. Cook in butter for 10 minutes on one side and 5 minutes on the other. Transfer to serving platter and keep warm.

For sauce: Melt butter and briefly sauté mushrooms. Stir in flour, salt and pepper. Gradually stir in milk and cook over medium heat until thickened and smooth. Pour over the patties.

Serves 4.

—Rose Strocen
Canora, Saskatchewan

CURRIED KIWI & CHICKEN SALAD

A LIGHT, REFRESHING SUMMER SALAD WITH A VERY SUCCESSFUL COMBINATION OF TEXTURES and flavours. Serve as a luncheon dish with fresh biscuits or muffins, or use as part of a cold dinner buffet.

½ cup olive oil
2 Tbsp. vinegar
2 Tbsp. lemon juice
½ tsp. paprika
½ tsp. curry
1 clove garlic
¼ tsp. salt

¼ tsp. pepper
4 cups cubed, cooked chicken
⅓ cup toasted slivered almonds (optional)
⅓ cup dark raisins **or** currants
¼ cup flaked coconut
3 kiwi fruit, peeled & thinly sliced

Combine oil, vinegar, lemon juice, paprika, curry, garlic, salt and pepper until well blended. Let sit for 30 minutes, then remove the garlic clove.

Toss chicken in a bowl with almonds, raisins and coconut. Just before serving, line a glass serving bowl with the sliced kiwi fruit. Mix chicken mixture with dressing and pile in centre of bowl. Garnish with kiwi slices.

Serves 4 to 6.

—Irene Louden
Port Coquitlam, British Columbia

CHICKEN BROCCOLI SALAD

PERFECT PICNIC FARE, THIS SALAD CAN BE ADAPTED TO MAKE USE OF A VARIETY OF GREEN vegetables – use whatever is in season. Homemade mayonnaise could be spiced up with garlic or blue cheese to give more zest to the dressing.

1 whole chicken breast, cooked & chopped
1 head broccoli, cut into florets & steamed
1 avocado, chopped
3 green onions, chopped
2 cups dry macaroni shells, cooked & cooled

1 tsp. lemon juice
1 cup mayonnaise
½ tsp. dry mustard
1 tsp. basil
salt & pepper

Combine chicken, broccoli, avocado, onions and macaroni. Sprinkle with lemon juice. Add mayonnaise, mustard, basil and salt and pepper, and toss lightly. Chill.

Serves 6.

—Penny Hartshorn
Banning, California

RICH CHICKEN LIVER PÂTÉ

"I MAKE THIS SMOOTH, RICH PÂTÉ AT CHRISTMAS AND GIVE IT AWAY IN SMALL, EARTHENWARE pots."

1 Spanish onion, finely chopped
4 Tbsp. melted chicken fat
4 Tbsp. rich chicken stock
1 lb. chicken livers
cinnamon, nutmeg & cloves

½ cup heavy cream
2 eggs, lightly beaten
1 Tbsp. cornstarch
4 Tbsp. dry sherry
melted butter

Simmer onion in fat and chicken stock until golden. Add livers and spices. Cover and simmer until tender. When livers are firm, drain and put through food processor. Add cream and eggs. Dissolve cornstarch in sherry and mix thoroughly with livers. Pack into loaf pan or small pots and cook in a water bath at 325 degrees F for 1½ to 2 hours or until firm. Cover top with melted butter and chill for at least 3 days before using.

—Crissie Hunt
Crysler, Ontario

PÂTÉ À L'ORANGE

A DELICIOUS PÂTÉ, THIS RECIPE ELIMINATES THE NEED FOR EGGS, PORK FAT AND A LONG cooking time but retains the rich, luxurious taste.

1 lb. poultry livers
1 lb. lean ground pork
1 onion, chopped
1½ cups butter

1 tsp. coriander
¼ cup Cointreau **or** orange liqueur
½ tsp. pepper
grated orange peel

Sauté livers, pork and onion in ¾ cup butter until cooked through. Put meat mixture, remaining butter, coriander, Cointreau and pepper in blender or food processor. Chop until mixture is smooth. (It may be slightly soupy but will become firm when chilled.) Place in mold and chill for at least 4 hours.

To serve, cut into thin slices and garnish with grated orange peel.

Serves 12 to 16.

—J.R. Galen
Conestoga, Pennsylvania

CHICKEN LIVER PÂTÉ

"THIS IS A RECIPE WHICH ORIGINATED WITH AN AUSTRIAN FRIEND. IT IS EXCELLENT, SMOOTH and buttery and keeps well in the refrigerator for about 3 weeks."

2 onions, chopped
1 clove garlic, chopped
1 Tbsp. butter
nutmeg

salt & pepper
2 cups chicken livers
1 cup butter
1 Tbsp. brandy

Sauté onions and garlic in butter until golden brown. Add nutmeg and salt and pepper. Add chicken livers and cook until liver is firm and not pink. While still hot, put mixture into blender or food processor. Add butter and brandy, and blend until smooth.

Makes approximately 3 cups.

—Joan Morrison
North Gower, Ontario

CHICKEN WITH MUSHROOMS, PINE NUTS & FETA

2 Tbsp. olive oil
¼ lb. mushrooms, sliced
3 Tbsp. pine nuts
1 clove garlic, minced
½ lb. feta cheese, crumbled
1 Tbsp. minced parsley

pepper
3-lb. chicken
salt & pepper
¼ cup butter, melted
3 Tbsp. lemon juice
1 tsp. Dijon mustard

Heat oil, then add mushrooms, pine nuts and garlic. Sauté for 5 minutes, then stir in feta cheese, parsley and pepper. Remove from heat and cool.

Sprinkle chicken with salt and pepper. Fill with cooled stuffing. Combine butter with lemon juice and mustard, then brush over chicken. Roast chicken for 5 minutes on each side at 425 degrees F, reduce heat to 350 degrees F and roast, breast side up, for 30 to 40 minutes.

Serves 4.

BUTTER-BRAISED PHEASANT

2 2-3-lb. pheasants
2 cups red wine
2 bay leaves
¼ cup oil

1 Tbsp. juniper berries
¼ tsp. peppercorns
3 Tbsp. butter

Clean and quarter pheasants, then rinse well in cold water. Combine wine, bay leaves and oil. Coarsely crush juniper berries and peppercorns and add to marinade. Place pheasant in shallow dish, pour marinade over, cover, and refrigerate for 3 days, turning several times.

In Dutch oven, brown pheasants in butter. Remove from heat, add marinade and bake, covered, at 400 degrees F for 1 to 1½ hours, or until tender.

Serves 6 to 8.

—J.R. Galen
Conestoga, Pennsylvania

WILD RICE, SAUSAGE & ALMOND STUFFING

THIS IS A WONDERFULLY CRUNCHY STUFFING FOR CHICKEN, GOOSE, DUCK OR EVEN PORK. IT CAN be baked in a greased casserole dish by itself, if you wish, to accompany pork chops or baked chicken breasts.

½ cup dry wild rice
½ lb. sausage meat
1 small onion, chopped
½ cup chopped celery
½ cup sliced mushrooms
½ cup coarsely chopped almonds

3 slices dry whole wheat bread, cubed
½ tsp. salt
½ tsp. pepper
¼ tsp. sage
savory
thyme

Place wild rice in strainer and rinse thoroughly under cold water. Drain well. Place in saucepan and pour 1½ cups boiling water over. Return to boil. Reduce heat and simmer for 45 minutes, or until tender but not mushy. Drain well and transfer to a large bowl.

In large skillet, cook sausage meat over medium heat until no longer pink, breaking it up as it cooks. Stir in onion, celery and mushrooms, and cook until tender – about 5 minutes.

With slotted spoon, transfer sausage-vegetable mixture to wild rice. Add remaining ingredients, stirring gently. Taste and adjust seasoning. Pack loosely into the cavity of a 10-lb. bird, or place in greased casserole dish and bake, covered, at 350 degrees F for 45 minutes.

—Sandy Robertson
Port Robinson, Ontario

SELF-BASTING ROAST TURKEY

1 turkey, stuffed with your favourite dressing
6-8 strips bacon

Attach strips of bacon evenly over turkey breast, fastening with toothpicks. Place turkey, breast up, on rack in roasting pan. Place roasting pan and turkey inside 2 large brown-paper grocery bags – one from each end.

Preheat oven to 450 degrees F. Place turkey in oven and immediately reduce heat to 350 degrees F. Roast for 18 to 20 minutes per pound of turkey. If not browned enough, remove bags for last 30 to 40 minutes of cooking time.

—Kathleen S.H. Moore
Denver, Colorado

TURKEY DRESSING

2 cups dry brown & white rice
½ lb. bacon
1½ cups dried fruit (peaches, pears, apples)
¾ cup butter
2 cups diced celery

1 cup diced leeks
1½ tsp. salt
2 Tbsp. tarragon
1 Tbsp. mint
½-1 cup sliced mushrooms

Cook rice in 4½ cups water for 45 minutes. Fry bacon and crumble. Soak dried fruit in ⅔ cup boiling water. Melt butter in large heavy pan, and sauté celery and leeks. Add salt. Remove from heat and stir in rice, bacon, fruit, seasonings and mushrooms. Stuff bird and cook as usual.

Enough stuffing for a 12-pound bird.

—Diane Ladouceur
Calgary, Alberta

STUFFED CORNISH GAME HENS WITH ORANGE SAUCE

Stuffing
1 cup sliced mushrooms
4 Tbsp. butter
1 cup chopped spinach
¼ cup sliced green onion
¼ cup chopped parsley
1 cup cooked white rice
1 cup cooked wild rice
1 cup mandarin orange sections
¼ cup walnut pieces

Sauce
2 Tbsp. sugar
1 cup water
2 Tbsp. grated orange peel
½ cup frozen orange juice concentrate
1½ Tbsp. cornstarch, mixed with 2 Tbsp. water
2 Tbsp. Grand Marnier **or** orange-flavoured liqueur

4 Cornish game hens

To make stuffing, brown mushrooms in 2 Tbsp. butter. Add spinach, onion and parsley and cook for 1 minute. Remove from heat. Add rices, orange sections and walnuts. Spoon into hens, then arrange hens in shallow baking dish and dot with remaining butter. Roast at 400 degrees F for 45 minutes, basting occasionally with pan drippings.

Meanwhile, prepare orange sauce. Combine sugar, water, orange peel and orange juice in heavy pot and bring to a boil. Stir cornstarch mixture into sauce, and cook, stirring, until thickened. Stir in liqueur. Roast hens for 15 minutes more, basting with orange sauce.

Serves 4.

—*Laura Rance*
Sanford, Manitoba

STUFFED DUCK WITH APPLE-CINNAMON GLAZE

"THIS GLAZE HAS A VERY FLAVOURFUL, MILDLY SPICY, APPLE TASTE. ITS SWEETNESS GOES WELL with the duck. It is easy to prepare, as both stuffing and sauce can be made ahead of time and refrigerated."

Stuffing
1 onion, chopped
1 stalk celery & leaves, chopped
1 cooking apple, cored & diced
4 Tbsp. butter
2 cups mashed potatoes
1½ cups bread crumbs
1 tsp. savory
½ tsp. marjoram
¾ tsp. salt
¼ tsp. pepper

Glaze
½ cup apple juice **or** cider
¼ cup apple jelly
1 Tbsp. cider vinegar
¼ tsp. cinnamon
¼ tsp. salt
⅛ tsp. dry mustard
1 Tbsp. cornstarch mixed with 1 Tbsp. water

4-5-lb. duck, wings tied back

For stuffing: Combine onion, celery, apple and butter in saucepan. Sauté until translucent. Mix with potatoes, bread crumbs, savory, marjoram, salt and pepper. Stuff duck. Bake, uncovered, at 350 degrees F for 2¾ to 3 hours, occasionally removing excess fat.

Meanwhile, prepare glaze. Heat juice, ½ cup water, jelly, vinegar, cinnamon, salt and mustard. Blend cornstarch mixture slowly into sauce and cook until thickened. After about 2¾ hours, brush duck generously with glaze. Bake for 20 to 25 minutes longer or until duck is done. Serve with extra sauce.

Serves 3 to 4.

—*Madonna Levesque*
Stayner, Ontario

VERMONT STYLE SKILLET-ROASTED DUCK

"EVERYTHING ABOUT THIS IS WONDERFUL," SAYS OUR VERMONT TESTER. "THE SKIN IS CRISPY and sweet, the meat is moist, and there is a natural congruity to the flavours."

4-5-lb. duck
salt & pepper
3 'MacIntosh' apples
   (1 whole; 2 peeled, cored & sliced)

1 cup maple syrup
½ cup diced raw bacon
juice of ½ lemon

Remove excess fat from duck, rub inside with salt and rinse well in cold water. Place whole apple inside and truss legs. Rub with salt and pepper and place in hot cast-iron skillet. Sear on all sides until well browned.

Heat oven to 400 degrees F. Roast duck, in skillet, for about 1½ hours. For the last 30 minutes, reduce temperature to 325 degrees F and brush with maple syrup, two or three times, using about ¼ cup. When duck is done and drumstick wiggles freely, remove from skillet and stand on end to drain fat.

In skillet, cook bacon until crisp, remove excess fat and add sliced apples. Toss for a few seconds, then add remaining maple syrup and lemon juice. Cut duck in half and spoon bacon and apples over duck.

Serves 2.

—James F. Lehane
Holly, Michigan

CANARD À L'ORANGE

2 ducks
2 tsp. salt
2 tsp. grated orange peel
½ tsp. thyme
½ tsp. pepper
2 Tbsp. finely chopped onion
¼ tsp. sage

Basting Sauce
wing tips & giblets
2 Tbsp. butter
2 Tbsp. finely chopped onion
1 tsp. dried parsley
1 bay leaf
3 Tbsp. sugar
¼ cup vinegar
1 tsp. grated orange peel
2 Tbsp. cornstarch
½ cup port wine

Remove giblets, wash and dry ducks and cut off wing tips at the first joint. Reserve, with giblets, for sauce. Combine salt, orange peel, thyme, pepper, onion and sage. Rub mixture on skin and inside the cavity of each duck. Tie legs together, then place ducks on rack in roasting pan. Roast at 350 degrees F for 2½ to 3 hours, or until drumstick moves and skin is crisp and golden.

Meanwhile, prepare sauce. Brown wing tips and giblets in butter. Add onion and cook until lightly browned. Add parsley, bay leaf and 3 cups water. Cover and simmer for 1 hour. Strain and cook liquid until reduced to 2 cups. Combine sugar and vinegar and cook until sugar caramelizes to a dark brown. Add stock, orange peel and cornstarch mixed with ¼ cup of port wine. Cook, stirring, until thickened.

About half an hour before ducks are done, remove them from pan. Drain off the fat and add ¼ cup port to pan. Heat and scrape browned particles into liquid. Add this to basting sauce. Replace ducks and baste until done. Serve extra sauce over sliced duck.

Serves 4 to 6.

—Laurie Noblet
Kalamazoo, Michigan

DUCK WITH BLUEBERRIES & VEGETABLES

OUR CAMDEN EAST TESTER RAVED ABOUT THIS RECIPE. ALTHOUGH UNUSUAL, THE FLAVOUR combinations were most successful and the appearance of the completed dish was very attractive.

3-lb. duck
salt
1 Tbsp. butter
¼ cup sugar
1 cup orange juice
½ cup red wine vinegar

1 cup blueberries
½ cup small white onions
½ cup baby carrots
1 cup whole green beans
2 potatoes, scooped into balls
butter

Place duck on rack in roasting pan and tie legs and wings to body. Sprinkle with salt, then bake, uncovered, at 500 degrees F for 25 minutes. Reduce heat to 400 degrees F and bake for another 45 minutes.

Melt butter and sugar, stirring until caramelized. Add orange juice and continue cooking until reduced. Add red wine vinegar and continue to reduce until consistency of marmalade. Add blueberries and baste duck once or twice with this.

Steam vegetables until just cooked, then sauté lightly in butter and keep hot.

Carve duck, arranging slices of meat on platter with vegetables around duck. Place sauce in gravy boat and serve.

Serves 2.

—Billie Sheffield
North Gower, Ontario

VENISON STROGANOFF

"WONDERING HOW TO PREPARE THE PIECE OF VENISON YOU'VE BEEN PRESENTED WITH NEED never be a problem again. This simple recipe does not require the extensive marinating often called for when cooking game. Venison should be well trimmed of all fat and strong membrane before use."

1-lb venison steak
flour
4 Tbsp. butter
½ cup chopped onion
1 clove garlic, minced
½ lb. mushrooms, sliced

3 Tbsp. flour
1 Tbsp. tomato paste
1½ cups beef stock
2 Tbsp. white wine
1 cup sour cream
cooked noodles

Cut meat into ¼-inch strips, against the grain, and dust with flour. Heat 2 Tbsp. butter in large skillet. When foam dies down, add meat and brown quickly. Add onion, garlic and mushrooms, adding more butter if necessary. Sauté for 3 to 5 minutes, or until onion and mushrooms are tender. Remove meat mixture and add 2 Tbsp. butter to pan. Blend in flour and tomato paste. Stir in stock and cook, stirring, until thickened. Return meat mixture to skillet. Stir in wine and sour cream. Heat gently but do not boil. Serve over hot buttered noodles.

Serves 4.

—Susan Baker
Holland Centre, Ontario

WILD GAME STEAKETTES

2 lbs. venison **or** moose steaks, sliced
   ½" thick
½ cup flour
1½ cups bread crumbs
salt & pepper
¼ tsp. thyme
¼ tsp. sage
¼ tsp. celery salt
½ tsp. basil
2 eggs
2 Tbsp. milk
oil for cooking
2 onions, sliced

Pound steaks to tenderize. Combine flour, bread crumbs, salt and pepper, thyme, sage, celery salt and basil. Beat eggs and milk together. Dip meat into egg mixture, then into bread crumbs. Fry in hot oil until crisp, remove from pan and set aside. Place onions in skillet, reduce heat to low, then return meat to pan. Cook for 7 to 10 minutes.

Serves 4.

—Stella Zachkewich
Boyle, Alberta

BREADED VENISON STEAKS

1½ lbs. boneless venison steak
½ cup flour
½ tsp. salt
⅛ tsp. pepper
¾ tsp. paprika
1 egg, lightly beaten
1 Tbsp. milk
1 cup fine dry bread crumbs
2 Tbsp. grated onion
1 clove garlic, crushed
½ tsp. basil
½ tsp. thyme
½ cup oil

Pound steaks to tenderize. Combine flour, salt, pepper and ¼ tsp. paprika in one bowl, egg and milk in a second and bread crumbs, onion, garlic, basil, thyme and remaining ½ tsp. paprika in a third.

Dip meat first in flour, then egg, then bread crumb mixtures. Be sure entire surface of meat is covered. Sauté steak in oil to desired doneness.

Serves 2.

—Dorothy Cage
Beaverlodge, Alberta

RABBIT, ASPARAGUS & APPLE SALAD

SERVE THIS SALAD ON A BED OF GREENS AND TOP WITH A FEW ALFALFA SPROUTS.

⅓ cup cooked, chopped rabbit
½ cup steamed asparagus, cut into 1" pieces, cooking water reserved
¼ cup diced apple

Dressing
1 Tbsp. cider vinegar
1 Tbsp. oil
1 tsp. honey
salt
chopped parsley

Combine rabbit, asparagus and apple. Mix together vinegar, oil, honey, salt and parsley. Toss with salad, adding a little asparagus water if needed.

Serves 2.

—Gabriele Klein
Montreal, Quebec

BEER-BRAISED RABBIT

1½-2 lbs. rabbit, cut up
salt & pepper
3 Tbsp. oil
3 potatoes, peeled & halved
2 cups carrots, cut into 1″ pieces
1 onion, sliced
1 cup beer

¼ cup chili sauce
1 Tbsp. brown sugar
½ tsp. salt
1 clove garlic, minced
⅓ cup water
3 Tbsp. flour

Generously season rabbit with salt and pepper. Heat oil in 10-inch skillet and brown rabbit. Add potatoes, carrots and onion. Combine beer, chili sauce, brown sugar, salt and garlic and pour over rabbit. Bring to a boil; cover, reduce heat and simmer for 45 minutes or until tender. Remove rabbit and vegetables to a serving platter and keep warm.

Measure pan juices, adding additional beer or water if needed to make 1½ cups liquid. Return pan juices to skillet. Blend ⅓ cup water into flour and stir into juices. Cook, stirring, until thickened and bubbly. Continue cooking for 1 to 2 minutes more. Serve with rabbit.

Serves 4.

—Kristine Mattila
Quesnel, British Columbia

MICHIGAN DUTCH-STYLE RABBIT

DESPITE ITS SIMPLICITY, THIS DISH IS FULL OF FLAVOUR. SERVE OVER MASHED POTATOES.

1 cup flour
salt & pepper
1 rabbit, cut into serving-sized pieces

¼ cup butter
½ tsp. thyme
1 cup heavy cream

Combine flour and salt and pepper in paper bag. Place one piece of rabbit in bag at a time and shake to coat completely. Melt butter in deep, heavy skillet that has a lid, and brown meat on both sides. Sprinkle with thyme and add cream. Cover and simmer over very low heat for about 1½ hours or until tender. If cream gets too thick, stir in a little water.

Serves 4.

—Teresa Carel
Winona, Missouri

YOGURT FRIED RABBIT

¼ cup whole wheat flour
1 tsp. thyme
salt & pepper
1 rabbit, cut up
3 Tbsp. oil

½ cup yogurt
1 egg, beaten
1 tsp. basil
⅛ cup heavy cream

Combine flour, thyme, salt and pepper. Dust rabbit with flour mixture. Heat oil and fry rabbit until golden. Cover pan tightly and simmer for 30 minutes or until meat is tender. Remove meat and keep warm.

Combine yogurt and egg, then stir into pan juices to blend. Add basil, then cream. Pour over rabbit and serve.

Serves 4.

—Helen Campbell
Loughborough Inlet, British Columbia

COVEY HILL BRAISED RABBIT

HESITANT FRIENDS WILL BE CONVERTED TO THE JOY OF EATING RABBIT ONCE THEY HAVE tasted this moist, tender preparation. Fresh herbs provide a flavour bonus, but if only dried are available, use ½ tsp. of each.

1 cup flour
1 tsp. paprika
¼ tsp. salt
¼ tsp. pepper
1 tsp. each chopped savory, basil, parsley
   & thyme
3-4-lb. rabbit, cut up

1 onion, chopped
2 cloves garlic, crushed
⅓ cup oil
1 bay leaf
2-3 carrots, chopped
2 stalks celery, chopped

Mix flour and seasonings in plastic bag. Moisten rabbit with water or milk and shake in flour mixture until each piece is well coated. Brown onion and garlic in oil in heavy skillet. Brown rabbit pieces, adding oil if needed. Place in clay baker or covered casserole dish with bay leaf. Add remaining flour mixture to skillet and add 2 to 3 cups water. Heat and stir until gravy has thickened. Arrange carrots and celery around rabbit, then cover with gravy.

Bake, covered, at 300 degrees F for 2 to 3 hours, turning the pieces every 45 minutes or so. More liquid may be added if gravy becomes too thick. Uncover for the last half hour of cooking. Remove bay leaf before serving.

Serves 4.

—E. Ransom Hodges
Montreal, Quebec

HERBED RABBIT

SIMILAR IN AROMA TO GIN, JUNIPER BERRIES ARE PRIZED FOR SEASONING GAME AND BEAN DISHES.

Marinade
3 Tbsp. olive oil
3 Tbsp. red wine vinegar
1 onion, sliced
8 peppercorns
8 juniper berries, crushed
1 tsp. rosemary
1 tsp. salt

1 rabbit, cut into 8 pieces

¼ cup butter
½ cup chopped ham **or** bacon
2 onions, sliced
1 cup chopped celery
1 cup sliced carrots
3 Tbsp. flour
2 cups rabbit **or** chicken stock
¼ cup apricot jelly
¼ cup white wine
1 tsp. lemon juice

Combine marinade ingredients. Add rabbit and marinate overnight. Drain and dry rabbit pieces, saving marinade.

Melt butter and fry rabbit until browned, then remove and set aside. Fry ham, onions, celery and carrots until onions are limp – 8 minutes. Add flour, stirring well. Remove from heat and stir in marinade. Return to heat, bring to a simmer and add rabbit and stock to cover.

Cover and cook over low heat for 2½ to 3 hours or until tender. Stir in jelly, wine and lemon juice.

Serves 4.

—Gabriele Klein
Montreal, Quebec

Meat

"Mustard's no good without roast beef."

—*Chico Marx*

"The Norman takes his vegetables in the form of animals," humorist A.J. Liebling once observed. "Herbivores eat grass. Man, a carnivore, eats herbivores."

Liebling was wrong, of course. Humans are omnivores. In fact, modern humans in Western society are omnivores who are finding it healthier to revert to a more herbivorous life style. For our forebears, a diet heavy in red meat made good sense: beef, pork and game provided the protein and energy to fuel their heavy labours, and the traditional "Sunday joint," glistening with fat and juices, went unchallenged in our North American culture until the relatively recent warnings of nutritionists and cardiologists.

Those who now take their beef in smaller, less frequent portions can refer to Thomas Jefferson as a role model, citing a passage he wrote at the age of 76: "I have lived temperately, eating little animal food and that not as an aliment so much as condiment to the vegetables that constitute my principal diet."

Those who love beef can lick their lips and counter with English novelist William Makepeace Thackeray's assertion that there is nothing better than "the old, rich, sweet taste of steak."

Harrowsmith readers obviously run the nutritional gamut on the question of meat, and the recipes that make up this chapter should get the juices flowing in both those who use meats as "condiments" and those who relish a hearty chop or roast. Clearly, travellers and newcomers to the North American mosaic have brought alternatives to the Anglo approach to meat cookery. Combined with vegetables and grains and cleverly herbed, there is nothing predictable about the meat dishes that follow.

Fortunately, both beef and pork are considerably leaner than they were even 20 years ago, trimmed more intelligently and bred to appeal to the new fat-conscious consumer. Leanness requires some adjustments in the way one prepares meat, and overcooking should be assiduously avoided. Economical cuts can benefit from cooking methods that tenderize: stewing, braising and marinating.

Lamb, too, has become much meatier through selective breeding, and we particularly recommend the Kashmiri-Style Leg of Lamb, which is marinated for two days in a spicy blend of yogurt, curry seasonings, pistachios and almonds, then roasted.

We always prefer to seek out fresh local lamb, finding it much superior to the rock-hard frozen New Zealand product, and we tend to look for nearby sources of other meats as well. Sadly, mass-produced modern beef and pork can carry highly undesirable medicinal contaminants, and we prefer to put our trust in local farmers and butchers whenever possible.

VEAL IN PAPRIKA & CAYENNE CREAM SAUCE

THE MADEIRA IN THIS DISH ADDS BOTH FLAVOUR AND BODY TO THE SAUCE.

paprika
4-6 pieces veal, pounded thinly
½ lb. butter
1 large Spanish onion, chopped
salt & pepper

¼ tsp. cayenne
2½ cups light cream
2 Tbsp. chopped parsley
2 oz. Madeira

Sprinkle paprika generously on both sides of veal slices, pressing firmly with fingers to make it stick. In heavy skillet, melt ⅓ of butter, add onion and sauté until soft. Set aside and keep warm. Add remaining butter to skillet and sauté veal slices one minute per side, then remove veal and keep warm in oven.

Return butter and onions to butter in skillet, add salt and pepper, cayenne and cream and stir over medium heat for 5 to 10 minutes, allowing cream to reduce and thicken. Add parsley and Madeira, stir and return veal and juices to sauce. Cover meat with sauce. Heat for one minute and serve with hot buttered noodles.

Serves 4 to 6.

—Nancy Gray
Islington, Ontario

ROAST TENDERLOIN WITH LEMON-TARRAGON CREAM SAUCE

THE SHALLOTS AND TARRAGON — BOTH IN UNCOMMONLY LARGE QUANTITIES HERE — COMBINE TO produce a sauce that is rich and tasty. Be sure to use French tarragon — Russian will result in an unpleasantly bitter flavour.

4-lb. veal or beef tenderloin
pepper
2 Tbsp. butter
2 Tbsp. oil
¾ cup minced shallots
1 cup chicken stock

1 cup dry vermouth
2 Tbsp. lemon juice
¼ cup packed, chopped tarragon
1½ cups heavy cream
salt

Pat tenderloin dry and season with pepper. Melt butter and oil in large heavy skillet over medium-high heat. Brown tenderloin well on all sides. Transfer to roasting pan.

In tenderloin drippings, cook shallots over low heat until softened — about 5 minutes. Add stock, vermouth, lemon juice and tarragon and boil until reduced to 1 cup. Add 1 cup cream and boil again until reduced to 1 cup. Add salt and pepper.

Roast tenderloin, uncovered, at 450 degrees F for about 15 minutes (for rare). Meanwhile, whip remaining ½ cup cream and fold into warm sauce. Slice meat thinly and pass sauce separately.

Serves 8.

—Ray Rewcastle
Charlie Lake, British Columbia

BULGOGI

THIS IS A TRADITIONAL KOREAN STIR-FRY. SERVE OVER FRIED NOODLE PANCAKES ACCOMPANIED by stir-fried snow peas and mushrooms. The flavour of this dish is very delicate so it is important not to overcook it.

12-oz. fillet steak, sliced into thin strips

Marinade
1 Tbsp. chopped leek
1 green onion, chopped
½ shallot, chopped
1 clove garlic, minced
¼ tsp. sugar
½ tsp. salt
4 Tbsp. light soy sauce
1 Tbsp. sesame oil
3-4 drops Tabasco sauce
⅔ cup peanut oil

Sauce
¼ tsp. salt
¼ tsp. sugar
1 tsp. bean paste
½ tsp. cayenne
1 tsp. sesame seeds
½ tsp. minced garlic
4 Tbsp. soy sauce
1 Tbsp. sesame oil

Combine marinade ingredients, pour over steak and marinate for 3 to 4 hours. Drain. Combine sauce ingredients and mix well. Stir-fry beef with sauce ingredients.

Serves 2.

—Marney Allen
Edmonton, Alberta

NETHERLANDS BEEF STROGANOFF

"THIS RECIPE PRODUCES A FLAVOURFUL BUT LIGHT STROGANOFF WITH A DISTINCTIVE PEPPERY taste. It was given to me by a friend who is a doctor. He got it from a grateful patient from the Netherlands."

2 lbs. steak
¼ lb. butter
1 onion, diced
½ tsp. pepper
2 oz. vodka
3 Tbsp. chili sauce
½ Tbsp. tomato paste

1 tsp. paprika
1½ Tbsp. flour
3-4 drops Tabasco sauce
cayenne
2 cups light cream
salt & pepper

Slice steak into small strips. Melt butter and brown meat for 1 minute. Place meat in warm oven.

Sauté onion and pepper in same skillet until onion is transparent. Add vodka, ignite and let all liquid burn out. Add chili sauce, tomato paste, paprika and flour and mix until smooth. Add Tabasco sauce, cayenne and cream. Cook, stirring, for 5 minutes. Season with salt and pepper. Return meat to skillet and mix gently.

Serves 4 to 6.

—William H. Combs
Ashland, New Hampshire

HOT STIR-FRIED BEEF

1 lb. lean beef
2 stalks celery
1 chili pepper
1 Tbsp. cornstarch
1 egg white
oil
1 Tbsp. soy sauce

½ tsp. sugar
1 tsp. hot pepper oil
3 cloves garlic
2 Tbsp. sweet rice wine
1 Tbsp. black bean sauce
½ tsp. minced gingerroot

Cut beef into very thin strips, slice celery and crush chili pepper. Blend cornstarch and egg white, add beef and toss. Heat oil and deep-fry beef for 3 minutes. Remove meat from oil. Heat 1 Tbsp. oil in another skillet. Sauté celery for 2 minutes, stir in beef and remaining ingredients and stir-fry until heated through.

Serves 2.

—Mary-Lee Judah
Hinton, Alberta

BEER STEW

4 slices bacon
2 lbs. stewing beef, cut into 1″ cubes
2½ cups chopped onions
2 cloves garlic, minced
salt & pepper

12 oz. beer
1 cup beef stock
1 Tbsp. vinegar
¼ tsp. thyme
2 Tbsp. flour

Fry bacon until crisp, remove from pan and set aside. Brown meat in bacon drippings with onions, garlic and salt and pepper. Add beer, stock, vinegar, thyme and reserved bacon and simmer for 2½ hours.

Stir a little of the hot juice into the flour until smooth, then stir back into stew, cooking until gravy is slightly thickened.

Serves 4.

—Reo Belhumeur
Gatineau, Quebec

MAPLE STEW

THIS IS A RICH, HEARTY STEW THAT CAN BE SIMMERED ON THE STOVE OR BAKED IN THE OVEN. It has quite a sweet flavour.

¼ cup flour
salt & pepper
1 clove garlic, crushed
¼ tsp. celery salt
1½ lbs. stewing beef, cut into 1″ cubes

19-oz. can tomatoes
½ cup dry red wine
¼ cup maple syrup
4 potatoes, diced
2 carrots, sliced

Combine flour, salt and pepper, garlic and celery salt. Toss beef in this. Place in casserole dish or saucepan. Add remaining ingredients and ½ cup water. Cover and simmer over low heat for 2½ to 3 hours, or bake at 300 degrees F for 4 hours.

Serves 4.

—Rosalind Mechefske
Guelph, Ontario

ANGLO-IRISH STEW

"MY MOTHER USED WARTIME RATIONING AS AN EXCUSE FOR NOT TEACHING ME TO COOK WHEN I was growing up in England. However, I watched her make Irish Stew so often that I discovered I could make it years later. My recipe has never let me down and has been passed on to sons, daughters-in-law and countless friends."

¾ cup flour	1 leek (optional)
salt & pepper	3 onions
1-1½ lbs. stewing beef **or** lamb	4 large potatoes
3 Tbsp. shortening	small turnip (optional)
beef stock	thyme
2 bay leaves	1 tsp. curry powder
3 large carrots	2 tsp. Worcestershire sauce

Put flour and salt and pepper into paper bag and shake to combine. Cut meat into cubes approximately 1½ inches square. Toss a few at a time into the bag and shake until coated. Melt shortening in large skillet and brown meat well.

Fill a large heavy pot about two-thirds full with stock or water and bring to a full boil. Add bay leaves and browned meat, including any drippings from the skillet. Bring back to full boil, then simmer for approximately 1 hour.

Slice carrots and leek and chop onions, potatoes and turnip. Add all vegetables to pot. Add remaining ingredients, using at least a teaspoon of whole thyme, more if you like its flavour. Stir well, return to boil and then lower heat until the stew is just bubbling gently. Taste and correct seasoning. Cook for 20 minutes. Serve with dumplings if desired.

Serves 6.

—Barbara Brennan
Sidney, British Columbia

FRENCH POT ROAST

"THIS FILLS THE HOUSE WITH A WONDERFUL SMELL AND PRODUCES TENDER MEAT WITH LOTS OF rich sauce."

4-5-lb. rump **or** round roast	2 cups beef stock
salt & pepper	2 cloves garlic, crushed
2 Tbsp. shortening, lard **or** suet	1 small bay leaf
2 Tbsp. butter	thyme
12-16 small white onions	chopped parsley
12-16 small carrots	4 Tbsp. cornstarch, mixed with
1 cup dry red wine	1 cup water

Rub roast with salt and pepper. In large pot, brown roast on all sides in hot shortening. Remove roast and set aside.

Add butter to pot and brown onions and carrots lightly. Remove vegetables and set aside. Return meat to pot, add wine, stock, garlic, bay leaf, thyme and parsley. Cover and cook slowly for about 1½ hours. Add onions and carrots, cover and cook slowly for about 1 hour longer, or until meat is tender. Remove bay leaf and discard.

Transfer meat to warm platter and surround with vegetables. Add cornstarch mixture to liquid in pot and boil until sauce is slightly thickened. Spoon a little sauce over the roast and serve remainder in a gravy boat.

Serves 6.

—Mrs. D.J. Zurbrigg
Pickering, Ontario

STEAK & KIDNEY PIE

PREPARE THE FILLING FOR THIS PIE A DAY AHEAD TO ALLOW THE FLAVOURS TO BLEND TOGETHER properly. Use beef, veal or lamb kidneys.

Filling

1 lb. kidneys
2½ lbs. round steak
½ cup flour
6 Tbsp. oil
1 cup thinly sliced onions
½ lb. mushrooms, sliced
½ tsp. salt

½ tsp. pepper
½ tsp. rosemary
½ tsp. tarragon
1 Tbsp. tomato paste
2 tsp. Worcestershire sauce
1 cup red wine
1 cup beef stock

Pastry

1½ cups flour
½ tsp. salt

½ cup shortening
1 egg yolk, beaten

To make filling: Clean kidneys, split, remove fat and soak in salted water for 1 hour. Dry and cube. Cut steak into cubes. Toss steak and kidneys with flour to coat. Heat oil and brown meat, removing it as it browns. Add onions and mushrooms to drippings, adding oil if necessary. Sauté for 5 minutes, until onions and mushrooms are lightly browned, stirring frequently. Return meat to skillet, add remaining filling ingredients and simmer for 2 hours or until meat is tender. Cool, then refrigerate overnight.

To prepare crust: Sift flour and salt into bowl, then cut in shortening until mixture resembles coarse cornmeal. Mix egg yolk with 3 Tbsp. ice water and add to flour, tossing with a fork until particles cling together. Form into a ball and refrigerate overnight.

To assemble: After removing any congealed fat from the surface of the filling, place filling in greased 2-quart casserole dish. Roll out pastry until it is 2 inches larger around than the top of the casserole dish. Place dough on top of filling, turning it under at the edges. Cut steam vents and bake at 400 degrees F for 30 minutes, reduce heat to 350 degrees F and bake for another 15 to 20 minutes.

Serves 4 to 6.

—Shirley Mullen Hooper
Kuna, Idaho

SESAME STEAK

PRESENT THIS IN A TERRA-COTTA DISH. IT IS A NUTTY, SLIGHTLY SWEET KOREAN METHOD OF preparing meat.

2 lbs. steak
1 Tbsp. toasted & pulverized sesame seeds
3 green onions, finely chopped
4 cloves garlic, crushed
¼ cup plus 1 Tbsp. soy sauce

2 Tbsp. sesame oil
¼ cup sugar
2 Tbsp. sherry
⅛ tsp. pepper

Slice meat thinly, diagonally across the grain; score each piece lightly with an X. Combine remaining ingredients in a bowl, mixing well. Add steak and stir to coat well. Refrigerate for at least 30 minutes. Grill for 2 minutes. Serve with rice.

Serves 4 to 6.

—J.W. Houston
Willowdale, Ontario

SAUERBRATEN

A VERY POPULAR GERMAN DISH, THIS IS SIMILAR IN CONCEPT TO CORNED BEEF. THE BEEF NEEDS to marinate for 4 days. Serve with potato pancakes.

4-lb. blade roast
1 large onion, sliced
8-10 peppercorns
3 cloves
2 bay leaves
¼ cup sugar

2 cups vinegar
2 tsp. salt
1 lemon, sliced
2 Tbsp. plus ¼ cup butter
¼ cup flour
½ cup sour cream

Wipe meat and place in deep crock with cover. In stainless-steel or enamel pot, combine 2 cups water, onion, peppercorns, cloves, bay leaves, sugar, vinegar and salt. Heat but do not boil, then pour over meat and cool. Add lemon slices, cover and refrigerate for 4 days, turning daily. Remove meat from marinade and drain well. Strain marinade and reserve.

Heat 2 Tbsp. butter in deep Dutch oven over low heat. Add meat and brown slowly. Gradually add 2 cups marinade and bring to a boil. Reduce heat, cover and simmer for 2½ to 3 hours, or until meat is tender. Add liquid if necessary. Remove meat, set aside and keep warm. Set aside cooking liquid as well.

In same pot, melt ¼ cup butter and blend in flour, cooking until golden. Remove from heat and slowly add 3 cups liquid (cooking liquid, more marinade and hot water if needed). Bring to a rapid boil, stirring constantly, until gravy thickens. Reduce heat and slowly stir in sour cream, making certain it does not curdle. Serve with meat.

Serves 6 to 8.

—Anton Gross
North Augusta, Ontario

BEEF ROULADEN

THIS ROULADEN COMES FROM THE HARZ MOUNTAIN REGION OF GERMANY. IT IS A DELICIOUS dish for horseradish lovers. Have your butcher cut the rouladen for you.

8 rouladen, ³/₁₆″ thick
¼ cup mustard
¼ cup horseradish
salt & pepper
4 slices bacon, chopped

1½ onions, thinly sliced
oil
½ cup red wine
1 cup beef stock

Pound rouladen with mallet until very thin—almost falling apart. Mix mustard and horseradish together and spread on meat. Sprinkle generously with salt and pepper. Lightly sauté bacon and onions, then place on meat. Roll each piece up tightly, folding in ends. Secure with toothpicks.

Heat oil in large skillet and brown meat very well. Add wine and stock to cover, and simmer, covered, for 2 to 2½ hours, adding liquid as required. Reduce sauce slightly before serving.

Serves 4.

—M
Hasting

ORANGE MARINATED BEEF

"THIS ROAST IS DELICIOUS SERVED ON A WARM PLATTER WITH BUTTERED YAMS. BUT IT JUST might be even better the next day, sliced very thinly and served cold."

4-lb. boneless round **or** rump roast
½ cup red wine vinegar
2 cups orange juice
2 onions, chopped

1 Tbsp. pickling spice
12 peppercorns
1 bay leaf
2 Tbsp. oil

Pierce roast all over with fork. Combine vinegar, juice, onions, pickling spice, peppercorns and bay leaf and bring to a boil. Simmer for 5 minutes, then cool. Pour marinade over roast. Refrigerate for 48 hours, turning roast frequently.

Remove from marinade and brown in oil in Dutch oven. Pour marinade over beef, cover and cook over low heat for 3 to 3½ hours, turning occasionally.

Serves 6 to 8.

—Kathryn MacDonald
Yarker, Ontario

LONDON BROIL WITH LIME & GINGER MARINADE

LIME AND GINGER BRING AN UNEXPECTED BUT DELICIOUS FLAVOUR TO THIS STEAK DISH.

3 cloves garlic, minced
2-3 pieces gingerroot, minced
½ cup soy sauce
4 tsp. sugar
2 tsp. sesame oil

juice of 1 lime
2 Tbsp. sherry
½ tsp. pepper
2-3 lbs. flank steak

Combine all ingredients except steak and mix well. Pour over meat and marinate for at least 6 hours but preferably overnight. Broil in oven or on grill, about 10 minutes per side.

Serves 4 to 6.

—Kathy Lempert
Strong, Maine

SWEET & SOUR MEATLOAF

SERVE THIS HOT OR COLD — IT MAKES EXCELLENT SANDWICHES ON THICK SLICES OF RYE BREAD with mustard.

Meatloaf
1½ lbs. ground beef
1 onion, chopped
½ cup tomato sauce
1 cup bread crumbs
¼ tsp. salt
1 egg, beaten

Sauce:
½ cup tomato sauce
2 Tbsp. vinegar
2 Tbsp. brown sugar
2 Tbsp. Dijon mustard

Combine meatloaf ingredients and mix well. Press into greased loaf pan, leaving 1-inch space on all sides.

Combine sauce ingredients with 1 cup water, and mix well. Pour over meatloaf. Bake, uncovered, at 350 degrees F for 1½ hours, basting frequently.

Serves 6.

—Bette Warkentin
Matsqui, British Columbia

TORTILLA STACK

THIS RESULTS IN A LAYERED DISH THAT LOOKS LIKE A TORTE OR CRÊPE PYRAMID. THE FILLING tastes wonderful and is very hearty.

1 lb. ground beef
4 oz. canned green chilies, seeded & diced
4 oz. canned jalapeño peppers, seeded
  & diced
1 onion, diced
2-3 cloves garlic, minced

2 cups tomato sauce
1 Tbsp. cumin
1 Tbsp. coriander
4 cups cooked pinto beans
20 corn tortillas
1 lb. Monterey Jack cheese, grated

Brown ground beef, then add chilies, peppers, onion and garlic and sauté until onion is translucent. Add tomato sauce, cumin, coriander and beans and simmer for 15 minutes.

Quickly fry tortillas on both sides in hot, dry skillet until crisp.

To assemble, coat bottom of greased casserole dish with a little sauce. Layer tortillas, sauce and cheese to top of dish. Bake, uncovered, at 350 degrees F for 15 minutes, or until heated through and cheese is melted.

Serves 6.

—Sandra Senchuk-Crandall
Santa Rosa, California

CHILI CORNPONE PIE

THIS MAKES A HEARTY MEAL AFTER A WINTER DAY SPENT OUTSIDE.

Chili
3 onions, chopped
1 lb. ground beef
1 green pepper, chopped
2 stalks celery, sliced
3½ cups tomato sauce
6-8 mushrooms, sliced
2 tsp. chili powder
2 pinches dried chilies
Tabasco sauce
1 tsp. Worcestershire sauce
¼ tsp. pepper
1 tsp. celery seed

1 clove garlic, crushed
1 tsp. basil
1 tsp. thyme
3½ cups cooked kidney beans

Topping
1 cup flour
¾ cup cornmeal
2½ tsp. baking powder
⅛-¼ tsp. curry
1 egg
1 cup milk
¼ cup oil

Sauté onions and ground beef, adding green pepper and celery just as meat is almost cooked. Add 2 to 3 Tbsp. water and simmer until meat is cooked. Add remaining chili ingredients, and simmer for 15 minutes.

Meanwhile, prepare topping: Sift together flour, cornmeal, baking powder and curry. Combine egg, milk and oil and mix gently into dry ingredients.

Pour chili into greased 9" x 13" baking pan. Spread batter on top and bake at 400 degrees F for 40 to 45 minutes.

Serves 4 to 6.

—Shelley Bishop
Swastika, Ontario

GERMAN MEATLOAF

THE APPLESAUCE GLAZE ON TOP OF THIS MEAT LOAF MAKES IT REALLY ATTRACTIVE — A GOOD combination of apple, beer and meat.

2 lbs. ground beef
1 lb. ground pork
1 egg
1 small onion, finely chopped
½ cup fine dry bread crumbs
1 medium apple, peeled, cored & chopped

1 tsp. savory
1 tsp. salt
¼ tsp. pepper
1 cup beer
1 cup thick applesauce

Combine all ingredients but applesauce and mix well. Turn into greased shallow baking pan and shape into a loaf. Bake for 45 minutes at 350 degrees F, then spread with applesauce. Bake, uncovered, for another 30 to 45 minutes. Serve hot or cold.

Serves 6 to 8.

—Louise Poole
Yellowknife, Northwest Territories

SATURDAY NIGHT PIE

A VARIATION OF SHEPHERD'S PIE, THIS RECIPE BASES ITS CRUST ON CORNMEAL RATHER THAN ON mashed potatoes.

Filling
1 lb. ground beef
1 cup chopped onion
1 cup chopped green pepper
2 cups tomato sauce
1-2 Tbsp. chili powder
1 tsp. salt
1 tsp. pepper
1 cup corn

Topping
2 eggs
½ cup buttermilk
1 Tbsp. butter
1 Tbsp. flour
1 tsp. baking soda
¼ tsp. salt
¾ cup cornmeal

Brown beef and onion in skillet. Add remaining filling ingredients, bring to a boil, reduce heat, cover and simmer for 15 minutes. Pour into ungreased deep 10 " pie plate.

For topping: Beat together eggs, buttermilk and butter. Beat in remaining ingredients until smooth. Spread evenly over filling and bake, uncovered, at 350 degrees F for 20 minutes.

Serves 6.

—Patricia Daine
Dartmouth, Nova Scotia

SWEDISH MEATBALLS

¾ cup milk
4 slices bread, crumbled
1 lb. ground steak
½ lb. ground veal
½ lb. ground pork
1 onion, grated
2 tsp. salt

⅛ tsp. nutmeg
⅛ tsp. allspice
1 clove garlic, crushed
¼ tsp. pepper
oil
1½ cups beef stock

Pour milk over bread and beat until consistency of paste. Add remaining ingredients except oil and stock and mix well. Form into meatballs, 1 inch in diameter. Fry in a little oil until browned on all sides. Place in casserole dish, pour stock over and bake, uncovered, at 350 degrees F for 30 minutes.

Makes approximately 36 meatballs.

Swedish Ginger Cookies, page 28; Chocolate Peanut Butter Squares, page 24; Orange Pecan Muffins, page 11

Landlubber's Gumbo, page 64

Flaming Apple Brandy Crêpes, page 240

Vita Quencher, page 268

Lemon Cheese Crown, page 260

Curried Pasta Salad, page 139

Eggs in Nests, page 44

Steamed Sole with Tomato Coulis, page 151

BEEF & TOMATO COBBLER

THIS COBBLER TOPPING OVER A SLOPPY-JOE-TYPE BEEF MIXTURE IS A QUICK AND EASY CASSEROLE.

3 Tbsp. oil
2 large onions, chopped
2 Tbsp. flour
2 cups tomato juice
2 Tbsp. tomato purée
¼ tsp. thyme
¼ tsp. basil
¼ tsp. oregano
salt & pepper

1½ lbs. ground beef

Cobbler
1 cup flour
2 tsp. baking powder
salt
3 Tbsp. butter
milk

Heat oil and sauté onions until transparent. Stir in flour and cook for 2 to 3 minutes. Gradually add tomato juice, purée, thyme, basil, oregano and salt and pepper. Add meat and simmer for 10 minutes, breaking up lumps. Transfer to casserole dish, cover and bake at 350 degrees F for 1 hour.

Meanwhile, prepare cobbler: Mix flour, baking powder and salt. Cut in butter to form crumbs, and add milk until dough can be rolled. Roll ½ inch thick and cut into rounds.

Remove cover from casserole dish, place biscuits on meat and bake for 15 minutes more.

Serves 6.

—Midge Denault
Lee Valley, Ontario

PASTITSIO

A GREEK DISH, PASTITSIO IS A MACARONI, TOMATO AND MEAT CASSEROLE THAT IS TOPPED WITH a custard and baked. Ground lamb may be used instead of ground beef, if it is available.

1 lb. ground beef
1 large onion, chopped
1 clove garlic, minced
2 cups canned tomatoes
½ tsp. salt
pepper
⅛ tsp. cinnamon

2 cups dry macaroni, cooked
½ cup Parmesan cheese
3 Tbsp. butter
¼ cup flour
2 cups milk
3 eggs

Cook beef, onion and garlic until meat is browned, then drain. Add tomatoes, ¼ tsp. salt, pepper and cinnamon and simmer for 15 minutes. Add macaroni to meat mixture with ¼ cup cheese. Place in 9″ x 13″ pan and set aside.

Make a white sauce by melting butter, stirring in flour and remaining ¼ tsp. salt and cooking for 2 to 3 minutes. Stir in milk and cook, stirring, until thickened. Cool slightly, then beat in eggs one at a time, followed by remaining ¼ cup cheese. Pour over meat mixture. Bake, uncovered, at 375 degrees F for 35 minutes, or until knife inserted in the centre comes out clean.

Serves 6.

—Adele Dueck
Lucky Lake, Saskatchewan

SWEET & SOUR MEATBALLS WITH PRUNES

2 lbs. ground beef
2 eggs
1 cup bread crumbs
1 onion, chopped
1 tsp. salt
6 prunes
3 tsp. raisins

8-10 peppercorns
2-3 bay leaves
20 oz. tomato juice
¼ cup sugar
juice of 2-3 lemons
½ cabbage, coarsely chopped

Combine beef, eggs and bread crumbs, mix well and form into meatballs. Bring 4 cups water to a boil, then add onion, salt, prunes, raisins, peppercorns, bay leaves and meatballs. Cook for 20 minutes, then add tomato juice, sugar, lemon juice and cabbage. Simmer, covered, for 1 hour.

Serves 6 to 8.

—Lynn Andersen
Lumsden, Saskatchewan

ITALIAN MEATBALLS

4 slices stale bread
2 eggs, beaten
1 lb. ground beef
¼ cup Parmesan cheese
2 Tbsp. snipped parsley

1 tsp. salt
¼ tsp. oregano
pepper
2 Tbsp. oil

Trim crusts from bread and soak bread in ½ cup water for 2 to 3 minutes. Wring out bread and discard excess water. Tear bread up into large bowl. Add eggs and mix well with egg beater. Combine with beef, cheese, parsley, salt, oregano and pepper. With wet hands, form into small balls. Brown slowly in hot oil, turning often so they don't stick to the bottom. Add meatballs to your favourite sauce and simmer for 30 minutes. Serve over hot spaghetti. Pass extra Parmesan cheese.

Makes 20 meatballs.

—Joyce M. Holland
Pawcatuck, Connecticut

MEATBALL STROGANOFF

1 lb. ground beef
1 clove garlic, crushed
2 Tbsp. oil
1 onion, sliced
¼ lb. mushrooms, sliced
2 Tbsp. flour

1 cup beef stock
2 Tbsp. red wine
2 Tbsp. tomato sauce
¾ tsp. Dijon mustard
½ cup sour cream

Combine beef and garlic and form into meatballs. Heat oil and sauté onion and mushrooms until lightly browned. Set aside, and in the same pan sauté meatballs, turning to brown all sides. Remove meatballs. Stir flour into pan drippings and cook for 3 to 4 minutes. Add stock and cook, stirring, until sauce thickens. Add wine, tomato sauce and mustard and mix well. Return meatballs, onions and mushrooms to skillet. Cover and simmer for 20 minutes. Stir in sour cream and heat through without boiling.

Serves 4.

—Ann Chambers
London, Ontario

BACON & LIVER BAKE

6 slices bacon, chopped
1 cup chopped onion
½ cup flour
1 tsp. salt
pepper

1 lb. calf's liver, cut into serving-sized
  pieces
1½ cups milk
¼ cup fine bread crumbs
1 Tbsp. butter, melted

Combine bacon and onion in skillet and cook until bacon is crisp and onion is tender. Remove and set aside, reserving drippings in skillet. Combine flour, salt and pepper, and coat liver with this. Reserve leftover flour mixture. Brown liver in skillet, then remove to baking dish. Blend reserved flour with pan drippings until smooth and bubbly, then add milk. Cook, stirring, until thickened and bubbly. Pour sauce over liver and sprinkle with bacon and onion pieces. Combine bread crumbs with melted butter and sprinkle over all. Bake, uncovered, at 350 degrees F for 25 minutes.

Serves 4.

—LaRae DuFresne Bergo
Grove City, Minnesota

LIVER STROGANOFF

1 lb. beef liver
4 bacon slices
1 small onion, chopped
1 cup sliced mushrooms

1 cup beef stock
1 Tbsp. flour
¼ cup sour cream

Cut liver into ½-inch-wide strips and set aside. Cook bacon until crisp, remove from skillet and drain. Cook liver, onion and mushrooms in bacon drippings until liver is lightly browned. Add beef stock and simmer for 20 minutes, or until liver is fork-tender. Stir flour into 3 Tbsp. water until smooth and add to skillet. Cook until thickened. Add crumbled bacon and sour cream.

Serves 2.

—Linda Russell
Exeter, Ontario

LIVER WITH MUSHROOMS & BACON

1 lb. calf's liver
8 slices bacon, chopped
10-12 mushrooms, sliced
1 large onion, chopped
1 clove garlic, minced

1-2 tsp. flour
½-1 cup beef stock
salt & pepper
parsley

Slice liver into thin strips and set aside. Sauté bacon, mushrooms, onion and garlic until bacon is quite crisp. Remove from skillet with slotted spoon. Add flour to a very small amount of heated stock. Blend well and continue adding stock until you have ½ cup. Set aside.

Cook liver over medium-high heat in bacon fat until lightly coloured. Add bacon mixture and stock. Cook until thickened, adding salt and pepper and parsley.

Serves 3 to 4.

—Colleen Suche
Winnipeg, Manitoba

CHINESE-STYLE LIVER

SERVE THIS TASTY, UNUSUAL LIVER DISH ON A BED OF FRIED BEAN SPROUTS.

3 Tbsp. soy sauce
1 Tbsp. honey
1 Tbsp. brown sugar
2 Tbsp. wine vinegar
1 small piece gingerroot, chopped
1 large clove garlic, minced
1 Tbsp. peppercorns

1 lb. beef liver, sliced in thin strips
1 Tbsp. cornstarch
½ cup chicken stock
2 Tbsp. oil
2-3 onions, quartered
10 mushrooms, sliced

Combine soy sauce, honey, sugar, vinegar, ginger, garlic and peppercorns. Pour over liver and let stand for at least 2 hours but preferably overnight, stirring occasionally.

Remove liver from marinade, then strain marinade. Combine marinade with cornstarch and stock, then set aside.

Heat oil and sauté onions and mushrooms until limp. Add to marinade. Sauté liver until lightly coloured. Pour marinade-onion mixture into pan and cook until thickened, stirring constantly.

Serves 2.

—Colleen Suche
Winnipeg, Manitoba

SWEET & SOUR PORK WITH PEACHES

THIS HAS A COLOURFUL APPEARANCE AND A NICELY BALANCED FLAVOUR, MAKING USE OF healthful and accessible ingredients.

1½ lbs. boneless pork, cut into 1" pieces
2 Tbsp. soy sauce
3 Tbsp. oil
1 clove garlic
pepper
2 onions, cut into eighths
1 green pepper, chopped

½ cup sugar
2 Tbsp. cornstarch
¼ tsp. salt
⅓ cup vinegar
2 Tbsp. tomato paste
2 cups sliced peaches
1 large tomato, cut into small wedges

Toss pork cubes in mixture of soy sauce and 1 Tbsp. oil, then marinate for 15 minutes. In large skillet, brown garlic in 2 Tbsp. oil over medium heat. Remove garlic. Brown pork cubes in garlic-flavoured oil, then reduce heat and cook for 15 to 20 minutes longer, stirring often. Sprinkle with pepper. Add onions and green pepper and stir-fry for 2 to 3 minutes.

While meat and vegetables are cooking, make the sauce in a small saucepan. Mix together sugar, cornstarch and salt. Stir in vinegar, 1 cup water and tomato paste. Bring to boil, stirring, until smooth and clear. Drain any excess fat from the frying pan, add sauce to pork mixture, simmer for a minute, taste and adjust seasoning. Add peaches and tomato, cover pan, and cook gently just until heated through.

Serves 4.

—Mrs. D.J. Zurbrigg
Pickering, Ontario

PORK WITH PORT & GARLIC

several cloves garlic
2½-lb. rolled loin of pork
1 Tbsp. oil
1 cup port wine

1 tsp. rosemary
½ tsp. salt
1 Tbsp. butter
1 Tbsp. flour

Cut garlic into slivers and stick into folds of pork loin. In Dutch oven, brown pork on all sides in oil. Pour off fat and add port, rosemary and salt. Bring to a boil. Bake, tightly covered, at 325 degrees F for about 2 hours, adding water if necessary. Soften butter and mix with flour. When pork is tender, remove to a platter and mix butter-flour mixture into pan juices a little at a time, just until sauce begins to thicken. Add salt to taste.

Serves 4 to 6.

—*Ruth Ellis Haworth*
Toronto, Ontario

PORK IN RED WINE WITH APPLE RINGS

START THIS THE EVENING BEFORE YOU PLAN TO SERVE IT BY SOAKING THE DRIED APPLE RINGS in water overnight.

2 Tbsp. oil
2 onions, chopped
2 lbs. pork tenderloin, cubed
1¼ cups red wine
⅔ cup chicken stock
2″ cinnamon stick
2 slivers lemon rind

salt & pepper
2-3 Tbsp. tomato paste
2 Tbsp. chopped parsley
½ cup dried apple rings, soaked
  overnight
2 Tbsp. cornstarch

Heat oil and sauté onions until soft. Add pork and cook until browned. Add wine, stock, cinnamon, lemon rind, salt and pepper and tomato paste. Cover and simmer for 1 hour. Stir in parsley and apple rings and cook for 30 minutes more. Discard cinnamon and lemon rind. Dissolve cornstarch in a bit of the hot liquid, then stir into pot and cook, stirring, until gravy is thickened.

Serves 6.

—*Ellen Wicklum*
Perth, Ontario

BUTTERMILK PORK ROAST

3-4-lb. boned pork shoulder
salt
2 Tbsp. oil
2 cups buttermilk
2 Tbsp. cider vinegar
1 onion, sliced

1 bay leaf
3 peppercorns, crushed
6 carrots, sliced
2 large potatoes, quartered
6 small white onions
cornstarch

Sprinkle meat with salt. Heat oil in Dutch oven, brown meat well on all sides, and remove excess fat. Add buttermilk, 1 cup water, vinegar, onion, bay leaf and peppercorns. Bring to a boil, cover and simmer for 2½ hours, or until meat is tender. Add carrots, potatoes and onions and cook for another 30 minutes. Thicken gravy with cornstarch dissolved in water.

Serves 6 to 8.

—*Anna J. Lee*
Sault Ste. Marie, Ontario

SZEKELY GOULASH

"I acquired this recipe in a cooking course I took in 1977. It was described by the Hungarian instructor as 'chunks of pork in creamy delectable kraut.' I make it frequently, as it is very popular."

2 Tbsp. flour
2 tsp. paprika
1½ lbs. lean pork, cubed
1 onion, finely chopped

2 Tbsp. oil
1 qt. sauerkraut
1½ cups thick sour cream

Combine flour and paprika in plastic bag, then toss pork in this to coat well. Cook onion in oil until soft. Add meat and brown on all sides. Add 2 to 3 Tbsp. hot water, cover and simmer for 45 to 60 minutes, stirring occasionally and adding water as needed. Add sauerkraut and 2 cups hot water. Bring to a boil, cover and simmer for 30 more minutes, or until meat is tender.

Remove from heat. Gradually blend 1½ cups cooking liquid into sour cream, then stir this back into liquid and meat.

Serves 4 to 6.

—Dianne Baker
Tatamagouche, Nova Scotia

PEPPER PORK EN BROCHETTE

2 large cloves garlic, crushed
3 Tbsp. soy sauce
2 Tbsp. sherry
1 Tbsp. cracked pepper
1 tsp. coriander
1 tsp. brown sugar

½ tsp. cumin
2 green peppers, diced
2 onions, quartered
2 lbs. lean pork roast, cubed
⅓ cup oil

Combine all ingredients except oil and marinate for 1 to 2 hours. Thread pork and vegetables on skewers and barbecue. Add oil to marinade and baste meat and vegetables. Serve with rice or pita bread.

Serves 4.

—Colleen Bruning Fann
Clare, Michigan

STUFFED PORK CHOPS

4 pork chops, 1" thick
2 Tbsp. butter
2 Tbsp. chopped onion
1 clove garlic, crushed
1 cup bread crumbs

¼ tsp. savory
¼ tsp. salt
pepper
2-4 Tbsp. orange juice

Trim fat from chops. Melt butter in frying pan and brown chops on both sides. Remove chops and add onion and garlic to pan. Cook until onion is tender, stirring frequently. Add bread crumbs and seasonings and stir together. Remove from heat. Stir in enough juice to make mixture crumbly but not soggy. Scrape pan to remove all drippings. Cut meat to bone to form a pocket, being careful not to tear meat. Pack each chop with ¼ cup stuffing. Wrap in foil and seal tightly.

Bake at 350 degrees F for 1 hour, opening foil for last 15 minutes to brown.

Serves 4.

—M. Raven
Powassan, Ontario

PORK & BEANS PADDINGTON BEAR

WE ALL REMEMBER PADDINGTON BEAR'S CONSTANT CRAVING FOR ORANGE MARMALADE. HERE IS a baked-bean recipe we are certain he would enjoy—it is rich and hearty and the marmalade adds a pleasant, sweet tang.

1 lb. dried lima beans
2 lbs. lean boneless pork, cubed
3 Tbsp. oil
2 tsp. celery salt
2 bay leaves
1 tsp. rosemary
2 cups tomato sauce

1 cup sliced mushrooms
1 onion, chopped
⅓ cup orange marmalade
2 Tbsp. cider vinegar
1 Tbsp. Worcestershire sauce
2 tsp. dry mustard

Rinse beans, cover with 6 cups water and boil for 2 minutes. Remove from heat, cover and let stand for 1 hour.

Brown pork in oil in heavy skillet. Add beans and cooking liquid, celery salt, bay leaves and rosemary. Cover, bring to a boil, reduce heat and simmer for 2 hours. Remove bay leaves. Stir in remaining ingredients and place in casserole dish. Bake, covered, at 350 degrees F for 1 hour. Uncover, stir well, re-cover and bake for 30 minutes more.

Serves 12.

—Midge Denault
Lee Valley, Ontario

CARNITAS BURRITOS

"I'VE DEVELOPED THIS RECIPE OVER THE YEARS I'VE LIVED IN ARKANSAS. I'M A LIFELONG FAN OF Mexican cooking, and used to have ready access to it when I lived in southern California. I use jalapeño peppers out of my own garden, freezing them in the fall for use over the winter."

2 lbs. cooked pork roast, cut into ½" slices
4 cloves garlic, minced
3 jalapeño peppers
1 lb. dry pinto beans
1 Tbsp. salt

3 Tbsp. bacon fat
oil
tortillas
salsa

Place pork, 2 cloves garlic and 1 jalapeño pepper in heavy pot with enough water to just cover. Bring to a boil, cover tightly and reduce heat to medium-low. Simmer for 2 to 3 hours, stirring occasionally and adding water in small amounts only if meat is in danger of boiling dry. Shred meat and keep covered on low heat. Ten minutes before serving, remove cover, increase heat and cook until all liquid is gone.

Meanwhile, rinse and sort beans. Place in heavy saucepan and cover with water to depth of 3 inches. Bring to a boil and cook for 10 minutes. Add salt, remaining 2 cloves garlic, remaining 2 jalapeño peppers and 2 Tbsp. bacon fat. Cover and reduce heat to medium-low. Boil slowly for 2 to 3 hours, stirring frequently and adding water as needed.

Once beans are tender, heat ¼ inch oil and 1 Tbsp. bacon fat in large skillet. Add beans carefully to hot oil, shaking excess liquid from them first. Fill skillet half full with beans and fry for 1 minute, stirring constantly. Mash beans in skillet, add more beans and continue the process until all beans are fried and mashed.

Serve refried beans and shredded pork with tortillas and salsa.

Serves 4 to 6.

—Tommie Majors-McQuary
Lead Hill, Arkansas

PORK CHOPS WITH ARTICHOKE HEARTS

PEOPLE OFTEN RELEGATE PORK CHOPS TO THE "ONLY WHEN I'M IN A HURRY AND CAN'T THINK OF anything else" category. All of these recipes prove this approach wrong – pork chops can be as elegant as any other meat.

6 loin pork chops, 1" thick
¼ cup butter
2 Tbsp. oil
½ lb. mushrooms, sliced
¼ cup chopped green onions
1 clove garlic, crushed

1 large can artichoke hearts, drained
¼-½ cup sherry
1 tsp. tarragon
½ tsp. basil
salt & pepper

Trim fat from chops. Heat 2 Tbsp. butter and oil in large heavy skillet and brown chops, two at a time, over medium heat, turning once. Remove from pan and set aside.

Add 2 Tbsp. butter to drippings. Over low heat, sauté mushrooms, onions and garlic for 5 minutes, or until mushrooms are golden. Cut artichoke hearts in half, add to skillet and sauté 1 to 2 minutes longer. Stir in sherry, tarragon, basil and salt and pepper.

Return chops to pan. Cover and simmer for 20 to 25 minutes, basting frequently.

Serves 6.

—Barbara Denz
Baltimore, Maryland

PORK CHOP OVEN DINNER

TENDER PORK, ATTRACTIVE APPEARANCE AND A PLEASANT COMBINATION OF FLAVOURS ARE produced by this recipe. The initial steps can be done ahead of time – the night before or early in the morning. It is then a simple matter of popping the casserole in the oven for 30 minutes and preparing a salad to accompany it.

3 Tbsp. flour
¾ tsp. salt
pepper
6 pork chops
oil
½ cup cooking sherry
1 Tbsp. parsley

¼ tsp. cloves
3 peppercorns
1 bay leaf
6 carrots, halved & cut in 2" pieces
6-8 small potatoes, halved
1 onion, sliced

Combine flour, salt and pepper in plastic bag, and shake with chops to coat. Brown chops in oil in ovenproof skillet. Set aside. Combine 1 cup water, sherry, parsley, cloves, peppercorns and bay leaf in skillet, bring to a boil, add vegetables and bring back to a boil.

Arrange chops on top of vegetables and bake, covered, at 350 degrees F for 1 hour, then uncovered for 30 minutes.

Serves 6.

—Ruth Stevens
Sault Ste. Marie, Ontario

MAPLE PORK CHOPS

"I SERVE THIS WITH A CREAMY SQUASH SOUP FIRST. ACCOMPANY THE CHOPS WITH CARROTS, oven-browned potatoes and a crunchy green vegetable. End the meal with crème caramel." Made with homegrown pork and thick, fresh maple syrup, this dish turns plain pork chops into company fare.

4 pork chops, 1" thick
¼ cup apricot brandy
½ tsp. dry mustard
2 slices gingerroot

1½ tsp. cornstarch
3 Tbsp. maple syrup
salt & pepper

Brown chops in large frying pan and drain off fat. Pour 2 Tbsp. brandy over top, then add ¼ cup water, mustard and ginger. Cover tightly and simmer, turning occasionally, until tender—about 1 hour.

Remove chops to warm platter. Blend cornstarch with 1 Tbsp. water and stir into remaining sauce in pan along with 2 Tbsp. brandy, maple syrup and salt and pepper. Boil, stirring constantly, until thickened and clear. Pour sauce over chops.

Serves 4.

—Linda Russell
Exeter, Ontario

VIETNAMESE SWEET & SOUR PORK

THE TRADITIONAL WAY TO SERVE THIS DISH IS TO LINE A LARGE PLATTER WITH ROMAINE lettuce, add a layer of peeled, sliced cucumber and a layer of sliced tomato. Place pork on top of tomato, garnish with chopped cilantro, and serve sauce in a separate bowl.

Sauce
⅓ cup sugar
4 tsp. cornstarch
½ cup rice vinegar
1¼ cups chicken stock
½ cup slivered red **or** green pepper

2 lbs. pork spareribs

1 egg, lightly beaten
1 Tbsp. flour
2 Tbsp. cornstarch
1 tsp. pepper
¼ cup oil
4 or more cloves garlic, chopped
⅓ cup fish sauce

Make sauce by mixing sugar and cornstarch in saucepan. Add remaining sauce ingredients and simmer until thickened, stirring, then cook over low heat for a few minutes. Set aside, but keep at room temperature.

Cut ribs into small pieces. Combine egg, 3 Tbsp. water, flour, cornstarch and pepper and mix well. Place ribs in this and turn to coat.

Heat oil in skillet. Fry ribs until batter is crisp. Pour out oil, but do not wipe out pan. Cook garlic briefly—10 seconds—then add fish sauce. Return ribs and turn to coat with garlic and fish sauce. Stir in sauce and heat through.

Serves 3 to 4.

—Donna J. Torres
Santa Barbara, California

SPARERIBS BARBECUE

"THIS IS A RECIPE I RECEIVED FROM A FAVOURITE AUNT WHO IS AN EXCELLENT COOK. I OFTEN substitute pork chops for spareribs, and it is still delicious."

4-6 lbs. spareribs
2 onions
2 stalks celery
1 cup sliced mushrooms
1 green pepper
2 Tbsp. brown sugar
3 Tbsp. vinegar

4 Tbsp. lemon juice
1 Tbsp. Worcestershire sauce
1 tsp. prepared mustard
1 cup tomato sauce
½ cup hot water
1 tsp. salt

Cut ribs into pieces of 2 to 3 ribs each and place in roasting pan. Chop onions, celery, mushrooms and green pepper and add to ribs. Combine remaining ingredients and pour over ribs and vegetables. Cover and bake at 350 degrees F for 1½ hours, basting several times.

Serves 4 to 6.

—*Lorraine Guilfoyle*
Farrellton, Quebec

MAPLE BARBECUED SPARERIBS

TASTY AND UNUSUAL, THIS IS NOT AT ALL LIKE TRADITIONAL BARBECUE OR SWEET AND SOUR recipes.

3 lbs. spareribs
1 cup maple syrup
1 Tbsp. chili sauce
1 Tbsp. vinegar
1 Tbsp. Worcestershire sauce

1 onion, finely chopped
½ tsp. salt
¼ tsp. dry mustard
⅛ tsp. pepper

Roast ribs on rack in roasting pan at 425 degrees F for 30 minutes. Drain fat from pan and cut ribs into serving-sized pieces. Place in 9" x 13" pan.

Combine remaining ingredients in saucepan and boil for 5 minutes. Pour over ribs and bake, uncovered, at 375 degrees F for 1 hour, basting occasionally and turning ribs after 30 minutes.

Serves 4.

—*Donna Jubb*
Fenelon Falls, Ontario

SPARKY'S SWEET & SOUR RIBS

3-4 lbs. pork spareribs
¼ cup vinegar
3 Tbsp. soy sauce
1 tsp. sugar
½ tsp. pepper

4 Tbsp. flour
3 Tbsp. oil
½ cup vinegar
1½ cups brown sugar
1 Tbsp. cornstarch

Parboil ribs in ¼ cup vinegar and water to cover for 1 hour. Drain, leaving ribs in pot. Pour soy sauce, sugar, pepper and flour over ribs, turning to cover each piece.

Heat oil in skillet and brown ribs, then place in large casserole dish.

Combine ½ cup vinegar, brown sugar, 1 cup water and cornstarch dissolved in a bit of water in saucepan. Cook over medium heat until slightly thickened. Pour over ribs and bake, uncovered, at 350 degrees F for 30 to 60 minutes.

Serves 4.

—Pat de la Ronde
Terrace, British Columbia

BAKED HAM WITH BEER

THIS RECIPE PRODUCES A DARK-SKINNED HAM WITH A FLAVOUR SIMILAR TO THAT OF BLACK Forest ham. Save the cooking juice to add to baked beans.

1 large ham
1 cup brown sugar
1 Tbsp. dry mustard
1 pint beer

Place ham in roasting pan with lid. Sprinkle ham with sugar and mustard, then pour the beer over, along with 4 cups water. Bake, uncovered, at 350 degrees F for 2 hours, basting every 30 minutes and adding water if necessary. Cool, covered, before slicing.

—Linda Palaisy
Cantley, Quebec

BAKED HAM WITH PORT WINE SAUCE

1½ cups firmly packed brown sugar
1 Tbsp. wine vinegar
1 Tbsp. prepared mustard
2-3-lb. ham
1 cup white wine

Sauce
1 cup currant jelly
1 cup port
1 Tbsp. butter

Make a paste of the brown sugar, vinegar and mustard. Remove skin from ham and spread with paste. Let stand overnight.

Place in roasting pan with wine. Cover and bake at 350 degrees F for 1½ hours, uncover and bake for 30 minutes longer at 400 degrees F. Remove from oven and let stand for 30 minutes.

Meanwhile, prepare sauce. Heat together currant jelly, port and butter, but do not allow to boil. Slice ham and serve with sauce.

Serves 4 to 6.

—Dolores De Rosario
Hamilton, Ontario

BAKED HAM WITH RAISIN SAUCE

THIS DISH MAKES EXCELLENT "FEAST FARE." IT WILL SERVE A CROWD (JUST INCREASE THE SAUCE recipe and use a bigger ham) and is fancy enough for a Thanksgiving or Christmas dinner. Serve with scalloped potatoes, broccoli, corn and a salad.

Ham
4-lb. ham
1 onion, halved
1 carrot, halved
1 stalk celery, chopped
2 sprigs parsley
¼ tsp. thyme
1 bay leaf
⅓ cup brown sugar
¼ tsp. mace
juice and grated rind of 1 orange
1¼ cups apple cider **or** juice

Sauce
½ cup sugar
⅓ cup raisins
1 Tbsp. Worcestershire sauce
2 Tbsp. butter
2½ Tbsp. wine vinegar
Tabasco sauce
salt & pepper
mace
¼ cup red currant jelly

Place ham, onion, carrot, celery, parsley, thyme and bay leaf in saucepan with water to cover ham. Cover and simmer gently for 35 minutes per pound. Drain and remove skin.

Place ham in roasting pan, fat side up. Score in diagonal pattern. Combine sugar, mace, orange juice and rind and brush over ham. Pour cider or juice around ham and bake, covered, for approximately 30 minutes, uncovering for last 5 minutes of cooking time.

Meanwhile, prepare raisin sauce: Dissolve sugar in ½ cup water, then boil for 5 minutes. Add remaining ingredients and simmer until jelly dissolves. Serve warm.

Serves 4 to 6.

—Eleonora MacDonald
Etobicoke, Ontario

APPLES, YAMS & SAUSAGE

THE FLAVOURS OF THE SAUSAGE, YAMS AND APPLES COMBINE IN A VERY TASTY FASHION IN THIS simple dish.

1 lb. bulk sausage
2 yams, peeled & cut into 1" chunks
3 medium apples
1 Tbsp. flour

1 Tbsp. brown sugar
½ tsp. cinnamon
salt & pepper

Brown sausage in skillet, cutting into large chunks. Drain off excess fat and place in 2-quart casserole. Add yams. Peel, core and slice apples, then add to casserole and mix gently.

Combine dry ingredients and add to meat, yams and apples, mixing well. Add ½ cup water, cover, and bake for 50 to 60 minutes at 375 degrees F, or until apples and yams are tender.

Serves 3.

—Judith Almond-Best
Madoc, Ontario

SAUSAGE SPINACH STUFFED BRIOCHE

THE FLAVOUR OF THIS SPECTACULAR-LOOKING BRIOCHE DEPENDS VERY MUCH ON THE TYPE OF sausage used. We recommend a garlic or even hotter sausage, but for a milder brioche, use a regular sausage.

Sausage Spinach Filling
½ lb. garlic sausage, crumbled
1 onion, minced
1 clove garlic, crushed
1 pkg. spinach, chopped
½ tsp. pepper
¼ tsp. salt
¼ tsp. thyme
¼ tsp. hot pepper sauce
1 egg

Brioche
¼ cup milk
⅓ cup butter, cut up
3 Tbsp. sugar
¼ tsp. salt
1 Tbsp. yeast
¼ cup warm water
2¼-2¾ cups flour
2 eggs

Brown sausage well in large skillet. Remove and set aside. In drippings, sauté onion and garlic until tender, stirring occasionally. Stir in sausage, spinach, pepper, salt, thyme and pepper sauce. Cook, stirring, for 5 minutes. Cool slightly.

Beat egg and set aside 1 tsp. of it. Stir remaining egg into sausage mixture and mix well. Combine 1 tsp. egg with ¼ tsp. water and reserve for glaze.

To make brioche: Scald milk in small saucepan. Add butter and stir until melted. Stir in sugar and salt and cool to lukewarm. In large bowl, dissolve yeast in ¼ cup warm water. Stir in milk mixture and 1 cup flour. Beat well. Add eggs and 1 cup flour, or enough to make thick batter. Beat until well blended. Cover and let rise until doubled – about 1 hour. Stir down.

Place large tablespoonful of dough on heavily floured surface and form into smooth ball with well-floured hands. Set aside.

Place half remaining dough in greased, deep 1½-quart casserole dish. Press some dough evenly against sides of dish to form hollow. Fill with sausage-spinach mixture. Place remaining dough over filling and pat to cover filling evenly. Press edges to seal. Make small indentation in centre and press in dough ball. Cover and let rise until almost doubled – 30 minutes. Brush with egg-water glaze. Bake at 400 degrees F for 25 minutes, covering with foil after 10 to 15 minutes. Loosen sides with spatula and turn out. Serve warm.

Serves 4 to 6.

—Christine Taylor
Norbertville, Quebec

SAUSAGE-STUFFED APPLES

8 baking apples
8 mushrooms
1 lb. garlic sausage meat

Wash, dry and core apples. Place in 9″ x 13″ baking dish. Stem mushrooms, chop stems and mix with sausage meat. Brown over medium heat, then drain fat. Stuff apples with sausage and top with mushroom caps. Bake, uncovered, at 350 degrees F for 30 minutes.

Serves 6.

—Laurie Bradley
Surrey, British Columbia

GREEN PEPPERS STUFFED WITH PORK & VEAL

SERVE THESE STUFFED PEPPERS WITH A LIGHTLY FLAVOURED TOMATO SAUCE IF DESIRED — THE pepper filling is delicate, so be sure not to overpower it with sauce.

2 Tbsp. plus 1 tsp. butter
4 large green peppers
1 large onion, chopped
½ lb. pork sausage
½ lb. ground veal
1 cup dry bread crumbs

2 Tbsp. milk
1 tsp. salt
½ tsp. pepper
⅛ tsp. nutmeg
½ tsp. thyme

With 1 tsp. butter, grease baking dish large enough to hold peppers. Set aside.

Wash peppers, then slice off and discard 1 inch from tops of peppers. Remove and discard pith and seeds. Melt remaining butter over medium heat. When foam subsides, add onion and cook for 5 to 7 minutes, stirring occasionally, until onion is soft and translucent. Add sausage and veal and stir to break up. Cook, stirring, until meat has lost its pink colour.

Stir in remaining ingredients and cook for another 5 minutes. Spoon filling into peppers, then place peppers in baking dish. Bake, uncovered, at 375 degrees F for 40 to 50 minutes, or until peppers are cooked.

Serves 4.

—Dolores De Rosario
Hamilton, Ontario

CHILI VERDE MEXICAN SALSA

HOT AND SPICY, THIS IS A WONDERFUL SALSA RECIPE. SERVE IT ON TORTILLAS, POTATOES, EGGS, whatever. It makes a good dip too. We suggest you start with the smaller quantities of peppers, then add more if you want a hotter taste.

1 Tbsp. shortening
1 lb. pork, diced
2 onions, chopped
2 28-oz. cans tomatoes, chopped
10-12 oz. canned green chilies, seeded &
  diced

4-8 oz. jalapeño peppers, seeded & diced
2 tsp. salt
½ tsp. pepper
2 cloves garlic, minced
2 Tbsp. oil
2 Tbsp. flour

Melt shortening and brown pork. Add onions and cook until they are translucent. Add tomatoes, chilies, jalapeños, salt, pepper and garlic and simmer. Heat oil in another skillet and stir in flour, cooking until browned. Add to other ingredients, cover and simmer for 3 hours, stirring occasionally.

—Rosemary Huffman
Kennewick, Washington

MUSTARD MARINADE FOR PORK

2-3 Tbsp. Dijon mustard
2 cloves garlic, crushed
2 Tbsp. dry white wine

2 Tbsp. olive oil
½ tsp. pepper

Combine all ingredients and mix well. Brush on meat and let sit at room temperature for at least 30 minutes before proceeding with preparation.

—Trudi Keillor
Berwyn, Alberta

HERB MARINADE FOR LAMB

2 Tbsp. oil
1 Tbsp. lemon juice
1 clove garlic, crushed
½ tsp. marjoram
½ tsp. rosemary

½ tsp. thyme
½ tsp. sage
½ tsp. mint
½ tsp. pepper
½ tsp. salt

Combine all ingredients and mix thoroughly. This can be brushed on a leg of lamb or added to a marinade for cubed lamb. Let sit at room temperature for at least 30 minutes.

—Trudi Keillor
Berwyn, Alberta

BLACK BEAN SAUCE WITH GARLIC & GINGER

KEEP THIS SAUCE ON HAND TO DRESS UP SPARERIBS, SHRIMP, CHICKEN OR TOFU IF UNEXPECTED company drops in. Simply add to cooked meat and heat through, thickening with cornstarch if desired.

3 Tbsp. oil
3-4 cloves garlic, crushed
2 Tbsp. chopped cooked black beans
2-3 onions, quartered

1 cup chicken stock
½ inch gingerroot, grated
2 Tbsp. soy sauce
1 tsp. honey

Heat oil, add garlic and black beans and sauté for 30 seconds. Add onions, sauté for 2 to 3 minutes, then add remaining ingredients. Cover and simmer for 1 to 2 minutes. Cool. Refrigerate if not using immediately.

Makes enough sauce for 2 pounds of spareribs.

—Margaret Graham
Greenwood, British Columbia

SAVOURY LAMB SHANKS

4 lamb shanks
3 large cloves garlic, slivered
salt & pepper
1 tsp. rosemary
2 Tbsp. chopped parsley
1 tsp. oregano

2 onions, thinly sliced
1 lb. fresh Italian plum tomatoes, peeled,
    seeded & coarsely chopped or 2 cups
    canned Italian plum tomatoes
¾ cup dry white wine
¾ cup olive oil

Remove excess fat and tendons from shanks. Insert garlic into meat in 2 or 3 crevices, then sprinkle remainder on top. Season with salt and pepper. Arrange shanks in baking dish and roast, uncovered, at 425 degrees F for 20 minutes. Reduce heat to 350 degrees F and sprinkle rosemary, parsley, oregano and onions over meat. Spoon tomatoes over meat and pour wine over all. Drizzle olive oil on top.

Return to oven and cook for 1 to 1½ hours, or until tender. Remove shanks to serving dish. Reduce liquid slightly and season with salt and pepper.

Serves 4.

—Ann L. Combs
Ashland, New Hampshire

KASHMIRI-STYLE LEG OF LAMB

"I DISCOVERED THIS DISH WHILE LIVING IN DUBAI. IT IS NOT TOO HOT, JUST TENDER AND flavourful. Serve it with Spiced Cauliflower and Potatoes." All the work is done two days before serving, which makes this a convenient dish to serve guests.

5-lb. leg of lamb
1 Tbsp. grated gingerroot
4 cloves garlic, crushed
3 tsp. salt
1 tsp. cumin
1 tsp. turmeric
½ tsp. pepper
½ tsp. cinnamon
½ tsp. cardamom

¼ tsp. cloves
½ tsp. chili powder
2 Tbsp. lemon juice
1 cup yogurt
2 Tbsp. blanched almonds
2 Tbsp. pistachios
1 Tbsp. turmeric
3 tsp. honey

Remove excess fat from lamb and make deep slits all over the leg. Place in glass or stainless-steel casserole dish. Combine ginger, garlic, salt, cumin, 1 tsp. turmeric, pepper, cinnamon, cardamom, cloves, chili powder and lemon juice. Rub over lamb, pressing into slits.

Blend together yogurt, almonds, pistachios and 1 Tbsp. turmeric and spread over lamb. Drizzle honey over lamb. Cover and marinate, refrigerated, for 2 days, turning occasionally.

Roast, covered, at 450 degrees F for 30 minutes, reduce heat to 350 degrees F and roast for another 1¾ hours. Uncover and serve at room temperature.

Serves 8.

—Cynthia R. Topliss
Montreal, Quebec

LAMB WITH FENNEL & TOMATOES

ALSO KNOWN AS FINOCCHIO, FENNEL IS AN ANISE-FLAVOURED VEGETABLE. THE ROOT LOOKS much like a celery heart, and the stalks end in dill-like, feathery leaves. It can be eaten raw, made into soup, braised or added to casseroles. If using the leaves for seasoning, be discreet, as the anise flavour is very strong.

5 Tbsp. olive oil
2-lb. boned leg of lamb, cubed
1 onion, chopped

2 cups peeled, seeded & mashed tomatoes
salt & pepper
1½ lbs. fennel, quartered

Heat oil in heavy casserole dish, then brown meat on all sides. Stir in onion and sauté for 5 minutes more, then add tomatoes and salt and pepper. Reduce heat, cover and simmer for 40 minutes, adding water if necessary.

Cook fennel in boiling salted water for 20 minutes. Drain, reserving 1 cup liquid. Add fennel and 1 cup liquid to lamb and cook for 20 minutes more.

Serves 4.

—Carroll MacDonald
Pierre Fundy, Quebec

RIVERSLEA LAMB SHANKS

"LAMB SHANKS ARE OFTEN BONED AND USED FOR STEW, BUT THE MEAT IS PERHAPS THE MOST tasty cut of lamb. This delicious recipe makes great use of an inexpensive cut."

4 lamb shanks
flour
oil
1 cup pitted prunes

½ cup brown sugar
½ tsp. cinnamon
½ tsp. allspice
3 Tbsp. vinegar

Dust shanks with flour and brown all over in a little hot oil. Mix remaining ingredients and 1 cup water and pour over shanks. Cover and bake at 350 degrees F for 2 hours, turning shanks over occasionally.

Serves 4.

—Jean Rivers
Vancouver, British Columbia

Desserts

"I doubt whether the world holds for anyone a more soul-stirring surprise than the first adventure with ice cream."

—*Heywood Brown*

"I stood transfixed before the windows of the confectioners' shops," Simone de Beauvoir once wrote, "fascinated by the luminous sparkle of candied fruits, the cloudy lustre of jellies . . . I coveted the colours themselves as much as the pleasure they promised me. . . . "

While most of us understand these sentiments, we have an acquaintance who eschews any food containing sugar, no matter how little. We appreciate his position, but in these days of increasing reliance on artificial sweeteners, good old "white death" sugar starts to look pretty safe. As one study after another has associated carcinogenicity and nervous disorders with chemical sweetening agents, the problems related to real sugar appear simple.

"Sugar is one of nature's remedies," the alchemist Paracelsus asserted, and we can attest to the restorative effects of the sight of a warm blueberry crisp, a bubbling crème brûlée or the dewy sparkles bidding invitation on a chilled apple meringue pie.

Traditionally, dessert baking—especially pies—has been the true test of a cook's skill in North America, no doubt a legacy from rural church suppers where a wife's pastry skills were there for all to see and taste. Crusts, in fact, can prove tricky for some, and a few basic tips are probably in order here.

The most important rule is always to handle lightly and quickly. If you have a food processor, by all means take advantage of its ability to incorporate the ingredients in seconds.

Before beginning, thoroughly chill all the ingredients (the water should be ice-cold) and utensils, including the bowl, fork, food processor blade or pastry cutter. We like to keep our flour in the freezer to prevent bug infestation and use it straight from the cold for pie making.

Measure accurately: too much fat will make a greasy crust, too much flour will toughen it, and too much water will make it impossible to roll. Flour the counter and rolling pin before beginning. What fat to use is a matter of debate, with the old school swearing that lard produces the flakiest crusts. Others rely on butter, margarine, vegetable shortening or a combination. In our experience, the most significant factor in making a good pastry crust is not the choice of fat but the way the dough is handled.

The dough will be easier to work, particularly if it is made with butter, if it has been covered in plastic wrap and refrigerated for up to 12 hours before rolling. Remove it from the refrigerator approximately one hour before it is to be used, and roll it out as gently as possible.

Finally, if you need to rationalize partaking of a particularly sinful dessert, tell yourself that it is not the first serving that causes the problem but, rather, the second and the third.

ROYAL CHEDDAR CHEESECAKE

THIS IS A VERY RICH, CREAMY CHEESECAKE WITH A TANG OF LEMON AND A HINT OF CHEDDAR.

Crust
1½ cups graham cracker crumbs
3 Tbsp. sugar
1 tsp. grated lemon rind
6 Tbsp. butter, melted

Filling
4 8-oz. pkgs. cream cheese
1 cup finely grated Cheddar cheese
1¾ cups sugar
5 eggs
½ cup heavy cream
½ tsp. vanilla
1 tsp. lemon rind

To make crust: Mix crumbs, 3 Tbsp. sugar, 1 tsp. lemon rind and butter. Press evenly in the bottom and up the sides of a 9″ springform pan. Chill.

To make filling: In a food processor or with an electric mixer, beat cream cheese and Cheddar cheese together thoroughly. Mix in 1¾ cups sugar until creamy smooth. Beat in eggs, one at a time, then cream, vanilla and 1 tsp. lemon rind. Pour into prepared crust. Bake in very hot oven (500 degrees F) for 12 minutes; reduce heat to 300 degrees and bake for 2 hours, or until firm in the centre. Cool cake completely in pan on wire rack. Chill.

To serve, loosen cake around edges with a knife and remove springform. May be covered with any sliced fresh fruit.

—Kristine Mattila
Quesnel, British Columbia

HONEY CHEESECAKE

Crust
1½ cups graham cracker crumbs
½ cup butter, melted
2 Tbsp. sugar

Filling
16 oz. cream cheese
⅓ cup honey
2 tsp. cinnamon
2 eggs
2 heaping Tbsp. sour cream
1 tsp. vanilla

Topping
½ pint plus 2 Tbsp. sour cream
1 tsp. vanilla
2 Tbsp. honey
juice of ⅓ lemon

Sauce
1½ cups sliced strawberries
½ cup brandy

Combine crust ingredients and press into large springform pan. Bake at 350 degrees F for 10 minutes, then cool for 5 minutes.

Mix all filling ingredients together and spoon into cooled crust. Bake at 325 degrees F for 30 minutes. Turn heat off and leave pie in oven for 10 more minutes..

Combine topping ingredients and pour over filling. Bake for 8 minutes at 400 degrees F, or until set. Combine berries and brandy, and spoon over cake.

—Lisa Reith
Cranbrook, British Columbia

GINGER CHEESECAKE

A REFRESHINGLY DIFFERENT CHEESECAKE, THIS ONE BLENDS FRESH GINGERROOT AND crystallized ginger.

Crust
1½ cups graham cracker crumbs
6 Tbsp. butter, melted
2 Tbsp. sugar

Filling
16 oz. cream cheese
½ cup (or less) sugar
2 eggs

3 tsp. lemon juice
2 Tbsp. freshly ground **or** grated
   gingerroot

Topping
1½ cups sour cream
5 Tbsp. sugar
3 Tbsp. (or more) chopped crystallized
   ginger

Make crust by combining crumbs, butter and sugar. Press into springform pan. Bake at 350 degrees F for 8 minutes.

Beat filling ingredients together until smooth. Pour into crust. Bake at 350 degrees F for 20 to 25 minutes.

Mix topping ingredients together. Spread over cheesecake while it is still hot from the oven. Turn oven off and place cheesecake back in oven for a few minutes. Remove and chill well before serving.

Serves 8.

—Marian da Costa
Etobicoke, Ontario

MAPLE CHEESECAKE

TRULY A CHEESECAKE FOR MAPLE-SYRUP LOVERS, THIS ONE IS RICH, CREAMY AND SMOOTH.

Crust
1¾ cups graham cracker
   crumbs
¼ cup butter, melted
3 Tbsp. brown sugar

Filling
½ cup flour
¼ tsp. baking soda
¼ tsp. salt
3 eggs

¾ cup sugar
8 oz. cream cheese
1¼ cups heavy cream
1 cup maple syrup
1 tsp. vanilla

Topping
1 cup heavy cream
½ cup maple syrup

pecans for garnish

For crust: Mix together crust ingredients and press into springform pan. Bake at 350 degrees F for 10 minutes.

For filling: Sift together flour, baking soda and salt. Beat eggs thoroughly. Add sugar and blend well. Cream the cream cheese until fluffy. Add cream slowly and beat until smooth. Blend in 1 cup maple syrup, egg mixture and flour mixture. Add vanilla and mix well.

Pour filling into crust. Bake at 350 degrees F for 1½ hours, or until centre has set. Turn off oven and let sit for 15 minutes. Chill.

Just before serving, whip cream and ½ cup maple syrup together and spread over cheesecake. Garnish with pecans.

—Jane Durward
Lindsay, Ontario

APPLE BAVARIAN TORTE

Crust
⅓ cup softened butter
⅓ cup sugar
½ tsp. salt
1 cup flour

Filling
1 cup cottage cheese
⅓ cup sugar
½ tsp. vanilla
1 egg

Topping
4 cups sliced apples
sugar to taste
1 tsp. cinnamon

Crumble
3 Tbsp. butter
⅓ cup flour
⅓ cup sugar

¼ cup sliced almonds for garnish

Make crust by mixing ingredients together and pressing into bottom of an 8″ x 8″ pan.

Mash cottage cheese, then stir in sugar, vanilla and egg until well blended. Spread on top of crust. Place ingredients for topping with 3 Tbsp. water in saucepan and cook over low heat until apples are just slightly tender. Spread carefully over filling.

Combine ingredients for crumble and sprinkle over topping. Arrange almonds on top. Bake at 425 degrees F for 20 minutes, lower heat to 375 degrees and bake for 40 minutes more, or until golden brown. Garnish with sliced almonds. Torte must be cut in pan.

Serves 6 to 8.

—Juanita Bryant
Pembroke, Ontario

RHUBARB DESSERT TORTE

THE RICH SHORTBREAD-LIKE BASE OF THIS RECIPE IS TOPPED WITH A RHUBARB CUSTARD AND meringue, producing a mouthwatering dessert with very little effort.

Base
1 cup butter
2 cups flour
2 Tbsp. sugar

Custard
5 cups finely chopped rhubarb
2 cups sugar
1 cup cream
6 egg yolks

4 Tbsp. flour
¼ tsp. salt
juice & rind of 2 oranges

Meringue
6 egg whites
¾ cup sugar
2 tsp. vanilla
coconut

Combine ingredients for base and blend well. Press into 9″ x 13″ pan and bake at 350 degrees F for 10 minutes.

Combine custard ingredients and pour into baked crust. Bake at 350 degrees F for 45 minutes.

Beat egg whites until peaks form, adding sugar 2 Tbsp. at a time. Add vanilla and spread on baked custard. Top with coconut and bake at 400 degrees F until browned – 10 minutes.

Serves 10.

—Dave & Essie Bergen
Clearwater, Manitoba

CHOCOLATE CREAM PIE

"PUT ON A POT OF COFFEE, LIGHT A FIRE AND PUT THE KIDS TO BED. THIS PIE IS THE PERFECT accompaniment – creamy, rich, chocolatey and delicious."

Pastry
1½ cups flour
½ tsp. salt
½ cup very cold butter
1 egg yolk

Filling
1 cup plus 2 Tbsp. sugar
½ tsp. salt

1 Tbsp. flour
4 Tbsp. cornstarch
3⅔ cups whole milk
6 Tbsp. cocoa
2 Tbsp. oil
2 eggs, beaten
2 Tbsp. butter
1 tsp. vanilla
whipped cream

To make pastry: Combine flour and salt. Cut in butter until crumbly. Add egg yolk and ¼ cup, or more, cold water and toss until dough forms a ball. Put into a plastic bag and knead a few seconds. Chill for at least 1 hour. Roll out on lightly floured board and place in 10-inch pie plate. Crimp edges and prick all over with a fork. Bake at 350 degrees F for 20 minutes, remove from oven and prick again if crust has puffed up. Bake for 20 minutes more.

To make filling: Combine sugar, salt, flour, cornstarch, milk, cocoa and oil. Heat to boiling, stirring constantly until mixture thickens. Remove from heat. Stir about half of chocolate mixture into eggs until completely blended. Pour mixture back into saucepan and continue cooking, stirring constantly until mixture boils again. Remove from heat and blend in butter and vanilla. Pour into crust and chill. Serve with whipped cream.

—Julia Dement
Stockton, California

AMARETTO YOGURT CREAM CHEESE PIE

THIS IS A VERY RICH AMARETTO-LADEN DESSERT THAT IS QUICK AND EASY TO PREPARE. BE SURE to allow it to set overnight.

Crust
2 cups crushed ladyfingers
⅓ cup finely chopped lightly toasted
   almonds
¼ cup Amaretto
3 Tbsp. butter, melted

Filling
8 oz. cream cheese, softened
½ cup yogurt
½ tsp. vanilla
¼ cup honey
⅓ cup Amaretto

¼ cup finely chopped lightly toasted
   almonds

Combine crust ingredients and mix well. Press firmly into bottom and sides of 8-inch pie pan. Bake at 325 degrees F for 10 minutes. Cool.

To make filling: Combine all ingredients and beat until completely smooth. Spread in pan. Chill overnight and top with ¼ cup almonds before serving.

—Nancy Scott
Port Matilda, Pennsylvania

APPLE MERINGUE PIE WITH HAZELNUT PASTRY

MULTILAYERED FLAVOURS MAKE THIS PIE EXCEPTIONAL.

Pastry
¾ cup plus 2 Tbsp. flour
1 tsp. baking powder
½ cup plus 1 Tbsp. sugar
½ tsp. vanilla
¼ tsp. almond extract
⅛ tsp. cloves
1 tsp. cinnamon
1 egg white and ½ yolk (reserve other half)
½ cup plus 2 Tbsp. unsalted butter, cut up
½ cup plus 2 Tbsp. ground hazelnuts
1 Tbsp. milk

Filling
10 tart green apples

juice of 1 lemon
⅔ cup sugar, plus more as needed
¼ tsp. cinnamon
4 Tbsp. butter
2 Tbsp. flour

Meringue
4 Tbsp. Frangelico (hazelnut) liqueur
2 Tbsp. cornstarch
6 large egg whites
¾ cup sugar
salt
1 tsp. vanilla

2 Tbsp. raspberry jam

To make crust: In large bowl, sift together flour and baking powder. Add sugar, vanilla, almond extract, spices and egg and mix together well. Add butter and hazelnuts and knead quickly with fingers to blend. Divide dough in half, reserving one half in freezer. Press other half evenly over bottom and sides of a 9-inch pie plate. Mix reserved ½ egg yolk with 1 Tbsp. milk and brush crust all over. Repeat process with other half. Bake at 350 degrees F for 25 to 30 minutes.

To make filling: Pare and core apples and cut into ¼-inch slices. Mix with lemon, sugar and cinnamon. In large frying pan with lid, melt butter, add flour and cook for 1 minute. Add apple mixture and stir to coat evenly. Cover and cook until just tender, stirring occasionally. Taste for sweetness and add more sugar to taste.

To make meringue: In small saucepan, mix Frangelico and cornstarch until smooth, then add 1 cup boiling water. Put over high heat, stirring briskly until just clear. Chill completely, in freezer. In large bowl, beat egg whites until just foamy. Continue beating while adding sugar until mixture is stiff but not dry. Beat in cornstarch mixture in thirds. When smooth, add salt and vanilla.

To assemble: Brush raspberry jam evenly over crusts. Spoon apple mixture into crusts. Mound meringue on top, making decorative peaks with the back of a spoon. Bake at 350 degrees F for 10 minutes, or until browned.

Makes 2 pies.

—Sandra Lance
Cos Cob, Connecticut

BURGUNDY BERRY PIE

2 cups cranberries
2 cups blueberries
½ cup honey
3 Tbsp. cornstarch

⅛ tsp. salt
⅛ tsp. nutmeg
pastry for 9-inch pie shell

Thaw and drain cranberries and blueberries if frozen. Mix honey, cornstarch, salt and nutmeg. Add berries and pour into pie shell. Bake at 425 degrees F for 15 minutes, lower oven temperature to 375 degrees and bake for 35 to 50 minutes longer.

—Judy Mueller
Dawson, Nebraska

RHUBARB CREAM PIE

DEVELOPED BY THE CONTRIBUTOR'S PENNSYLVANIAN MOTHER-IN-LAW FOR FARMHANDS DURING haying, this rhubarb pie is for cinnamon lovers.

pastry for 9-inch pie shell
2 lbs. rhubarb, cut into ½" pieces
1½ cups brown sugar
3 Tbsp. quick-cooking tapioca

2 eggs
¼ cup heavy cream
2 Tbsp. cinnamon
2 Tbsp. butter

Line pie plate with pastry. Combine rhubarb, sugar, tapioca, eggs, cream and cinnamon. Toss gently to coat rhubarb. Place in pastry and dot with butter. Bake at 425 degrees F for 10 minutes, reduce heat to 350 degrees and bake for another 20 to 30 minutes.

—Patricia P. Marzke
Orlando, Florida

DAKOTA PRAIRIE PUMPKIN PIE

"THIS RECIPE HAS BEEN HANDED DOWN WITH PRIDE THROUGH SIX GENERATIONS SINCE CHARLES and Ann Ashton settled in South Dakota in 1881. No family gathering would be complete without it."

4 cups pumpkin purée
4 cups sugar
1 tsp. salt
2 tsp. cinnamon
1 tsp. nutmeg
6 eggs, lightly beaten

4 cups milk
1 cup light cream
1 Tbsp. vanilla
pastry for 3 9-inch pie shells
whipped cream & chopped walnuts
  for garnish

Combine pumpkin, sugar, salt, cinnamon and nutmeg. Blend in eggs, milk, cream and vanilla. Pour into pie shells and bake at 400 degrees F for 50 minutes, or until firm. Cool on a rack. Garnish with whipped cream and chopped walnuts.

Makes 3 pies.

—Mrs. Charles Weinberger
Artesian, South Dakota

THE BEST OF ALL BUTTERMILK PIE

"MY DAUGHTER AND I TRIED MANY BUTTERMILK PIE RECIPES THROUGH THE YEARS AND FINALLY found the right combination: neither too sweet nor too sour."

3 cups sugar
½ cup flour
6 eggs
1 cup buttermilk

¾ cup butter, melted
1 Tbsp. vanilla
pastry for 9-inch pie shells

Mix sugar and flour and set aside. Whisk eggs, add buttermilk, butter and vanilla. Mix well. Slowly add flour-sugar mixture and beat thoroughly. Pour into unbaked pie shells. Bake at 325 degrees F for 1 hour.

Makes 2 pies.

—Peggy Peabody
Dallas, Texas

SWEET POTATO PECAN PIE

"THIS PIE HOLDS A SPECIAL PLACE IN MY CHILDHOOD MEMORIES."

¼ cup butter
½ cup sugar
1 cup cooked, mashed sweet potato
3 eggs
⅓ cup milk

½ tsp. salt
1 tsp. vanilla
1 cup chopped pecans
pastry for 9-inch pie shell

Cream butter and sugar until smooth. Add sweet potato and eggs and blend well. Mix in milk, salt, vanilla and pecans. Pour into pastry shell and bake at 425 degrees F for 10 minutes. Reduce oven temperature to 325 degrees and bake for another 45 minutes.

—Christine Taylor
Norbertville, Quebec

ALMOND ORANGE PIE WITH GRAND MARNIER CREAM

"A MELT-IN-YOUR-MOUTH INDULGENCE FOR AFTER THAT TRIP THROUGH CUSTOMS WITH YOUR coveted bottle of Grand Marnier. While not an instant recipe, it is well worth the effort."

Pastry
1½ cups pastry flour
½ tsp. ginger
½ tsp. nutmeg
⅛ tsp. salt
⅔ cup butter
⅔ cup sugar
½ cup ground almonds
1 large egg yolk

Filling
2 navel oranges, rind grated & reserved
1 cup plus 3 Tbsp. sugar

2 Tbsp. fresh lemon juice
3 Tbsp. softened butter
1 tsp. vanilla
½ tsp. almond extract
2 Tbsp. flour
2 eggs plus 2 egg whites
2 Tbsp. Grand Marnier

Glaze
1 large egg yolk beaten with 1 tsp. heavy
  cream

⅓ cup sliced almonds

To make pastry: Blend flour, spices and salt with butter until mixture resembles coarse meal. Blend in sugar, ground almonds and egg yolk plus 1 to 2 tsp. cold water to form a soft dough. Form into 2 balls and chill for 30 minutes. Roll half the dough between sheets of waxed paper to ⅛-inch thickness and fit into 9-inch pie plate, leaving ½-inch overhang. Roll the other half to ⅛-inch thickness, and chill for 30 minutes.

To make filling: Section oranges, removing pith and membranes. In stainless-steel or enamel pot, combine sections with orange rind, 3 Tbsp. sugar, lemon juice and ½ cup water. Bring to a boil and reduce to ¾ cup. Cool. Cream butter and remaining 1 cup sugar. Add vanilla, almond extract, flour, eggs and egg whites. Mix well. Add orange mixture and Grand Marnier and pour into shell.

Cut remaining dough into strips and lay across pie in a lattice pattern. Fold in overhang and crimp edges. Pour glaze over pie. Sprinkle with sliced almonds.

Bake at 350 degrees F for 45 minutes, or until almonds are golden and filling puffs up through lattice. May be served with a topping of 1½ cups heavy cream whipped with 3 Tbsp. confectioners' sugar and 2 Tbsp. Grand Marnier if desired.

—Anne Creighton
Maberly, Ontario

FRUIT PLATZ

"THIS IS A RECIPE GIVEN TO US BY AN ELDERLY GENTLEMAN WHO RECALLED IT FROM HIS YOUTH on the Prairies, stating they often used wild berries in summer and dried apples in winter."

Crust
1¾ cups flour
1 tsp. baking powder
½ tsp. salt
⅓ cup butter
1 egg, beaten

Filling
2½ cups sliced fruit

Topping
½ cup sugar
1 Tbsp. softened butter

To assemble: Make crust by combining dry ingredients and cutting in butter. Add ½ beaten egg and ¼ cup cold water to make a soft dough. Press dough into greased 8" x 8" pan, pressing mixture about 1 inch up the sides. Add fruit, spreading evenly over crust. Combine topping ingredients and spread over fruit. Bake at 350 degrees F for 50 to 60 minutes.

Serves 6 to 8.

—Judith Almond-Best
Madoc, Ontario

PATCHBERRY PIE

A VARIATION OF THE STANDARD RHUBARB PIE THAT IS DELICIOUS SERVED WARM WITH ICE cream. Frozen rhubarb or currants can be used for a midwinter treat.

Filling
2 eggs
⅝ cup flour
½ tsp. salt
2 Tbsp. butter, melted
2½ cups sugar
2 cups red currants
7 cups chopped rhubarb, cut into 1" pieces

pastry for three 9-inch pie shells

Crumb Topping
⅔ cup flour
1 cup brown sugar
1 tsp. salt
⅔ cup butter, melted
2 cups rolled oats

Beat eggs lightly, then combine with flour, salt, 2 Tbsp. butter and sugar. Add currants and rhubarb and fill crusts. Combine crumb topping ingredients and sprinkle on top. Bake at 425 degrees F for 10 minutes, then at 350 degrees for 40 to 50 minutes.

Makes 3 pies.

—Kim Allerton
Desboro, Ontario

MAPLE CUSTARD

½ cup maple syrup
3 eggs, beaten
2 cups milk

salt
mace

Add syrup to eggs and beat well. Beat in milk and salt. Spoon into 4 custard cups and sprinkle with mace. Place cups in pan with 1 inch water. Bake at 350 degrees F for 40 minutes.

Serves 4.

—Mrs. L.M. Cyre
Logan Lake, British Columbia

PUMPKIN PECAN TARTS

Make these tarts with frozen pumpkin purée for a midwinter flavour pick-up. To freeze pumpkin, bake at 300 degrees F until soft (baking time will depend on size of pumpkin), remove filling from shells, discard seeds, purée, then freeze.

Filling
½ cup milk
½ cup light cream
2 eggs
1½ cups puréed pumpkin
⅔ cup brown sugar
1 tsp. cinnamon
½ tsp. salt
½ tsp. ginger
½ tsp. cloves
½ tsp. allspice

1 tsp. vanilla

24 unbaked tart shells

Topping
1 cup chopped pecans
⅔ cup brown sugar
3 Tbsp. butter, melted

whipped cream for garnish
pecan halves for garnish

Place all filling ingredients in blender or food processor and blend for 2 minutes. Pour into tart shells and bake at 425 degrees F for 15 minutes. Reduce heat to 275 degrees and bake for 30 minutes more, or until a toothpick inserted in the centre comes out clean. Let tarts cool.

For topping: Mix nuts and sugar. Stir in butter until mixture is uniformly moist. Sprinkle over tarts. Broil about 5 inches from heat for 1 to 2 minutes. Serve with whipped cream and pecan halves.

Makes 24 tarts.

—*J.W. Houston*
Willowdale, Ontario

STEAMED CRANBERRY PUDDING

"This recipe was given to me by a good friend whose family serves it at every Christmas dinner. It has since become a holiday favourite for our family too." The pudding has a tart cranberry taste, well complemented by the sweetness of the sauce.

Pudding
2 cups cranberries
½ cup molasses
2 tsp. baking soda
1½ cups flour

Hot Butter Sauce
½ cup butter
1 cup sugar
½ cup light cream
1 tsp. vanilla

Cut cranberries in half and pour molasses over them. Dissolve baking soda in ½ cup boiling water, then add to cranberries. Stir in flour. Place in well-greased 1-lb. can, and cover with foil. Place in covered kettle with boiling water and steam for 1½ hours.

Meanwhile, prepare sauce: Cream butter and sugar together. Add cream, then place in double boiler and cook until sugar is dissolved. Do not boil. Stir in vanilla. Spoon over pudding while hot.

Serves 8 to 10.

—*Susan Holec*
Brooklyn, Wisconsin

BAKED MAPLE PUDDING

Sauce
1 cup maple syrup
2 tsp. butter

Pudding
1 cup flour

1½ tsp. baking powder
⅓ cup demerara sugar
1 Tbsp. shortening
1 egg
⅓ cup milk
½ cup unsweetened coconut

Bring maple syrup and 1 cup water to a boil, then remove from heat. Add butter and set aside.

Sift together flour and baking powder. Cream sugar and shortening together. Beat in egg. Add dry ingredients alternately with milk to creamed mixture. Beat until smooth. Spread cake batter into greased 8″ x 8″ pan. Pour sauce over and sprinkle coconut evenly over top. Bake at 350 degrees F for 35 minutes. Serve warm.

Serves 6 to 8.

—Shelley Bishop
Swastika, Ontario

LEMON CUSTARD PUDDING

¾ cup sugar
1 Tbsp. butter
2 eggs, separated

2 Tbsp. flour
1 cup milk
juice of 1 lemon

Cream sugar and butter together. Beat egg yolks and add to sugar-butter mixture. Mix in flour, milk and lemon juice. Beat egg whites until stiff and fold into batter. Pour into small, buttered ovenproof dish. Place dish in pan containing ½ inch water. Bake at 325 degrees F for about 50 minutes.

Serves 2 to 3.

—Ruth Henly
Victoria, British Columbia

BAKED ORANGE PUDDING

"THIS RECIPE HAS BEEN IN MY FAMILY FOR WELL OVER 50 YEARS AND IS STILL GOING STRONG. Easy to make, it is simply scrumptious with whipped cream."

Sauce
1 cup sugar
1 Tbsp. flour
1 Tbsp. butter
juice & rind of 1 or more oranges

Batter
½ cup sugar
1 cup flour
1 tsp. baking powder
1 tsp. butter
½ cup milk
⅛ tsp. salt

Make sauce by mixing sugar and flour in saucepan. Melt butter in 2 cups hot water. Add to saucepan with orange juice and rind. Bring to a boil and pour into greased 9″ x 9″ baking dish.

Mix batter ingredients together and spoon over sauce. Bake, uncovered, at 350 degrees F for 40 to 50 minutes, or until golden brown. Serve warm.

Serves 4.

—H. Jean Brown
Toronto, Ontario

FIGS & PEARS IN RUM CUSTARD SAUCE

½ cup sugar
1 cup water
½ tsp. vanilla
1 tsp. grated orange rind
1 tsp. grated lemon rind
24 fresh figs **or** dried figs that have been
  soaked
8 fresh pears, peeled & halved
½ cup dark rum

Rum Custard Sauce
1 Tbsp. cornstarch
1½ cups milk
4 egg yolks
¼ cup sugar
⅛ tsp. salt
½ cup juice from marinade
2 tsp. dark rum
2 cups heavy cream, whipped

Combine sugar, water, vanilla and grated rind in saucepan. Stir over low heat until mixture comes to a boil. Cut 12 figs in half and leave remainder whole. Add fruit to saucepan, reduce heat and simmer 3 to 4 minutes if the figs are fresh, 10 minutes if dried. Add rum. Marinate fruit in this syrup for 1 to 2 hours in a cool place.

Prepare custard by dissolving cornstarch in ¼ cup cold milk. Add egg yolks and beat lightly. Add remaining 1¼ cups milk, sugar and salt and bring to a simmer, stirring, in a double boiler. Add ½ cup juice from marinade and cook until thickened. Cool. Add rum and chill.

To serve: Place fruit in a large serving bowl. Pour the sauce over and top with whipped cream.

Serves 6 to 8.

—Ingrid Birker
Montreal, Quebec

FROZEN SOUFFLÉ WITH HOT STRAWBERRY SAUCE

OUR VERMONT TESTER SAYS, "DELICIOUSLY DIFFERENT AND VERY EASY TO PREPARE, THIS WAS gone as soon as I put it out for testing."

½ gallon vanilla ice cream
12 almond macaroons, crumbled
5 Tbsp. Grand Marnier **or** orange liqueur
2 cups heavy cream
½ cup chopped, toasted almonds
icing sugar

Sauce
2 quarts strawberries, halved
½ cup sugar
6 Tbsp. Grand Marnier **or** orange liqueur

Soften ice cream slightly, then stir in macaroons and liqueur. Whip cream until thick, then fold into ice cream. Spoon into angel-food pan and sprinkle surface with almonds and icing sugar. Cover with plastic wrap and freeze until firm—at least 5 hours, but preferably overnight.

Prepare sauce just before serving. Place berries in saucepan with sugar and simmer until just soft. Remove from heat and stir in liqueur.

Unmould soufflé and top with sauce.

Serves 12 to 16.

—Sherry Mowat Spruit
Mountain, Ontario

BERRIES IN LEMON MOUSSE

4 cups blueberries, raspberries **or**
    strawberries
1 cup sugar
5 eggs, separated

juice of 2 large lemons
1 cup heavy cream, whipped
2 Tbsp. grated lemon rind

Wash berries, remove stems and drain well. Pour into glass serving bowl and sprinkle with ¼ cup sugar. In top of double boiler, beat egg yolks with remaining ¾ cup sugar until light yellow in colour. Add lemon juice and continue to cook over simmering water, whisking constantly, until mixture is thick enough to heavily coat a spoon. Remove from heat and allow to cool. Beat egg whites until stiff but not dry. Fold gently into cooled lemon mixture. Fold in whipped cream and lemon rind. Be sure everything is well incorporated and the mousse is very smooth. Chill well. Immediately before serving, cover berries with mousse.

Serves 4 to 6.

—*Holly Andrews*
Puslinch, Ontario

BLUEBERRY CRISP

4 cups blueberries, fresh **or** frozen
¾ cup sugar
1 tsp. nutmeg
⅓ cup butter

⅓ cup brown sugar
6 Tbsp. flour
¾ cup oatmeal
1 tsp. cinnamon

Place berries in greased 9-inch casserole dish. Mix sugar and nutmeg and pour over berries. Cream butter and brown sugar. Add flour, oatmeal and cinnamon. Crumble over berries. Bake at 350 degrees F for 30 minutes. Good warm or cold, topped with ice cream or yogurt.

Serves 4 to 5.

—*Valerie L. Arnason*
Cheverie, Nova Scotia

PEARS IN CHOCOLATE

THIS VERY ELEGANT DESSERT IS MUCH EASIER TO PREPARE THAN THE FINAL PRODUCT WOULD lead you to believe.

6 ripe but firm pears (Bartlett or Anjou),
    with stems intact
1 cup sugar
2 4″ cinnamon sticks
4 cloves

juice of 1 small lemon
2 Tbsp. crème de menthe
4 oz. semisweet chocolate
¼ cup butter

Carefully peel pears and cut bottoms flat so they will stand upright. In heavy pan, heat sugar, 4 cups water, spices, lemon juice and crème de menthe. Simmer for 15 minutes. Add pears and stew in syrup, turning frequently, for about 30 minutes, or until tender. Chill overnight in syrup.

Melt chocolate and butter in double boiler over hot water. Drain pears and pat dry. Dip pears in chocolate sauce, coating evenly. Place on waxed paper and chill. Allow to return to room temperature before serving.

Serves 6.

—*Kathryn MacDonald*
Yarker, Ontario

FLAMING APPLE BRANDY CRÊPES

"I INVENTED THIS EASY YET ELEGANT DISH SO NEW YEAR'S EVE GUESTS COULD RING IN 1987 with delicious (but inexpensive) style. Serve with cream."

Crêpes
2 Tbsp. butter, melted
1½ cups milk
⅔ cup flour
½ tsp. salt
3 eggs
oil for frying

Filling
4 large tart cooking apples
1 Tbsp. flour
1 Tbsp. butter
½ cup brown sugar
1 tsp. cinnamon
⅛ tsp. nutmeg
4 oz. brandy

In medium bowl, with wire whisk, beat all crêpe ingredients together, except oil, until smooth. Cover and refrigerate batter for at least 2 hours.

Heat and swirl a scant teaspoon of oil in 10-inch skillet. Pour a scant ¼ cup batter into pan and swirl to coat. Cook for about 2 minutes over medium heat, or until top is just set and bottom is browned. With metal spatula, loosen crêpe all around and turn over. Cook other side until just browned – about 30 seconds. Slide cooked crêpe onto a plate. Repeat with remaining batter, stacking crêpes as they are cooked.

Prepare filling: Pare and slice apples as if for pie. Toss with flour to coat, then set aside. In saucepan, melt butter, then add sugar and spices. Add apples and stir to coat. Add half the brandy. Over low heat, simmer and stir often until apples are tender – about 15 minutes. If mixture becomes a little dry, add a bit of water or more brandy.

To serve: Fill and roll 4 crêpes. Transfer each crêpe to a serving plate. Gently heat remaining 2 oz. of brandy. Divide among crêpes, and set alight. Pass pitcher of cream for drizzling over each serving.

Serves 4.

—Sandy Robertson
Port Robinson, Ontario

CRÈME BRÛLÉE

SERVE THIS VERY RICH PUDDING WITH FRESH FRUIT FOR A TASTY AND COLOURFUL DESSERT.

4 egg yolks
1 Tbsp. castor sugar
2 cups heavy cream

1 vanilla bean, split
handful unblanched almonds
sugar

Mix egg yolks and castor sugar well. Place cream and vanilla bean in top of double boiler. Cover and bring to scalding point, remove vanilla bean and pour cream onto egg yolks, whisking well. Return to pan and cook until thickened, stirring constantly. Do not allow to boil. Pour into serving bowl and let stand overnight.

Prepare praline: Place almonds in heavy saucepan. Heat until nuts begin spitting. Add sugar to cover nuts and bottom of pan. Cook without stirring over medium heat until sugar has turned dark caramel in colour. Pour onto well-oiled plate and cool. When cold, pound in mortar and pestle until praline is in small pieces. Two hours before serving, place pralines on pudding.

Serves 6.

—Crissie Hunt
Crysler, Ontario

ORANGES GLACÉES

6 oranges
2 Tbsp. orange liqueur
1½ cups sugar

Remove a thin layer of peel from 2 oranges. Cut into strips and soak in liqueur. Peel oranges. Slice as thinly as possible, removing seeds. Arrange on shallow heatproof serving dish. Boil sugar and ½ cup water together, stirring constantly until golden. Pour carefully over oranges. Garnish with liqueur-soaked peel. Refrigerate for at least 8 hours.

Serves 6.

—Patricia Daine
Dartmouth, Nova Scotia

STRAWBERRY AMBROSIA

"WHILE CROSS-COUNTRY SKIING IN THE AMERICAN BERKEBEINER IN 1977, I WAS BILLETED AT A home in Hayward, Wisconsin, where I was treated to superb meals each day. The one dessert which so impressed me that I sat down and wrote out the recipe from the woman's cards was this one. It was a real treat to try broiled fruit, and the contrast with the ice cream was not only delightful to the taste buds but visually appealing as well. It was hot, cold and crunchy."

2 ripe bananas, sliced
1 cup halved **or** quartered strawberries
2 oranges, peeled & cut into bite-sized
   pieces
1 Tbsp. lemon juice

1 cup brown sugar
6 Tbsp. butter, melted
⅔ cup sliced almonds

French vanilla ice cream

Toss together bananas, strawberries, oranges and lemon juice. Place in a 10-inch pie plate. Stir together sugar, butter and almonds. Sprinkle over fruit. Broil 6 to 8 inches from heat until sugar melts and almonds are lightly toasted. Cool for a few minutes. Spoon over ice cream in individual dishes.

Serves 4.

—Lorne A. Davis
Parkhill, Ontario

POPPY SEED FRUIT SALAD DRESSING

3 Tbsp. onion juice
1 cup honey
1 Tbsp. dry mustard
2 tsp. salt

⅔ cup cider vinegar
2 cups oil
3 Tbsp. poppy seeds

Make onion juice by grinding a large onion in a blender or food processor, then scraping pulp into a strainer over a bowl. Press pulp with a spoon to remove juice. Set aside.

Mix honey, mustard, salt and vinegar in blender on slow speed. Add onion juice and continue blending. Add oil to blender a few drops at a time, still on slow speed, then in a thin stream, until dressing is thick. At the very last, add poppy seeds, blending just to incorporate. Store in refrigerator. Serve on fruit such as melons, green grapes, pineapple, pears or as a dressing for fruit salad.

—Kristine Marie Halls Reid
Floyd, Virginia

CANTALOUPE SHERBET

"WHEN THE EIGHT CANTALOUPE PLANTS IN OUR FIRST GEORGIA GARDEN YIELDED MORE THAN 40 luscious cantaloupes in three weeks, we developed this recipe. Since frozen melon purée works just as well as fresh, we can now remember midsummer during the dark and dreary days of winter; the beautiful green-flecked orange sherbet tastes just like fresh, ripe cantaloupes."

2 cups heavy cream
1 cup sugar
2 medium cantaloupes (7 cups purée)
½ cup lemon juice

¼ cup lime juice
finely grated rind of 1 lime
2 Tbsp. Cointreau **or** Triple Sec

Heat cream to scalding. Stir in sugar until dissolved. Chill. Seed, peel and purée cantaloupe in food processor. Add lemon and lime juices and grated rind to purée. Chill thoroughly. Mix in chilled cream and liqueur. Freeze in ice-cream maker according to its directions.

Makes ½ gallon. Note: To enjoy cantaloupe sherbet all year, add lemon and lime juices to fresh purée and freeze in glass jars with lids. Leave 1-inch headspace for expansion.

—Susan Hodges & Tim Denny
Winterville, Georgia

GOLDEN DRESSING FOR FRUIT

"THIS IS A SWEET BUT TANGY COOKED DRESSING THAT IS DELICIOUS SERVED OVER FRUIT SALAD for brunch or over fruit for dessert."

¼ cup orange juice
¼ cup lemon juice
¼ cup pineapple juice

2 eggs, beaten
½ cup sugar
½ cup heavy cream, whipped

Heat juices and add eggs and sugar, stirring. Cook until spoon is coated. Set pan in cold water and stir until cool. When cool, add whipped cream.

—Mary-Eileen McClear
Baden, Ontario

LEMON ICE CREAM

THIS RECIPE WILL LAST FOR MONTHS IN THE FREEZER—BUT IS NOT LIKELY TO IF ICE-CREAM lovers know where it is.

2 lemons
3 eggs, separated

¾ cup sugar
1 cup heavy cream

Squeeze juice from lemons to make 5 Tbsp. Finely grate peel from 1 lemon. Place egg whites in large bowl and beat until stiff peaks form. Gradually add ¼ cup sugar, continuing to beat. Sprinkle with lemon peel. Place yolks in another bowl and whisk with remaining ½ cup sugar and lemon juice. Fold into egg whites until just blended.

In another bowl, whip cream until soft peaks form. Fold into egg mixture, gently but thoroughly. Place in freezer container and freeze for several hours.

Serves 6 to 8.

—Laurabel Miller
Denbigh, Ontario

BEST VANILLA ICE CREAM

TOPPED WITH RHUBARB SAUCE, THIS ICE CREAM MAKES A VERY SPECIAL EARLY-SUMMER TREAT. Simply cook sliced rhubarb until tender, then add sugar and cinnamon to taste. The use of buttermilk makes this recipe very unusual – the result is less rich and the taste is lovely.

1½ cups sugar	3 cups milk
1 Tbsp. flour	2 cups cold buttermilk
¼ tsp. salt	3 cups heavy cream
4-5 eggs, beaten	3 tsp. vanilla

Combine sugar, flour and salt, then add to beaten eggs. Heat milk to scalding and slowly add egg mixture. Cook over low heat, stirring constantly, until thick enough to coat a spoon. Set pot in ice water and stir until cooled to room temperature.

Add buttermilk, cream and vanilla, then churn in ice-cream maker, following instructions on machine.

Makes approximately 1 gallon.

– Susan Hodges & Tim Denny
Winterville, Georgia

RUTH'S PECAN ICE CREAM

"I DEVELOPED THIS RECIPE WHEN I WAS A TEENAGER, SOMEHOW MANAGING TO CONVINCE MY mother that just one more test was needed to make sure I had it right! One day I ran out of ice for the ice-cream machine in the midst of the procedure, which would have been disastrous except that, just then, it began to hail. I was able to finish cranking using hailstones instead of ice, and the ice cream turned out just fine." Make vanilla sugar by placing a vanilla bean in a jar of white sugar and letting it sit for several weeks.

4 cups milk	2 cups vanilla sugar
2 cups heavy cream	1 Tbsp. cornstarch
1 small vanilla bean	½ tsp. salt
2 egg yolks	¼ cup sugar
4 eggs	¼ lb. pecans

Scald milk and cream with vanilla bean. Discard bean (or rinse well and keep for re-use).

Blend together yolks, eggs, vanilla sugar, cornstarch and salt. Cook in top of double boiler, stirring constantly. When warm, slowly stir in milk-cream mixture. Continue heating until thick enough to coat the back of a spoon. Chill.

Place sugar and pecans in heavy skillet and cook over low heat until sugar has melted and is light brown. Cool, then crush.

When custard is very cold, freeze in ice-cream machine, following manufacturer's instructions. Mix in pecans when done.

Makes approximately 3 quarts.

– Ruth Ellis Haworth
Toronto, Ontario

Baking

"Woulds't thou eat thy cake and have it?"

—*George Herbert*

If most of cooking is intuition, inspiration and good taste, baking is a realm where science cannot be trifled with. Meats, soups, vegetables and even many desserts can be created on the whim of the cook, but cakes and breads require the presence of certain ingredients in fairly specific proportions if one has any hope of achieving the desired result. This is no small comfort to those who like to follow recipes to the letter and leave chance to the improvisers.

"What I love about cooking," novelist Nora Ephron once wrote, "is that after a hard day, there is something comforting about the fact that if you melt butter and add flour and then hot stock, *it will get thick*! It's a sure thing! It's a sure thing in a world where those of us who long for some kind of certainty are forced to settle for crossword puzzles."

If Ephron likes gravy making, she must love baking, where success is virtually a sure thing if the cook appreciates the importance of being precise and accurate when following a recipe. When making a cake, for instance, ½ cup of cocoa means just that and not a little more or a little less, for the amounts of liquid and leavening ingredients have been calculated to complement exactly that amount of cocoa. We cannot guarantee the success of a recipe if oil is substituted for butter or whole wheat flour for unbleached white or molasses for sugar. Ingredients must be added and combined in the order indicated. The dough or batter must be placed in a pan of the correct size and then baked as instructed. One cannot throw a cake in whatever pan comes to hand and toss it into the oven at a lower heat so it can bake a little longer just to accommodate the cook's other activities.

If baking requires discipline, it can also be deeply gratifying. With experience, most bakers can make the leap to experimentation, learning what substitutions work (3 tablespoons of cocoa and 1 tablespoon of fat for 1 tablespoon of unsweetened chocolate) and juggling seasonings, flavourings, fruits and nuts to suit their own tastes. Invariably, a cook will find his or her own signature recipes, perhaps even achieving a bit of local renown for chocolate cake, apple torte or a particular specialty bread.

The baking sections of our cookbooks are always a favourite of contributors and readers alike. What we are able to offer is the best of the best – the three chocolate cake recipes included here, for example, were chosen only after dozens of others failed to pass our evaluation and test-kitchen screening.

Our baking tester grew fat as he repeatedly failed in his intention to "eat just enough to know whether or not it's good and then freeze the rest." We thank him for his dedication but hope our readers can show more restraint.

OCTOBER CELEBRATION CAKE

"EVERY COOK HAS HIS/HER TRADEMARK — THIS IS MINE. WEIGHING IN AT JUST UNDER FOUR pounds, this glorious bit of chocolate and hazelnut heaven was created three years ago to celebrate two Iowa harvests — the first 'Ioa Teritory' harvest gathered in by my great-great-grandfather, Joel Riley Hough, in the fall of 1841 and our own corn and soybean harvest more than 140 years later."

1 cup softened butter
¼ cup shortening
2 cups brown sugar
2 Tbsp. white corn syrup
3 eggs
½ cup sour cream
2 Tbsp. orange liqueur
4 oz. unsweetened chocolate, melted
2 oz. German sweetened chocolate, melted
2 tsp. baking soda
2 tsp. vanilla
½ tsp. salt

2 cups flour
½ cup plus 2 Tbsp. hot coffee
1 cup chopped, roasted hazelnuts

Chocolate Glaze
½ cup chocolate chips
1 Tbsp. butter
1 Tbsp. milk
1 Tbsp. white corn syrup
½ tsp. vanilla
sliced almonds for garnish

In large bowl, cream together butter, shortening, sugar and corn syrup. Add eggs one at a time, beating well after each addition. Add sour cream, orange liqueur, chocolates, baking soda, vanilla and salt. Beat until well blended. Add flour and coffee alternately, beating well after each addition. Fold in hazelnuts. Pour into greased and floured bundt pan and bake at 325 degrees F for 65 to 70 minutes, or until toothpick inserted deep into cake comes out clean. Cool in pan for 10 minutes, then turn out onto serving plate and cool completely.

Meanwhile, prepare glaze: Measure ingredients (except almonds) into small saucepan and place over medium heat. Bring to a full boil, remove from heat and spoon over cake, allowing glaze to run down the sides. Garnish with almonds.

Serves 16.

—*Ellen Ross*
Underwood, Iowa

BEST EVER BANANA CAKE

AN OLD FAVOURITE, THIS BANANA CAKE ADDS A BROILED CARAMEL TOPPING FOR A DELICIOUS new twist.

½ cup butter
1½ cups sugar
2 eggs, well beaten
1 cup mashed bananas
1 tsp. vanilla
2 cups flour
½ tsp. baking powder
¾ tsp. baking soda

½ tsp. salt
¼ cup sour milk

Caramel Topping
⅓ cup coconut **or** chopped nuts
3 Tbsp. butter, melted
½ cup brown sugar
1 Tbsp. cream

Cream butter and sugar together, then beat in eggs, bananas and vanilla. Sift together flour, baking powder, baking soda and salt. Add to creamed mixture alternately with milk, beating well after each addition. Bake in greased and floured 9" x 9" pan at 350 degrees F for 50 to 60 minutes.

Meanwhile, combine topping ingredients. Spread over warm cake in pan and brown under broiler until bubbling.

—*Niva Rowan*
Newtonville, Ontario

GREEK WALNUT CAKE

THE HONEY SYRUP FOR THIS CAKE CAN ALSO BE USED FOR BAKLAVA.

Cake
¾ cup oil
½ cup honey
3 eggs
2 tsp. grated orange rind
1 cup flour
1½ tsp. baking powder
½ tsp. cinnamon
¼ tsp. salt
⅛ tsp. nutmeg

⅓ cup milk powder
1½ cups finely chopped walnuts

Honey Syrup
1 lemon
1 cup sugar
2" stick cinnamon
2 whole cloves
1 cup honey
1 Tbsp. brandy

To make cake: Beat oil and honey until light—about 5 minutes. Beat in eggs, one at a time. Add orange rind. Sift together all dry ingredients except walnuts. Add to liquid mixture alternately with ¼ cup water. Stir in walnuts. Bake in a greased 9" x 9" pan at 350 degrees F for 35 minutes, or until a toothpick inserted in the centre comes out clean.

To make honey syrup: Juice the lemon, reserving 1½ tsp. of juice. Place the lemon rind in a heavy saucepan with 1 cup water, sugar, cinnamon stick and cloves. Bring to a boil, lower heat and cook without stirring for about 25 minutes, or until 230 degrees F is reached on a candy thermometer. Pick out rind and spices. Stir in lemon juice, honey and brandy. Cool. Makes 2 cups.

—Susan O'Neill
Bella Coola, British Columbia

RUTH'S PINEAPPLE CAKE

"AN EASY PINEAPPLE CAKE—IT WAS A DELICATE BRONZE COMING OUT OF THE OVEN. Excellent pineapple flavour," says our Vermont tester.

2 cups flour
1½ cups sugar
2 eggs
2 tsp. baking soda

½ tsp. salt
1 tsp. vanilla
2 cups crushed pineapple, undrained
1 cup chopped walnuts

Combine all ingredients and beat until smooth. Pour into greased jelly-roll pan and bake at 325 degrees F for 35 minutes.

—Linda A. Petree
Kennewick, Washington

TRADITIONAL LITHUANIAN HONEY CAKE

4 eggs
¾ cup sugar
¾ cup honey
½ cup oil
1 cup milk

3 tsp. baking powder
½ tsp. baking soda
2½ cups flour
1 Tbsp. mixed spices (cinnamon, cloves, ginger, cardamom)

Beat eggs, then add sugar, honey, oil and milk. Sift together baking powder, baking soda, flour and spices, and add to liquid ingredients. Stir to blend. Pour into greased bundt pan, and bake at 350 degrees F for 1 hour.

—Linda Barsauskas
Gloucester, Ontario

NUTMEG FEATHER CAKE

THIS IS A LIGHT-TEXTURED YELLOW CAKE THAT CALLS YOU BACK FOR SECONDS BECAUSE IT IS NOT too rich.

¼ cup butter
¼ cup shortening
1½ cups sugar
3 eggs, beaten
1 tsp. vanilla
2 cups flour

salt
2 tsp. nutmeg
1 tsp. baking soda
2 tsp. baking powder
1 cup buttermilk

Cream together butter, shortening and sugar. Add eggs and vanilla. Sift together flour, salt, nutmeg, baking soda and baking powder. Add to creamed ingredients alternately with buttermilk. Pour into greased 9″ x 13″ pan and bake at 350 degrees F for 35 to 40 minutes.

—Doris M. Denicola
Hartselle, Alabama

COCONUT BLACK WALNUT POUND CAKE

THIS IS A DELICIOUS, MOIST, HEAVY CAKE, EQUALLY SUCCESSFUL WITH BLACK OR REGULAR walnuts.

2 cups sugar
1 cup oil
4 eggs, beaten
3 cups flour
½ tsp. baking soda
½ tsp. salt

½ tsp. baking powder
1 cup buttermilk
1 cup chopped black walnuts
1 cup flaked coconut
2 tsp. coconut extract

Combine sugar, oil and eggs and beat well. Mix together flour, baking soda, salt and baking powder. Add to sugar mixture alternately with buttermilk, beating well after each addition. Stir in walnuts, coconut and extract. Pour into greased and floured 10-inch bundt pan and bake at 325 degrees F for 65 minutes.

—Dorothy Hollis
Blanchard, Oklahoma

CREAM CHEESE POUND CAKE WITH CRANBERRIES

FOR ORANGE RIND RICH WITH FLAVOUR, DRY ORANGE PEELS (PREFERABLY FROM MANDARIN oranges), then grind them. They can be stored in a tightly capped jar or in the freezer.

1 cup butter
½ lb. cream cheese
4 eggs
2 cups brown sugar
1 tsp. vanilla

1 Tbsp. dried orange rind
    soaked in 1½ Tbsp. lemon juice
2¼ cups flour
1½ tsp. baking powder
1 cup cranberries with ¾ tsp. orange rind

Beat butter and cream cheese until fluffy. Add eggs one at a time, beating until fluffy after each addition. Add sugar and beat well, then add vanilla and orange rind-lemon juice mixture. Sift flour and baking powder together, then fold into creamed mixture. Drop half the batter into bundt pan that has been greased and dusted with brown sugar. Sprinkle liberally with cranberries and top with remaining batter. Bake at 350 degrees F for 60 to 70 minutes.

—Helen P. Slama
Whitehorse, Yukon

BLUE RIBBON SPICE CAKE

"THIS IS MY GRANDMOTHER'S RECIPE. SHE WAS THE COOK AT THE TOLEDO WOMEN'S CLUB FOR many years. I entered this in the Monroe County Fair and it was a first-prize winner. Do not worry about overbeating this cake – the more it is beaten, the better the texture."

1 cup butter
2¼ cups sugar
5 eggs
1 Tbsp. cloves
1 Tbsp. cinnamon

salt
1 tsp. baking soda
1 cup sour milk
3 cups flour

Cream together butter and sugar until fluffy. Add eggs, one at a time, beating well after each addition. Add cloves, cinnamon and salt and beat well. Dissolve baking soda in milk, then add to creamed mixture alternately with flour, beating well. Pour into greased and floured bundt pan and bake at 350 degrees F for 45 to 50 minutes.

—*Evelyn Nofziger*
Temperance, Michigan

RUSSIAN POPPY SEED CAKE

LOADED WITH POPPY SEEDS, THIS IS AN IRRESISTIBLE CAKE. ALL THE TASTERS IN VERMONT ATE more of this cake than they needed and still came back for more.

2 cups poppy seeds
2 cups milk
1 cup honey
1½ cups butter
1 cup sugar
5 eggs, separated

1 tsp. almond extract
1½ cups whole wheat flour
1½ cups white flour
2 tsp. baking powder
½ tsp. salt

Heat poppy seeds, milk and honey to boiling point, then set aside to cool.

Cream together butter and sugar, then add egg yolks and almond extract. Sift together flours, baking powder and salt. Add flour mixture and poppy seed mixture alternately to creamed mixture, beating well. Gently fold in stiffly beaten egg whites. Pour into greased and floured bundt pan. Bake at 350 degrees F for 40 to 50 minutes.

—*Christine A. Lichatz*
Westerly, Rhode Island

SOUTHERN SPICY GINGERBREAD

SERVED WARM WITH FRESHLY MADE APPLESAUCE OR WHIPPED CREAM, THIS GINGERBREAD IS hard to beat.

2 eggs
¾ cup brown sugar
¾ cup molasses
¾ cup melted shortening
2½ cups flour
2 tsp. baking soda

2 tsp. ginger
2 tsp. cinnamon
½ tsp. cloves
½ tsp. nutmeg
½ tsp. baking powder

Beat eggs, then add sugar, molasses and shortening. Sift together dry ingredients, then add to creamed mixture. Stir in 1 cup boiling water. Pour cake into greased 9" x 13" pan and bake at 350 degrees F for 30 to 40 minutes.

—*Carole Creswell*
St. Chrysostome, Quebec

BLACKBERRY JAM CAKE

"This cake is a favourite to take to picnics and cake sales. The flavours of the blackberry jam and bananas blend to produce an exceptionally moist and tasty cake."

1 cup packed brown sugar
½ cup butter
1 cup blackberry jam
1 cup mashed bananas
2 cups flour
¼ tsp. cloves
¼ tsp. cinnamon

¼ tsp. nutmeg
1 tsp. baking powder
1 tsp. baking soda
½ cup buttermilk
2 eggs, beaten
1 cup chopped walnuts

Cream together sugar and butter. Add jam and bananas and mix well. Sift flour with cloves, cinnamon, nutmeg and baking powder. Dissolve baking soda in buttermilk. Add flour mixture alternately with buttermilk to creamed mixture, beginning and ending with flour. Mix well, add eggs and mix again. Add walnuts. Pour into greased and floured 9" x 13" baking pan and bake at 350 degrees F for 40 minutes.

—James Mottern
Knoxville, Tennessee

OATMEAL CAKE

"This cake is the favourite at all our Hill gatherings and of our friends from out of town."

1½ cups boiling water
1 cup oats
1 cup brown sugar
1 cup white sugar
½ cup shortening

2 eggs
1½ cups flour
1 tsp. salt
1 tsp. baking powder
1 tsp. baking soda

Pour boiling water over oats and let stand for 20 minutes. Cream together sugars and shortening, then beat in eggs, one at a time. Combine dry ingredients and add alternately with oats to creamed mixture. Bake in greased bundt pan at 350 degrees F for 35 minutes.

—Patricia DeVelder
Conesus, New York

DOUBLE CHOCOLATE ZUCCHINI CAKE

A great way to get zucchini into zucchini haters, this cake improves in flavour if allowed to sit for a day before it is eaten.

3 cups flour
1½ tsp. baking powder
1½ tsp. cinnamon
1¼ tsp. salt
1 tsp. baking soda
⅛ tsp. cloves
1½ cups oil

2⅓ cups packed brown sugar
4 eggs
2 oz. unsweetened chocolate, melted
3 zucchini, grated
1 cup chocolate chips
1 cup chopped nuts

Combine flour, baking powder, cinnamon, salt, baking soda and cloves and set aside. Beat together oil and sugar, then add eggs, one at a time, beating well after each addition. Gradually beat in melted chocolate, then dry ingredients. Beat until smooth. Fold in zucchini, chocolate chips and nuts. Pour into greased and floured bundt pan and bake at 350 degrees F for 1 hour 20 minutes. Frost with Chocolate Cake Glaze (page 257).

—Debra J. Eddy
Charlotte, Michigan

RHUBARB CAKE

½ cup butter
1½ cups brown sugar
1 egg
1 tsp. baking soda
1 cup buttermilk
2 cups flour
2 cups chopped rhubarb
1 tsp. vanilla

1 tsp. cinnamon
¼ tsp. cloves

Topping
½ cup sugar
1 tsp. cinnamon
1 Tbsp. butter

Cream together butter, sugar and egg. Dissolve baking soda in buttermilk. Combine flour, rhubarb, vanilla, cinnamon and cloves. Add buttermilk and flour mixture to creamed ingredients and stir until just mixed. Pour into greased 9″ x 9″ pan.

Combine topping ingredients and sprinkle over cake. Bake at 350 degrees F for 40 to 45 minutes.

—Annemarie Berryman
Greenwood, British Columbia

COCONUT CARROT CAKE

2 cups flour
2½ tsp. baking soda
1½ tsp. cinnamon
2 tsp. salt
1 cup oil
2 cups sugar

3 eggs
1 cup crushed pineapple
2 cups grated carrots
1½ cups grated coconut
½ cup chopped nuts

Mix together flour, baking soda, cinnamon and salt. Beat together oil, sugar and eggs thoroughly, then add flour mixture and beat until smooth. Fold in pineapple, carrots, coconut and nuts. Pour into a greased 9″ x 13″ baking pan and bake at 350 degrees F for 50 to 60 minutes. Frost with Coconut Cream Frosting (page 257).

—Paddi Caldwell
Newburgh, Ontario

TIGER CAKE

THIS CAKE COMBINES WITH GREAT SUCCESS THE FLAVOURS OF CHOCOLATE AND ORANGE. IT IS A cake that can be made in a hurry and served simply sprinkled with confectioners' sugar.

½ cup butter
1 tsp. salt
½ tsp. vanilla
1¼ cups sugar
2 eggs
2½ tsp. baking powder

2 cups flour
⅔ cup milk
1 oz. unsweetened chocolate
  or 3 Tbsp. cocoa
2 Tbsp. grated orange rind

Cream together butter, salt, vanilla and sugar, then add eggs, one at a time, beating well. Sift together dry ingredients and add to creamed mixture alternately with milk. Divide batter in half.

Melt chocolate (or dissolve cocoa in 2 Tbsp. water) and add to half of batter. Add orange rind to other half. Pour orange batter into greased 9″ x 9″ pan. Pour chocolate batter on top and cut through with a knife, just enough to create a marbled effect. Bake at 350 degrees F for 30 minutes. Frost with Orange Frosting (page 257).

—Donna Parker
Pictou, Nova Scotia

CRUSTY BLUEBERRY BATTER CAKE

"ALTHOUGH ORIGINALLY MADE BY MY GRANDMOTHER, MY MOTHER DESERVES THE CREDIT FOR this cake. It was she who figured out the proper measurements from my grandmother's 'two handfuls of this and a pinch of that.' This cake has a crisp, sweet top crust, with a delicious moist cake layer and, best of all, a sweet, thickened layer of blueberries."

2 cups blueberries	1 tsp. baking powder
juice of ½ lemon	¼ tsp. salt
1¾ cups sugar	½ cup milk
3 Tbsp. butter	salt
1 cup flour	1 Tbsp. cornstarch

Grease a 9" x 13" pan and line with blueberries. Sprinkle with lemon juice. Cream together ¾ cup sugar and butter. Sift together flour, baking powder and ¼ tsp. salt. Add milk, alternating with flour, to creamed mixture. Pour evenly over berries – do not mix berries into batter. Combine remaining 1 cup sugar with salt and cornstarch and sprinkle over batter. Pour 1 cup boiling water over all.

Bake at 375 degrees F for 1 hour. Serve cold from pan.

—*J.L. Moorehouse*
Chicago, Illinois

PUMPKIN BUNDT CAKE

OUR CAMDEN EAST TESTER SAYS, "THIS CAKE WILL BECOME A FAMILY FAVOURITE IN OUR HOUSE. It mixes up fast and is a moist, lightly spiced cake."

3 cups flour	2 cups sugar
2 tsp. baking soda	1¼ cups oil
2 tsp. baking powder	2 cups cooked, mashed pumpkin
3 tsp. cinnamon	½ cup chopped pecans
1 tsp. salt	½ cup chocolate chips
4 eggs, beaten	

Sift flour, baking soda, baking powder, cinnamon and salt together twice. Beat eggs and sugar together. Add oil and pumpkin, then blend in flour mixture. Fold in pecans and chocolate chips. Bake in greased and floured bundt pan at 350 degrees F for 60 minutes. Let cool in pan for 10 minutes, then turn out onto cooling rack.

—*Gladys Sykes*
Regina, Saskatchewan

PUMPKIN YOGURT CAKE

"LAST YEAR I HAD AN EXTRAORDINARILY GOOD CROP OF PUMPKINS, AND EVERY DAY FOR A WEEK, I adapted recipes to use pumpkin. This one was a definite success."

2½ cups flour	1 cup sugar
1 tsp. baking soda	2 eggs
½ tsp. cinnamon	1 cup yogurt
½ tsp. ginger	1 cup cooked, mashed pumpkin
½ cup butter	

Combine flour, baking soda, cinnamon and ginger. Melt butter, then stir in sugar and eggs, beating well. Add flour mixture and yogurt and pumpkin alternately. Mix well. Pour into 2 greased 9-inch cake pans and bake at 350 degrees F for 30 to 35 minutes. Frost with Vanilla Butter Frosting (page 257).

—*Marcia D. Powers*
East Thetford, Vermont

SWEET POTATO CAKE

½ cup shortening
1 cup sugar
2 eggs
1 cup cooked, mashed sweet potato
2 cups flour
½ tsp. salt
2 tsp. baking powder

¼ tsp. baking soda
¼ tsp. cloves
½ tsp. cinnamon
½ tsp. nutmeg
½ cup milk
½ cup chopped nuts

Cream together shortening and sugar, then add eggs, beating after each addition. Add sweet potato. Sift together flour, salt, baking powder, baking soda, cloves, cinnamon and nutmeg. Add to creamed mixture alternately with milk. Fold in nuts. Bake in greased bundt pan at 350 degrees F for 45 to 50 minutes.

—Betty Hay
Lexington, Kentucky

SOUR CREAM CHOCOLATE CAKE

THIS CAKE HAS A REALLY GOOD SWEET-AND-SOUR TASTE COMPLEMENTED BY A DENSE TEXTURE.

3 oz. semisweet chocolate
2 Tbsp. butter
3 eggs, separated

1½ cups sugar
1 cup sour cream
1 cup flour minus 2 Tbsp.

Melt chocolate in double boiler, then add butter. Beat egg whites with 1 cup sugar until peaks hold their shape, then set aside. Beat yolks with remaining ½ cup sugar until thick. Fold chocolate and sour cream into yolks. Alternately, one third at a time, fold egg whites and flour into chocolate mixture, mixing only until smooth.

Line bottom of two 8″-round cake pans with waxed paper, then butter bottom and sides and flour lightly. Divide batter between pans and bake at 325 degrees F for 25 minutes. Cool briefly in pans, then invert onto cooling rack. Frost with Chocolate Cream Frosting (page 257).

—Bobbi Hobbs
El Cajon, California

OLD SARATOGA COUNTY HOUSE FRUIT CAKE

PRODUCING A HEAVY, DENSE CAKE, STRONG WITH MOLASSES FLAVOUR, THIS RECIPE CAME TO THE contributor from a former cook at the Saratoga County House, Saratoga Springs, New York.

1 cup sugar
1 cup shortening
2 eggs, lightly beaten
2¼ cups dark molasses
1 rounded Tbsp. baking soda
5 cups flour, sifted several times
½ tsp. salt

1 tsp. cinnamon
1 tsp. cloves
½ tsp. nutmeg
1 tsp. allspice
1 cup raisins
4 cups chopped apples

Cream together sugar and shortening. Beat in eggs and 2 cups molasses. Dissolve baking soda in remaining ¼ cup molasses, then stir into sugar mixture. Sift flour, salt, cinnamon, cloves, nutmeg and allspice together, then stir into creamed mixture. Fold in raisins and apples. Spoon into well-greased bundt pan and bake at 275 degrees F for 1½ hours or until done.

—Kenneth P. Sherman
Porter Corners, New York

CHOCOLATE BROWNIE CAKE

"A FRIEND, KNOWING MY LOVE OF CHOCOLATE, CREATED THIS CAKE FOR MY BIRTHDAY A FEW years ago—it's a chocolate-lover's dream come true."

6 oz. unsweetened chocolate
¾ cup butter, softened
2¼ cups sugar
4 eggs
1 tsp. vanilla

2 cups flour
1½ tsp. baking powder
¼ tsp. salt
1½ cups milk

Melt chocolate and set aside to cool. Cream together butter and sugar until light and fluffy. Beat in eggs, one at a time, then beat in chocolate and vanilla. Sift flour, baking powder and salt together, then add to creamed mixture alternately with milk. Grease and flour three 9-inch cake pans and divide batter among them. Bake at 350 degrees F for 25 to 30 minutes.

—Bobbie Nelson
Alcove, Quebec

LINCOLN'S FAVOURITE CAKE

"THIS RECIPE IS FROM MY GRANDMOTHER'S COOKBOOK. THE STORY SHE WROTE ALONG WITH IT IS this: 'Long ago, a certain French caterer in Lexington, Kentucky, made a wonderful white cake in honour of his countryman, Lafayette, who visited the city. The snow-white cake was beautifully decorated with coloured sugar. The recipe for this famous cake originated in the household of Mary Todd, who later made the cake for Abraham Lincoln.' Whether or not the recipe's history is accurate, this is definitely the best white cake I have ever eaten."

1 cup butter
2 cups sugar
3 cups flour
3 tsp. baking powder
1 cup milk

1 tsp. vanilla
1 cup chopped blanched almonds, floured
6 egg whites
¼ tsp. salt

Lightly cream together butter and sugar. Sift together flour and baking powder and add to creamed mixture alternately with milk. Add vanilla and nuts. Beat egg whites with salt until stiff, then fold into batter. Pour into two 9"-round cake pans. Bake at 350 degrees F for 35 minutes.

—Penny Fetter
Johnstown, Ohio

COCOA APPLESAUCE CAKE

"I RECEIVED THIS RECIPE FROM MY GERMAN MOTHER-IN-LAW. IT HAD BEEN IN HER FAMILY FOR years, and I am passing it on to mine. If you can keep eager eaters away from it, this cake tastes better after ageing for three or four days."

1 cup sugar
½ cup shortening
1½ cups applesauce
2 cups flour
2 tsp. baking soda
3 Tbsp. cocoa

1 tsp. cinnamon
¼ tsp. cloves
pinch nutmeg
pinch allspice
pinch salt
1 cup chopped pecans

Cream together sugar and shortening, then stir in applesauce. Sift together flour, baking soda, cocoa, cinnamon, cloves, nutmeg, allspice and salt. Add to creamed mixture, mix well, then fold in nuts. Bake in greased bundt pan at 350 degrees F for 50 to 60 minutes.

—Frances Slater
Hillsboro, Oregon

APPLESAUCE CAKE

"THIS IS MY GRANDMOTHER'S RECIPE—IT TAKES ME BACK TO MY VISITS TO HER HOUSE, WHERE the kitchen was filled with the smell of cinnamon and cloves."

1 cup sugar	salt
½ cup butter	1 tsp. cinnamon
1 egg	1 tsp. allspice
1 cup applesauce	1 cup raisins
1 tsp. baking soda	1 cup chopped walnuts
1 cup flour	

Cream together sugar and butter, then beat in egg. Mix together applesauce and baking soda. Sift together flour, salt, cinnamon and allspice. Add applesauce and dry ingredients alternately, in thirds, to creamed mixture. Fold in raisins and nuts. Pour into greased loaf pan and bake at 375 degrees for 50 to 60 minutes.

—Jeanne Reitz
Yreka, California

PRIZE DATE & ORANGE CAKE

"THIS WAS ONE OF MY FAVOURITE CAKES WHEN MY MOTHER USED TO MAKE IT. IT IS DELICIOUS and moist. I glaze the cake with ½ cup sugar dissolved in the juice of one orange."

½ cup butter	2 cups flour
½ cup sugar	1 tsp. baking powder
½ cup chopped walnuts	1 cup sour milk
1 cup chopped dates	1 tsp. baking soda, dissolved in
rind of 1 orange, grated	1 tsp. warm water

Cream together butter and sugar. Fold in nuts, dates and orange rind. Sift together flour and baking powder and add to creamed mixture alternately with milk. Stir in dissolved baking soda. Bake in greased bundt pan at 325 degrees F for 40 minutes.

—Mrs. John R. Stanley
Lenore, Manitoba

GÂTEAU MARGUERITE

"THIS RECIPE ORIGINATED IN A BELGIAN CONVENT. IT IS DENSE AND RICH—JUST DUST WITH icing sugar to serve." Our Camden East tester says this is one of the three best cakes he has ever eaten.

1 cup butter	3 cups flour
1¼ cups sugar	1 Tbsp. baking powder
¼ tsp. salt	8 oz. semisweet chocolate, chopped
juice of 1 lemon	2 cups ground hazelnuts
4-5 eggs, separated	

Beat together butter, sugar, salt, lemon juice and egg yolks until creamy. Stir in flour, baking powder, chocolate and nuts. Beat egg whites until stiff, then gently fold into batter. Pour into well-greased and floured 9½-inch springform pan. Bake at 350 degrees F for 1 to 1½ hours, or until toothpick inserted in middle comes out clean.

—Trudi Keillor
Berwyn, Alberta

UPSIDE-DOWN MACAROON CAKE

⅓ cup butter
2 cups sugar
3 eggs, separated
1¼ cups milk
1 cup flour

1 tsp. baking powder
coconut
2 Tbsp. cornstarch
salt
1 tsp. vanilla

Cream together butter and ½ cup sugar. Add 2 egg yolks, ½ cup milk, flour and baking powder and mix well. Place in two 8-inch cake pans lined with waxed paper. Beat 3 egg whites with 1 cup sugar until stiff and glossy. Spread over cakes and sprinkle with coconut. Bake at 350 degrees F for 20 to 30 minutes, or until golden brown.

Meanwhile, prepare filling: Combine remaining ½ cup sugar, cornstarch, salt, remaining egg yolk and vanilla in heavy pot. Add remaining milk slowly while cooking over medium heat. Cook until thickened. Spread as filling between cooled cake layers.

—Jane Matthews
Stirling, Ontario

MAMA'S JOHNNY CAKE

"My grandmother lived in a grand house in Toronto and entertained a great deal. This recipe was served often, even to the likes of Mrs. Timothy Eaton Senior, who summoned my grandmother's cook for the recipe."

¼ cup butter
1 cup sugar
2 eggs, beaten
1 cup flour

3 tsp. baking powder
1 cup cornmeal
2 Tbsp. beef **or** chicken stock
1 cup milk

Cream butter then blend in sugar and eggs. In another bowl, sift together flour and baking powder, then stir in cornmeal. Add stock to milk. Mix dry ingredients and milk mixture alternately into butter-sugar mixture.

Pour into a 9" x 9" pan and bake at 375 degrees F for 30 to 40 minutes. Serve warm as an alternative to rolls or bread.

—Mary Matear
London, Ontario

GRANDMA GARVEY'S SWEDISH MERINGUE CAKE

½ cup butter
½ cup sugar
4 eggs, separated
1 cup plus 2 Tbsp. flour
2 tsp. baking powder
⅓ cup milk

1 tsp. vanilla
¼ tsp. cream of tartar
1 cup sugar
¾ cup finely chopped walnuts
1 cup heavy cream
2 Tbsp. powdered sugar

Cream together butter and sugar. Add egg yolks, one at a time, beating well after each addition. Combine flour with baking powder, and milk with vanilla. Add alternately to creamed mixture and mix well. Spread evenly in two greased 8"-round cake pans.

Beat egg whites and cream of tartar until frothy. Add sugar very slowly, continuing to beat until meringue holds stiff peaks. Spread evenly over batter. Top one of the pans with nuts.

Bake at 300 degrees F for 40 minutes, or until meringue starts to brown. Whip together cream and powdered sugar. Using the nut-topped cake as the bottom layer, stack the cakes, with whipped cream between the layers.

—Diane Milan
Northfield, Minnesota

CHOCOLATE CREAM FROSTING

5 oz. semisweet chocolate
½ cup sugar
3 eggs

2 Tbsp. coffee liqueur
1 cup softened butter

Melt chocolate and let cool. Mix sugar and eggs in top of double boiler and cook, stirring constantly, until thickened. Remove from heat and pour into glass or metal bowl. Fold in chocolate and coffee liqueur, then beat in butter in chunks until smooth. Chill.

Frosts a 2-layer cake.

—Bobbi Hobbs
El Cajon, California

ORANGE FROSTING

1 egg yolk, beaten
3 Tbsp. butter
2 cups icing sugar

3 Tbsp. orange juice
1 tsp. grated orange rind
salt

Combine all ingredients and beat well.

Frosts a 9″ x 9″ cake.

—Donna Parker
Pictou, Nova Scotia

VANILLA BUTTER FROSTING

4 Tbsp. softened butter
2 Tbsp. yogurt

1 tsp. vanilla
2 cups icing sugar

Beat butter until light and fluffy, then add remaining ingredients. Beat well.

Frosts a 2-layer cake.

—Marcia D. Powers
East Thetford, Vermont

COCONUT CREAM FROSTING

1 cup coconut
3 oz. cream cheese
¼ cup butter

3 cups icing sugar
1 Tbsp. milk
½ tsp. vanilla

Toast coconut and cool. Cream cheese with butter, then add sugar, milk and vanilla. Beat until smooth, then stir in half the coconut. Frost cake and top with remaining coconut.

Frosts a 9″ x 13″ cake.

—Paddi Caldwell
Newburgh, Ontario

CHOCOLATE CAKE GLAZE

1 cup icing sugar
1 Tbsp. butter, melted
salt

2 Tbsp. corn syrup
½ tsp. vanilla
1 oz. semisweet chocolate curls

Beat together sugar, butter and salt, then add corn syrup, 2 Tbsp. water and vanilla, stirring until smooth. Garnish cake with chocolate curls after spreading with glaze.

Frosts a bundt cake.

—Debra J. Eddy
Charlotte, Michigan

BOHEMIAN KOLACHE

"BOHEMIA FORMS THE WESTERNMOST PART OF CZECHOSLOVAKIA. THIS IS MY GRANDMOTHER'S recipe. She lived in Wilson, Kansas, which is known as the Czech capital of Kansas.

1 pkg. yeast
⅓ cup plus 1 tsp. sugar
¾ cup milk, scalded
⅓ cup shortening
½ tsp. salt
½ tsp. grated lemon peel

¼ tsp. mace **or** nutmeg
3¼-3½ cups flour
2 eggs, beaten
1 lb. dried apricots **or** prunes
sugar
1 Tbsp. lemon juice

Dissolve yeast in ¼ cup warm water, then add 1 tsp. sugar. Combine milk, ⅓ cup sugar, shortening, salt, lemon peel and mace. Cool, then stir in 1 cup flour. Beat vigorously for 2 minutes, then add yeast and eggs and beat well. Add enough flour to make a soft dough. Turn out on a floured board and knead for 5 minutes, or until smooth and elastic, kneading in ⅓ to ½ cup flour.

Place dough in greased bowl, cover and let rise for 1 hour. Punch down and divide in half. Cover and let rise for 10 minutes. Shape each half into 3-inch balls. Place on cookie sheet, until doubled—about 45 minutes.

Prepare filling: Cover apricots or prunes with water and cook until soft. Drain water and grind fruit. If using apricots, add sugar to taste and lemon juice.

Make depressions in dough and place filling in each ball. Bake at 350 degrees F for 15 to 20 minutes.

—Joan McKeegan
Boise, Idaho

MRS. ROCKENSUESS' BRÜNEN SPÄTZLE

"THE FOLLOWING IS AN OLD GERMAN RECIPE GIVEN TO MY GREAT-GRANDMOTHER AND PASSED on to me. 'Brünen' means well or spring, and 'spätzle' means a dough ball from which small pieces are cut. The result is a slightly sweet pastry, best eaten when fresh, that truly melts in your mouth."

¼ cup evaporated milk
2 Tbsp. yeast
1 Tbsp. sugar
3 cups flour
½ cup butter

½ tsp. salt
3 eggs
1 tsp. vanilla
½ cup sugar
1 cup chopped nuts

Combine milk with ¼ cup hot water. When lukewarm, add yeast and sugar, and stir to dissolve. Using pastry blender, combine 1½ cups flour with butter and salt. Combine flour and yeast mixture and let stand 20 minutes. Beat eggs lightly and add vanilla. Add to the flour-yeast mixture. Add remaining flour and combine well. Tie dough in a cheesecloth bag, or towel sprinkled with flour, leaving enough room for expansion, and place in a bowl or pail of cool water (this is called water-proofing). Bag should rise to the top in about an hour. Drain and turn out onto a platter.

Break off pieces the size of an egg, roll into "fingers" and twist into figure 8's. Push into sugar and then into nuts. Place on greased cookie sheet, cover and let rise 15 minutes in a warm place. Bake at 375 degrees F for 12 to 15 minutes.

—Amy Kegel
Colville, Washington

BLACK PEPPER CHEESE BREAD

"I REMEMBER COMING HOME FROM SCHOOL JUST AS MY MOTHER WAS TAKING THESE LOAVES from the oven. I would have the 'heel' of the loaf with butter and a cool mug of buttermilk. We used to put on so much butter that we were sent outside to sit on the step to prevent drips on the floor."

½ tsp. dry mustard
6-6½ cups flour
1 Tbsp. salt
3 tsp. pepper
1¾ cups warm milk

2 Tbsp. active dry yeast
2 Tbsp. sugar
2 Tbsp. vegetable oil
2 large eggs
1½ cups grated Cheddar cheese

Combine mustard and ½ tsp. warm water. Set aside for 10 minutes to develop flavour. Combine 3 cups flour with salt and 2 tsp. pepper. Set aside.

Place warm milk and yeast in large bowl. Let stand for 10 minutes. Stir well and add sugar, oil, eggs and mustard-water mixture. Stir. Gradually beat in the flour mixture. Beat well. Stir in cheese. Stir in enough of the remaining flour to make a stiff dough.

Turn out onto a floured board and knead until smooth and elastic (about 10 minutes), adding more flour as needed. Place in a lightly greased bowl, turning to grease the top. Cover and let rise in a warm place until doubled in bulk – about 1 hour. Punch down and form into 2 loaves. Place each in a greased 9" x 5" x 3" loaf pan and cover. Let rise until doubled.

Brush the loaves with milk, sprinkle with the remaining 1 tsp. of black pepper. Bake at 375 degrees F for about 50 minutes, or until bread is golden and sounds hollow. If loaves are browning too quickly, cover lightly with foil. Turn out on wire rack to cool.

Makes 2 loaves.

—Irene Louden
Port Coquitlam, British Columbia

HONEY NUT BREAD

THE COTTAGE CHEESE ADDS AN INTERESTING DIMENSION TO THIS EXCEPTIONALLY MOIST AND flavourful bread.

3 cups white flour
2 Tbsp. yeast
1 tsp. salt
1 cup cottage cheese
4 Tbsp. butter

½ cup honey
2 eggs
2-2½ cups whole wheat flour
½ cup rolled oats
⅔ cup chopped walnuts

In a large bowl, mix 2 cups white flour, yeast and salt. Heat 1 cup water, cottage cheese, butter and honey in a saucepan until just warm. Add to flour mixture. Beat in eggs. Stir in whole wheat flour, oats and nuts. Add remaining white flour. On a floured surface, knead dough until smooth and elastic, adding more white flour if dough is sticky. Let dough rise in a warm place until it has doubled in size – about 1 hour.

Punch down dough and divide into thirds. Shape loaves and place in greased bread pans. Let rise until doubled – about half an hour. Bake at 350 degrees F for 45 minutes, or until the loaf sounds hollow when tapped.

Makes 3 loaves.

—Shirley Miller
Stella, Ontario

LEMON CHEESE CROWN

"THIS IS A BRAIDED BREAD WHICH IS BEAUTIFUL TO LOOK AT. I HAVE OFTEN SERVED IT WITH A delicate soup such as Cream of Almond Soup (Vol. 2, pg. 42). The combination of cardamom, lemon and Swiss cheese has a very pleasing 'bite' to it."

3-4 cups flour	½ tsp. salt
1 Tbsp. yeast	1 cup finely grated Swiss cheese
2 tsp. lemon peel	1 egg
1 tsp. ground cardamom	1 egg yolk
1 cup milk	1 beaten egg white
⅓ cup sugar	1 Tbsp. sugar
¼ cup butter	1 Tbsp. sliced almonds

In a large bowl, combine 1½ cups flour, yeast, lemon peel and cardamom. In a saucepan, heat milk, sugar, butter and salt just until warm and butter melts. Add to flour mixture. Add cheese, egg and yolk. Beat very well until the mixture is stretchy. Using a spoon, stir in as much of the remaining flour as possible. Knead in enough flour to make a stiff dough. Knead for 6-8 minutes. Shape into a ball and let rise till doubled in size. Punch down.

Make two balls, one with ⅔ of the dough and one with ⅓ of the dough. Cover and let rest for 10 minutes. Divide big ball into three loose strands and roll into strips. Braid. Place on a greased sheet to form a circle. Repeat with the smaller piece of dough to form three 18-inch-long ropes. Place second braid on top of first. Seal ends together. Cover and let rise until doubled—about 1 hour. Brush with egg white, sprinkle with 1 Tbsp. sugar. Sprinkle almonds on top. Bake at 350 degrees F for 35 to 40 minutes, or until done. Cover the loaf with foil after about 20 minutes to prevent overbrowning.

—Maureen Marcotte
Farrellton, Quebec

ETHEREAL PUFFS

"I HAVE BEEN BAKING THESE MUFFIN-SHAPED ROLLS FOR 20 YEARS. ALWAYS VERY LIGHT IN texture, they go well with any lunch or dinner menu."

1 Tbsp. yeast	1 tsp. salt
1⅓ cups sifted flour plus 1 cup flour	2 Tbsp. sugar
¼ tsp. baking soda	1 tsp. sesame seeds
1 cup creamed cottage cheese	1 egg
½ tsp. grated onion	2 Tbsp. untoasted wheat germ
1 Tbsp. butter	

Mix together yeast, sifted flour and baking soda in a large bowl. In a saucepan, heat ¼ cup water, cottage cheese, onion, butter, salt, sugar and sesame seeds. After butter has melted and cheese mixture feels warm, add egg and wheat germ. Add to yeast-flour mixture. Using electric mixer, beat 30 seconds on low, then 3 minutes on high. Stir in remaining flour with a wooden spoon.

Place in a well-greased bowl, turning over to grease top. Cover and let rise 1½ hours or until doubled in size. Beat down dough. Pour into 12 greased muffin tins. Cover and let rise for 40 minutes. Bake at 400 degrees F for 12 to 15 minutes. Cool in muffin tins for 5 minutes before removing to a rack.

Makes 12 rolls.

—Janet E. Stanford
Ligonier, Pennsylvania

CARROT CORNMEAL DINNER ROLLS

"THIS WAS ONE OF MY MOTHER'S FAVOURITE RECIPES. AS I WAS RAISING MY FOUR CHILDREN, 'Grandma's rolls' were always a special treat—especially when served straight from the oven, dripping with butter and homemade blackberry jelly."

1 cup packed grated carrots	1½ tsp. salt
1 pkg. yeast	3-3½ cups flour
2 tsp. sugar	¾ cup cornmeal
¼ cup softened butter	1 Tbsp. sugar
1 egg, beaten	melted butter

Simmer carrots in 1¼ cups boiling water for 5 minutes. Set aside to cool to lukewarm.

Soften yeast and 2 tsp. sugar in ¼ cup warm water. Combine butter, egg, yeast mixture, carrots and carrot water. Add salt and 2 cups flour and beat well. Stir in cornmeal and 1 Tbsp. sugar and beat. Gradually add flour to make a soft dough. Knead on floured board for 10 minutes, adding flour as needed.

Place in greased bowl, cover and let rise until doubled—about 1 hour. Punch down, then shape into 36 balls. Place 2 balls in each greased cup of muffin pan. Brush with melted butter, cover and let rise until doubled—30 minutes. Bake at 375 degrees F for 15 minutes.

Makes 18 rolls.

—Frances Walker
Halifax, Nova Scotia

STOUT BREAD

"WHEN I FIRST TASTED MUESLI, A SWISS-STYLE BREAKFAST CEREAL, I WANTED TO INCORPORATE it into a bread recipe. This is the result—a dark, flavourful bread full of texture. My husband brews his own beer and stout. This is what is used, including the rich mineral sediment in the bottom of the bottle, but commercial stouts will work too."

4 pkgs. yeast	¼ cup dill seed
2 Tbsp. sugar	rind of 3 oranges, grated
12 oz. stout	2 eggs, beaten
1 cup molasses	4-5 cups whole wheat flour
½ cup shortening	4-5 cups white flour
2 tsp. salt	2 cups muesli

Dissolve yeast and sugar in 1 cup lukewarm water. Gently heat stout, ½ cup water, molasses and shortening to 140 degrees F. Pour into large mixing bowl with salt, dill and orange rind. Add eggs, yeast mixture and ⅓ of the flours. Mix on medium speed of electric mixer for 5 minutes.

Process muesli in blender, then add to dough. Stir in enough flour to make a smooth dough. Knead on floured surface for at least 5 minutes, adding flour as needed to make a smooth elastic dough.

Place in large, greased bowl, cover and let rise until doubled—1 to 2 hours. Punch down and let rest for 5 minutes. With greased hands, knead again for 5 minutes.

Divide dough into thirds, form into loaves and place in greased loaf pans. Cover and let rise until doubled—1 hour. Bake at 400 degrees F for 10 minutes, lower heat to 350 degrees and bake for 30 minutes longer.

Makes 3 loaves.

—Christine Amy-Peterson
Philomath, Oregon

GRANDMA BECKSTEAD'S THREE-DAY BUNS

"MY GRANDMOTHER'S HOUSE ALWAYS SMELLED OF THESE BUNS IN SOME DEGREE OF PROGRESS. They were covered with a gingham tea towel and served with lots of fresh butter and jam."

1 tsp. sugar	1 egg
1 Tbsp. yeast	1 tsp. salt
7 cups flour	½ cup oil
¾ cup sugar	

Day 1, a.m.: In a large bowl, dissolve 1 tsp. sugar in ½ cup cold water. Sprinkle yeast over and let stand until evening. Add 1 cup of flour and 2 cups of water. Mix well and let stand overnight.

Day 2, a.m.: Mix together ¾ cup sugar, egg, salt, oil and yeast mixture. Stir in remaining flour, adding more if dough is too sticky. Knead 10 minutes on a floured board, adding flour as needed. Put in a greased bowl and let stand. In evening, punch down, shape into small balls and put in greased pans. Cover and let stand overnight. Buns will almost triple in size.

Day 3, a.m.: Brush tops with butter. Bake at 350 degrees F for approximately 15 minutes.

Yield 4-5½ dozen buns.

—Donna Beckstead
Kingston, Ontario

DINNER ROLLS

"MY ATTEMPTS AT DIFFERENT RECIPES FOR ROLLS ALWAYS PRODUCED HEAVY, ALBINO HOCKEY pucks until a friend of mine taught me how to make these buns." These rolls are light and moist and make a perfect accompaniment to any meal, especially when warm and fresh from the oven.

2⅔ cups milk	7 cups bread flour
6 Tbsp. butter	2 eggs **or** ⅓ cup plain yogurt
8 Tbsp. sugar	1 Tbsp. salt
2 Tbsp. yeast	

Scald milk, add butter and sugar and cool to lukewarm. Add yeast and let stand for 20 minutes in a warm place. Add 3 cups flour and eggs or yogurt and beat well. Add salt and remaining flour. Dough should be quite elastic and only slightly sticky to the touch. Cover and let rise until doubled. Stir down and let rise for another 45 minutes.

On a well-floured surface, work ¼ of the dough at a time. Knead gently just until dough is not sticky. Roll to ¾" thickness and cut into 3" circles. Place buns on greased cookie sheet. Rework trimmings of dough into the next quarter batch. Let rise for 1 hour. Bake at 400 degrees F for 12 to 15 minutes.

Rolls may be brushed gently with melted butter just before baking, if desired. These make great hamburger buns.

Makes 5 to 6 dozen rolls.

—Jeannette McQuaid
Read, Ontario

GRAHAM BREAD

WE FOUND THIS BREAD TO BE LIGHT, SLIGHTLY SWEET AND VERY AROMATIC. IT WAS DELICIOUS served warm and was still moist and flavourful the next day.

13-oz. can evaporated milk
¼ cup melted butter
3 Tbsp. sugar
1 Tbsp. salt

1 pkg. yeast
3 cups medium graham flour
5-6 cups white flour

Combine milk with equal amount hot water, butter, sugar and salt and let stand until lukewarm.

Dissolve yeast in ½ cup warm water and add to milk mixture. Beat in graham flour with a wooden spoon, then add enough white flour to make a smooth dough.

Turn out onto floured board and knead, adding additional flour as needed to make a smooth, elastic dough. Place in greased bowl, cover, and let rise until doubled — about 1 hour. Turn out, knead briefly, then form into 2 large loaves. Place in greased bread pans and let rise, covered, until dough reaches the top of the pans. Bake at 375 degrees F for 1 hour.

Makes 3 loaves.

—Laurabel Miller
Denbigh, Ontario

SPECIAL SWEDISH RYE BREAD

THIS BREAD IS ABOUT AS NUTRITIOUS AS A BREAD CAN GET, AS IT USES BOTH RYE FLOUR AND bran-wheat cereal, as well as carrots. It is still a light bread, however, because of the white flour.

2 Tbsp. yeast
½ tsp. sugar
¼ tsp. ginger
½ cup molasses
¼ cup brown sugar
¼ cup oil
½ cup nonfat milk powder

2 tsp. (or less) salt
½ cup finely shredded carrots
2 Tbsp. grated orange peel
3 cups rye flour
6½ cups unbleached white flour
1½ cups bran-wheat cereal

Dissolve yeast in ½ cup warm water. Add sugar and ginger and let stand 3 minutes. In a large bowl, combine 3 cups hot water with molasses, brown sugar, oil, milk powder, salt, carrots and orange peel. When cooled to lukewarm, add yeast mixture, rye flour, 3 cups white flour and cereal. Blend at low speed on mixer or by hand. Stir in remaining flour. Dough will be soft and sticky.

Turn out onto a floured board and knead about 10 minutes, incorporating another 1 to 2 cups white flour. Place dough in a greased bowl and let rise in a warm place until doubled. Punch down and divide into thirds. Shape into loaves and place in 3 greased loaf pans. Let rise until doubled. Bake at 350 degrees F for 40 to 45 minutes.

Makes 3 loaves.

—Judy Mueller
Dawson, Nebraska

JANNE'S DARK RYE BREAD

"I GOT THIS RECIPE FROM A DANISH FELLOW STUDENT WHEN I WAS AT COLLEGE. IT IS A DENSE European rye bread, full of whole-grain flavour and is best sliced very thinly."

¼ cup sugar
½ cup plus 1 Tbsp. strong coffee
¼ cup softened butter
1½ cups bran
½ cup wheat germ
¼ cup molasses
2 tsp. salt

2½ tsp. sugar
2 Tbsp. yeast
3 cups rye flour
2½-3 cups unbleached white flour
½ tsp. sugar
1 egg white

Place sugar in small, heavy pot and heat, stirring constantly, over medium heat until sugar is melted and dark golden brown. Remove from heat, add ½ cup coffee and return to heat. Cook, stirring constantly, until mixture is blended. Remove from heat.

Place 1¾ cups boiling water in large bowl. Add butter and stir until melted. Add bran, wheat germ, molasses, sugar-coffee mixture and salt. Cool to lukewarm.

Dissolve 2 tsp. sugar in ½ cup warm water. Add yeast and let stand for 10 minutes. Stir into lukewarm mixture, along with rye flour. Beat well, then gradually add white flour until a ball forms.

Knead on floured surface for 10 minutes, adding flour as needed to make a firm dough. Cover and let rise until doubled – about 1½ hours. Punch down and form into 2 loaves. Cover and let rise until doubled – about 45 minutes.

Combine remaining 1 Tbsp. coffee, remaining ½ tsp. sugar and egg white. Brush over loaves. Bake at 375 degrees F for 45 minutes, brushing twice more with glaze.

Makes 2 loaves.

—Heidi Juul
North Battleford, Saskatchewan

MAPLE OATMEAL BREAD

THIS IS A VERY GOOD FARMERS' MARKET BREAD THAT IS EASY TO PREPARE. IT ALSO MAKES wonderful toast.

¼ cup butter
1½ cups old-fashioned oats
½ cup maple syrup
2 tsp. salt

1 Tbsp. yeast
1 Tbsp. brown sugar
6-8 cups unbleached white flour

In a large bowl, combine butter, oats, maple syrup and salt. Pour 2 cups of boiling water over and stir. In a small bowl, mix yeast and brown sugar with ½ cup warm water. Set small bowl on top of ingredients in large bowl – it keeps the yeast warm and prevents spills as yeast foams up. After yeast has doubled and oat mixture has cooled to warm, mix the two. Add flour, 2 cups at a time, and beat well until it is all incorporated.

Knead until dough is elastic and not sticky. Allow to rise in a warm place for 1 hour. Punch down, knead briefly and divide dough in half. Shape loaves and place in greased loaf pans. Let rise for another 30 to 45 minutes. Bake at 350 degrees F for 30 to 45 minutes, or until golden brown.

Makes 2 loaves.

—Mary Jirik
West Rutland, Vermont

APPLE CIDER BREAD

"THE SWEETNESS IN THIS BREAD COMES FROM THE APPLE CIDER. ALLOW 4 TO 5 HOURS TO complete this recipe – it's worth the wait!" It rises beautifully, although the recipe calls for only whole wheat flour.

1½ Tbsp. yeast
3¼ cups warm apple cider (85°-105° F)
7-9 cups whole wheat flour

1 Tbsp. salt
¼ cup oil **or** melted butter
1½ Tbsp. cinnamon

Dissolve yeast in warm cider. Stir in 3 to 4 cups whole wheat flour to make a thick batter. Beat well with spoon. Cover loosely, and let rise for 1 hour. Stir in salt, oil and cinnamon. Mix in additional flour until dough comes away from sides of bowl.

Knead on floured board until dough is smooth – about 15 minutes. Use more flour as needed to keep dough from sticking to the board. Cover and let rise for 50 minutes. Punch down. Cover and let rise for 40 minutes. Punch down.

Shape into two loaves and place in two greased loaf pans. Let rise for 20 minutes, or until doubled. Bake in a preheated 350 degree F oven for 40 minutes to 1 hour. Remove from pans and let cool, or enjoy right away.

Makes 2 loaves.

—*Judy Sheppard-Segal*
Falmouth, Maine

RAISIN PUMPERNICKEL BREAD

WE TESTED THIS RECIPE LARGELY BECAUSE IT CAME TO US BEAUTIFULLY HAND LETTERED, BUT once we tasted the bread, it stood on its own merits.

1 tsp. honey
2 Tbsp. yeast
2 Tbsp. oil
½ cup molasses
2 tsp. salt
2 tsp. fennel seeds
3 tsp. caraway seeds

2½ cups white flour
2 cups whole wheat flour
½ cup cornmeal
1½ cups raisins
2 cups rye flour
melted butter
1 egg white

In a large bowl, dissolve honey in ½ cup warm water and add yeast. When yeast is foamy, add 2 cups warm water, oil, molasses, salt, fennel and caraway seeds, white flour and whole wheat flour. Beat for at least 5 minutes with a wooden spoon. Sprinkle cornmeal, raisins and rye flour over the dough and beat well to combine.

Turn dough out onto a floured board and knead until smooth. Extra white flour may be added but use restraint, as too much flour will make the bread dry. The stickiness disappears after the dough rises. Let rise in an oiled bowl covered with a damp cloth for 1 hour. Punch down and let rise a second time for 30 minutes. Prepare two cookie sheets by greasing and dusting with cornmeal. Punch dough down, knead a bit and cut in half. Let rise 15 minutes.

Shape into 2 ovals, place on cookie sheets, slash tops diagonally and brush with melted butter. Let rise again until almost doubled. Bake at 350 degrees F for 40 minutes. After 30 minutes, loaves may be glazed with egg white beaten with 1 Tbsp. water.

—*Michael & Dyan Walters*
Kitchener, Ontario

Holiday

"Strange to see how a good dinner and feasting reconciles everybody."

—*Samuel Pepys*

We are not sure it holds true that large families have more steadfast holiday rituals, but it can certainly be argued that there are more of us to remember the essentials and to protest if traditions seem to be slipping. Having grown up in a family with six children, one of our editors remembers well the howls of dismay on the Christmas her mother decided to drop the pickled crabapples from the menu of the annual feast. Everyone conveniently forgot that no one had ever liked the mouth-puckering condiments, but there was no lack of agreement that they were just supposed to be there. There also were firm rules about the coveted turkey legs, and when the children were young and less given to harmonious sharing, a list was kept from year to year to record just who had partaken of what during the previous Yule dinners. Woe betide the carver if he failed to count properly or forgot whose turn it was!

Part of the ritual of family holidays is the presentation of the expected, foods whose aromas are permanently imprinted in our minds as essential to the year's special feasts and gatherings. Times certainly have changed, but the need for these rituals has not. In recent years, we have tended to celebrate in a more communal way, with each guest bringing a component of the meal. Perhaps because the pressure is more evenly distributed, things seem more relaxed, and I can say that we have had some wonderful meals this way.

This final chapter is, by necessity, an eclectic assortment of recipes; you will see that many have a long and meaningful heritage for those who submitted them. The choices are truly international, reflecting the proud ethnic roots of our hybrid society. Baking, desserts and beverages tend to dominate here, partly because the main course items appear elsewhere but also because these are the most coveted and personal recipes. Potential gifts—Chocolate Rum Balls, Carrot Mincemeat, Fresh Cranberry Nut Bread—abound, along with a hearty assortment of temptations to dabble in the holiday cuisines of other cultures.

We also break our rules of strict impartiality and present an old family Christmas cake recipe. Dark, laden with fruit and nuts, wrapped in rum-soaked cheesecloth and allowed to age from sometime in October until Christmas, it is more of an event than a recipe, and it comes to you with more history than can be repeated here. This is a cake—weighing in at 12 pounds—that has been mailed to far-flung family weddings and other gatherings in England and Australia. In the spirit of the *Harrowsmith* cookbooks—some 20,000 recipes from private family collections have been submitted in the last six years—we offer it to you.

CRANBERRY BRANDY

"Here in Alaska, wild berries of all kinds are plentiful — this recipe also works well with raspberries or blueberries. Serve this brandy over vanilla ice cream, or just sip it plain. It also makes a wonderful gift."

3 quarts cranberries
32 oz. brandy

4 cups sugar
3 cups water

Mash berries in large bowl, then add brandy. Cover and let stand for 24 hours, stirring twice. Separate juice from pulp, using jelly strainer or coffee filter, and discard pulp.

Cook sugar in water, stirring, until mixture becomes clear. Cool. Mix sugar syrup with brandy and stir well. Pour into clean bottles and cap.

Makes approximately 80 oz.

—Chris Thorsrud
Tok, Alaska

VITA QUENCHER

1 qt. raspberries **or** blackberries
1 cup white vinegar

sugar

Place berries in stainless steel or glass bowl. Mix vinegar with 1 cup water and pour over berries. Let stand, covered, for 24 to 48 hours, then squeeze through strainer.

Measure juice, pour into stainless steel pot and add an equal amount of sugar (approximately 3 cups). Boil, stirring occasionally, for 20 minutes. Cool, then refrigerate for up to several weeks or freeze.

To serve, use 3 Tbsp. concentrate mixed with water to make one 8-oz. glass.

Makes 1 quart concentrate.

—Anita L. Weidemoyer
Gassaway, West Virginia

EGGNOG SUPREME

"This is my mother's recipe and is, quite simply, the best eggnog I have ever tasted."

12 eggs, separated
1 cup sugar
13 oz. brandy
26 oz. rye **or** rum

2 cups light cream
3 cups heavy cream
nutmeg

Combine egg yolks and sugar in large punch bowl. Beat until thick and lemon-coloured, then slowly add brandy, rye or rum and light cream. Beat to blend well, then chill for at least 1 hour.

Beat egg whites until stiff. Whip heavy cream till stiff in large bowl, then fold in egg whites. Add gently to alcohol mixture. Sprinkle with nutmeg.

Serves 12 to 16.

—Lynne Collier
Kaministiquia, Ontario

MARY'S WASSAIL

"I SERVE THIS DRINK EVERY YEAR AT MY OPEN HOUSE. IT'S VERY WARMING BUT NOT SO alcoholic that I worry about my guests driving afterwards. In fact, the wine can be left out altogether. In that case, increase the amount of sugar to 1 cup."

1 gallon apple cider
⅓ cup brown sugar
6-oz. can frozen lemonade
6-oz. can frozen orange juice
12 cloves

6 whole allspice
1 tsp. nutmeg
4" stick cinnamon
1 bottle port wine
½ tsp. Angostura bitters

Combine cider, sugar, lemonade and orange juice in large kettle. Tie cloves and allspice in a small piece of cloth (or place in a tea ball) and add to juices. Add nutmeg and cinnamon stick and simmer gently for 20 minutes. Add wine and heat to steaming, but do not boil. Remove spice bag.

Serves approximately 20.

—Mary Irwin-Gibson
Dunham, Quebec

MABEL'S CRANBERRY SALAD

"MADE ORIGINALLY BY MY GRANDMOTHER, THIS COOL, SWEET-TART SALAD IS AS MUCH A PART of my holiday as the turkey."

4 cups fresh cranberries
2 cups sugar
2 cups halved seedless red grapes

½ cup chopped nuts
1 cup heavy cream, whipped

Mince cranberries in a grinder or food processor. Mix in sugar. Place in a colander and set colander in a bowl deep enough to allow cranberries to drain. Cover with foil and let drain in refrigerator overnight. Don't shortcut this step. Mix drained cranberries with remaining ingredients and chill. It can be kept for several days in the refrigerator.

Makes 6 servings.

—Margo Hamilton
Cologne, Minnesota

HOLIDAY STUFFING

3 cups chopped tart apples
¼ cup brandy
1¼ cups chopped onions
1-2 cloves garlic, minced
½ cup chopped celery
¾ cup chopped celery leaves
½ cup butter

1½ tsp. salt
¾ tsp. thyme
½ tsp. sage
1½ tsp. white pepper
1 bay leaf
10 cups dry bread cubes

Marinate apples in brandy for 15 minutes. Sauté onions, garlic, celery and celery leaves in butter for 3 to 5 minutes. Mix seasonings and toss with bread. Add all other ingredients to bread and mix well. Stuff turkey and roast according to personal preference.

Makes enough to stuff a 20-lb. turkey.

—Julie Hustvet
Mondovi, Wisconsin

TORTIÈRE

Rated "the best" by the Camden East test kitchen, this recipe originated in a high-school home-economics class. Both the tortière and the herb sauce freeze well.

Special Dough for Crust
2¼-2½ cups flour
2 tsp. baking powder
1 tsp. salt
½ lb. shortening
½ cup hot water
2 tsp. lemon juice
1 egg, well beaten

Filling
1 lb. lean ground pork
1 onion, finely chopped
½ tsp. salt
¼ tsp. pepper
½ tsp. thyme

½ tsp. sage
½ tsp. dry mustard
½ tsp. cloves
1 potato, boiled & mashed

Herb Sauce
1 stalk celery with leaves, minced
2½ cups consommé
½ tsp. sage
½ tsp. thyme
¼ cup butter
¼-½ cup flour
1 Tbsp. parsley
1 cup chopped mushrooms

For crust: Combine flour, baking powder and salt in large mixing bowl. Measure ⅔ cup cold shortening and cut into flour until mealy. Completely dissolve remaining ½ cup shortening in hot water (heat as necessary to dissolve). Cool. Add lemon juice and egg to water-shortening mixture. Mix liquid into flour mixture until dough leaves sides of bowl. Turn onto lightly floured board and knead for about 1 minute, or until all flour is blended. Wrap in waxed paper, refrigerate for 1 to 12 hours. Roll out ⅔ of the dough and line a casserole dish. Reserve ⅓ for top crust.

For filling: Simmer meat and ½ cup water for 45 minutes. Add onion and seasonings and simmer for 15 minutes. Mix in mashed potato and cool. Place in bottom crust, top with remaining dough and slit crust. Bake at 400 degrees F for 30 minutes.

For sauce: Simmer all ingredients except flour, parsley and mushrooms for 1 hour. Mix flour with 1 cup cold water. Add to sauce and stir until thickened, then add parsley and mushrooms. Simmer for 10 minutes. Serve with tortière.

Serves 8 to 10.

—Kim Allerton
Desboro, Ontario

CARROT MINCEMEAT

2 cups grated carrots
2 cups raisins
1 whole lemon
5 cups chopped apples
1 cup mixed fruit peels
2 cups sugar

1 tsp. salt (optional)
2 tsp. cinnamon
1 tsp. cloves
½ cup molasses
½ cup cider **or** apple juice

Grind together carrots, raisins and lemon. Add apples, fruit peels, sugar, salt, cinnamon and cloves. When thoroughly mixed, add molasses and cider or juice. Cook over low heat until carrots and apples are tender. Can be sealed in jars while hot or packed in containers for freezing. Use for pies or tarts.

Makes about 2½ quarts.

—Mrs. V.T. Stone
Hampden, Maine

NORWEGIAN FRUIT SOUP

"Served as a dessert every Christmas Eve in our home, this recipe for 'Sot Suppe' came from Norway in 1913 and makes a tasty sauce over sponge cake or ice cream."

1 lb. dark raisins
1 lb. pitted prunes
2 cinnamon sticks, broken
10 whole cloves
6 cups water **or**
   3 cups water & 3 cups red wine

3 Tbsp. minute tapioca
½ cup sugar
1 orange, quartered & thinly sliced
1 apple, unpeeled, cored & quartered
1 cup orange juice

Slowly bring raisins, prunes, cinnamon sticks, cloves and water to a boil. Add tapioca and sugar. Cook until tapioca is transparent. Add orange and apple. Cook for 2 to 3 minutes. Add orange juice. Serve warm or cold, with cream if desired.

Serves 8.

—Mary Linstad
Porterfield, Wisconsin

CARDAMOM BREAD

"My dad made this bread every Christmas for years, and I have carried on the tradition, with my own recipe evolving over time."

6 cups milk
½ cup butter
¾ cup honey
1½ tsp. ground cardamom
1 Tbsp. yeast
4 eggs, lightly beaten
6 cups whole wheat flour
12-15 cups unbleached white flour
2 Tbsp. salt

Egg Wash
1 egg
3 Tbsp. water

Glaze
½ cup icing sugar
2 tsp. hot milk
¼ tsp. vanilla

almond halves

Scald milk. Combine with butter, honey and cardamom. Let cool to lukewarm in large bowl. Meanwhile, proof yeast by combining yeast and 1⅓ cups warm water. Let sit until it doubles in volume—approximately 10 minutes. When milk mixture is cool, add yeast mixture, eggs, whole wheat flour and 3 cups white flour. Beat with wooden spoon at least 100 strokes, or until dough becomes elastic. Cover and let sit in a warm place for about 1 hour.

Stir down sponge and stir in salt and 9 to 12 cups flour, 2 cups at a time. Turn out onto a board and knead dough until smooth and elastic—about 10 minutes. Put in greased bowl, cover with a damp cloth and put in a warm place until doubled. Punch down and let rise again. Punch down and turn out onto a lightly floured board.

Cut dough into 8 sections. Cut each section into 3 pieces. With your hands, roll each piece into a rope 15 to 18 inches long. Braid 3 pieces together, pinch ends and tuck underneath. Repeat for remaining dough. Place 2 braids side by side on foil-lined cookie sheets. Cover and let rise until doubled.

Mix egg and water together (egg wash) and brush each loaf. Bake at 350 degrees F for 20 to 25 minutes. Let cool. Mix glaze and drizzle over loaves, pressing almond halves into glaze for decoration.

Makes 8 large braids.

—Leslie Pierpont
Santa Fe, New Mexico

FESTIVE WILD RICE

WILD RICE IS ACTUALLY A GRASS, NOT A RICE, AND NUTRITIONALLY IS CLOSER TO WHEAT THAN to rice. Its nutty taste is incomparable, but for economy, a blend of wild and brown or basmati rice could be substituted. To prepare, wash well several times, then cook, without stirring, in boiling water (4 cups water to 1 cup rice) for 40 minutes. One cup dry rice makes 3 cups cooked rice.

2 Tbsp. oil
2 green peppers, chopped
2 onions, chopped
1 clove garlic, minced
2 cups canned tomatoes
½ cup raisins

½ cup blanched almonds
1 tsp. curry
1 tsp. thyme
salt & pepper
2 cups cooked wild rice

Heat oil and sauté green peppers, onions and garlic. Add tomatoes, ¼ cup raisins, ¼ cup almonds, curry, thyme and salt and pepper. Simmer for 10 minutes. Put rice in greased casserole dish and cover with sauce. Sprinkle with remaining raisins and nuts. Cover and bake at 400 degrees F for 45 minutes.

Serves 6 to 8.

—Rachel Grapentine
Maple, Wisconsin

FLAKY SWEDISH BUNS

"THESE BUNS ARE MY MOM'S RECIPE. SHE LEARNED TO MAKE THEM BY WATCHING MY grandmother, and the recipe was never written down until my sister and I wanted it. We watched Mom and never let her add a thing until we knew what it was and how much! They are a little time-consuming to make, but well worth the effort."

3 pkgs. yeast
2 Tbsp. plus 1 cup sugar
1½ tsp. salt
4 tsp. ground cardamom
5 cups scalded milk
4 eggs, beaten
10-10½ cups flour
⅔ cup butter, softened

Almond Icing
¼ cup soft butter
2 cups icing sugar
1 tsp. almond extract
few drops of milk

crushed walnuts

Dissolve yeast in ½ cup warm water with 2 Tbsp. sugar and let sit for 10 minutes. In large bowl, combine 1 cup sugar, salt and cardamom. Pour in scalded milk and mix. Add eggs and beat in well. Cool to lukewarm. Add yeast and mix well. Add 4 cups flour and beat in. Knead in another 6 to 6½ cups flour. Butter counter before rolling out. Roll out half the dough and spread with butter. Cut dough into quarters and pile pieces on top of each other. Roll out and butter again, continuing until half the butter is used up. Place dough in freezer.

Roll out second half of dough in the same manner. Put second piece of dough in freezer and take out first. Roll out dough. Cut into strips 5 inches by ½ inch, twist tightly and tie in a knot. Repeat with second half of dough. Place on cookie sheets, cover and let rise for 2 to 2½ hours. Bake at 350 to 375 degrees F for 15 to 20 minutes (until brown). Cool and ice with almond icing, and roll in crushed walnuts.

For icing: Cream butter, gradually adding the icing sugar. Add the almond extract and mix well. If too stiff to spread, add a few drops of milk.

Makes approximately 4 dozen buns.

—Lynne Collier
Kaministiquia, Ontario

HOT CROSS BUNS

"THIS IS MY MOTHER'S RECIPE AND HAS BEEN IN OUR FAMILY FOR MANY YEARS."

1 Tbsp. yeast
1 tsp. sugar
2 cups milk
½ cup sugar
1½ tsp. salt
1 egg, beaten
⅓ cup butter, melted

5-6 cups flour
¾ tsp. cinnamon
¾ cup raisins

Icing
1 cup icing sugar
milk

Add yeast and 1 tsp. sugar to ½ cup warm water. Let sit for 10 minutes. Warm milk in saucepan, add ½ cup sugar, salt, egg and butter. Pour into large bowl, add yeast mixture and stir. Add 5 cups flour, cinnamon and raisins. Mix well. If dough is very sticky, add 1 more cup flour. Knead as for bread dough until smooth. Cover and let rise until doubled. Punch down, knead briefly and cut into buns. Place buns on a 9" x 13" cookie sheet and cut a cross in the top of each. Let rise until doubled in size. Bake at 325 degrees F for 25 minutes, or until golden brown. After they have cooled a bit, put icing in each cross. Icing sugar blended with enough milk to form a paste works well.

Makes 24 buns.

—Sharon McKay
Riverview, New Brunswick

PANNETONE – ITALIAN CHRISTMAS BREAD

"WHEN AN ITALIAN VISITING CANADA TASTED THIS, HE DECLARED IT TO BE AS GOOD AS THOSE sold in fancy blue boxes in Italy. It has become our traditional Christmas breakfast accompanied by champagne cocktails and coffee."

1 Tbsp. yeast
5-6 cups flour
1 tsp. anise extract **or** fennel seed
½ tsp. salt
¾ cup butter, melted
2 whole eggs, plus 4 yolks

1 cup sugar
½ cup seedless raisins
½ cup white raisins
½ cup finely chopped citron
2 Tbsp. butter, melted

Sprinkle yeast over ¼ cup warm water. When yeast is soft, add ½ cup flour and mix to form a small ball. Cover and let rise 1½ to 2 hours.

Put 2 cups flour in a large bowl, add dough and ½ cup warm water. Knead in the bowl to make a ball. Cover and let rise 2 hours.

To dough, add 1½ cups flour, anise or fennel, salt and ¾ cup butter. Beat eggs plus yolks, sugar and ½ cup warm water together and add to dough. Knead in the bowl and add fruits. Turn out onto a floured board and knead, incorporating remaining flour. Cover and let rise 2 to 4 hours. Punch down and leave in refrigerator overnight.

The next day, grease two 8-inch flat-bottomed casserole dishes. Punch down bread and divide in half. Press dough evenly into dishes, cover and let rise 2 to 4 hours in a warm place. Mark a cross in the top of each loaf. Bake at 400 degrees F for 5 minutes, then pour 1 Tbsp. melted butter in each cross. Bake 15 minutes longer. Lower heat to 375 degrees and bake for 40 minutes. Loaves will be mushroom-shaped.

Makes 2 loaves.

—Hazel R. Baker
Coombs, British Columbia

PULLA – FINNISH COFFEE BREAD

"Pulla is an age-old bread that can be enjoyed year-round, although I often give it as Easter or Christmas gifts. It is best enjoyed with a fresh cup of coffee after an invigorating, steamy sauna."

2 cups milk
14-18 cardamom pods
1 pkg. yeast
1 cup sugar

4 eggs, lightly beaten
8-9 cups white flour
¼ cup butter, melted

Scald milk and let cool to lukewarm. Remove cardamom seeds from pods and crush. Dissolve yeast in ½ cup warm water. Add cardamom, yeast mixture, sugar and all but 1 Tbsp. eggs to milk. Pour into large bowl. Add 4 cups flour, then melted butter. Mix well. Continue adding flour, one cup at a time, until dough is firm enough to knead. Knead for 10 minutes on a floured board, incorporating the remaining flour. Cover and let rise in a greased bowl – 1½ to 2 hours.

Punch down, divide dough in half and knead for a few minutes. Let rest for 15 minutes. Divide each portion into 3 pieces, shape each piece into a rope about 1 foot long and braid together. Brush with remaining 1 Tbsp. egg. Let rise, covered, for 30 minutes. Bake at 350 degrees F for about 30 minutes, or until golden.

Makes 2 loaves.

—Shari Suter
Stäfa, Switzerland

HUNGARIAN FILLED PASTRIES

Although time-consuming to prepare, these festive pastries are well worth the effort. The pastry is rich and flaky.

Pastry
5 cups flour
½ tsp. salt
2 cups shortening **or** lard **or** butter
5 egg yolks
½ cup red wine
1 pint sour cream
1 tsp. baking powder

Filling
4 egg whites
2 cups crushed walnuts
1 cup sugar
2 tsp. vanilla

Mix pastry ingredients with pastry cutter until chunky. Refrigerate for 1 hour.

Meanwhile, prepare filling: Beat egg whites until soft peaks form. Fold in nuts, sugar and vanilla.

Divide dough into quarters. On surface well dusted with confectioners' sugar, roll one quarter at a time into 10-inch squares. Cut each into sixteen 2½-inch squares. Place ¼ to ½ tsp. filling in centre of each. Fold corners into centre. Bake on ungreased cookie sheets at 375 degrees F for 12 to 15 minutes, or until edges turn golden.

Makes approximately 60 pastries.

—Dianne Baker
Tatamagouche, Nova Scotia

KENTUCKY JAM CAKE

"IN KENTUCKY, JAM CAKE IS A HOLIDAY TRADITION ALONG WITH TURKEY, COUNTRY HAM AND Christmas cookies."

1 cup butter	1 tsp. baking soda
2 cups sugar	1 tsp. nutmeg
3 eggs	1 tsp. ground cloves
1 cup jam, preferably blackberry	1 cup buttermilk
3 cups white flour	½ cup orange juice

Cream butter and sugar together. Mix in eggs and jam. Mix together flour, baking soda, nutmeg and cloves. Add butter mixture to dry ingredients alternately with buttermilk and orange juice. Beat well. Pour into a greased tube pan. Bake at 325 degrees F for 45 to 60 minutes.

—Sharon Fuller
Ravenna, Kentucky

FRESH CRANBERRY NUT BREAD

THE SLIGHTLY TART CRANBERRIES ARE ESPECIALLY APPRECIATED BY THOSE WHO DISLIKE THE usual rich holiday fare.

2 cups cranberries, chopped	5 cups flour
2½ cups sugar	7 tsp. baking powder
2 eggs, lightly beaten	1 tsp. salt
⅓ cup butter	1 cup chopped walnuts
2 cups milk	

Mix cranberries with ½ cup sugar and set aside. Cream remaining 2 cups sugar and eggs. Cream in butter and add milk. Sift flour, baking powder and salt, then add dry ingredients to the creamed mixture. Stir in cranberries and walnuts. Turn into 2 greased 9" x 5" loaf pans. Bake at 350 degrees F for 1 hour.

Makes 2 loaves.

—Kathryn MacDonald
Yarker, Ontario

CHOCOLATE RUM BALLS

"THESE ARE A CHRISTMAS TRADITION IN OUR HOME, BUT THEY ALSO MAKE A LOVELY GIFT ANY time of the year."

1½ cups graham cracker crumbs	¼ cup honey
1 cup icing sugar	3 Tbsp. dark rum
1 cup ground almonds	semisweet chocolate, melted
2-3 Tbsp. cocoa	

Mix together graham cracker crumbs, sugar, almonds and cocoa. Gently warm honey and stir in rum. Mix into dry ingredients. Form into 1-inch balls and roll in melted chocolate.

Makes approximately 2½ dozen.

—Susan O'Neill
Bella Coola, British Columbia

RUSSIAN WAFERS

"My daughter brought this recipe home in a collection of recipes showing how Christmas is celebrated around the world."

1 cup butter	2 cups flour
1 cup sugar	3 tsp. baking powder
2 eggs, well beaten	½ tsp. salt
2 tsp. vanilla	nutmeg

Cream butter and sugar together. Beat in eggs and vanilla. Add dry ingredients, mixing until very smooth. Chill dough overnight.

Roll dough out on a cookie sheet and cut into wafer-sized rectangles with sharp knife. (Cookies will break apart like crackers when cooked and cooled.) Sprinkle with sugar and nutmeg. Bake at 400 degrees F for about 8 minutes.

—Linda Palaisy
Cantley, Quebec

CHRISTMAS CAKE

Editor's note: This is my mother's Christmas Cake recipe. She has been making it for as long as I can remember and now I make it too. It has been used for each child's wedding cake and is given away as gifts every Christmas. Traditional fruitcake pans are three pans, round or square, of 6-, 4- and 2-pound size. Put the cakes in the oven, largest first, so that all will be done at the same time.

½ lb. currants	½ lb. butter
1 lb. raisins	¼ cup molasses
½ lb. candied cherries	5 eggs
4 oz. preserved citron	1 tsp. cinnamon
4 oz. mixed fruit peel	½ tsp. each cloves, nutmeg, allspice,
1½ candied pineapple rings	baking soda, salt
¼ lb. dates	½ cup grape juice
½ lb. almonds	½ cup orange juice
2 cups flour	½ cup lemon juice
½ lb. sugar	

Wash currants and raisins. Halve cherries. Chop citron, peel, pineapple and dates. Combine all fruit with almonds. Dredge in ¼ cup flour. Allow to stand for 8 hours.

Cream sugar and butter, add molasses and eggs and beat well. Sift remaining flour with dry ingredients. Add to sugar-butter mixture alternately with juices. Beat thoroughly. Pour over fruit and blend well.

Prepare Christmas cake pans by greasing thoroughly and lining with 2 layers of foil. Bake cakes at 250 degrees F for 30 to 45 minutes per pound.

Makes 6 lbs. of cake.

—Flora Cross
Waterloo, Ontario

DUTCH CHERRY CAKE

"THIS IS A GOOD DESSERT THAT IS NOT OVERLY SWEET. WE OFTEN HAD THIS ON VALENTINE'S Day when I was a child."

Crust
1¼ cups flour, sifted
½ tsp. baking powder
¼ tsp. salt
1 Tbsp. sugar
½ cup cold butter
1 egg

½ cup sugar
1 Tbsp. flour
¼ tsp. cinnamon
2 Tbsp. butter

Topping
1 cup sour cream
1 egg

Filling
3 cups frozen red sour cherries **or** 3 cans
    sour cherries, drained

To make crust: Combine flour, baking powder, salt and sugar, mixing well. Cut in butter until mixture resembles coarse crumbs. Add egg and mix with a fork; then, using hands, work into a stiff dough. Press mixture into 9" x 9" pan. Crust should come up about 1 inch on the sides.

Scatter cherries evenly over crust. Combine sugar, flour and cinnamon. Cut in butter to make a crumb mixture; sprinkle over cherries. Bake at 350 degrees F for 55 minutes. If a topping is desired, beat sour cream and egg together and spoon over top. Return cake to oven, turn oven off and let sit for 5 to 10 minutes. Serve warm or cold.

Serves 6.

—Nancy R. Franklin
San Jose, California

FILBERT CONFECTION CREAMS

1 cup filberts
½ cup butter
1 egg
¼ cup sugar
2 Tbsp. cocoa
2 tsp. vanilla
¼ tsp. salt (optional)
1¾ cups vanilla wafer crumbs
½ cup flaked coconut

Icing & Glaze
⅓ cup butter
1 egg
½ tsp. vanilla **or** peppermint extract
2 cups sifted powdered sugar
4 squares semisweet chocolate

Chop filberts but do not grind too finely. Spread them in a shallow pan, toast at 350 degrees F for 5 to 10 minutes, stirring occasionally, until lightly browned.

In saucepan, combine butter, egg, sugar, cocoa, vanilla and salt. Cook over low heat until mixture thickens and becomes glossy. Combine filberts, crumbs and coconut in large bowl. Add cocoa mixture to this, blending well. Pack evenly into a greased 9" x 9" pan. Set aside.

To make icing and glaze: Cream butter and add egg and extract. Beat well. Beat in sugar until smooth and creamy. Spread over cocoa base. Chill in freezer for a few minutes to firm it. Melt chocolate squares over hot water and spread over icing. When partially set, cut into 1½-inch squares. Refrigerate until ready to serve.

Makes 36 squares.

—Sybil D. Hendricks
Plymouth, California

CALSENGEL

"MY GRANDPARENTS CAME TO AMERICA FROM NORTHERN ITALY IN 1910, AND WE STILL ENJOY many of the recipes my grandmother cooked. This rich, filled cookie was always anxiously anticipated at Christmastime." The filling improves if it is made one to two days in advance.

Filling
1 lb. raisins
½ lb. almonds, ground
grated rind of 1 orange
½ tsp. cinnamon
1 cup sugar
½ cup honey

Pastry
6 cups flour
3 tsp. salt
3 tsp. baking powder
1 cup shortening

oil for deep frying
egg wash (1 egg beaten with 2 Tbsp.
    water)
2 cups honey

For filling: Wash raisins and mix with almonds, orange rind, cinnamon and sugar in saucepan. Cover with water and cook for 15 to 20 minutes, stirring often. Mix in ½ cup honey, cool and refrigerate.

For pastry: Mix flour, salt, baking powder and shortening until mixture resembles coarse meal. Add 1½ cups cold water until dough sticks together. Knead a few minutes. Roll dough out to ⅛-inch thickness on a floured surface. Cut into 2-by-3-inch rectangles with a pastry cutter. Place about 2 Tbsp. of filling on each rectangle. Brush edges with egg wash. Cover with another rectangle and crimp edges with a fork to seal. Deep-fry each cookie until lightly browned and crisp. Drain on paper towelling.

Heat about 2 cups honey in saucepan. Using a slotted spoon, dip each cookie in hot honey to coat. Cool. May be stored in a cool, dry place.

Makes 3 to 4 dozen.

—*Michelle Sollohub*
Schenectady, New York

PEBERNØDDER

PEBERNØDDER DIRECTLY TRANSLATES TO "PEPPER NUTS." THEY ARE A TRADITIONAL Christmas cookie in Denmark, where they are placed in woven heart "baskets" and hung on the Christmas tree.

½ cup plus 3 Tbsp. butter
1⅔ cups flour
⅔ cup sugar

½ tsp. vanilla
½-¾ tsp. white pepper
2 Tbsp. cream

Cut butter into flour. Add remaining ingredients, mixing well. Roll dough into long, thin ropes about the size of your little finger. Cut into ½-inch sections. Place on cookie sheet and bake at 350 degrees F for about 10 minutes.

—*Kristine Marie Halls Reid*
Floyd, Virginia

STEAMED CARROT PUDDING

"THIS PUDDING WAS TRADITIONALLY SERVED AT CHRISTMAS IN MY FAMILY. COINS WERE ALWAYS stuck into the pudding before cooking, and anyone finding a coin was guaranteed good luck."

2 Tbsp. sour milk
½ tsp. baking soda
1 tsp. salt
1 tsp. cinnamon
½ tsp. allspice
⅛ tsp. nutmeg
½ cup flour
1 cup grated carrot
1 cup grated potato
1¼ cups soft bread crumbs
1 cup raisins (mix light & dark)

1 cup currants
1 cup packed brown sugar
¾ cup suet **or** ½ cup shortening

Spiced Rum Sauce
1 cup packed brown sugar
2 Tbsp. cornstarch
¼ cup dark rum
¼ tsp. nutmeg
2 Tbsp. butter

Combine milk and baking soda. Mix salt, cinnamon, allspice and nutmeg with flour. Add milk mixture and remaining pudding ingredients and place in well-greased ceramic pudding mould, bowl or canning jar. Make sure you leave space for expansion during steaming. If using mould or bowl, wrap in a cloth. Steam for 3 hours.

For sauce: In heavy saucepan, mix together brown sugar and cornstarch. Stir in 1½ cups water. Bring to a boil, stirring constantly. Reduce heat, add rum, nutmeg and butter and simmer for 2 minutes. Makes 2 cups.

Serves 8.

—Mary Lou Garlick
Pine Point, Northwest Territories

Index

Special thanks for assistance:

Elizabeth Alexander
Glen E. Anglin
Lynne Ashworth
The Fish House, Kingston, Ontario
Flowers & Things, Kingston, Ontario
Richard and Jocelyn Hession
Mitchell Kelsey
Lisa Kershaw
Ruth King
Suzanne Legaré
Jane Masor
Sari Mayer
Caroline Miller
Staples Natural Foods, Newburgh, Ontario
Claire Still
The Squire's House, Camden East, Ontario
Donna Watts
Susan Woodend

PAGE 83, *location:* ALLAN MACPHERSON HOUSE, NAPANEE, ONTARIO

PAGE 84, *location:* ALLAN MACPHERSON HOUSE, NAPANEE, ONTARIO

PAGE 85, *butter dish & cups:* MARGARET E. HUGHES, POTTER
KINGSTON, ONTARIO

PAGE 86, *location:* ALLAN MACPHERSON HOUSE, NAPANEE, ONTARIO

PAGE 87, *location:* THE MARINE MUSEUM OF THE GREAT LAKES
KINGSTON, ONTARIO

PAGE 201, *location & props:* POLLIWOG CASTLE ANTIQUE DOLL & TOY MUSEUM
KINGSTON, ONTARIO

PAGE 203, *china & cutlery:* KEIRSTEAD GALLERY, KINGSTON, ONTARIO

PAGE 207, *china & cutlery:* KEIRSTEAD GALLERY, KINGSTON, ONTARIO

PAGE 208, *location:* HOTEL BELVEDERE, KINGSTON, ONTARIO